SYMPATHY IN EARLY MODERN LITERATURE AND CULTURE

This is the first comprehensive study of sympathy in the early modern period, providing a deeply researched and interdisciplinary examination of its development in Anglophone literature and culture. It argues that the term *sympathy* was used to refer to an active and imaginative sharing of affect considerably earlier than previous critical and historical accounts have suggested. Investigating a wide range of texts and genres, including prose fiction, sermons, poetic complaint, drama, political tracts, and scientific treatises, Richard Meek demonstrates the ways in which sympathy in the period is bound up with larger debates about society, religion, and identity. He also reveals the extent to which early modern emotions were not simply humoral or grounded in the body, but rather relational, comparative, and intertextual. This volume will be of particular interest to scholars and students of Renaissance literature and history, the history of emotions, and the history and philosophy of science.

RICHARD MEEK is Lecturer in English at the University of Hull. He is the author of *Narrating the Visual in Shakespeare* (2009) and co-editor of *Shakespeare's Book: Essays in Reading, Writing and Reception* (2008), *The Renaissance of Emotion: Understanding Affect in Shakespeare and His Contemporaries* (2015), and *Ekphrastic Encounters: New Interdisciplinary Essays on Literature and the Visual Arts* (2019).

SYMPATHY IN EARLY MODERN LITERATURE AND CULTURE

RICHARD MEEK
University of Hull

Shaftesbury Road, Cambridge CB2 8EA, United Kingdom

One Liberty Plaza, 20th Floor, New York, NY 10006, USA

477 Williamstown Road, Port Melbourne, VIC 3207, Australia

314–321, 3rd Floor, Plot 3, Splendor Forum, Jasola District Centre, New Delhi – 110025, India

103 Penang Road, #05–06/07, Visioncrest Commercial, Singapore 238467

Cambridge University Press is part of Cambridge University Press & Assessment, a department of the University of Cambridge.

We share the University's mission to contribute to society through the pursuit of education, learning and research at the highest international levels of excellence.

www.cambridge.org
Information on this title: www.cambridge.org/9781009280242

DOI: 10.1017/9781009280259

© Richard Meek 2023

This publication is in copyright. Subject to statutory exception and to the provisions of relevant collective licensing agreements, no reproduction of any part may take place without the written permission of Cambridge University Press & Assessment.

First published 2023
First paperback edition 2025

A catalogue record for this publication is available from the British Library

Library of Congress Cataloging-in-Publication data
NAMES: Meek, Richard, 1975– author.
TITLE: Sympathy in early modern literature and culture / Richard Meek.
DESCRIPTION: Cambridge ; New York, NY : Cambridge University Press, 2023. | Includes bibliographical references and index.
IDENTIFIERS: LCCN 2022043253 | ISBN 9781009280266 (hardback) | ISBN 9781009280259 (ebook)
SUBJECTS: LCSH: English literature – Early modern, 1500–1700 – History and criticism. | Sympathy in literature.
CLASSIFICATION: LCC PR428.S96 M44 2023 | DDC 820.9/353–dc23/eng/20230113
LC record available at https://lccn.loc.gov/2022043253

ISBN 978-1-009-28026-6 Hardback
ISBN 978-1-009-28024-2 Paperback

Cambridge University Press & Assessment has no responsibility for the persistence or accuracy of URLs for external or third-party internet websites referred to in this publication and does not guarantee that any content on such websites is, or will remain, accurate or appropriate.

Contents

List of Figures	*page* vi
Acknowledgements	vii
Note on Texts	x
Introduction: 'Solemn Sympathy'	1
1 'A sympathy of affections': Sympathy, Love, and Friendship in Elizabethan Prose Fiction	35
2 'Compassion and mercie draw teares from the godlyfull often': The Rhetoric of Sympathy in the Early Modern Sermon	72
3 'Grief best is pleased with grief's society': Female Complaint and the Transmission of Sympathy	103
4 'O, what a sympathy of woe is this': Passionate Sympathy in Late Elizabethan Drama	139
5 'Soveraignes have a sympathie with subjects': The Politics of Sympathy in Jacobean England	176
6 'As God loves Sympathy, God loves Symphony': Sympathy at a Distance in Caroline England	215
Coda	253
Bibliography	267
Index	289

Figures

1. *Natural magick by John Baptista Porta, a Neapolitane: in twenty books ... Wherein are set forth all the riches and delights of the natural sciences* (London, 1658), title page. Wellcome Collection, London. — *page* 7
2. Frontispiece to Kenelm Digby, *Eröffnung unterschiedlicher Heimlichkeiten der Natur, worbey viel ... Reden von nützlichen Dingen ... und vornemlich von einem wunderbaren Geheimnüss in Heilungen der Wunden ... durch die Sympathiam*, trans. M. H. Hupka (Frankfurt, 1677). Wellcome Collection, London. — 9
3. William Shakespeare, *Lucrece* (London, 1594), sigs. H3v–H4r. STC 22345 copy 1. Used by permission of the Folger Shakespeare Library. — 104
4. John Trussell, *Raptus I. Helenae. The First Rape of Faire Hellen* (London, 1595), title page. STC 24296. Used by permission of the Folger Shakespeare Library. — 126
5. *Bel-vedére, or, The Garden of the muses* (London, 1600), sigs. K7v–K8r (pp. 142–3). STC 3189. Used by permission of the Folger Shakespeare Library. — 137
6. Print made by James Barry, *King Lear and Cordelia* (1776), Etching and aquatint with India ink, published state, Yale Center for British Art, Paul Mellon Collection, B1977.14.11064. — 200
7. Francis Bacon, *Sylva sylvarum, or, A naturall history in ten centuries* (London, 1627), title page. STC 1169 copy 1. Used by permission of the Folger Shakespeare Library. — 219
8. Robert Fludd, *Anatomiae amphitheatrum effigie triplici* (Frankfurt, 1623), title page. Wellcome Collection, London. — 223

Acknowledgements

This book has been a long time in the making, and during that time I have benefited from the advice and support of various individuals and institutions. I am very grateful to the Leverhulme Trust for granting me a two-year Early Career Fellowship, which enabled me to carry out the initial research for this project. I am also grateful to the Faculty of Arts, Cultures and Education at the University of Hull for two subsequent periods of research leave, and for funding an enjoyable and productive trip to the Folger Shakespeare Library in the summer of 2019. At the Folger, it was rewarding to discuss my project and spend time with the other scholars there, in particular Tobias Gregory, Adam G. Hooks, Joseph Mansky, Emily Mayne, Bruce Janacek, Jonathan Sawday, and Michael Whitmore.

Parts of the project have been presented at various conferences and seminars over the years, and my thanks to all those colleagues who offered feedback and suggestions. I would like to single out Katharine A. Craik's seminar 'Passionate Shakespeare' at the International Shakespeare Conference in 2012, where I first presented my work on sympathy in *Titus Andronicus*. Katharine has been an enthusiastic champion of the project ever since, and I am grateful for her collegial support and professional advice. I also benefited a great deal from the (certainly for me) very timely conference 'Compassion in Early Modern Culture 1500–1700' at Vrije University Amsterdam in 2015. Many thanks to Kristine Steenbergh for organizing such a stimulating event, and to Katherine Ibbett and Eric Langley for their compassionate and sympathetic comments. I was fortunate to be awarded an International Visitor Fellowship at the Australian Research Council Centre of Excellence for the History of Emotions, which enabled me to travel to Perth and Sydney to work on the book in the spring of 2017. It was a pleasure to be part of that lively and convivial scholarly community, albeit briefly, and I would like to thank the organizers of the '*Hamlet* and Emotions' conference at the University of Western Australia, as well as the other attendees – especially fellow travellers Kevin Curran and Naya Tsentourou. Thanks to Bob White for his hospitality during my fellowship and his professional support more generally.

Several friends and colleagues formed a sympathetic network by responding to my enquiries and reading parts of the manuscript – which was certainly appreciated during the lockdowns of recent years. My thanks to Jennifer Clement, Kirk Essary, Brett Greatley-Hirsch, Kevin Killeen, Mary Morrissey, Laurence Publicover, Emma Rhatigan, and Kristine Steenbergh. The late Katherine Heavey helpfully answered my questions about translations of Ovid's Medea with her customary knowledge and good sense – she will be much missed. I would like to thank my early modern colleagues at the University of Hull – Janet Clare, Ann Kaegi, Jason Lawrence, and Stewart Mottram – for their support and encouragement throughout the writing process; I am particularly grateful to Jason for reading and commenting on Chapter 5 in the final stages. Many thanks also to Neil Rhodes, who made some insightful comments on an early description of the project and shared some of his own work with me prior to publication. My collaborations with Erin Sullivan have played a significant part in shaping my thinking about the history of emotions and early modern sympathy; my thanks to Erin for her advice and friendship, and for her careful reading of the Introduction.

I would like to extend my thanks to the two anonymous readers at Cambridge University Press for their detailed and generous reports on the manuscript, which encouraged me to bring out the wider significance of my arguments and to pursue the religious aspects of the project. My thanks are also due to Sarah Stanton for her enthusiastic response to the initial proposal, and to Emily Hockley for her professionalism and efficiency in steering the book through the peer-review process. I am grateful to the staff at the various libraries in which I worked: the British Library, the Brotherton Library, the Brynmor Jones Library, the Folger, and the Huntington Library.

I would like to thank my family for their love and support, and for putting me up, and up with me, during various research trips to London. I should also thank my other family, the Rickards, for their kindness and hospitality as well as their long-standing interest in my work. My final thank-you is to Jane Rickard, who has lived with the project for as long as I have, and has been unfailingly patient in providing advice and guidance – not least by reading multiple drafts of the chapters and helping me to work out the book's structure. She has also provided the encouragement and emotional support I needed at various points, so heartfelt thanks to Jane for her love, care, and indeed sympathy.

A shorter version of Chapter 2 appeared in Kristine Steenbergh and Katherine Ibbett (eds.), *Compassion in Early Modern Literature and Culture: Feeling and Practice* (Cambridge University Press, 2021), and part of Chapter 4 appeared as '"O, what a sympathy of woe is this": Passionate Sympathy in *Titus Andronicus*', *Shakespeare Survey*, 66 (2013), 287–97.

Note on Texts

When quoting from early modern texts, I have silently modernized *j*, *u*, *v*, and long *s*. Quotations from Shakespeare are taken from *The Riverside Shakespeare*, ed. G. Blakemore Evans, 2nd ed. (Boston: Houghton Mifflin, 1997), unless otherwise stated.

Introduction
'Solemn Sympathy'

Towards the end of Shakespeare's narrative poem *Venus and Adonis* (1593), the distraught Venus discovers Adonis's body after he has been killed by the boar. She observes not only the 'wide wound' made by the boar's tusk but also the effect of Adonis's death on the surrounding landscape: 'No flower was nigh, no grass, herb, leaf, or weed / But stole his blood, and seemed with him to bleed'.[1] Here the environment appears to be capable of appropriating Adonis's blood and even partaking in his suffering; although the word *seemed* raises the possibility that this may be an illusion. Nevertheless, the terms in which the narrator describes this seeming correspondence between Adonis and the natural world – and Venus's subsequent reaction – are highly suggestive:

> This solemn sympathy poor Venus noteth.
> Over one shoulder doth she hang her head.
> Dumbly she passions, franticly she doteth;
> She thinks he could not die, he is not dead.
>   Her voice is stopped, her joints forget to bow,
>   Her eyes are mad that they have wept till now.   (1057–62)

This stanza describes Venus's passionate response to Adonis's death and her attempts to express her sorrows. The narrator employs an unusual verbal form of *passion* to mean 'To show, express, or be affected by passion or deep feeling' (*OED*, v., 3). Shakespeare uses the word elsewhere to mean a spoken articulation of grief, yet Venus expresses her sorrows silently: 'Dumbly she passions'.[2] In this way, while Venus herself is silent,

---

[1] *Venus and Adonis*, in *The Complete Sonnets and Poems*, ed. Colin Burrow (Oxford University Press, 2002), 1055–6.
[2] Don Amado's letter, which is read out in the opening scene of *Love's Labour's Lost*, includes the phrase 'but with this I passion to say wherewith' (1.1.260–61), while Julia uses the term *passioning* in her description of an imaginary performance as Ariadne in *The Two Gentlemen of Verona*: 'Madam, 'twas Ariadne, passioning / For Theseus' perjury and unjust flight' (4.4.167–8). For further discussion of this passage see Chapter 4, below.

I

the narrator of the poem makes creative use of an existing emotion word to describe her bodily expressions of woe. But what is especially striking here is the phrase 'solemn sympathy'. The term *sympathy* – which could refer to natural or cosmic correspondences in the period – implies an occult affinity between Adonis and the landscape; yet the qualifier *solemn* imbues it with an emotional quality.[3] The poem thus shifts its attention from the natural environment to Venus's emotions: the apparent 'sympathy' of the grassland is both a figure and prompt for her extreme grief. On another level, however, this passage dramatizes a wider shift in early modern culture, whereby the concept of sympathy is increasingly associated with, and used to express, human feelings. This solemn sympathy is less a magical quality of the landscape and more a powerful metaphorical means for Shakespeare to describe Venus's sorrow for Adonis's death.

The predicament that Shakespeare depicts here – which involves the relationship between emotional experience, emotional expression, and the concept of sympathy – is the central subject of the present book. The chapters that follow offer a new conceptual and semantic history of sympathy in the early modern period. I argue that the emergence and development of the term *sympathy* is related to wider changes in the affective culture of early modern England, in which emotions were increasingly seen as things that individuals do rather than forces that act upon them. *Venus and Adonis* itself hints at this shift in its innovative use of *passions*, an earlier term for emotions, as a verb.[4] The poem's fascination with sympathy – and its experimentation with this verbal form of *passion* – points not only to a complex understanding of fellow-feeling but also to an active form of emotional experience. This shift would eventually lead to the word *passions*, with its implications of passivity, being superseded by the term *emotions*.[5] As we shall see throughout this book, Renaissance representations of sympathy often have a self-consciously semantic dimension, with

---

[3] Burrow writes that 'This sense [of occult affinities] is played off against the human meaning "compassion": the landscape responds both with arcane *sympathy* to Adonis's death, and with human compassion' (note to 1057). *Solemn* could mean 'performed with due ceremony and reverence' (*OED*, 1) and 'Of a serious, grave, or earnest character' (*OED*, 6). This latter usage could refer to actions, feelings, or persons.

[4] See R. S. White offers a wide-ranging discussion of Shakespeare's use of the term *passion* in '"False Friends": Affective Semantics in Shakespeare', *Shakespeare*, 8 (2012), 286–99.

[5] See Amélie Oksenberg Rorty, 'From Passions to Emotions and Sentiments', *Philosophy*, 57 (1982), 159–72; Susan James, *Passion and Action: The Emotions in Seventeenth-Century Philosophy* (Oxford: Clarendon Press, 1997); and Thomas Dixon, *From Passions to Emotions: The Creation of a Secular Psychological Category* (Cambridge University Press, 2003). See also Dixon, '"Emotion": The History of a Keyword in Crisis', *Emotion Review*, 4 (2012), 338–44, and David Thorley, 'Towards a History of Emotion, 1562–1660', *The Seventeenth Century*, 28 (2013), 3–19. The *OED* suggests that *passion*

characters either dissatisfied with the language they use, or seeking out new words to describe their feelings. By tracing this history the book challenges well-established critical and historical narratives regarding the 'development' of sympathy in pre-modern Europe, as well as offering a wider reassessment of early modern emotions, thought, and ethics.

In recent years there has been a resurgence of scholarly interest in sympathy, particularly amongst literary historians and philosophers, which is arguably part of the wider 'affective turn' across the humanities.[6] However, scholars have generally worked under the assumption that the crucial period for the development of sympathy was the eighteenth century. In the pre-modern world of the Renaissance, the argument goes, sympathy was an essentially passive phenomenon, in which individuals were affected by physical and physiological processes. In an important article from 1998, for example, Andrew Cunningham writes that, 'Prior to the Enlightenment … "sympathy" usually referred not to a coming together of mental states, but to a coming together of physical objects, whether this took the form of simple attraction, of the mutual assimilation of qualities, or of mutual interaction towards some common end'.[7] Similarly, Ildiko Csengei's study of eighteenth century sensibility emphasizes the prevalence of the scientific model of sympathy in earlier periods: 'During the seventeenth century, sympathy was defined as an attraction that made similar material particles migrate towards each other'.[8] Jeanne M. Britton goes further by describing this earlier conception of sympathy as 'an unreflective, somatic communication' that 'persists well into the early nineteenth century and often … relies on untraceable, immaterial

---

could denote 'any strong, controlling, or overpowering emotion … an intense feeling or impulse' (*OED*, n., 6a), as well as 'The fact or condition of being acted upon; subjection to external force; *esp.* (*Grammar*) passivity (opposed to *action*)' (*OED*, 11a).

[6] See Sophie Ratcliffe, *On Sympathy* (Oxford University Press, 2008); Jonathan Lamb, *The Evolution of Sympathy in the Long Eighteenth Century* (London: Pickering and Chatto, 2009); Ildiko Csengei, *Sympathy, Sensibility and the Literature of Feeling in the Eighteenth Century* (Basingstoke: Palgrave Macmillan, 2012); Mary Fairclough, *The Romantic Crowd: Sympathy, Controversy and Print Culture* (Cambridge University Press, 2013); Kirsty Martin, *Modernism and the Rhythms of Sympathy* (Oxford University Press, 2013); James Chandler, *An Archaeology of Sympathy: The Sentimental Mode in Literature and Cinema* (Chicago University Press, 2013); Seth Lobis, *The Virtue of Sympathy: Magic, Philosophy, and Literature in Seventeenth-Century England* (New Haven and London: Yale University Press, 2015); Eric Langley, *Shakespeare's Contagious Sympathies: Ill Communications* (Oxford University Press, 2018); and Jeanne M. Britton, *Vicarious Narratives: A Literary History of Sympathy, 1750–1850* (Oxford University Press, 2019). On the affective turn see, for example, Patricia Clough and Jean Halley (eds.), *The Affective Turn: Theorizing the Social* (Durham and London: Duke University Press, 2007).

[7] Andrew S. Cunningham, 'Was Eighteenth-Century Sentimentalism Unprecedented?', *British Journal for the History of Philosophy*, 6 (1998), 381–96 (p. 383).

[8] Csengei, *Sympathy, Sensibility and the Literature of Feeling*, p. 41.

affinities between organs or across bodies'.[9] And, in her study of *Emotions in History: Lost and Found* (2011), Ute Frevert has presented the emotional form of sympathy as an invention of modernity:

> Empathy and sympathy/compassion serve as great examples of emotions that are 'invented' and 'found' in the modern period … Since the eighteenth century, empathy and sympathy have been regarded as civil society's primary emotional resources, connecting citizens and fine-tuning their mutual relations. They have fuelled humanitarian movements, from abolitionism to campaigns against cruelty, from giving shelter to escaping slaves to donating money for grief-stricken citizens in the present world.[10]

This passage perhaps raises more questions than it answers. Are emotions 'invented' or 'found' in particular periods? Certainly new emotion words come into being, including *sympathy*, which first appears in English printed texts in the 1560s, and *empathy*, which emerges at the start of the twentieth century. But the question of whether those words create new feelings or provide new ways of describing pre-existing ones is a complex and contentious one. What is the relationship between emotional expression and emotional experience? Frevert does admit that there was a vibrant early modern history of emotions; but her comments here reinforce the conventional view that the crucial period for the development of sympathy was the eighteenth century. The present book argues that, *pace* Frevert, sympathy and compassion were primary emotional resources prior to the eighteenth century; that Shakespeare and his contemporaries were fascinated by ideas of pity and fellow-feeling; and that there was a culture of sympathy – and an emerging discourse of sympathy – in the early modern period.

We might begin by thinking about the history of the term *sympathy*, which had multiple and shifting meanings during the sixteenth and seventeenth centuries. The *OED* suggests that the word was primarily understood to mean 'A (real or supposed) affinity between certain things, by virtue of which they are similarly or correspondingly affected by the same influence … (esp. in some occult way), or attract or tend towards each other' (*OED*, 1a; first cited usage 1586). This earlier conception of sympathy – a physical or occult attraction between people, objects in the cosmos, parts of the body, the body and the soul, or even musical vibrations – appears in the work of several Latin authors from antiquity who were influential in

---

[9] Britton, *Vicarious Narratives*, p. 10.
[10] Ute Frevert, *Emotions in History: Lost and Found* (Budapest and New York: Central European University Press, 2011), p. 12.

the Renaissance, including Galen, Plutarch, and Pliny.[11] For example, in book 20 of his *Natural History*, Pliny the Elder writes that:

> The Greeks have applied the terms 'sympathy' and 'antipathy' [sympathiam et antipathiam] to this basic principle of all things: water putting out fire; the sun absorbing water while the moon gives it birth; each of these heavenly bodies suffering eclipse through the injustice of the other … the magnetic stone draws iron to itself while another kind of stone repels it … Other marvels, equally or even more wonderful, we shall speak of in their proper place.[12]

Here Pliny draws our attention to the fact that sympathy is a word and concept borrowed from the Greeks: the Latin *sympathia* comes from the ancient Greek συμπάθεια, or *sumpatheia* ('having a fellow feeling'). He goes on to describe an elaborate system of hidden sympathies and antipathies, which offers a wonderfully comprehensive way of explaining various natural phenomena, including why objects attract or repel each other; why the sun absorbs water; why magnets work; and (perhaps most tenuously) why the blood of a goat can break diamonds. It is a curious mixture of natural philosophy, magic, and folklore.

These Latin authors were an influence on European Renaissance writers on occult philosophy, including Heinrich Cornelius Agrippa and Giambattista Della Porta.[13] Agrippa's *De occulta philosophia* (first published 1531–3) and Della Porta's later study of *Magia naturalis* (first published 1558), which were both written in Latin and display their indebtedness to Pliny, invoke the ancient system of sympathies and antipathies. For example, Della Porta offers this admirable example from Pliny: 'A Dog is most friendly to a man; and if you lay him to any diseased part of your body, he takes away the disease to himself; as *Pliny* reporteth'.[14] He also makes a suggestive analogy between the parts of the world and the parts of the body:

> The Platonicks termed Magick to be the attraction or fetching out of one thing from another, by a certain affinity of Nature. For the parts of this

---

[11] Neil Rhodes discusses the earlier physiological theory of sympathy in 'The Science of the Heart: Shakespeare, Kames and the Eighteenth-Century Invention of the Human', in Stefan Herbrechter and Ivan Callus (eds.), *Posthumanist Shakespeares* (Basingstoke: Palgrave, 2012), pp. 23–40 (esp. pp. 26–7).

[12] Pliny, *Natural History, Volume VI: Books 20–23*, trans. W. H. S. Jones (Cambridge, MA: Harvard University Press, 1951), pp. 2–3.

[13] See Brian P. Copenhaver, 'Magic', in Katharine Park and Lorraine Daston (eds.), *The Cambridge History of Science, Volume 3: Early Modern Science* (Cambridge University Press, 2006), pp. 518–40. See also Copenhaver, *Magic in Western Culture: From Antiquity to the Enlightenment* (Cambridge University Press, 2015), and Ann Moyer, 'Sympathy in the Renaissance', in Eric Schliesser (ed.), *Sympathy: A History* (Oxford University Press, 2015), pp. 70–101.

[14] *Natural magick by John Baptista Porta, a Neopolitane: in twenty books … Wherein are set forth all the riches and delights of the natural sciences* (London, 1658), p. 10.

huge world, like the limbs and members of one living creature, do all depend upon one Author, and are knit together by the bond of one Nature: therefore as in us, the brain, the lights [lungs], the heart, the liver, and other parts of us do receive and draw mutual benefit from each other, so that when one part suffers, the rest also suffer with it … (p. 13)

For Della Porta, the world is like the human body, and vice versa, with their individual components responding sympathetically to each other.[15] The implication is that the transference of suffering between individuals is also a natural process of attraction and affinity (rather than a cognitive or imaginative response). *Magia naturalis* was widely read across Europe, and translated into various languages including Italian, Dutch, German, and French.[16] It is one of the few sources cited by Michel Foucault in his influential characterization of sympathy as the most significant and powerful form of resemblance in the early modern period.[17] The fact that Agrippa and Della Porta's works were also translated into English in the mid-seventeenth century (see Figure 1) suggests that such concepts remained influential, even if some readers were beginning to doubt the evidential basis of such claims.[18]

The classical concept of sympathy also finds its way into various English texts in the sixteenth century. The Latin term *sympathia* appears in Thomas Elyot's Latin Dictionary (1538), which defines it as 'a mutuall combination of thynges naturall in the operation of theyr powers and qualities, as water in coldenesse dothe participate with erthe, in moysture with the ayre, the ayre with the fyre in heate, with water in moysture'.[19] *Sympathia* also appears in Thomas Gale's translation of Galen's works from 1586, which includes a discussion of the ways in which parts of the body affect each other: 'at this time the causes of these intemperatives are to be considered, whether these be common to all the whole bodie, or else proper of some partes, which should infest the ulcerate member by societie, the Greekes call it *Simpathia*'.[20] In the same year early modern readers could

---

[15] Cf. the *OED*: 'A relation between two bodily organs or parts (or between two persons) such that disorder, or any condition, of the one induces a corresponding condition in the other' (*OED*, 'sympathy', 1b; first cited usage 1603).
[16] See Moyer, 'Sympathy in the Renaissance', p. 90.
[17] See Michel Foucault, *The Order of Things: An Archaeology of the Human Sciences* (1970; rpt. London: Routledge, 2002), pp. 26–8. He writes that 'Sympathy is an instance of the *Same* so strong and so insistent that it will not rest content to be merely one of the forms of likeness; it has the dangerous power of *assimilating*, of rendering things identical to one another, of mingling them, of causing their individuality to disappear' (p. 26).
[18] See Copenhaver, 'Magic', p. 531.
[19] *The dictionary of syr Thomas Eliot knyght* (London, 1538), s.v. 'Sympathia'. Elyot's dictionary is the earliest example of *sympathia* listed on Early English Books Online (EEBO).
[20] *Certaine workes of Galens, called Methodus medendi*, trans. Thomas Gale (London, 1586), p. 84.

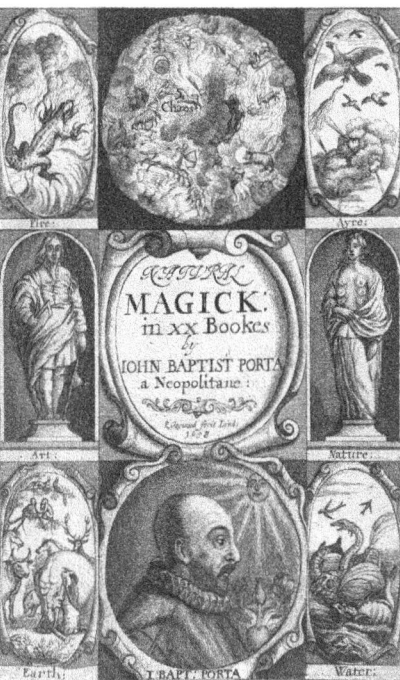

Figure 1   *Natural magick by John Baptista Porta, a Neapolitane: in twenty books ... Wherein are set forth all the riches and delights of the natural sciences* (London, 1658), title page. Wellcome Collection, London.

have encountered the concept of sympathy in Timothy Bright's *A treatise of melancholie*, which uses the Anglicised form *simpathy* to describe how the brain communicates with the heart, and how both parts then affect the rest of the body: 'these being troubled carie with them all the rest of the partes into a simpathy, they of all the rest being in respect of affection of most importance. The humours then to worke these effectes, which approch nigh to naturall perturbations grounded upon just occasion, of necessity, alter either brayne or hart'. The heart is then 'moved to a disorderly passion'.[21] By the 1580s, then, *sympathy* was used by medical writers to describe a form of compassionate contagion between bodily parts and understood in humoral terms.

[21] Timothie Bright, *A treatise of melancholie, Containing the causes thereof, & reasons of the strange effects it worketh in our minds and bodies* (London, 1586), p. 93.

The idea of sympathy as correspondence and transmission persists into the seventeenth century. In Philemon Holland's 1603 translation of Plutarch's *Morals*, for example, *sympathy* is included in the list of 'certeine obscure words' that are helpfully glossed at the back of the volume: '*Sympathie*, that is to say, A fellow feeling, as is betweene the head and stomacke in our bodies: also the agreement and naturall amitie in divers senslesse things, as between iron and the load-stone'.[22] And in *The Passions of the Minde in Generall* (1604) Thomas Wright likens the process of moving others to notions of physical transference and induction: 'If my hand be hot for the fire, the fire must bee more hot it selfe: if my chamber be lightsome for the beames of the sunne, the sunne it selfe must be more lightsome: If I must bee moved by thy perswasions, first thou must shew me by passion, they perswaded thy selfe'.[23] Wright conceives of emotional transference in the same way that he regards the transference of heat and light between physical bodies or spaces. Half a century later, in *A Late Discourse … Touching the Cure of Wounds by Sympathy* (1658), Kenelm Digby describes his famous 'powder of sympathy' – which could cure wounds without touching them – and suggests that laughing and sadness are also transmitted by an automatic process:

> Now lets consider how the strong imagination of one man doth marvailously act upon another man who hath it more feeble and passive … If one come perchance to converse with persons that are subject to excesse of laughter, one can hardly forbear laughing, although one doth not know the cause why they laugh. If one should enter into a house, where all the World is sad, he becomes melancholy, for as one said, *Si vis me flere dolendum est primum ipsi tibi* …[24]

Here Digby refers to Horace's often-cited Latin tag '*si vis me flere*' – the rhetorical ideal that in order to move others you have to be moved yourself.[25] Digby invokes this familiar rhetorical trope but suggests that such

---

[22] Plutarch, *The Philosophie, Commonlie Called the Morals*, trans. Philemon Holland (London, 1603), sig. 6a1v.
[23] Thomas Wright, *The Passions of the Minde in Generall. In Six Books. Corrected, enlarged, and with sundry new Discourses augmented* (1604; rpt. London, 1630), p. 173.
[24] Sir Kenelm Digby, *A Late Discourse … Touching the Cure of Wounds by Sympathy, With Instructions how to make the said Power; whereby many other Secrets of Nature are unfolded* (London, 1658), p. 93. See also Lobis, *The Virtue of Sympathy*, ch. 2 (esp. pp. 58–9).
[25] See Horace, *The Art of Poetry*, in D. A. Russell and M. Winterbottom (eds.), *Classical Literary Criticism* (Oxford University Press, 1989), pp. 98–110 (p. 100). For useful discussions of this rhetorical ideal see Joseph R. Roach, *The Player's Passion: Studies in the Science of Acting* (Newark: University of Delaware Press, 1985), and Robert Cockcroft, *Rhetorical Affect in Early Modern Writing* (Basingstoke: Macmillan, 2003). For further discussion of Horace and classical rhetoric see below.

Figure 2 Frontispiece to Kenelm Digby, *Eröffnung unterschiedlicher Heimlichkeiten der Natur, worbey viel ... Reden von nützlichen Dingen ... und vornemlich von einem wunderbaren Geheimnüss in Heilungen der Wunden ... durch die Sympathiam*, trans. M. H. Hupka (Frankfurt, 1677). Wellcome Collection, London.

emotional transference has a physiological basis, continuing with the reflection that 'Women and Children being very moist and passive, are most susceptible of this unpleasing contagion of the imagination' (p. 93). Using language that recalls Renaissance antitheatricalists, Digby proposes that the transmission of sorrow is a form of contagion that affects weak and passive individuals.[26] Such examples offer a compelling picture of sympathy in the sixteenth and seventeenth centuries: the term, it would seem, simply described the process by which two things influenced each other, or were attracted to one another (see Figure 2).

---

[26] On the relationship between fellow-feeling and theatrical contagion see Heather James, 'Dido's Ear: Tragedy and the Politics of Response', *Shakespeare Quarterly*, 52 (2001), 360–82 (pp. 361–4).

This picture of early modern sympathy – as a form of likeness and correspondence, and part of a wider analogical worldview – is corroborated by the history of the word that we find in the *OED*. The more general sense of 'Agreement, accord, harmony, consonance, concord; agreement in qualities, likeness, conformity, correspondence' (*OED*, 2) has the earliest citation (Geoffrey Fenton's 1567 translation of Bandello: 'If he had bene aunswerd with a *sympathia* or equalitie of frendshipp'). The idea of sympathy as 'The quality or state of being thus affected by the suffering or sorrow of another; a feeling of compassion or commiseration' (*OED*, 3c) does not, we are told, appear until 1600; while the more complex idea of sympathy as 'the fact or capacity of entering into or sharing the feelings of another or others; fellow-feeling' (*OED*, 3b) only appears in 1662. The *OED*'s account of the development of *sympathy* might thus confirm the standard view that the 'modern' understanding of the term – as a complex, imaginative engagement with the other – only emerges fully in the long eighteenth century with the philosophical writings of David Hume and Adam Smith.[27]

Critics are beginning to recognize that this standard history of sympathy needs revision: Seth Lobis's *The Virtue of Sympathy* (2015) has argued for the earlier emergence of a culture of sympathy, but his study focuses on later seventeenth-century writers, including Margaret Cavendish, Katherine Philips, and John Milton, and thus neglects the key developments that took place in the late sixteenth and early seventeenth centuries.[28] Other critics working in later periods have acknowledged that there was not a clear and decisive shift from one model to the other; as Lily Gurton-Wachter suggests in a recent discussion of sympathy in the eighteenth and early nineteenth centuries, 'fellow feeling didn't simply replace the natural or physiological sympathies', but rather 'the two overlapped and intertwined', and 'the latter never fully disappeared'.[29] I agree

---

[27] In *The Theory of Moral Sentiments* (1759), Adam Smith writes that 'By the imagination we place ourselves in [the sufferer's] situation, we conceive ourselves enduring all the same torments, we enter as it were into his body, and become in some measure the same person with him … by changing places in fancy with the sufferer … we come either to conceive or to be affected by what he feels' (Smith, *The Theory of Moral Sentiments*, ed. Knud Haakonssen (Cambridge University Press, 2002), p. 12). On Smith and theatricality see, for example, David Marshall, *The Surprising Effects of Sympathy: Marivaux, Diderot, Rousseau, and Mary Shelley* (University of Chicago Press, 1988), and Stephanie Degooyer, '"The Eyes of Other People": Adam Smith's Triangular Sympathy and the Sentimental Novel', *ELH*, 85 (2018), 669–90. See also Geoffrey Sayre-McCord, 'Hume and Smith on Sympathy, Approbation, and Moral Judgement', in Schliesser (ed.), *Sympathy: A History*, pp. 208–46.

[28] Lobis identifies the seventeenth century, and the middle of the century especially, as the 'critical period of transition in conceptions of sympathy' (*The Virtue of Sympathy*, p. 3).

[29] Lily Gurton-Wachter, 'Sympathy between Disciplines', *Literature Compass*, 15/3 (March 2018), (p. 5), https://doi.org/10.1111/lic3.12443. See also Britton, *Vicarious Narratives*.

with Gurton-Wachter that the transition from one model to the other was not linear or uninterrupted, but would argue that scepticism regarding the natural or physiological model can be traced back to the sixteenth century. Indeed when we turn to literary, dramatic, and religious texts from this period we can see the gradual emergence of the more 'modern' usages of the term considerably earlier than the *OED* suggests. This more complex usage of *sympathy* grows out of, and extends, an early modern fascination with ideas of pity and compassion; and even before the term is used in this sense, literary and dramatic representations of fellow-feeling point to a complex imaginative and cognitive engagement with the other.

My investigation into this conceptual and semantic history poses some complex methodological questions: how can one be sure that a word that is shifting in meaning is being used in a particular way in any given text? Does the appearance of a new emotion word create new possibilities of feeling? How far can one identify the nascent presence of a concept, even when the word is absent? This book does not seek to provide definitive answers to these questions, but it does examine a wide range of usages of the words *sympathy* and *sympathize*, as well as the period's fascination with fellow-feeling and compassion, and attempts to map the gradual coalescing of the two. This history could of course be traced back further – for example to the medieval concept of 'pitee' (deriving from the Latin *pietas*), and to classical poetics.[30] Yet there is a marked intensification in articulations of compassion and pity in the late sixteenth century, when earlier terms such as *rue* and *ruth* start to become obsolete and *sympathy* offers a new way of conceptualizing and articulating a correspondence of woe. It is thus an important example of the phenomenon described by Eric Auerbach: 'on the basis of its semantic development a word may grow into an historical situation and give rise to structures that will be effective for many centuries'.[31] As we shall see, certain developments in the sixteenth and seventeenth centuries meant that a word from natural philosophy evolved into a more specifically affective term used to describe emotional correspondence between individuals. In this way, my particular focus on the history of the term *sympathy* is not merely etymological or philological but rather part of a broader argument about changes in social and religious

---

[30] See Jill Mann's account of 'The Feminized Hero' in *Feminizing Chaucer* (Cambridge: D. S. Brewer, 2002), ch. 5. On Aristotle's ideas of pity and fear see, for example, Stephen Halliwell, 'Tragic Pity', in *The Aesthetics of Mimesis: Ancient Texts and Modern Problems* (Princeton University Press, 2002), ch. 7.
[31] Eric Auerbach, *Scenes from the Drama of European Literature: Six Essays* (New York: Meridian Books, 1959), p. 76.

life in the period – which I will return to later in this Introduction – and the shifting understanding of human emotions and relationships.

In our own period, *sympathy* has arguably been replaced by *empathy* as the primary term for describing compassion and fellow-feeling.[32] And yet, as Lauren Wispé has written, 'The concepts of sympathy and empathy are frequently confused, and both have been variously and vaguely defined'.[33] More recently, Remy Debes has suggested that the two terms are 'eclectic concepts, which only the most dogmatical ignorant pretend to separate objectively and without stipulation'.[34] As we noted earlier, *empathy* is the more recent term, and first appears in English in 1909 (Edward Titchener's translation of Theodore Lipps's term *Einfühlung*). It is thus another loan word, from another language. The term suggests 'The quality or power of projecting one's personality into or mentally identifying oneself with an object of contemplation, and so fully understanding or appreciating it' (*OED*, 2a). In modern and contemporary usage, empathy is generally regarded as an imaginative process, in which one imagines oneself in the situation of the suffering other, while sympathy involves feeling pity and compassion for the other from one's own perspective. But this book will argue that both of these ideas were formerly contained within the word *sympathy*; in other words, it is only in the last century that the term *empathy* has come to denote a distinct type of engagement with others. As we shall see, early modern representations of fellow-feeling involve complex forms of imaginative projection and identification that could certainly be described as empathetic. The semantic history of *sympathy* thus demonstrates the extent to which these different aspects of pity, compassion and emotional transference are closely related and often overlap.

The present book, then, does not seek to offer a complete or comprehensive history of sympathy; rather it illuminates a crucial period in its development in Anglophone culture. What is especially striking in tracing this history is that some of the earliest examples of the word *sympathy* appear in literary texts and are associated with emotional correspondence. These specifically emotional usages – often describing a 'sympathy of affections' between friends or lovers – first appear in translations of European

---

[32] See Amy Coplan and Peter Goldie (eds.), *Empathy: Philosophical and Psychological Perspectives* (Oxford University Press, 2011).
[33] Lauren Wispé, 'The Distinction between Sympathy and Empathy: To Call Forth a Concept, a Word Is Needed', *Journal of Personality and Social Psychology*, 50 (1986), 314–21 (p. 318).
[34] Remy Debes, 'From *Einfühlung* to Empathy: Sympathy in Early Phenomenology and Psychology', in Schliesser (ed.), *Sympathy: A History*, pp. 286–322 (p. 287).

vernacular texts.³⁵ For example, in Thomas Hudson's 1584 translation of Du Bartas's *The Historie of Judith* we find a moving description of Judith and her husband: 'this chaste young-man & his most chastest wife, / as if their bodies twaine had but one life'. This text invokes the humanist idea of one soul in two bodies, in this case two individuals who are identical in thought and expression: 'what th' one did will, the other wild no lesse, / As by one mouth, their wils they do expresse'. This leads the narrator to reflect upon their emotional correspondence:

> And as a stroke given on the righter eye
> Offends the left, even so by *Simpathie*:
> Her husbands dolours made her hart unglad,
> And *Judiths* sorrowes made her husband sad.³⁶

The narrator includes the word *simpathie* to describe this emotional correspondence; as with other early usages, the word is italicized and capitalized, indicating that it is imported directly from the French original.³⁷ In this way, while Hudson finds English equivalents for many of the words in this passage, he retains the French term *simpathie* to describe the close affinity between Judith and her husband. At the back of Hudson's text we find 'a table of signification of some words as they are used before', in which *sympathie* is glossed as 'Concordance of nature and things'' (sig. H4v). As we have already seen, this was the standard definition of the word in the late sixteenth century. However, within the poem itself the term is clearly being used to describe an exchange of sorrows. The importance of this passage is further evidenced by the fact that Robert Allott reproduces it as the final extract in a section marked 'Sorrow' in his poetic anthology *Englands Parnassus* (1600).³⁸ The anthologizing of these four lines demonstrates that *sympathy* was being presented to English readers as a quotable and useful

---

[35] The earliest example of *sympathy* I have found appears in the Second Tome of William Painter's *The Palace of Pleasure* (London, 1567), which describes friendship as 'a certaine natural *Sympathie* & attonement to the affections of him who he loveth' (fol. 350r). I discuss this example in more detail in Chapter 1, below.
[36] Guillaume de Salluste Du Bartas, *The Historie of Judith*, trans. Thomas Hudson (London, 1584), pp. 57–8.
[37] The French original reads: 'Et comme un coup doné sur la droite partie / Respond dessus la gauche: ainsi par sympathie, / Les doleurs de l'epous Juidit triste sentoit: / Les douleurs de Judit l'epous triste portoit' (quoted from *The Works of Guillaume De Salluste Sieur Du Bartas: A Critical Edition with Introduction, Commentary, and Variants*, ed. Urban Tigner Holmes, Jr., John Coriden Lyons, and Robert White Linker, 3 vols (Chapel Hill: University of North Carolina Press (1935–40), vol. 2, p. 77). These four lines appear in the enlarged French edition of 1585, but not in the 1574 edition, which suggests that Hudson may have had access to a manuscript version of the expanded French text.
[38] *Englands Parnassus: or The choysest flowers of our moderne poets, with their poeticall comparisons* (London, 1600); see p. 428.

word for expressing grief and compassion. As we will see in Chapter 3, such anthologies and miscellanies played an important role in disseminating certain innovative emotion words, and provided new models of fellow-feeling and gender relations that became available in the wider culture.

While Hudson's translation imports the French word *sympathie* (and glosses it in its earlier sense of correspondence) we find a rather different case when we turn to John Harington's influential 1591 English version of Ariosto's *Orlando Furioso*. At the start of book 30, the narrator apologizes for his rude comments about women at the end of the previous book and asks for their clemency. His explanation is that he has been carried away by a kind of literary madness, and, more specifically, that he was moved with 'sympathy' for Orlando:

> Yet Ladies of your clemencies I hope
> Pittie I shall, not onely pardon finde,
> Although I somewhat swarve from reasons scope,
> And rash words flow from unadvised minde:
> She onely beare the blame that slayes my hope,
> And for true service shews her selfe unkinde:
> That I did speake was partly of compassion,
> With sympathy mov'd of *Orlandos* passion.   (book 30, stanza 3)

In the 1591 edition there is a marginal gloss to the left of this stanza, which tells us that 'Sympathy is in effect, as much as compassion or feeling of anothers misery'.[39] Harrington's poem thus offers clear evidence that the affective understanding of sympathy was available and conceivable as far back as the early 1590s. What makes this example even more suggestive is that, in Ariosto's original, the narrator compares his passion to Orlando's love-induced madness, but there is no reference to anything that we might call sympathy. The Italian *simpatia* does not appear; and the narrator simply says (to quote a modern prose translation) 'I am no less divorced from myself than was Orlando'.[40] This is Harington introducing the word and the concept of *sympathy* into his translation of an Italian text. This moment thus represents a creative imitation or outdoing of Ariosto, in which Harington is also introducing this definition of the term to his English readers.

In addition to such literary examples, there are various noteworthy instances of religious writers using the term *sympathy* to refer to fellow-feeling in the late sixteenth century. While writers of imaginative literature appear initially to have borrowed the term from continental texts, religious

---

[39] *Orlando Furioso*, trans. John Harington (London, 1591). p. 141.
[40] Lodovico Ariosto, *Orlando Furioso*, trans. Guido Waldman (Oxford University Press, 1983), p. 360.

writers seem to have derived it from classical and natural philosophical works. Early examples use the term in its wider sense of agreement to describe the affinity between the soul and the body, as we see in Richard Cavendish's *The image of nature and grace* (1571): 'And even naturall Philosophy teacheth this, that betweene the soule and the body, there is a certaine sympathy or knitting of affection: for who seeth not that in melancholy bodyes the mynde is heavy and solitary, in sanguine bodies mery and lyght'.[41] This interest is extended in various sermons from the 1580s onwards, which use the idea of sympathy between parts of the body – which we have already seen invoked in works of magic and medicine – as a way of describing the unity between members of the church. For example, William Burton's *An exposition of the Lords Prayer* (1594) includes an extended meditation on the first word of the Lord's prayer – 'our' – in the form of a catechism. The word not only unites the speakers in prayer but also in sympathy and fellow-feeling:

> it putteth us in minde of that sympathie and fellow-feeling of our brethrens miseries, which may move us to helpe them even when we can, & have fit occasion: for we are all as members of one and the same bodie by faith: therefore if one bee hurt, all must helpe; if one bee grieved, all must bee grieved; and if one rejoyce, all must rejoyce.[42]

As Burton suggests, if one person is grieved, all must be grieved, as all 'members' are part of the same body by faith; he combines 'sympathie' with 'fellow-feeling' to suggest this shared suffering. The marginal note points to various biblical verses on this theme, including Romans 12:15 ('Rejoyce with them that rejoyce, & wepe with them that wepe'), which was frequently quoted in the period, and which Burton duly paraphrases. His description of sympathy may suggest a straightforward or automatic form of emotional correspondence; and yet, as we shall see in Chapter 2, sermons increasingly associate sympathy with an imaginative response to the suffering of others. This kind of response often involved reflecting upon and imaginatively participating in Christ's passion, which was arguably the preeminent ethical example of intersubjective sympathy.[43]

---

[41] Richard Cavendish, *The image of nature and grace conteynyng the whole course, and condition of mans estate* (London, 1571), p. 16.

[42] William Burton, *An exposition of the Lords Prayer made in divers lectures, and now drawne into questions and answers for the greater benefite of the simpler sort* (London, 1594), p. 86.

[43] See Jan Frans van Dijkhuizen, *Pain and Compassion in Early Modern Literature and Culture* (Cambridge: D. S. Brewer, 2012). For further discussions of sympathy and compassion in early modern religious culture see Abram C. Van Engen, *Sympathetic Puritans: Calvinist Fellow Feeling in Early New England* (Oxford University Press, 2015), and Katherine Ibbett, *Compassion's Edge. Fellow-Feeling and Its Limits in Early Modern France* (Philadelphia: University of Pennsylvania Press, 2018).

As Thomas Bilson writes, in *The survey of Christs sufferings for mans redemption* (1604), 'this is that which you call sympathie, when both doe suffer paine together, the one from and with the other'.[44]

By the turn of the seventeenth century, then, *sympathy* could be used in the narrower sense of shared suffering and fellow-feeling, as well as the more general senses of agreement and physiological correspondence. One particularly influential writer from this period, Michel de Montaigne, refers to both of these understandings of sympathy in his *Essays*. English readers would have encountered the term *sympathy* in John Florio's 1603 translation, although – as we saw in the case of John Harington – Florio sometimes allows himself a degree of creativity and liberty in his usage of the word. In Florio's translation of 'An Apologie of *Raymond Sebond*' Montaigne explicitly mentions the earlier model of sympathy as correspondence and agreement: 'There are certaine inclinations of affection, which without counsell of reason arise somtimes in us, proceeding of a casuall temerity, which some call *Sympathie:* beasts as wel as men are capable of it'.[45] This is a fairly accurate translation of the French, which includes the term *sympathie*: 'que d'autres nomment sympathie'.[46] Clearly Montaigne is aware of the earlier concept, characterizing it as an unreasoned inclination of affection found in both humans and animals. However, in another essay, 'Of crueltie', Montaigne writes candidly about his own more complex feelings of pity and compassion:

> I have a verie feeling and tender compassion of other mens afflictions, and should more easily weep for companie sake, if possiblie for any occasion whatsoever, I could shed teares. There is nothing sooner mooveth teares in me, then to see others weepe, not onely fainedly, but howsoever, whether truely or forcedly ... As for me, I could never so much as endure, without remorse and griefe, to see a poore, sillie, and innocent beast pursued and killed ... And least any bodie should jeast at this simpathie, which I have with them, Divinitie it selfe willeth us to shew them some favour.[47]

Here Montaigne admits his readiness to weep, even if the weeping he responds to is produced 'fainedly'. He thus attests to his imaginative

---

[44] Thomas Bilson, *The survey of Christs sufferings for mans redemption and of his descent to Hades or Hel for our deliverance* (London, 1604), p. 29.
[45] 'An Apologie of *Raymond Sebond*', in *Essays written in French by Michael Lord of Montaigne*, trans. John Florio (1603; rpt. London, 1613), the second book, p. 261.
[46] The French text is quoted from *Les essais de Michel de Montaigne*, ed. Verdun Louis Saulnier and Pierre Villey (Paris: Presses Universitaires de France, 1965), p. 471.
[47] 'Of crueltie', trans. Florio, the second book, pp. 238–40.

Introduction: 'Solemn Sympathy'

capacity for entering into the feelings of others – whether humans or animals – and Florio once again borrows *simpathie* from the original French text. The word is used to describe sympathy with another creature ('a poore, sillie, and innocent beast') that is quite unlike the self, and thus recalls Montaigne's memorable reflections upon his cat that appear in 'An Apologie of *Raymond Sebond*'.[48] It seems clear that Montaigne used the French word in both senses: the physiological and the emotional. His essays thus provide further evidence that these two conceptions of sympathy coexisted in the Renaissance. The fact that the word could be used in both senses also suggests the close affinity – or perhaps sympathy – between these two definitions of the term.

There is another passage in Florio's translation that is even more suggestive: Montaigne's account of the execution of a thief in Rome, which also appears in 'Of crueltie'. This passage is highly concerned with pity and a community of feeling:

> It was my fortune to be at *Rome,* upon a day that one *Catena,* a notorious high-way theefe, was executed: at his strangling no man of the companie seemed to be mooved to any ruth; but when he came to be quartered, the Executioner gave no blow that was not accompanied with a pitteous voyce, and hartie exclamation, as if every man had had a feeling sympathie, or lent his senses to the poore mangled wretch. (p. 239)

Here, then, we have a moving account of this 'companie' sharing in this piteous spectacle. When Catena is hanged, no one is moved to 'ruth' – an earlier term for compassion and pity that was becoming increasingly archaic in the Renaissance. Yet they do have a 'feeling sympathie' that is expressed audibly, and which emerges as the man's torture continues. The passage thus describes the shared feeling of sympathy between this community of spectators, and how they projected those feelings onto the object of contemplation. We might also suggest that there is a kind of textual community being constructed here, as Montaigne, Florio, and their readers are drawn into this imagined community as well. And yet, in the French original, Montaigne does not use the word *sympathie*:

> On l'estrangla sans aucune émotion de l'assistance; mais, quand on vint à le mettre à quartiers, le bourreau ne donnoit coup, que le peuple ne suivit d'une vois pleintive et d'une exclamation, comme si chacun eut presté son sentiment à cette charongne [as if every one had lent his feelings to this carcass]. (p. 432)

---

[48] 'When I am playing with my Cat, who knowes whether she have more sport in dallying with me, then I have in gaming with hir?' ('An Apologie of *Raymond Sebond*', p. 250).

In the French text Montaigne uses the word *sentiment*, as well as *émotion*, which had yet to be absorbed into English, but not *sympathy*. Clearly, then, this is a moment when Florio wanted to amplify and extend Montaigne's vivid description of the crowd 'len[ding]' their feelings to the man. This sense of an outward movement from the self seems to have caught Florio's imagination and prompted him to add the word *sympathie* – used in the sense of feeling – into his translation. This example would suggest that the transmission of *sympathy* was more intricate and two-way than it might at first appear: the word both emerges from, and finds its way back into, translations of European texts.

Given these complex usages of the term *sympathy* it is perhaps surprising that early modern historians and critics have been so adamant that it was understood strictly in material and physical terms. This is related to a larger tendency in the study of early modern emotions to argue for the prevalence and importance of Galenic humoral theory. In 1999, Michael Schoenfeldt argued that the Renaissance was a period 'when the "scientific" language of analysis had not yet been separated from the sensory language of experience', and that 'the Galenic regime of the humoral self … demanded the invasion of social and psychological realms by biological and environmental processes'.[49] Similarly, Gail Kern Paster's *Humoring the Body* (2004) emphasized the ways in which early modern emotions were 'the stuff of the body' and inseparable from physiological experiences.[50] She argued that early modern texts point to a 'psychophysiological reciprocity between the experiencing subject and his or her relation to the world', and that the humoral body is 'characterized not only by its physical openness but also by its emotional instability and volatility, by an internal microclimate knowable, like climates in the outer world, more for changeability than for stasis' (p. 19). More recently, Mary Floyd-Wilson has suggested that some emotions could not be explained in such humoral terms; yet her approach is nevertheless similar to that of Paster, emphasizing the influence of occult sympathies and antipathies on women's bodies and emotions. Floyd-Wilson argues that

---

[49] Michael C. Schoenfeldt, *Bodies and Selves in Early Modern England: Physiology and Inwardness in Spenser, Shakespeare, Herbert, and Milton* (Cambridge University Press, 1999), p. 8.

[50] Gail Kern Paster, *Humoring the Body: Emotions and the Shakespearean Stage* (Chicago University Press, 2004), p. 4. For other studies influenced by the humoral model see Gail Kern Paster, Katherine Rowe, and Mary Floyd-Wilson (eds.), *Reading the Early Modern Passions: Essays in the Cultural History of Emotion* (Philadelphia: University of Pennsylvania Press, 2004); Matthew Steggle, *Laughing and Weeping in Early Modern Theatres* (Aldershot: Ashgate, 2007); Katharine A. Craik and Tanya Pollard (eds.), *Shakespearean Sensations: Experiencing Literature in Early Modern England* (Cambridge University Press, 2013); and Allison P. Hobgood, *Passionate Playgoing in Early Modern England* (Cambridge University Press, 2014).

Introduction: 'Solemn Sympathy' 19

sixteenth-century understandings of sympathy 'had surprisingly little to do with moral philosophy', and that, prior to the eighteenth century, 'sympathy was not just a somatic feeling but a somatic feeling that breached the boundaries of individual bodies'.[51] In this way, while Floyd-Wilson's study attempts to move beyond humoral theory her conception of sympathy and early modern emotion remains largely deterministic, passive, and bodily. According to her, the sympathy that existed between individuals was no different from the magical forces that bind the universe together.

The present book builds upon this scholarly interest in the passions and the transmission of affect, while at the same time questioning the emphasis upon humoral theory and the body. It thus joins with other recent studies that have argued for a more pluralistic and active conception of early modern emotional experience. Richard Strier – one of the most strident critics of the humoral approach – has argued that the 'new humoralists' are akin to new historicists in their questioning of individual agency, and that humoral theory is one of several tools used by scholars to characterize the period 'in dark and dour terms'. He writes that the focus of the new humoralists 'might be said to be on selves in the period as physiocultural rather than sociocultural formations'.[52] Meanwhile Cora Fox and Lynn Enterline have argued for greater attention to the influence of classical narratives and intertexts in studying the emotional culture of the period, with Enterline focusing on the ways in which Shakespeare's reflections on the passions 'involve meta-theatrical or meta-rhetorical reflections on classical figures, texts, and traditions'.[53] Other scholars working in the field have highlighted the importance of religious and philosophical frameworks. For example, Brian Cummings and Freya Sierhuis have called for a 'realignment' of the field, 'both with the ancient concerns of rhetoric and with contemporary reflections on intersubjectivity and self-reflection'.[54]

---

[51] Mary Floyd-Wilson, *Occult Knowledge, Science, and Gender on the Shakespearean Stage* (Cambridge University Press, 2013), p. 9.
[52] Richard Strier, *The Unrepentant Renaissance: From Petrarch to Shakespeare to Milton* (University of Chicago Press, 2011), p. 17. Elsewhere, Strier has commented that 'the problem of what is literal and what is metaphoric in early modern humors discourse is extremely tricky'. He continues: 'To think that people, then or now, directly experience (or experienced) their emotions in terms of scientific theories about the physiological bases of emotions seems to me a category mistake of a rather major kind' (Richard Strier and Carla Mazzio, 'Two Responses to "Shakespeare and Embodiment: An E-Conversation"', *Literature Compass*, 3 (2006), 15–31 (pp. 16–17)).
[53] Cora Fox, *Ovid and the Politics of Emotion in Elizabethan England* (Basingstoke: Palgrave Macmillan, 2009); Lynn Enterline, *Shakespeare's Schoolroom: Rhetoric, Discipline, Emotion* (Philadelphia: University of Pennsylvania Press, 2012), p. 27.
[54] Brian Cummings and Freya Sierhuis, 'Introduction' to *Passions and Subjectivity in Early Modern Culture* (Farnham: Ashgate, 2013), pp. 1–9 (p. 7). See also Richard Meek and Erin Sullivan (eds.),

More recently still, Steven Mullaney has voiced his scepticism about the ability of Galenic physiology to provide access to the feelings of the past, and about whether 'an etiological theory of the passions could become the basis for a phenomenology of emotions'. Arguing for a 'reformation of emotions' in the period, he suggests that this shift took place 'in the social and hence the lived world of feeling, as opposed to the theoretical or polemical discourses of medical treatises'.[55]

In contesting the conventional history of sympathy mapped out above, *Sympathy in Early Modern Literature and Culture* seeks to extend this critique of the medical-humoral model of early modern emotions. I argue that representations of pity and compassion from this period are far more concerned with imagination, projection, and self-recognition than has been previously recognized. This more complex form of sympathy, which we will see represented and explored in a wide range of literary and cultural texts, cannot simply be understood as a version of natural sympathy or a subset of Foucauldian similitude.[56] This approach is perhaps where the present study most clearly departs from the new humoralists; it proposes that early modern emotions were often the effect of human intersubjectivity and not solely or even primarily grounded in the body. Of course, one has to be careful to avoid projecting one's own conceptual and emotional frameworks onto the past; but we also have to recognize that such methodological concerns about anachronism are complicated when we are dealing with a word whose meaning is in flux. As we shall see in the chapters that follow, various early modern texts implicitly question the quasi-scientific model of sympathy as a way of explaining human emotions. Moreover, the conceptual history with which I am concerned invites reflection upon the ways in which emotions (and emotion words) were both shaped by and came to shape the workings of early modern culture. It also prompts us to think about present-day theoretical debates regarding whether emotions are socially constructed or biologically hardwired.[57]

The Renaissance of Emotion: Understanding Affect in Shakespeare and His Contemporaries (Manchester University Press, 2015); R. S. White, Mark Houlahan, and Katrina O'Loughlin (eds.), *Shakespeare and Emotions: Inheritances, Enactments, Legacies* (Houndmills: Palgrave Macmillan, 2015); and Cora Fox, Bradley J. Irish, and Cassie Miura (eds.), *Positive Emotions in Early Modern Literature and Culture* (Manchester University Press, 2021).

[55] Steven Mullaney, *The Reformation of Emotions in the Age of Shakespeare* (University of Chicago Press, 2015), p. 22.

[56] On the limitations of Foucault's argument see also Lobis, *The Virtue of Sympathy*, pp. 16–19.

[57] Dylan Evans, for example, drawing upon Paul Ekman's well-known (and controversial) work on emotions and facial expressions, writes that 'Our common emotional heritage binds humanity together … in a way that transcends cultural difference. In all places, and at all times, human

One attractive model that may provide a way out of this theoretical impasse appears in William Reddy's *The Navigation of Feeling* (2001). As Reddy pertinently asks, 'Must emotions be either cultural or biological?'[58] He takes a more nuanced view, proposing that emotions are 'largely (but not entirely) products of learning', and questions the idea that human experience is entirely malleable – or that suffering in distant times and places is 'just another byproduct of a cultural context' (p. xii). Reddy writes that 'history becomes a record of human efforts to conceptualize our emotional makeup, and to realize social and political orders attuned to its nature' (p. xii). He is especially interested in the language of feeling, asserting that 'Emotion and emotional expression interact in a dynamic way', and that 'this one aspect of emotional expression is universal' (p. xii). Reddy's position relates to what some twenty-first century critics have called 'soft essentialism' in their attempts to counterbalance the social constructivist critique of the self that was particularly influential in the 1980s and 90s.[59] This is not to argue for a kind of unchanging human nature, but rather to recognize that there are some aspects of human life – for example, the fact that human beings reflect upon the relationship between their own feelings and the emotional codes of their culture – that are transhistorical.

Drawing upon J. L. Austin's *How to Do Things with Words* (1962), Reddy proposes the term *emotives* for describing emotion words that are not simply performative or constative. This model arguably reflects Reddy's desire to reconcile the two theoretical poles of social constructivism and universalism, inasmuch as constative or descriptive statements (which describe a pre-existing world) are comparable to universalism, while performative utterances (which actually do things in the world) are comparable to social

---

beings have shared the same basic emotional repertoire' (*Emotion: The Science of Sentiment* (Oxford University Press, 2001), p. 11). Gail Paster, in contrast, emphasizes the difference between early moderns and ourselves, and suggests that, no matter how 'natural' an emotion might feel, it always occurs 'within a dense cultural and social context' (*Humoring the Body*, p. 8). For a useful overview of these debates see Jan Plamper, *The History of Emotions: An Introduction* (Oxford University Press, 2015).

[58] William M. Reddy, *The Navigation of Feeling: A Framework for the History of Emotions* (Cambridge and New York: Cambridge University Press, 2001), p. ix. Susan J. Matt comments that 'Historians of the emotions share the conviction that feelings are never strictly biological or chemical occurrences; neither are they wholly created by language and society. Instead, feelings are somewhere in between. They have a neurological basis but are shaped, repressed, expressed differently from place to place and era to era' ('Current Emotion Research in History: Or, Doing History from the Inside Out', *Emotion Review*, 3 (2011), 117–24 (p. 118)). See also Susan J. Matt and Peter N. Stearns's 'Introduction' to *Doing Emotions History* (Urbana: University of Illinois Press, 2014), pp. 1–14.

[59] See Andy Mousley, *Re-Humanising Shakespeare* (Edinburgh University Press, 2007), and his 'Introduction: Shakespeare and the Meaning of Life', *Shakespeare*, 5 (2009), 135–44 (esp. p. 136). See also John Lee, 'Shakespeare, Human Nature, and English Literature', *Shakespeare*, 5 (2009), 177–90, and Rhodes, 'The Science of the Heart'.

constructivism.[60] Reddy suggests that emotives not only have a real external referent, but also change what they refer to: 'Emotives are themselves instruments for directly changing, building, hiding, intensifying emotions, instruments that may be more or less successful … emotives are a two-edged sword in that they may have repercussions on the very goals they are intended to serve' (p. 105). This seems to me to be a fruitful concept for thinking about my central topic, as it addresses how the history of a word intersects with the history of a concept or feeling. It also highlights the ways in which new emotion words can be generated by and tested in cultural texts, and how verbal creativity can deepen and extend the affective vocabulary of an emotional community. As an important emotional 'keyword', *sympathy* provided early moderns with a new way of articulating (and intensifying) a highly complex emotional experience.[61]

Such debates regarding the relationship between emotional expression and emotional experience speak to wider scholarly discussions about the relationship between culture and identity. In early modern studies a number of critics have argued that selves and emotions are partly but not wholly shaped by culture. For example, Nancy Selleck's *The Interpersonal Idiom in Shakespeare, Donne, and Early Modern Culture* (2008) suggests that the new historicists' emphasis upon identity as a cultural artefact and social construct is too simplistic. In particular, she queries Stephen Greenblatt's suggestion that self-fashioning always takes place in relation to an 'other' that is alien, strange, or hostile. She suggests that 'Moving beyond a Self/Other dichotomy means conceptualizing others with the same ontological status as the self – others with whom the self can be interchanged, who can penetrate and alter the self, whose perspectives can shape and constitute the self'. Selleck argues that Renaissance articulations of selfhood point to the ways in which the self was 'interpersonally embedded'.[62] Building upon the writings

---

[60] See Plamper, *The History of Emotions*, p. 252. See also J. L. Austin, *How to Do Things with Words* (Oxford: Clarendon Press, 1962).

[61] See Raymond Williams, *Keywords* (London: Fontana, 1976). *Sympathy* does not have an entry in Williams's book, although I would suggest that it fits his definition of keywords – that is, 'significant, binding words in certain activities and their interpretation' and 'significant, indicative words in certain forms of thought' (p. 13).

[62] Nancy Selleck, *The Interpersonal Idiom in Shakespeare, Donne, and Early Modern Culture* (Basingstoke: Palgrave Macmillan, 2008), p. 3. See also James Kuzner, *Open Subjects: English Renaissance Republicans, Modern Selfhoods and the Virtue of Vulnerability* (Edinburgh University Press, 2011); Christopher Tilmouth, 'Passion and Intersubjectivity in Early Modern Literature', in Cummings and Sierhuis (eds.), *Passions and Subjectivity*, pp. 13–32; Patrick Gray and John D. Cox (eds.), *Shakespeare and Renaissance Ethics* (Cambridge University Press, 2014); and Bradley J. Irish, *Emotion in the Tudor Court: Literature, History, and Early Modern Feeling* (Evanston: Northwestern

of Mikhail Bakhtin, Selleck proposes a model of dialogic consciousness, which allows us to recognize 'the impact of the other not as that which deconstructs an already existing self, but as what the self is made on'.[63] In this way, the idea of early modern subjects being either authors of themselves or entirely determined by their context begins to look like a false dichotomy: rather we should see Renaissance selfhood – like our own perhaps – as being inherently relational, in which the self is defined and understood in relation to other selves and other stories.

This is why the case study of sympathy – which is precisely concerned with the role of mimesis and intersubjectivity in the experience of emotions – is so suggestive. The development of the word *sympathy* helps us to map the complex ways in which the feelings of pity and compassion intersect and interact with early modern culture. For, while some critics have argued that early moderns were fundamentally embedded in and affected by the natural world, it seems to me that this is a period when human selves were starting to regard themselves as separate from that environment, and as individuated beings able to imagine and participate in the feelings of another.[64] Indeed the shift from a physiological to a social understanding of sympathy illuminates the complex relationship between the self and the wider community. One is necessarily cautious about crediting the Renaissance with the invention of sympathy (or the birth of the 'modern' subject); and yet Nick Davis, in his study of *Early Modern Writing and the Privatization of Experience* (2013), has suggested that there was an identifiable change in the culture, 'by which special importance is transferred to the community-detached self as a locus of valued experience'. At the same time, however, he emphasizes the ways in which the early modern self was nevertheless connected to other selves:

> the intersubjective relation, however one wishes to inflect an account of it, defines an inherent and structural non-detachment from others of the individual ego; it implies that analysis of individual agency necessarily includes analysis of what the individual experiences as the agency of others.

University Press, 2018). Langley's *Shakespeare's Contagious Sympathies* is also concerned with the interpersonal aspects of early modern selfhood, but his 'medically inflected discussion' (p. 8) is quite different from my own and considers sympathy in relation to concepts of infection and contagion: 'the sympathetic subject is situated at the centre of viral networks, emitting and receiving imaginatively conveyed influences and influenzas' (p. 18).

[63] Selleck, *The Interpersonal Idiom*, p. 4. See M. M. Bakhtin, 'Bakhtin on Shakespeare: Excerpt from "Additions and Changes to *Rabelais*"', trans. and introduction by Sergeiy Sandler, *PMLA*, 129 (2014), 522–37.

[64] See, for example, Mary Floyd-Wilson and Garrett A. Sullivan, Jr (eds.), *Environment and Embodiment in Early Modern England* (Basingstoke: Palgrave, 2007).

Davis suggests that this history of privatization is 'a history of devices, practical and conceptual, *making for* a sense of individually lived separation from the lives of others', which includes 'the replacement of an architecture favouring communal life by one allowing for periods of personal isolation'.[65] A similar argument was made half a century ago by Lionel Trilling in his *Sincerity and Authenticity* (1972), which was also interested in such cultural developments and the processes that led to people perceiving themselves as 'individuals'.[66] As John Lee has written in a recent discussion of Trilling, 'this increasing awareness of one's own particularity made for a greater awareness of the singularity of others, and so of a public society made up of other, similarly distinct persons, as opposed to a social order defined by custom and underpinned by divine authority'.[67]

My research into the history of sympathy speaks to this longstanding interest in the development of the early modern self, not least because it is centrally concerned with the relationships between selves. The material developments identified by Trilling and Davies, together with other social changes – particularly the Reformation's emphasis upon the individual's relationship with God – and the expanding emotional vocabulary of the period, led to an increased theorization of pity and compassion, in which individuals came to be regarded as a connected network of distinct selves rather than a homogenous social group. In particular, the emergence of *sympathy* as a new emotion word appears to have prompted a reconsideration of the nature and boundaries of personhood in the period. It also reminds us that certain linguistic innovations – such as the advent of *sympathize* as a verb in the mid-1590s – can be an agent of social change. For, if engaging with others is an active and agential process, sympathy might paradoxically be regarded as a new form of separation and resistance, as individuals distinguish themselves from groups and collectives of one kind or another. This resistance emerges most clearly in the religious and political texts we will encounter in Chapters 2 and 5; but throughout the book

---

[65] Nick Davis, *Early Modern Writing and the Privatization of Experience* (London: Bloomsbury, 2013), pp. 5, 7. Davis explains that the period sees 'widespread provision of larger houses with closets, offset small rooms with lockable doors which might be used for prayer, study, conversation, sexual activities which were to go on unacknowledged, or the sequestration of valued possessions' (p. 7).

[66] Trilling is aware of the limitations of such periodization, and is uncertain whether the new form of selfhood he describes is the cause or result of increased opportunities for privacy: 'It is when he becomes an individual that a man lives more and more in private rooms; whether the privacy makes the individuality or the individuality requires the privacy the historians do not say' (*Sincerity and Authenticity* (London: Oxford University Press, 1972), pp. 24–5).

[67] John Lee, 'Agency and Choice', in John Lee (ed.), *A Handbook of English Renaissance Literary Studies* (Chichester: John Wiley & Sons, 2017), pp. 56–69 (p. 58).

we will see how a more rational and dissonant view of human relationships leads to – but also necessitates – an ability to imagine oneself in the position of another.

In addition to such material, social, and linguistic developments, the literary and rhetorical culture of the period seems to have been particularly significant in shaping these imaginative aspects of sympathy. After all, literary and dramatic texts involve storytelling, imitation, and role-playing, which are vital imaginative tools for negotiating the space between the self and the other – especially if the other is not identical to the self.[68] Such tools were also central to humanist education and classical rhetoric. Horace's tag '*si vis me flere*', taken from a key passage in *The Art of Poetry*, was frequently and enthusiastically quoted in the sixteenth and seventeenth centuries (for example by Kenelm Digby, as we saw earlier). This is the passage as it appears in Ben Jonson's translation:

> Men's faces still with such as laugh are prone
> To laughter; so they grieve with those that moan.
> If thou wouldst have me weep, be thou first drowned
> Thyself in tears, then me thy loss will move,
> Peleus or Telephus.[69]

The idea of moving another person to pity, and that in order to move others you have to be moved yourself, was a key concept in classical and Renaissance rhetoric. There is an implicit understanding in this passage that emotions could be passed spontaneously from one person to another, which might seem to confirm the sense that sympathy – or at least the idea of emotional transference and correspondence – was understood as a kind of automatic contagion. And yet, if we turn to Quintilian's *Institutio oratoria*, we find that this interest in emotion is part of a wider fascination with representational mimesis. In book 6, Quintilian describes the figure of *enargeia*, or vividness, as 'a quality which makes us seem not so much to be talking about something as exhibiting it. Emotions will ensue just as if we were present at the event itself'.[70] For Quintilian, vivid narrative descriptions should not only persuade the reader that they are in the presence of the thing being described, but also stir the emotions. Elsewhere in

---

[68] See Lisa Zunshine, *Why We Read Fiction: Theory of Mind and the Novel* (Columbus: The Ohio State University Press, 2006), and Suzanne Keen, *Empathy and the Novel* (Oxford University Press, 2007).
[69] Ben Jonson, *Horace, his Art of Poetry*, in Gavin Alexander (ed.), *Sidney's 'The Defence of Poesy' and Selected Renaissance Literary Criticism* (London: Penguin, 2004), lines 143–7 (p. 305).
[70] Quintilian, *The Orator's Education*, ed. and trans. Donald A. Russell, 5 vols (Cambridge, MA: Harvard University Press, 2001), vol. 3, p. 63 (6.2.34). Further references are included in the text.

the same book Quintilian recommends evoking 'an impression of reality', and seems to admit that there is something quite wily, or even cunning, about the emotional manipulation that he advocates:

> The heart of the matter as regards arousing emotions, so far as I can see, lies in being moved by them oneself. The mere imitation of grief or anger or indignation may in fact sometimes be ridiculous, if we fail to adapt our feelings to the emotion as well as our words and our face. Why else should mourners, at least when their grief is fresh, seem sometimes to show great eloquence in their cries? … Consequently, where we wish to give an impression of reality, let us assimilate ourselves to the emotions of those who really suffer; let our speech spring from the very attitude that we want to produce in the judge. (6.2.26)

Like Horace, Quintilian describes a form of emotional chain reaction, in which the orator feels the emotions of their client, which are then transferred onto the judge, audience, or reader. At the same time, however, this is a performance or a role that the orator has to play. The orator's emotional response to his client's case acts as a template for the response of the judge; but the orator's performed response has the potential to be more moving than the original emotions of the client.

Furthermore, Quintilian's understanding of emotional transference or correspondence also involves a form of imaginative substitution: 'when pity is needed, let us believe that the ills of which we are to complain have happened to us, and persuade our hearts of this … We shall thus say what we would have said in similar circumstances of our own' (6.2.34). Here Quintilian suggests that one has to summon up extreme emotions in order to create a compelling illusion of reality – yet one has to persuade one's own heart to have those emotions, in order to provoke them in another. This is produced through an imaginative process, whereby the orator imagines what he would have said, and by extension how he would have felt, if he been in the same predicament. Cicero makes a similar point in his *De Oratore*: 'compassion is awakened if the hearer can be brought to apply to his own adversities, whether endured or only apprehended, the lamentations uttered over someone else, or if, in his contemplation of another's case, he many a time goes back to his own experience'.[71] For these classical writers, then, compassion is not simply automatic or contagious, but involves the orator or hearer remembering his own experiences, or imagining what he would say in the situation of the suffering other. Both Cicero and Quintilian thus

---

[71] Cicero, *De Oratore*, trans. E. W. Sutton and H. Rackham, 2 vols (Cambridge, MA: Harvard University Press, 1942), vol. 2, p. 353.

imply that being an effective orator involves what we would now describe as empathy. Quintilian is quite explicit about the way in which role-play involves imaginative transposition and taking on the emotions of the part that we perform: 'Even in school, it is proper that the student should be moved by his subject and imagine it to be real – all the more indeed because we speak in school more often as litigants than as advocates. We play the part of an orphan, a shipwrecked man, or someone in jeopardy: what is the point of taking these roles if we do not also assume the emotions?'[72]

Such examples complicate the idea that the history of sympathy is one of linear progression, in which human beings invented a sophisticated model of projection and imaginative emotional engagement in the eighteenth century (or indeed the Renaissance). At the same time, however, Quintilian's comments about students being moved by their subject remind us of a specifically early modern practice that was part of the grammar school curriculum and bound up with humanist ideas of imitation.[73] The pedagogical practice of *ethopoeia* involved (predominantly male) students being instructed to imagine themselves in the role of tragic women from classical texts. Richard Rainholde's *A booke called the Foundacion of Rhetorike* (1563) describes ethopoeia as 'a certain Oracion made by voice, and lamentable imitacion, upon the state of anyone'. The first sort of ethopoeia is described as

> a imitacion passive, which expresseth the affection, to whom it partaineth: whiche altogether expresseth the mocion of the mynde, as what patheticall and dolefull oracion, Hecuba the quene made, the citee of Troie destroyed, her housbande, her children slaine.[74]

The most well-known literary response to this rhetorical exercise is to be found in act two of *Hamlet*, in which the First Player recites a moving account of Hecuba's grief, which prompts Hamlet to reflect upon his own emotional state in relation to the Player's performance. We might also think of Lucrece's reflections upon the figure of Hecuba in the long ekphrasis towards the end of *The Rape of Lucrece*.[75] On a more fundamental level, however, such rhetorical

---

[72] Quintilian, *The Orator's Education*, vol. 3, p. 63 (6.2.36).
[73] Enterline writes that 'School lessons in eloquence taught young orators that success was more than a matter of learning to imitate precedent Latin texts fluently and accurately. It also meant learning to feel for oneself, and convey to others, the many passions represented in them' (*Shakespeare's Schoolroom*, p. 121).
[74] Richard Rainholde, *A booke Called the Foundacion of Rhetorike* (London, 1563), sig. N1r.
[75] For a discussion of these passages see my *Narrating the Visual in Shakespeare* (Farnham: Ashgate, 2009), and my chapter '"For by the Image of My Cause, I See / The Portraiture of His": *Hamlet* and the Imitation of Emotion', in Brid Phillips, Paul Megna, and R. S. White (eds.), *Hamlet and Emotions* (London and New York: Palgrave, 2019), pp. 81–108.

training is a key context for understanding early modern emotions; perhaps more so than Galenic humoral theory. As we shall see in Chapter 4, the story of the fall of Troy – familiar to grammar school boys from their reading of Virgil's *Aeneid* – was a paradigmatic narrative for early moderns and their thinking about tragedy, and what Colin Burrow has termed 'situated affect'.[76] The emphasis in the *Aeneid* upon tragic storytelling, and its effect upon Dido, reminds us of the extent to which sympathy and compassion are often intertextual and relational. As Peter Goldie has emphasized, 'grief is an emotion best understood and explained through a narrative'.[77]

The idea that a moving representation can be just as effective as, or even more affecting than, the 'real thing' is explored in Philip Sidney's *Astrophil and Stella* (printed 1591). In Sonnet 45, Astrophil notes that Stella has been moved by a fictional narrative:

> Alas, if fancy drawn by imaged things,
> Though false, yet with free scope more grace doth breed
> Than servant's wrack, where new doubts honours brings;
> Then think, my dear, that you in me do read
>   Of lover's ruin some sad tragedy:
> I am not I, pity the tale of me.[78]

Katherine Duncan-Jones has suggested that this sonnet recalls the Aristotelian paradox that objects represented in art may have an emotive effect that they lack in life. The sequence as a whole, she writes, may constitute 'the tale of me'.[79] Astrophil asks Stella to imagine that he is a fictional character: then she would be moved by his plight. But of course Astrophil is himself an imaginary persona who may or may not represent a version of his author. This is a moment when, as Alastair Fowler puts it, 'Fiction … imitates empathy itself, interweaving subject and object so intricately that one may be at a loss to know where participation is to end'.[80] The kind

---

[76] Colin Burrow, *Shakespeare and Classical Antiquity* (Oxford University Press, 2013), p. 61. See also Burrow's earlier study of *Epic Romance: Homer to Milton* (Oxford: Clarendon Press, 1993). For further discussion of sympathy and empathy in Virgil see Leah Whittington, 'Shakespeare's Vergil: empathy and *The Tempest*', in Gray and Cox (eds.), *Shakespeare and Renaissance Ethics*, pp. 98–120, and Patrick Gray, 'Shakespeare and the Other Virgil: Pity and *Imperium* in *Titus Andronicus*', *Shakespeare Survey*, 69 (2016), 30–45.

[77] Peter Goldie, *The Mess Inside: Narrative, Emotion, and the Mind* (Oxford University Press, 2012), p. 56. See also Alessandro Giovannelli, 'In Sympathy with Narrative Characters', *The Journal of Aesthetics and Art Criticism*, 67 (2009), 83–95.

[78] *Astrophil and Stella*, in Katherine Duncan-Jones (ed.), *The Oxford Authors: Sir Philip Sidney* (Oxford University Press, 1989), Sonnet 45, lines 9–14 (p. 170).

[79] See Duncan-Jones's note to line 14.

[80] Alastair Fowler, *Renaissance Realism: Narrative Images in Literature and Art* (Oxford University Press, 2003), p. 79. Tom MacFaul, responding to Fowler, comments that he is 'suspicious of

of misdirection and manipulation that we find in Sidney's poem is thus a cunning rhetorical and mimetic strategy. It emphasizes the ways in which Renaissance explorations of pity can play with the distinction between representation and reality, and how drawing attention to a text's fictionality can paradoxically increase its affectivity.

Sidney's playful experimentation here with tales and tragedies may have been one inspiration for a highly self-reflexive passage in Shakespeare's *Richard II* (*c.*1595), which includes the new word *sympathize*.[81] In 5.1, Richard commands the Queen to spend the rest of her days in a nunnery, and enjoins her to tell his story in the context of other old, tragic tales. He goes on to offer a piece of narrative that is simultaneously about the power of narrative:

> Think I am dead, and that even here thou takest,
> As from my death-bed, thy last living leave.
> In winter's tedious nights sit by the fire
> With good old folks and let them tell thee tales
> Of woeful ages long ago betid;
> And ere thou bid good night, to quite their griefs,
> Tell thou the lamentable tale of me,
> And send the hearers weeping to their beds.
> For why, the senseless brands will sympathize
> The heavy accent of thy moving tongue,
> And in compassion weep the fire out,
> And some will mourn in ashes, some coal-black,
> For the deposing of a rightful king.   (5.1.38–50)

The play's editors do not quite agree on the meaning of *sympathize* here, in particular whether it carries the earlier sense of correspondence or the more 'modern' sense of emotional affinity. Charles Forker glosses the word as 'respond to, or match', while Andrew Gurr suggests that it means 'share the feelings of'.[82] Yet the response that Richard describes here is a specifically

---

the word empathy', describing it as 'a word and idea not really available in the Renaissance'. He prefers 'the more mediated and partial concept of sympathy' (*Shakespeare and the Natural World* (Cambridge University Press, 2015), p. 21). I would suggest, however, that it is not necessarily problematic to use modern words and ideas to discuss early modern texts. As Kirk Essary reminds us, 'The map is not the territory' ('Passions, Affections, or Emotions? On the Ambiguity of 16th-Century Terminology', *Emotion Review*, 9 (2017), 367–74 (p. 368)).

[81] Charles Forker also makes this connection with Sidney; see his Arden 3 edition of *King Richard II* (London: Methuen, 2002), note to 5.1.44. See my chapter, '"Rue e'en for ruth": *Richard II* and the Imitation of Sympathy', in Meek and Sullivan (eds.), *The Renaissance of Emotion*, pp. 130–52, for a fuller discussion of the representation of sympathy in the play.

[82] See Forker's note to 5.1.46–7, and Andrew Gurr (ed.), *Richard II* (Cambridge University Press, 1984), note to 5.1.46. The *OED* includes this passage as an example of meaning 3a, 'To agree with, answer or correspond to, match. *Obs.*'

emotional one. His speech can thus be read as an early example of the emotional form of *sympathize*, 'To feel sympathy; to have a fellow-feeling; to share the feelings of another or others' (*OED*, 4a; first cited usage 1607). This claim is complicated, of course, by the fact that the objects experiencing compassion are not human: Richard describes the piteous response of the 'senseless' embers of the fire, and thus recalls the 'senslesse things' described in Holland's translation of Plutarch's *Morals* quoted above. However, the fact that Richard's speech is concerned with an imaginary act of storytelling suggests that the function of the sympathetic brands is a poetic one: they offer Richard a powerful metaphorical means of expressing his faith in the ability of language to move others. While the notion of sympathetic magic is certainly evoked, this extraordinary speech emphasizes the figurative, aesthetic, and rhetorical possibilities of the concept. The senseless brands are said to be moved, not by an occult or physical process, but by the sad stories recounted by Richard's figured narrator.

As we shall see in Chapter 3, Shakespeare played an important role in the creation of such emotion words, including the verbal form *sympathize*. At the same time, however, this book is especially interested in the ways in which notable articulations or representations of sympathy were reworked and echoed by other writers, and how such layers of emotional intertextuality both represent and enact a transmission of feeling. For example, Christopher Middleton's *The legend of Humphrey Duke of Glocester* (1600) includes a moving description of the parting of Humphrey (who was the brother of Henry V), and his wife Ellinor, who is to be exiled; the depicted situation thus mirrors the parting of Richard and Queen Isabel in Shakespeare's *Richard II*. As they part, Humphrey says that he will spurn men's company and tell his sorrows 'to beastes and birds, / Trees, stones and rivers … till to my wofull words / They frame lamenting notes'.[83] He goes on to describe a form of emotional affinity between his grief and the natural environment:

> So lands and seas, poore fishes, beastes and birds,
> Hard stones, strong trees, and silver-running streames,
> Shall simpathize our woes, greeve at our words,
> And wish that they our sorrows might redeeme;
> Whilst wicked men, that wrought our misery,
> Feeles not the sting of hard extreamity.   (stanza 130)

This passage might seem to support the idea that early modern emotions existed in relation to the environment, which is itself alive and capable

---

[83] Christopher Middleton, *The legend of Humphrey Duke of Glocester* (London, 1600), stanza 129 (sig. E2r).

of feelings. Even hard stones, which were proverbially unsympathetic, will 'simpathize' with the protagonists' sorrow, and hope that it might be relieved.[84] And yet, Humphrey is not describing what is taking place within the fictional world of the poem, but rather offering a poetic description of his solitude and grief. He invokes the idea of natural sympathy as a way of describing an idealised audience for his woeful words, which will be magically moved to feel his sorrows. Like the speech from *Richard II* quoted above, which may well have influenced Middleton, this is a highly reflexive passage about the power of language that describes a figured emotional response. By the early seventeenth century, then, the cosmological understanding of the term was still invoked, but was available as a rich metaphorical concept that could be used to articulate an exchange of feelings. Rather than being an automatic or natural process, sympathy was increasingly regarded as an imaginative and cognitive activity that individuals could engage in, or – like the 'wicked men' described by Middleton – withhold.

This book is organized both chronologically and generically. My central case studies are drawn from a sixty-year period, roughly from the late 1570s, when appearances of the word *sympathy* in printed texts start to proliferate, to 1640. The book's primary mode of investigation is close textual analysis, although its methodology is necessarily more interdisciplinary than my previous monograph and involves a broader range of genres and approaches – including the history of science and intellectual history as well as literary history. The first four chapters chart the development of sympathy in the late Elizabethan period, and each focuses on a different genre: prose romances, sermons, complaint poems, and dramatic works. The next two chapters – which explore the Jacobean and Caroline periods – range across these genres and introduce two more: political tracts and scientific treatises respectively. My aim throughout the book is to explore the interactions between these different texts, their sources and analogues, and how they shaped the emotional culture of the period. I argue that the words *sympathy* and *sympathize* emerge through a complex process of translation, imitation, and transmission, which in turn makes the words increasingly available in the wider culture.

The first chapter explores some of the earliest appearances of the term *sympathy* in Elizabethan prose fiction, where it is used to refer to a naturally occurring affinity or resemblance between people. I consider how

---

[84] For the proverb 'A heart of (as hard as a) stone (flint, marble)' see See R. W. Dent, *Shakespeare's Proverbial Language: An Index* (Berkeley: University of California Press, 1981), H311 and D618.

such concepts are explored and interrogated in John Lyly's *Euphues: The Anatomy of Wit*, Sidney's *Old Arcadia*, and Thomas Lodge's *Rosalynde*. Lyly's *Euphues* represents an important transitional moment in the history of sympathy, as it employs both the earlier Latin form *sympathia* and the newer English word *sympathy* to describe the 'sympathy of manners' between two male friends: Euphues and Philautus. Within this discourse we can see the term *sympathy* increasingly used to describe a correspondence of woe, or what the narrator of Anthony Munday's translation of *Palmerin* suggestively refers to as a 'sympathy of afflictions'.

The second chapter examines the important cultural role played by early modern sermons in refining and developing the meaning of the term. In the 1580s preachers begin to use *sympathy* to describe a mutual suffering between people. The Protestant preacher William James, for example, combines the natural philosophical concept of sympathy with biblical ideas as a way of describing both the 'bodie' of the church and the emotional correspondence between its members. Drawing upon comparable works by Edwin Sandys, John Udall, and Henry Holland, I argue that sermons from this period play a key part in creating an imaginative understanding of sympathy, which parallels contemporary developments in poetic and dramatic culture. The chapter proposes that articulations of sympathy in sermons are significant in performative and rhetorical terms, inasmuch as they employ the idea of physiological agreement as a way of trying to unite a diverse audience into a single compassionate body – albeit one constituted of individual selves.

This process of associating *sympathy* with ideas of compassion and commiseration can also be discerned in poetic works. Chapter 3 considers the first appearances in print of the word *sympathize*, and argues that female complaints of the 1590s were particularly concerned to explore ideas of emotional imitation and transmission. The fact that these poems rework and echo each other makes their focus on imitation all the more suggestive and complex. The chapter examines Samuel Daniel's influential *The Complaint of Rosamond*, which offers an ambivalent retelling of Rosamond's story and includes various figured allegories of interpretation and reader response. While Daniel's poem does not use the word *sympathy*, it does appear in several complaint poems that followed, such as Thomas Lodge's *The Complaint of Elstred* and Shakespeare's *The Rape of Lucrece*. The chapter focuses on Lucrece's encounters with Tarquin, her maid, and the painted figure of Hecuba. The encounter between Lucrece and her maid in particular seems to have caught the imagination of various subsequent poets who reworked it; while poetic miscellanies from the turn of the seventeenth century reproduced several key passages from these

Introduction: 'Solemn Sympathy' 33

complaint poems, perpetuating this intriguing process of emotional and textual imitation.

Chapter 4 explores the drama of the 1580s and 90s, and how playwrights of the period were fascinated by ideas of pity and fellow-feeling, and how to articulate such emotions. I discuss how playwrights' grammar school training and reading of classical texts led to a fascination with intense emotional states, and the capacity of drama to move audiences to compassion. Marlowe's *Dido, Queen of Carthage* and Kyd's *The Spanish Tragedy* are important case studies here, inasmuch as they dramatize the complexities of emotional correspondence as well as highlighting the limitations of earlier emotion words such as *rue* and *ruth*. The influence of these plays is felt in Shakespeare's *Titus Andronicus*, which not only invokes (and interrogates) earlier models of physical and physiological sympathy but also depicts a 'sympathy of woe' between Titus, Marcus, and Lavinia. The chapter also considers the appearance of the verbal form *sympathize* in several plays from the late 1590s, including Samuel Brandon's 1598 closet drama *The Vertuous Octavia*. Such plays raise central questions about emotional agency: Octavia invokes the possibility that she might 'simpathize' with her husband, while simultaneously suggesting that she is capable of resisting such emotional forces.

The book then turns to the Jacobean period, where we find that the term *sympathy* is co-opted into political discourse – including King James's own writings – and that literary and dramatic texts are increasingly interested in the political aspects of pity and compassion. Chapter 5 suggests that, while some texts from this period present an optimistic vision of a nation united in political and emotional sympathy, others offer a more pessimistic and fragmented picture of Jacobean society. These debates about the political aspects of sympathy, and whether the monarch should feel sympathy for his subjects, inform Jacobean dramatic works, including William Alexander's *The Tragedy of Croesus* and Shakespeare's *King Lear*. I argue that *King Lear* does not simply advocate sympathy and fellow-feeling but rather exposes their limitations, and the ways in which concepts of compassion were complicated by an individual's class and status. The chapter also examines the representation of sympathy in royal elegies – which commemorated the deaths of Prince Henry and Queen Anne – alongside religious and political writings from the 1610s. I suggest that the increased bleakness of the 1623 text of *Lear* may reflect wider social anxieties about what Thomas Medeley calls 'this iron and flinty age'.

Finally, Chapter 6 explores the Caroline period, and argues that the affective meanings of *sympathy* and *sympathize* persisted despite a renewed interest in the natural philosophical conception of sympathy. I argue that the fascination with 'sympathy at a distance' in the 1620s and 30s has been taken as normative by critics and cultural historians, resulting in a skewed understanding of sympathy in the preceding decades. The chapter discusses several scientific and theological treatises that debated the magical properties of the weapon-salve (a precursor to Digby's powder of sympathy), including works by Francis Bacon, William Foster, and Robert Fludd. It argues that several plays that followed offered a highly sceptical response to these debates – in particular Henry Glapthorne's medical satire *The Hollander*, which presents the weapon-salve as a sham cure. The chapter also considers how the concept of natural sympathy feeds into and complicates religious writings during this period; it focuses on Charles Fitzgeffry's extraordinary set of sermons *Compassion towards captives*, which describes sympathy for those in bondage in terms that anticipate modern conceptions of empathy.

In the Coda I reflect further upon the importance of religious and literary writings in this history of sympathy, as well as the complex intersection between natural philosophical and emotional models. I also suggest that critics have presented 'contextual' writings – such as Edward Reynolds's *A treatise of the passions* – in ways that may have downplayed their complexity. I take Reynolds's treatise as my final case study and argue that his conception of the passions was primarily spiritual, intellectual, and rhetorical, rather than humoral or environmental. In this way, the book demonstrates the multiple ways in which sympathy functioned across several distinct literary and cultural realms; but it also reveals some surprising and intriguing connections, interactions, and sympathies between my chosen texts. Taken as a whole, my case studies provide a new account of affective relationships in the early modern period, and show how the materialist understanding of sympathy was channelled into a new version that prioritised affective relations between people. While the book argues that the development of sympathy in the Renaissance was not straightforward or linear, it nonetheless reveals that early modern individuals were not simply passive bodies affected by unseen forces, but rather thinking and feeling human beings, capable of putting themselves imaginatively into the positions of others.

CHAPTER I

'A sympathy of affections'
Sympathy, Love, and Friendship in Elizabethan Prose Fiction

One of the most important printed books of the mid-sixteenth century was William Painter's *The Palace of Pleasure* (1566), the first English miscellany of short stories in prose, some of which are possible sources for several Shakespearean works, including *Romeo and Juliet*.[1] A second volume followed in 1567 containing thirty-four additional stories, including the tale of Dom Diego, which concludes with a harmonious ending in which the characters are reconciled and their friendship celebrated:

> For a friend being a second himself, agreth by a certaine natural *Sympathie* & attonement to the affections of him who he loveth, both to participate his joyes and pleasures, and to sorrowe his adversitie, where Fortune shall use by some misadventures, to shewe hir accustomed mobility.[2]

The passage includes what may be the first example of the word *sympathy* in an English printed text. In the light of the standard picture of early modern sympathy I outlined in the Introduction, one might have expected the first example to occur in a natural philosophical or medical treatise; but this very early usage appears in a fictional text, and describes a relationship between people. It is used by Painter to express the familiar idea that a friend is like a 'second himself' who shares one's thoughts and feelings. The tale thus recalls various humanist ideas about male friendship – many of which were derived from Aristotle and Cicero – that were endlessly repeated in conduct books, courtesy manuals, and literary texts in the period.[3] It is in this context that the narrator describes a '*Sympathie* & attonement' of affections

---

[1] See Stuart Gillespie, *Shakespeare's Books: A Dictionary of Shakespeare's Sources*, 2nd ed. (London: Bloomsbury, 2016), pp. 324–6; and Neil Rhodes, 'Italianate Tales: William Painter and George Pettite', in Andrew Hadfield (ed.), *The Oxford Handbook of English Prose, 1500–1640* (Oxford University Press, 2013), pp. 91–105.
[2] William Painter, *The second Tome of the Palace of Pleasure* (London, 1567), fol. 350r.
[3] For useful discussions of the early modern discourse of male friendship see Laurie Shannon, *Sovereign Amity: Figures of Friendship in Shakespearean Contexts* (University of Chicago Press, 2002); William C. Carroll's 'Introduction' to *The Two Gentlemen of Verona* (London: Thomson Learning, 2004),

between friends. As with several other early usages, the word *sympathy* is combined with a parallel term, in this case *atonement* ('The condition of being *at one* with others; unity of feeling, harmony, concord, agreement' (*OED*, 1)). Such verbal coupling or bisociation replicates the agreement between people that these words denote.[4] This example also associates *sympathy* with *affections* – a term that, like *passions*, is a precursor to the later term *emotions*.[5] As we shall see, a simpler version of this phrase – 'a sympathy of affections' – was borrowed and recycled many times by various writers in the years that followed, pointing to a fascination in the period with the idea of two emotionally connected individuals. We should note that Painter here describes joyful as well as sorrowful emotions; but it is highly significant that this first appearance of the word *sympathy* in English associates the term with a correspondence of feelings.

What is even more significant, perhaps, is that the word is borrowed from another text, and indeed another language. Painter's version is a translation of the tale as it appears in François Belleforest's *Histoires Tragiques* (1559–82), which is itself a reworking of stories by the Italian writer Matteo Bandello. I have been unable to trace the term *sympathy* in Bandello, but the word *sympathie* does appear in the French version: 'ne peus qu'estre conduit par le sympathie naturelle des affections'.[6] In Painter, the word is capitalized and italicized, which emphasizes its status as an important loan word. Terttu Nevalainen has written that 'borrowing was the most common way of augmenting the early modern English word stock'. He writes that the influence of Latin was largely filtered through French in the Middle English period, but that by the Renaissance it was 'more common to find that loans go back

---

pp. 3–19; and Tom MacFaul, *Male Friendship in Shakespeare and His Contemporaries* (Cambridge University Press, 2007). Erasmus refers to the friend as 'another self' and a 'second self' in his *Adages* (see *Collected Works of Erasmus, Adages, vol. 31*, trans. Margaret Mann Phillips, annotated by R. A. B. Mynors (University of Toronto Press, 1982), p. 31).

[4] See *The Oxford Companion to the English Language*, ed. Tom McArthur, Jacqueline Lam-McArthur, and Lise Fontaine, 2nd ed. (Oxford University Press, 2018), s.v. 'bisociation': 'This kind of semantic parallelism has also occurred in Latin, which has absorbed many words from Greek, creating such pairs as Latin *compassio* and Greek *sympathia*. In many instances, such pairs have passed into English, leading to *trisociation*, as with Germanic *fellow feeling*, Latinate *compassion*, and Greek-derived *sympathy*.'

[5] Thomas Dixon suggests that affections were distinguished from passions and appetites, and 'were acts of the higher rational soul' (*From Passions to Emotions*, p. 21), although Kirk Essary has argued that the terms *passions* and *affections* were used interchangeably in the period ('Passions, Affections, or Emotions?', pp. 367–8).

[6] François Belleforest, *XVIII. Histoires tragiques: extraictes des oeuures italiennes de Bandel, & mises en langue françoise* (Paris, 1560), p. 437. The *Histoires tragiques* has a complicated publication history, and this tale is most easily read in *The French Bandello: a selection; the original text of four of Belleforest's Histoires tragiques*, ed. Frank S. Hook (Columbia: University of Missouri Press, 1948).

to Latin directly'.[7] However, this example from Painter suggests that *sympathy* first entered the English language via the French *sympathie* rather than directly from the Latin *sympathia*. Thus the translation of French vernacular texts played a key role in generating the English form of *sympathy*, and associating the term with an exchange of emotions.

While the earliest usages of *sympathy* appear in translations of continental works, such as André Thevet's *The new found worlde* (1568) and Thomas Paynell's translation of *The treasurie of Amadis of Fraunce* (1572), by the late 1570s the word can be found in several romances written in English.[8] The present chapter explores how these late Elizabethan prose texts used the term *sympathy* in relation to love and friendship. It argues that this phenomenon was part of a wider fascination with ideas of harmony, resemblance, and mutuality. As we shall see, this was a period when the word *sympathy* was still being used in its more general sense of affinity and correspondence; and yet such usages often occur alongside representations of pity, compassion, and fellow-feeling. The works discussed in this chapter – many of which refer or respond to one another – thus demonstrate the ways in which concepts of comparability and compassion were closely related. These texts play a foundational role in the complex process that I will be tracing throughout this book, whereby the classical and natural philosophical concept of sympathy comes to refer to human emotions. But they also indicate that the term was associated with human relationships and shared passions in some of its earliest appearances in English printed texts.

The chapter begins by examining John Lyly's *Euphues: The Anatomy of Wit* (1578) and its sceptical fascination with ideas of likeness and friendship. It goes on to explore the relationship between the articulation and sharing of feelings in Philip Sidney's *Old Arcadia* (c. 1580). It then considers the representation of emotional affinities in Thomas Lodge's *Rosalynde, Euphues Golden Legacie* (1590), which – like *Euphues* – employs the word *sympathy* to refer to the affinity or resemblance between two close friends.[9]

---

[7] Terttu Nevalainen, 'Early Modern English Lexis and Semantics', in Roger Lass (ed.), *The Cambridge History of the English Language* (Cambridge University Press, 2000), pp. 332–458 (p. 358).

[8] See Moyer, 'Sympathy in the Renaissance', p. 93. Thevet's *The new found worlde, or Antarctike* (London, 1568), uses the term in an explicitly Galenic discussion of the relationship between the temperateness of a country and the 'temperance' of its inhabitants, 'by folowing of maners for the *Simpathie* that the soule hath with the body, as *Galian* sheweth in the booke that he hath write' (fol. 4v).

[9] MacFaul argues that the humanist ideal of friendship is questioned and interrogated in the work of Shakespeare and other early modern dramatists: 'the Humanist ideal of equality is done away with in the drama, and replaced by a sense of sympathetic or symbiotic difference in which individuality is recognized in everyone' (*Male Friendship*, p. 26). He rightly emphasizes the increasing scepticism about the humanist ideal, although, as we shall see in the present chapter, such issues are not only explored in the dramatic works of the period.

The chapter argues that all three of these texts demonstrate that fellow-feeling inevitably involves a degree of projection, imagination, and self-recognition. Moreover, the fact they employ various terms derived from art and music to describe instances of emotional correspondence highlights the ways in which early modern representations of sympathy relate to wider debates regarding imitation and mimesis. Finally, the chapter explores how the word *sympathy* and its derivatives are imported into various reworkings of Sidney's *Arcadia*, highlighting the increasing currency of the term as we move into the 1590s and 1600s.

'[T]he sympathy of manners': Lyly's *Euphues: The Anatomy of Wit*

Painter's *The Palace of Pleasure* ushered in several similar story collections, including Geoffrey Fenton's competing collection of Bandello's tales, *Certaine tragicall discourses*, which appeared in the same year as the Second Tome of the *Palace of Pleasure*.[10] Fenton's prose miscellany does not include the word *sympathy*, but the Latin *sympathia* appears several times in the context of human relationships. In the tale of Livio and Camilla, for example, the narrator describes their courtship, and Livio's desire for a 'SYMPATHIA or equalitie of frendshipp' between them.[11] Another tale describes a young gentleman of Milan, Cornelia, and his pursuit of the fair Plaudina: 'wyth certeine sighes and secret wringing of the hande, and kisses gotten by stealthe in corners, whiche albeit argued a likelihod and SIMPATHYA of affection, ymparting an equalitie of desyer to the hartes of theim both' (fol. 96r). As these examples suggest, the earlier term *sympathia* was used to describe romantic love as well as friendship – an equality or correspondence of affections between two lovers.

When we turn to dictionaries and glossaries from the period, however, we find that the natural philosophical conception of the term was still predominant. The Latin form appears in Richard Huloet's revised and enlarged English-Latin dictionary (1572) under the entry for *combination*, although interestingly it includes the newer term *sympathie* as part of the definition: '*mutuall and naturall operation of thinges according to their kyndes, as water doth participate with ayre in moystnes, with the earth in coldnes. &c. Sympathia, ae. foe. g. Convenance, Sympathie*'.[12]

[10] See Rhodes, 'Italianate Tales', p. 92.
[11] *Certaine tragicall discourses written out of Frenche and Latin, by Geffraie Fenton* (London, 1567), fol. 40r.
[12] *Huloets dictionarie newelye corrected, amended, set in order and enlarged* (London, 1572), s.v. 'combination'. Huloet's definition borrows from Thomas Elyot's definition of *sympathia* in his 1538 Latin dictionary (quoted in the Introduction, above).

In the same year, the word appears in a literary text, Paynell's translation of *Amadis of Fraunce*, as a way of describing and explaining romantic love. In a speech from Amadis to Lucell he states that 'there is yet a more like nature among certain, that doth draw to one mutuall affection, the whyche wise men do call Simpathie, and yet engendreth a certayne entier, fervent, and inviolable amitie, of the which our firste love betweene you and me dothe gyve us witnesse'.[13] Amadis describes this mutual affection as a natural force that binds individuals together; he points to its arcane status by referring to sympathy as a phenomenon described by 'wise men', but nevertheless attests to its applicability and usefulness for articulating his feelings.

Paynell's text might thus confirm the critical commonplace – which I outlined in the Introduction – that sympathy in the period was conceived of as something bodily, automatic, or instinctive. Certain individuals who have a 'more like nature', as Amadis puts it, are attracted to each other via the magical forces of sympathy rather than human agency. Such beliefs are handled rather more sceptically in John Lyly's *Euphues: The Anatomy of Wit* (1578), a key English text that responds to the storytelling models of Painter and Bandello as well as their emotional vocabularies.[14] The plot of *Euphues* centres on Euphues's friendship with Philautus; his courtship of Lucilla (Philautus's beloved); his subsequent rejection by Lucilla; and his reconciliation with Philautus. The nature of friendship is debated and discussed throughout the text; but what is even more striking, for our purposes, is Lyly's related fascination with ideas of similitude and correspondence. This is a matter of form as well as content: it is apparent not only in Lyly's euphuistic style, which is characterized not only by antithesis and alliteration, but also in various extended similes that draw upon the fabulous qualities of the natural world.[15] As Jonas Barish has noted in a classic essay on Lyly's prose style, Lyly drew upon various encyclopaedic and occult interpretations of nature that 'emphasized the multitudes of correspondences that were supposed to govern the natural world, the mysterious sympathies as well as the mysterious antipathies between things'. Unlike other early modern writers, however, Lyly 'ranged the affinities and

---

[13] Thomas Paynell, *The moste excellent and pleasaunt booke, entitled; The treasurie of Amadis of Fraunce … Translated out of Frenche into English* (London, 1572), p. 260.

[14] On the links between *Euphues* and 'the emerging market for print narrative' see Andy Kesson, *John Lyly and Early Modern Authorship* (Manchester University Press, 2014), pp. 37–40 (p. 37).

[15] See Katherine Wilson, '"Turne your library to a wardrobe": John Lyly and Euphuism', in Hadfield (ed.), *The Oxford Handbook of English Prose, 1500–1640*, pp. 172–87 (esp. p. 175). On the difficulties of defining euphuism see Kesson, *John Lyly*, pp. 14–15.

antipathies side by side so as to unveil the contradictions in nature, the infinite inconsistency of the world'.[16]

This simultaneous fascination with, and scepticism towards, ideas of correspondence is apparent at the start of the narrative, when Euphues, on his way to Naples, listens to the counsel of old Eubulus. Eubulus's lecture is followed by a piece of 'choric moralizing' in which the narrator laments the fact that Euphues disregards Eubulus's advice.[17] The narrator goes on to describe friends who regard each other in terms of total likeness: 'Hereof cometh such great familiarity between the ripest wits when they shall see the disposition the one of the other, the "sympathia" of affections and, as it were, but a pair of sheets between their natures'.[18] This usage of the Latin *sympathia* recalls some of the earlier sixteenth-century usages quoted above, in particular Fenton's *Certaine tragicall discourses*. And yet the '*sympathia* of affections' that Lyly's narrator describes is more complex and ironic than it might appear; after all, Eubulus has already acknowledged that the apparent similarity between individuals can sometimes be overstated: 'Though all men be made of one metal, yet they be not cast all in one mould' (p. 38). From the outset, then, Lyly warns his readers against being too willing to identify similarities and correspondences between disparate people, objects, and ideas.

After receiving various warnings from Eubulus, Euphues encounters Philautus, and, impressed with his 'courtesie' and pleasant conceits, resolves to become his friend:

> Euphues showed such entire love towards him [Philautus] that he seemed to make small accompt of any others, determining to enter into such an inviolable league of friendship with him as neither time by piecemeal should impair, neither fancy utterly dissolve, nor any suspicion infringe. 'I have read,' saith he, 'and well I believe it, that a friend is in prosperity a pleasure, a solace in adversity, in grief a comfort, in joy a merry companion, at all times an other I, in all places the express image of mine own person ...' (p. 44)

Here Euphues attempts to describe and imagine his putative friendship with Philautus, including the correspondence of their feelings. Yet Euphues's reference to his reading is a tacit acknowledgement that these definitions of friendship – especially the notion that the friend is 'at all times an other

---

[16] Jonas Barish, 'The Prose Style of John Lyly', *ELH*, 23 (1956), 14–35 (pp. 22–3).
[17] See G. K. Hunter, *John Lyly, The Humanist as Courtier* (London: Routledge and Kegan Paul, 1962), p. 55.
[18] John Lyly, *Euphues: The Anatomy of Wit and Euphues and His England*, ed. Leah Scragg (Manchester University Press, 2003), p. 43.

I' – are second-hand, borrowed from various humanist writings on the subject.[19] Clearly, then, there is something imaginary about the friendship that Euphues describes (and constructs) here. Euphues does, however, remind himself not to get too carried away with this idea of unity:

> But whither am I carried? Have I not learned that one should eat a bushel of salt with him who he meaneth to make his friend; that trial maketh trust; that there is falsehood in fellowship? And what then? Doth not the sympathy of manners, make the conjunction of minds? Is it not a byword, 'like will to like'? ... I will therefore have Philautus for my fere, and by so much the more I make my selfe sure to have Philautus, by the more I view in him the lively image of Euphues. (p. 44)

This passage is cited by the *OED* as the first usage of the English form *sympathy* (as opposed to the Latin *sympathia*) in the sense of 'Agreement, accord, harmony, consonance, concord; agreement in qualities, likeness, conformity, correspondence' (*OED*, 2). Euphues suggests that the 'sympathy of manners' between himself and Philautus means that their minds are effectively conjoined. Lyly's *Euphues* thus represents an important transitional moment in the history of sympathy, as it employs both the earlier Latin form *sympathia* and the newer English word *sympathy* to describe the 'sympathy of manners' between two male friends.

Yet the fact that Euphues's meditations are made up of various proverbial ideas about male friendship questions the nature and extent of this apparent consonance between them.[20] Euphues imagines that when he looks at Philautus he will see his own 'lively image' reflected back at him. The word *lively* could refer to both intense feelings (*OED*, 3b) and vivid representation ('Of an image, picture, or description: lifelike ... that brings the subject to life; that represents the original faithfully' (*OED*, 4a)). Stephen Guy-Bray has suggested that this passage 'hints that this sameness is at least partly physical, and the emphasis in this passage is thus on how Philautus looks like Euphues, rather than on how he acts or

---

[19] In *The Boke Named the Governour* (1531), for example, one of the most influential English texts in this tradition, Thomas Elyot describes friendship as 'a blessed and stable connexion of sondrie willes, makinge of two parsones one in having and suffering. And therfore a frende is proprely named of Philosophers the other I' (*The Boke Named the Governour*, ed. Henry H. S. Croft, 2 vols (London: Kegan Paul, Trench, and Co., 1883), vol. 2, pp. 129–30). Croft cites Zeno, Cicero, Aristotle, and Bacon as authorities who used the phrase (p. 130, note). See also Carroll, 'Introduction', pp. 6–7, and MacFaul, *Male Friendship*, esp. ch. 4.

[20] Euphues's reflections include the proverbs 'Before you make a friend eat a bushel of salt with him' and 'Like will to like'. See Morris Palmer Tilley, *A Dictionary of the Proverbs in England in the Sixteenth and Seventeenth Centuries* (Ann Arbor: University of Michigan Press, 1950), F685 and L286.

thinks like him'.[21] But the phrase 'lively image' is perhaps more complex and ambiguous than Guy-Bray suggests. We might read this as an instance of imaginative projection, in which Euphues recognizes those aspects of himself that he wants to see in Philautus, rather than any actual physical resemblance. Indeed the fact that Euphues refers to himself in the third person is further evidence that he has imaginatively transferred his own identity onto Philautus. Thus Lyly seems to be testing the ideas about friendship that Euphues has read about, and the narrator warns of the precariousness of the affection between the pair: 'whosoever shall see this amity grounded upon a little affection will soon conjecture that it shall be dissolved upon a light occasion; as in the sequel of Euphues and Philautus you shall see, whose hot love waxed soon cold' (pp. 44–5). Lyly seems to be exposing the humanist model of friendship – and, by extension, the very notion of a 'sympathy of manners' – as an unattainable ideal.

The narrator's description of Euphues and Philautus's closeness is, once again, expressed in conventional terms: 'They used not only one board but one bed, one book (if so be it they thought not one too many). Their friendship augmented every day, insomuch that the one could not refrain the company of the other one minute. All things went in common between them, which all men accompted commendable' (p. 46). However, despite their willingness to share board, bed, and book – perhaps even implying that they have been reading the same book about friendship – there are some things that these two young men are unable to share. We learn that Philautus is in love with Lucilla, the daughter of one Don Ferardo. Philautus goes to visit her, but he makes the mistake of bringing Euphues with him. Philautus presents Euphues to Lucilla as his 'shadow' (p. 47), in the sense of 'One that constantly accompanies or follows another like a shadow' (*OED*, 8), and, perhaps more specifically, 'a companion whom a guest brings without invitation' (*OED*, 8a). Yet Euphues impresses Lucilla with his witty speeches, and she decides that Philautus suffers by the comparison:

> although I loved Philautus for his good properties, yet seeing Euphues to excel him I ought by nature to like him better … Is not the diamond of more value than the ruby because he is of more virtue? Is not the emerald preferred before the sapphire for his wonderful property? Is not Euphues more praiseworthy than Philautus, being more witty? (pp. 52–3)

---

[21] Stephen Guy-Bray, 'Same Difference: Homo and Allo in Lyly's *Euphues*', in Contance C. Relihan and Goran V. Stanivukovic (eds.), *Prose Fiction and Early Modern Sexualities in England, 1570–1640* (New York and Basingstoke: Palgrave Macmillan, 2003), pp. 113–27 (p. 119).

In this way, the apparent affinity between the two men invites others to compare and evaluate them, and thus increases our sense of their dissimilarity.

Later, as we discover Euphues reflecting upon his betrayal of Philautus, he reverses this dichotomy by figuring Philautus as his shadow: 'As Philautus brought me for his shadow the last supper, so I will use him for my shadow till I have gained my saint' (p. 55). Euphues now appropriates and redeploys the word *shadow* as a way of expressing the fact that Philautus has now been relegated to second place in Lucilla's affections. Philautus is now redescribed as Euphues's shadow, evoking the senses of 'a delusive semblance or image; a vain and unsubstantial object of pursuit' (*OED*, 6a), or perhaps even 'Applied rhetorically to a portrait as contrasted with the original; also to an actor or a play in contrast with the reality represented' (*OED*, 6b).[22] This description arguably makes explicit some of the more pejorative implications of Euphues's earlier description of Philautus as his 'lively image'. And yet, while Euphues might regard Philautus as a mere decoy or parasite, we find that Philautus is still concerned to imitate Euphues's sorrows: 'Thou hast hitherto found me a cheerful companion in thy mirth, and now shalt thou find me as careful with thee in thy moan. If altogether thou mayest not be cured, yet mayest thou be comforted' (p. 57). Philautus encourages Euphues to articulate his grief, proclaiming his care and concern for him; yet the tale that Euphues spins is a false one, as he claims to be in love with Livia, rather than Lucilla. Philautus's comments about this imaginary relationship, and how it compares to his own love for Lucilla, are particularly revealing:

> Concerning Livia, though she be fair yet is she not so amiable as my Lucilla, whose servant I have been the term of three years – but lest comparisons should seem odious, chiefly where both the parties be without comparison, I will omit that. And seeing that we had both rather be talking with them than tattling of them, we will immediately go to them. (p. 60)

Philautus suggests that he finds Lucilla to be superior to Livia, but then states that comparisons are odious, given that both women are so superior to others ('without comparison'). They are 'both of such honour as in all Naples there is not one in birth to be compared with any of them both' (p. 60). And yet, as we have already seen with Philautus and Euphues, comparability leads to evaluation. Indeed the irony of Philautus's speech is

---

[22] The word *shadow* is also used by Shakespeare in relation to sympathy in *Lucrece* and *Titus Andronicus*; see Chapters 3 and 4, below.

that the two men are in agreement with each other, inasmuch as Euphues also finds Lucilla to be the superior of the two. Even though Euphues seeks to position Philautus as his 'shadow', then, he nevertheless finds himself following Philautus in his opinions and desires.

We might also suggest that this episode highlights a wider discrepancy between form and content in *Euphues*. On the level of plot, Lyly repeatedly demonstrates the problems and limitations of perceiving two people in terms of absolute likeness. At the same time, however, Lyly's narrator and his characters employ a succession of comparative metaphors and similes, drawing endless comparisons between people, objects, and ideas.[23] This relates to Lyly's concern with the ways in which, as Barish puts it, 'things contain within them their own contraries'.[24] When Philautus is entirely taken in by Euphues's narrative, for example, the narrator warns against mistaking the surface for the substance: 'Here you may see, gentlemen, the falsehood in fellowship, the fraud in friendship, the painted sheath with the leaden dagger, the fair words that make fools fain' (p. 60). There appears to be a tension here between the desire to expose the unreliability of false appearances – and 'fair words' – and the desire to express such ideas in the most ornate and metaphorically elaborate style possible. In other words, this proliferation of metaphors and similes cuts against the moralizing thrust of the narrative, which warns us about the dangers of being seduced by ideas of similitude and correspondence. Philautus also rails against the deceptiveness of appearances when he realizes Euphues's duplicity:

> Ah most dissembling wretch Euphues! O counterfeit companion! Couldst thou under the show of a steadfast friend cloak the malice of a mortal foe; under the colour of simplicity shroud the image of deceit? … Couldst thou not remember, Philautus, that Greece is never without some wily Ulysses, never void of some Sinon, never to seek of some deceitful shifter? … I see

---

[23] In 'John Lyly's Prose Fiction: Irony, Humour and Anti-Humanism', *English Literary Renaissance*, 11 (1981), 3–21, Raymond Stephenson notes Lyly's characters' frequent recourse to analogies and comparisons, but argues that *Euphues* and *Euphues and His England* present such beliefs and precepts ironically: 'what one finds … is not some happy combination of the human and natural worlds governed by synonymous and unalterable Order of Truth, but rather a dramatization of the characters' failure to make the correspondence epistemologically adequate' (p. 8). He does not, however, specifically address the notion of sympathy. Guy-Bray suggests that the analogical aspects of Lyly's fiction relate to his representation of sexuality: 'On the level of plot, *Euphues* is concerned with both alloiosis and homonormativity and this concern is also visible on the level of the sentence' ('Same Difference', p. 116).

[24] Barish, 'The Prose Style of John Lyly', p. 20. Barish writes: 'The moral is always the same: that the more absolute of its kind a thing may appear to be, the more certain it is that somewhere within it lies its own antithesis, its anti-self' (p. 22).

> now that as the fish scolopidus in the flood Araris at the waxing of the moon is as white as the driven snow, and at the waning as black as the burnt coal, so Euphues, which at the first increasing of our familiarity was very zealous, is now at the last cast become most faithless. (p. 76)

Philautus realizes that the conjunction of their minds, if it ever existed, has come to an end. As we have seen, Euphues and Philautus employ various metaphors to describe their relationship – 'lively image', 'shadow', and now 'counterfeit' – that have increasingly pejorative connotations. Here Philautus compares Euphues to other duplicitous individuals, including Sinon, the figure who so fascinates and appals Shakespeare's Lucrece and Marlowe's Dido – as we will see in subsequent chapters. But perhaps some of these metaphorical comparisons stretch the limits of reasonableness. There is, surely, a considerable difference between the duplicitous Sinon, who persuaded the Trojans to admit the wooden horse into their city, and someone who steals his friend's fiancée. Even more strikingly, Philautus uses the idea of occult sympathy between a mythical fish (scolopidus) and the moon as a way of describing the decline of Euphues's character.[25] Ironically this example of natural sympathy is used as a metaphor for the lack of sympathy between himself and Euphues. What this passage highlights, perhaps, is the difficulty of avoiding using metaphors, and notions of likeness and similitude, despite an awareness that they might be problematic, or even misleading.

The main action of the narrative concludes with an acknowledgement of both the similarities and the differences between Euphues and Philautus.[26] The text thus implies that the idealized friendship described at the start was itself a kind of 'shadow'. Yet a form of reconciliation between the two men is accommodated nevertheless. We discover that Lucilla is not, in fact, interested in Euphues or Philautus. Lucilla reveals to Euphues that she is a fish that has already been caught, so to speak, by Curio. In a sense, the situation of Euphues and Philautus is thus comparable; they have, as Lucilla puts it, 'both drunk of one cup'. Lucilla does offer Euphues some consolation, however, reminding him that 'In misery, Euphues, it is great comfort to have a companion' (p. 81). This proverbial phrase suggests

---

[25] This mythological creature, which purportedly changed its colour according to the waxing and waning of the moon (see Scragg's note 3, p. 76), is also referred to in Lyly's *Endymion* (1588), when Endymion uses it as a metaphor for his supposed sympathy with Cynthia: 'I am none of those wolves that bark most when thou shinest brightest, but that fish – thy fish, Cynthia, in the flood Araris – which at thy waxing is as white as the driven snow and at thy waning as black as deepest darkness' (*Endymion*, ed. David Bevington (Manchester University Press, 1996), 2.1.33–7).
[26] There are various letters that follow, which discuss the issues raised by the text.

that emotional comparability – perhaps also shared imaginatively with the many others who have quoted the proverb – can lead to consolation.[27] In this way the two men will indeed share each other's emotions, but not through some sort of natural or occult sympathy, or humanist model of sympathetic friendship, but rather through a shared set of circumstances. Indeed Lucilla's inconstancy engenders a renewed sympathy between the two men, as Philautus once again feels pity for Euphues: 'Philautus, having intelligence of Euphues his success and the falsehood of Lucilla, although he began to rejoice at the misery of his fellow, yet seeing her fickleness could not but lament her folly and pity his friend's misfortune, thinking that the lightness of Lucilla enticed Euphues to so great liking'. *Euphues* ends with its two protagonists 'renew[ing] their old friendship' over Lucilla's rejection of them both. Euphues and Philautus agree to part, but state that the 'conjunction of their minds' (p. 87) will persist, despite their physical separation. This phrase echoes the description of their friendship at the start of the text. The irony, then, is that the 'sympathy of manners' between Euphues and Philautus is reasserted, but only in the context of their separation.

Euphues: The Anatomy of Wit is thus a key text in the history of the term *sympathy*, which simultaneously includes a thoroughgoing interrogation of concepts of agreement, harmony, and likeness. Lyly suggests that friendship does not simply make, as Elyot puts it, 'two parsones one in having and suffering', but rather involves two individuals who recognize both their shared experiences and their differences.[28] The characters' faith in their ability to find correspondences between themselves and others, and between the human and the natural world, is tested and ironized. In this way, the text invites us to reflect upon how Euphues and Philautus's friendship relates to Lyly's own partiality for comparative metaphors and similes. The fact that such notions of resemblance are often expressed in terms that recall pictorial art, and in such explicitly metaphorical and rhetorical terms, reminds us of the extent to which literary texts – including

---

[27] See Dent, *Shakespeare's Proverbial Language*, C571: 'It is good to have company in misery'. The phrase is reworked in Shakespeare's *Lucrece*: 'And fellowship in woe doth woe assuage' (790); see Chapter 3, below.

[28] *The Boke Named the Governour* (1531), ed. Croft, vol. 2, pp. 129–30. Pierre de La Primaudaye's *The French academie* (translated into English in 1586) includes a chapter entitled 'Of Friendship, and of a Friend', which suggests that 'a man may easily judge that this so excellent a sympathie and fellow feeling of two friends is very rare, and not easily found'. But like Lyly he sounds a sceptical note about how the model might work in practice: 'and by a more forcible reason it followeth, that it is altogither impossible that many such friends should be linked togither' (*The French academie*, trans. Thomas Bowers (London, 1586), p. 145).

Euphues itself – are inextricably bound up with rhetoric, imitation, and metaphor. The notion that the friend resembles a 'lively image' of the self is also adopted and developed in subsequent literary works, including what is arguably the most remarkable and influential romance of the Elizabethan period: Sidney's *Arcadia*.

'[T]o touch the right tune of their own woes': Sidney's *Arcadia*

Like Lyly's *Euphues*, Philip Sidney's *Old Arcadia* (completed *c.* 1580) offers a fictionalized exploration of early modern notions of friendship.[29] The main plot of the *Arcadia* centres on two princes, Pyrocles and Musidorus, who are cousins and great friends. Tom MacFaul has described this friendship as 'an instance of the humanist ideal', suggesting that 'there is no ironic mutual undermining of the concepts of love and friendship'.[30] We might suggest, however, that Sidney's depiction of the relationship between Pyrocles and Musidorus is somewhat more sceptical than MacFaul allows, and that Sidney's interest in friendship is part of a larger exploration of the aesthetics of pity and compassion. The word *sympathy* does not appear in the *Old Arcadia*, although there is a character called Sympathus who appears at the end of the text, and whose name suggests 'one who commiserates'.[31] Wendy Olmstead, who offers this gloss, has explored the relationship between emotion and rhetoric in the text, but she does not consider the significance of Sympathus's name in relation to the history of sympathy. Sidney's innovation is to associate this Latinate term, which does not appear in any other English text in the period, with a character notable for his piteous nature.[32] Meanwhile, Garrett A. Sullivan, Jr has discussed the relationship between the body and the environment in the *Old Arcadia*, and considered the role of the passions 'in generating an *affective landscape*

---

[29] On the date, see *The Countess of Pembroke's Arcadia (The Old Arcadia)*, ed. Jean Robertson (Oxford: Clarendon Press, 1973), pp. xv–xix. Quotations from the text are taken from this edition, unless otherwise stated.
[30] Tom MacFaul, 'Friendship in Sidney's *Arcadias*', *Studies in English Literature, 1500–1900*, 49 (2009), 17–33 (pp. 17, 20).
[31] Wendy Olmstead, *The Imperfect Friend: Emotion and Rhetoric in Sidney, Milton, and Their Contexts* (University of Toronto Press, 2008), p. 22. See also Jacqueline T. Miller, 'The Passion Signified: Imitation and the Construction of Emotions in Sidney and Wroth', *Criticism*, 43 (2001), 407–21; Jennifer Vaught, 'Men Who Weep and Wail: Masculinity and Emotion in Sidney's *New Arcadia*', *Literature Compass*, 2 (2005), 1–16; and Vaught's *Masculinity and Emotion in Early Modern Literature* (Aldershot: Ashgate, 2008).
[32] The name is reused by Nathaniel Ingelo in his prose romance *Bentivolio and Urania* (London, 1660), but I have not found it any other English printed text.

into which [the] subject is dissolved'.³³ For Sullivan, the passages in the text that make connections between the characters' emotions and the natural world constitute an early modern version of the pathetic fallacy:

> Thinking this way runs the risk of evoking the pathetic fallacy, but we are in fact dealing here with something quite different and quite distinctly early modern. The pathetic fallacy presupposes a clear separation between subject and environment as the precondition for the projection of human emotion on to that environment. But within the passion-suffused world of the forest, the separation that underwrites this fallacy simply does not exist, at least not as such. (p. 58)

Yet, in seeking to historicize the early modern passions, Sullivan perhaps overstates the extent to which Sidney's conception of the passions is humoral, physical, and environmental. As we shall see, Sidney's interest in emotion is decidedly literary, in the sense that we find various characters who write poems about their grief while other characters respond to and comment upon them. The *Old Arcadia* is thus fascinated not only by emotional correspondence but also by the ways in which the representation or narrativization of an individual's grief enables others to share it. The fact that later expansions and adaptations of the *Arcadia* do include the term *sympathy* – as we shall see below – suggests that later writers picked up on the text's fascination with grief and compassion, and that they found this innovative word apt for expressing and extending those concerns.³⁴

As the start of the text, Pyrocles and Musidorus fall in love with Philoclea and Pamela, the two daughters of Duke Basilius, and, in order to gain access to the pair, Pyrocles takes on the identity of an Amazon named Cleophila, while Musidorus disguises himself as a shepherd. The two princes go off with their respective partners, but are then reunited at the start of book 3. And, as they recount their adventures to one another, we have the following passage, which is explicitly concerned with mutuality, friendship, and emotion:

> they recounted one to another their strange pilgrimage of passions, omitting nothing which the open-hearted friendship is wont to lay forth, where there is cause to communicate both joys and sorrows – for, indeed, there is no sweeter

---

[33] Garrett A. Sullivan, Jr, *Sleep, Romance and Human Embodiment: Vitality from Spenser to Milton* (Cambridge University Press, 2012), p. 47 (italics in original).

[34] The word *sympathy* does appear in book 3 of the 1590 *Arcadia* in its 'occult' sense when the narrator describes Amphialus's encounter with the Forsaken Knight: 'His impresa was a catoblepta, which so long lies dead as the moon, whereto it hath so natural a sympathy, wants her light' (*The Countess of Pembroke's Arcadia (The New Arcadia)*, ed. Victor Skretkowicz (Oxford: Clarendon Press, 1987), p. 405).

taste of friendship than the coupling of their souls in this mutuality either of condoling or comforting, where the oppressed mind finds itself not altogether miserable, since it is sure of one which is feelingly sorry for his misery; and the joyful spends not his joy either alone or there where it may be envied, but may freely send it to such a well-grounded object, from whence he shall be sure to receive a sweet reflection of the same joy, and (as in a clear mirror of sincere goodwill) see a lively picture of his own gladness. (p. 168)

At first glance, this passage appears to be a fairly conventional description of the ideal of early modern friendship. The description of 'the coupling of souls' in a mutuality of 'condoling or comforting' may remind us of the sympathetic, though problematic, relationship between Euphues and Philautus. True friends do not simply offer each other company, but rather the friend is 'feelingly sorry for [the other's] misery'. In other words, this pity comes 'By or from actual personal feeling, knowledge or experience' (*OED*, 'feelingly', 4a). We have already seen how Philautus is described by Euphues as a 'lively image' of himself in Lyly's *Euphues*. Here once again we find the vocabulary of semblance and mirroring: the friend offers a 'lively picture' of one's emotional state, and a 'sweet reflection of the same joy'. The fact that Renaissance representations of emotion often refer to sympathetic individuals as 'lively' images of each other demonstrates the close affinity between concepts of sympathy and mimesis in the period.[35] And yet the idea of the other as a 'lively picture' of the self remains attractive but problematic. Can it really be the same emotion that the friend feels? The vocabulary of the passage – 'reflection', 'mirror', and 'picture' – seems to imply that sympathy involves recognizing oneself as well as feeling the sorrows of another.[36]

The notion that sympathy might involve a degree of self-recognition – which is hinted at in the passage above, but made more explicit at other points in the text – is arguably one of the most important and suggestive insights of the *Arcadia*. And indeed several of Sidney's characters not only

---

[35] Jonathan H. Holmes considers this trope in relation to dramatic performance in '"To Move the Spirits of the Beholder to Admiration": Lively Passionate Performance on the Early Modern Stage', *Literature Compass* 14/2 (2017), doi: 10.1111/lic3.12381. Clearly, however, this term was also used to describe representations of emotion in prose and poetry from the period. Erasmus discusses the proverbial sayings 'As though in a mirror' and 'As though in a picture' in his *Adages* (see *Collected Works of Erasmus, Adages, vol. 33*, trans. R. A. B. Mynors (University of Toronto Press, 1991), pp. 162–3). For further discussion of Erasmus's usage of these metaphors see Brian Cummings, 'Erasmus and the Invention of Literature', *Erasmus Yearbook*, 33 (2013), 22–54.

[36] For a stimulating discussion of metaphors involving 'active mirrors' in the period see Selleck, *The Interpersonal Idiom*: 'Renaissance mirrors have an active dimension, engaging the viewer with something beyond his or her actual self-image, and in some way *adding to* or *changing* the self they confront … By presenting something *other* than the self, such mirrors mean to produce a more complex process than just self-recognition – they provoke comparison and make one aware of the similarity or difference between oneself and the model' (pp. 102–3).

experience grief, loss, or love-sickness, but also recognize their feelings in those of others. At the start of book 2, for instance, Pyrocles's Amazonian disguise seems to be causing various problems for the inhabitants of Arcadia. Gynecia, the Duke's wife, realizes that Cleophila is a young man in disguise, and falls in love with him. At the same time, Gynecia realizes that the Duke is also in love with Cleophila, and we discover Gynecia bemoaning her predicament. She soon finds, however, that she is not the only person in a sorrowful state:

> Having spoken this, she [Gynecia] began to make a piteous war with her fair hair when she might hear not far from her an extremely doleful voice, but so suppressed with a kind of whispering note that she could not conceive the words distinctly. But as a lamentable tune is the sweetest music to a woeful mind, she drew thither near away in hope to find some companion of her misery. (p. 92)

Gynecia tries to seek out the source of this music, thinking that this 'lamentable tune' might offer her a way of expressing her own plight, perhaps in the same way that the woes of a 'companion' might resonate with her own, and thus offer her comfort. She hears a lute, excellently played, and some verses accompanying it that take the form of a sonnet. Given that the sonnet is about the painful effects of love and 'hot desire' (p. 93), it can be seen to anticipate the Petrarchan mode of *Astrophil and Stella* (1581–2). And indeed, like Astrophil, this piteous individual – who turns out to be Pyrocles in disguise as Cleophila – is unsatisfied with the ameliorative effects of his singing and playing. He castigates his lute after throwing it to the ground:

> Alas, poor lute, how much thou art deceived to think that in my miseries thou couldst ease my woes, as in careless times thou wert wont to please my fancies! ... The discord of my thoughts, my lute, doth ill agree to the concord of thy sweet strings; therefore, be not ashamed to leave thy master, since he is not afraid to forsake himself. (p. 93)

What we find here, then, is an apparent failure of musical sympathy. Using the vocabulary of musical concord and discord, Pyrocles suggests that his inward sufferings do not 'agree' with the harmony of his lute's sweet strings.[37] Pyrocles thus raises doubts about the efficacy of art and its

---

[37] For a wide-ranging discussion of musical sympathy see Ruth HaCohen, 'The Music of Sympathy in the Arts of the Baroque; or, the Use of Difference to Overcome Indifference', *Poetics Today*, 22 (2001), 607–50. Pyrocles's vocabulary is combined with the term *simpathy* in John Bennett's *Madrigalls to foure voyces* (London, 1599): 'No discord jarres, in our loves simpathy, no discord jarres, in our loves simpathy. / Our concords have some discords mixt among, / Discording concords makes the sweetest song, discording concords, makes the sweetest song' (sig. C4r).

ability to express an individual's inner grief, particularly when that expression is aesthetically 'sweet' and well-ordered. Yet we find that Pyrocles's griefs are in harmony with those of Gynecia, or at least so Gynecia thinks: 'Gynecia could not refrain to show herself, thinking such griefs could serve fitly for nothing but her own fortune' (p. 94). Interestingly, then, even though Pyrocles's attempts to express his grief through art do not seem to correspond with his own thoughts, they do appear to correspond with, even speak for, Gynecia's misfortunes.

Later in the same book we find another episode in which the sorrowful expressions of grief speak more effectively for the other than the self. Philoclea – who has begun to feel a strong affection for Cleophila – leaves her cottage, and comes across an unnamed lady by the riverside, bent over the river, whose tears fall into the water. This lady – who is, once again, Pyrocles – articulates her desire for the streams to carry the knowledge of her 'unfortunate fortune' (p. 118) to the sea, in order that the whole world might know it. She then takes a willow stick and writes a poem in the sand:

>Over these brooks, trusting to ease mine eye
>(Mine eyes e'en great in labour with their tears),
>I laid my face (my face wherein there lies
>Clusters of clouds, which no sun ever clears).
>   In wat'ry glass my watered eyes I see:
>   Sorrows ill eased, where sorrows painted be.
>
>My thoughts, imprisoned in my secret woes,
>With flamy breath do issue oft in sound:
>The sound to this strange air no sooner goes
>But that it doth with echo's force rebound
>   And make me hear the plaints I would refrain:
>   Thus outward helps my inward griefs maintain.
>
>Now in this sand I would discharge my mind,
>And cast from me part of my burd'nous cares:
>But in the sand my tales foretold I find,
>And see therein how well the writer fares.
>   Since stream, air, sand, mine eyes and ears conspire:
>   What hope to quench where each thing blows the fire? (p. 118)

This poem is explicitly about the act of writing, and the question of whether art eases grief or maintains and intensifies it. The first stanza suggests that sorrows are 'ill eased, where sorrows painted be'; that is, the very process of articulating one's sorrows, or turning them into art, may have the potential to increase rather than diminish them, inasmuch as the very process of articulation inevitably recalls, or even emphasizes, one's pain.[38] Indeed the second stanza suggests that, by articulating one's 'secret woes' and 'inward griefs', they may 'rebound' back to oneself, and thus remind one afresh of one's sufferings. Outward expressions of grief might thus simply 'maintain' the very inward griefs that they seek to depict.

In the third stanza the speaker finds that the sands have 'foretold' her cares, possibly in the sense that the two previous stanzas have already been written down. The poem is thus primarily concerned with the speaker's inability to mitigate or assuage her woes. And yet, as with Pyrocles's encounter with Gynecia, Philoclea finds that these verses do articulate, and thus ameliorate, her predicament: 'she was well content to hear her words which she thought might with more cause have been spoken by her own mouth' (p. 119). In this way, Sidney invites his readers to compare Pyrocles's encounter with Philoclea with his earlier encounter with Gynecia. Sidney thus not only explores the comparability of sorrows between two individuals but also invites his readers to compare these two sets of comparisons. Philoclea's writerly dilemma might also prompt us to reflect upon the difference between composing and consuming literary texts. Expressing our own grief does not necessarily help us, but recognizing our own grief in the words of others might: art helps the consumer, not the artist. This also relates to Astrophil's Petrarchan predicament in *Astrophil and Stella*: finding fit words 'to paint the blackest face of woe' may not mitigate his sorrows, but reading about them may move Stella to pity: 'Knowledge might pity win, and pity grace obtain'.[39]

This ambivalence towards pity is further explored in the fourth book. Duke Basilius seems to die after being given a potion by his wife that she thinks is an aphrodisiac. His death is merely apparent, however, and in typical romance fashion he revives in the final book. Yet, at least for a while, the Arcadians think that Basilius has died, and we get to hear their lamentations. At the start of the Fourth Eclogues, a shepherd named Geron laments Basilius's death, suggesting that the Arcadians' only strength has been taken away from them:

> To that all the other shepherds present uttered pitiful voices, especially the very born Arcadians. For … though humanity moved them to pity human cases, especially under a prince under whom they had found a refuge of

---

[38] A similar aesthetic dilemma occurs in Shakespeare's *Richard II*, when the Queen rejects her lady's suggestion that they tell sorrowful tales of their predicament: 'It doth remember me the more of sorrow; / Or if of grief, being altogether had, / It adds more sorrow to my want of joy; / For what I have I need not to repeat, / And what I want it boots not to complain' (3.4.14–18).
[39] *Astrophil and Stella* in Duncan-Jones (ed.), *The Oxford Authors: Sir Philip Sidney*, Sonnet 1, lines 4–5.

> their miseries and justice equally administered, yet they could not so naturally feel the lively touch of sorrow, but rather used the occasion to record their own private sorrows which they thought would not have agreed with a joyful time. (pp. 327–8)

The Arcadians' reaction to the King's death raises the possibility that there are times when one might not feel sympathy at all, and when individuals might use sorrowful occasions to reflect upon or give vent to their own sufferings. Once again we find the vocabulary of art and imitation employed to depict suffering, with the narrator suggesting that the shepherds could not feel 'the lively touch of sorrow'. The word *touch* could refer to 'Mental, spiritual, or emotional influence; impression upon the mind, emotions, etc., or the response caused by this; feeling' (*OED*, 22b), and thus suggests a feeling of concern between individuals.[40] It has even been suggested that the word is a precursor to terms such as *sympathy* and *fellow-feeling*, in the sense of being 'touched' by the sufferings of others.[41] And yet, by the late sixteenth and early seventeenth centuries, the term could also mean 'A mark made by touching' (*OED*, 10a) or 'A mark produced by a light or brief stroke with a brush, pencil, pen, etc.' (*OED*, 10b). The phrase 'the lively touch of sorrow' thus reminds us that stirring the passions was one of the central goals of art, whether literary, pictorial, or musical.[42] But what is striking here is that the Arcadians do not feel sorrow, precisely because the Duke's death has not been translated into narrative, pictorial art, or music. In this way, the passage suggests that early moderns conceived of emotional transference via concepts of literary or artistic imitation as well as environmental or humoral frameworks.

Perhaps the most suggestive occurrence of the word *touch*, used in the sense of artistic and affective correspondence, appears at the start of book 1. When Pyrocles and Musidorus fall in love with the Duke's two daughters they both experience extreme grief and love melancholy. And perhaps the most suggestive description of their shared grief is the following passage, in which Musidorus confesses his woes to Pyrocles:

> Musidorus did so lively deliver out his inward griefs that Cleophila's friendly heart felt a great impression of pity withal – as certainly all persons

---

[40] The *OED* cites the Countess of Pembroke's translation of the Psalms: 'And looke how much / The neerly touching touch / The father feeles towards his sonne most deare' (Psalm 103, lines 57–9).
[41] See David Wootton, 'Never Knowingly Naked', *London Review of Books*, 26/8 (15 August 2004), pp. 26–7. As the *OED* notes, the verb *touch* could mean 'To affect with some feeling or emotion; to move or stir the feelings of; to produce an emotion in; *spec.* to affect with tender feeling, as pity or gratitude' (*OED*, 24a; first cited usage 1340).
[42] See Timothy J. Reiss, 'Cartesian Aesthetics', in Glyn P. Norton (ed.), *The Cambridge History of Literary Criticism, Volume 3: The Renaissance* (Cambridge University Press, 1999), pp. 511–21.

> that find themselves afflicted easily fall to compassion of them who taste of like misery, partly led by the common course of humanity, but principally because, under the image of them, they lament their own mishaps; and so the complaints the others make seem to touch the right tune of their own woes. (pp. 42–3)

The narrator suggests that compassion is, in part, a kind of generalized fellow-feeling with 'the common course of humanity'. At the same time, however, he suggests that compassion also (and indeed principally) involves a recognition of our own woes as we contemplate the sufferings of others. Thus Sidney asks us to reflect upon the relationship between these two aspects of sympathy – a generalized recognition of our shared humanity, and a recollection of our own specific experiences of woe – and invites us to consider their interdependence. This does not necessarily suggest that sympathy is bound up with self-interest; after all, how can we recognize the common course of humanity without recalling or drawing upon our own experiences? It provides further evidence that the early modern self was 'interpersonally embedded' rather than primarily embedded in, or affected by, the environment.[43]

The passage concludes with the suggestion that individuals find that the 'complaints the others make ... touch the right tune of their own woes'; once again it is the articulation of suffering that leads to others being touched by grief. This idea is complicated, however, by the fact that the complaints of others only 'seem' to correspond with our own, raising the possibility that this harmony of disposition may be a matter of perception. Nonetheless, the notion of affective tuning is particularly suggestive, and invites comparison with eighteenth-century explorations of sympathy. In *The Theory of Moral Sentiments*, Adam Smith acknowledges the limits of fellow-feeling, and the fact that compassion 'can never be exactly the same with original sorrow'. Yet he goes on to suggest that a form of emotional harmony may be possible, employing a suggestive musical metaphor: 'These two sentiments ... may, it is evident, have such a correspondence with one another, as is sufficient for the harmony of society. Though they will never be unisons, they may be concords, and this is all that is wanted or required'.[44] Such musical metaphors imply that there may be harmony or agreement between two individuals, despite – or perhaps because of – the fact that they are not identical. We find a similar figure in *The Defence of Poesy*, in which Sidney writes that 'a feigned example hath as much force

---

[43] See Selleck, *The Interpersonal Idiom*, p. 3.
[44] Smith, *The Theory of Moral Sentiments*, ed. Haakonssen, p. 27.

to teach as a true example', for 'the feigned may be tuned to the highest key of passion'.[45] As this example suggests, Sidney is interested not only in the sympathetic harmony between individuals (and thus addressing some of the same philosophical concerns as Adam Smith) but also in the correspondence between the real and the 'feigned', and the capacity of literary representations to correspond with, and thus elicit, real passions.

We have seen how much of the *Arcadia* is concerned with the comparability of sorrows, and that it features various figured audience and spectator figures. The fifth book makes this aspect of the text even more explicit. The action of this final book consists of a public trial, in which Euarchas, the King of Macedonia, arrives to act as a judge of these 'late evils'. Matthew Woodcock has written that 'language and rhetoric are not simply a medium and means of ornament in the text but are fundamental to what the *Old Arcadia* is "about"', and that the final book 'returns rhetoric to its judicial origins'.[46] There is one specific aspect of rhetoric that Sidney seems to be particularly interested in here; that is, the notion of *movere*, and the capacity of judicial rhetoric to move onlookers and audiences.[47] This is signalled by the presence of Sympathus, who is moved by a 'kindly compassion' (p. 403) by one of Musidorus's speeches. The figured audience within the text, of which Sympathus is an especially sympathetic member, serves as a way for Sidney to explore the diversity and complexity of his readers' responses. Particularly telling in this regard is Gynecia's impassioned confession, in which she acknowledges that she is solely responsible for Basilius's death. She herself states that there may be various reasons why onlookers might feel sympathy for her: 'Let either the remembrance how great she was move thy heart to some reverence, or the seeing how low she is stir in thee some pity' (p. 381). Such is the power of Gynecia's speech that the entire audience seem to react in sympathetic harmony with one another, although their responses are not necessarily uniform:

> With that, she crossed her arms and sat down upon the ground, attending the judge's answer. But a great while it was before anybody could be heard speak, the whole people concurring in a lamentable cry; so much had

---

[45] Sidney, *The Defence of Poesy*, in Duncan-Jones (ed.), *The Oxford Authors: Sir Philip Sidney*, p. 224.
[46] Matthew Woodcock, *Sir Philip Sidney and the Sidney Circle* (Tavistock: Northcote House, 2010), pp. 25–6.
[47] As Quintilian puts it, 'The life and soul of oratory, we may say, is in the emotions' (*The Orator's Education*, ed. Russell, vol. 3, p. 49 (6.2.7)). Cicero writes that 'for purposes of persuasion the art of speaking relies wholly upon three things: the proof of our allegations, the winning of our hearers' favour, and the rousing of their feelings to whatever impulse our case may require' (*De Oratore*, trans. Sutton and Rackham, vol. 2, p. 281). See also Alexander (ed.), *Selected Renaissance Literary Criticism*, p. xxxv.

> Gynecia's words and behaviour stirred their hearts to a doleful compassion. Neither, in truth, could most of them in their judgements tell whether they should be more sorry for her fault or her misery, for the loss of her estate or loss of her virtue. But most were most moved with that which was under their eyes, the sense most subject to pity. (p. 382)

The audience concur in their response; and yet, according to the narrator, they are uncertain of the precise cause of that response, and whether it is the nature of Gynecia's predicament or her words, and whether it is her original fault or the misery resulting from that fault. Once again, then, Sidney is concerned to dramatize the ways in which sympathy is the result of a complex and overlapping combination of automatic and considered responses. The narrator suggests that most people were moved by 'that which was under their eyes', and that sight is the sense 'most subject to pity'. We might note, however, that Euarchas is unmoved by what the narrator calls Gynecia's 'tragical phrases' (p. 382). These verbal descriptions of her grief, we are told, are 'apter to stir a vulgar pity than his mind which hated evil in what colours soever he found it' (pp. 382–3), suggesting that we ought to be sceptical of articulations of grief that are overly rhetorical or artful. Yet the *Arcadia* as a whole seems to suggest that verbal expressions of grief, for all their reliance upon the colours of rhetoric, are necessary for moving others to a doleful compassion.

Earlier we saw how Sidney suggests that one can see a 'lively picture' of one's own emotions reflected in one's friends. And we have seen how the term *lively* is used in various passages to describe both the representation and experience of grief. Sidney implies that the translation of suffering into language – and, perhaps by extension, into literary art – is a fundamental part of sympathy. Like Lyly's *Euphues: The Anatomy of Wit*, Sidney's *Arcadia* acknowledges the extent to which human relationships are more multi-faceted than the humanist rhetoric of friendship suggests; Sidney also explores the ways in which pity and compassion inevitably involve a degree of imaginative projection. In this way, Sidney invites us to reflect upon what Sophie Ratcliffe has called the 'dilemma' of sympathy – the dilemma of our encounters with fiction, and the problem of other minds.[48] When we read fictional works, to what extent is our response shaped by what Sidney calls 'the common course of humanity', and to what extent does reading involve self-recognition, in which individuals 'lament their own mishaps' and see their own sufferings reflected in the text? The *Arcadia* suggests that these two models of pity – and sympathetic reading – are inextricably linked.

---

[48] Ratcliffe, *On Sympathy*, p. 58.

'[C]an there be sympathy between a king and a beggar?': Thomas Lodge's *Rosalynde, Euphues Golden Legacie*

The influence of Sidney's *Arcadia* and Lyly's *Euphues* books can be discerned in various prose romances that followed, including Robert Greene's *Menaphon: Camillas alarum to slumbering Euphues* (1589) and the most important work by Greene's protégé, Thomas Lodge: *Rosalynde, Euphues Golden Legacie* (1590). Unlike Sidney's *Old Arcadia*, Greene's *Menaphon* does include the term *sympathy*; and this is not unusual for Greene, who uses the word over sixty times across his dramatic and prose works. Greene usually uses *sympathy* in the earlier sense of agreement and correspondence; for example, when Menaphon attempts to court the noble Sephestia, who has disguised herself as the rustic Samela, he worries about their lack of compatibility: 'Hath love then respect of circumstance? Else it is not love, but lust; for where the parties have no simpathie of Estates, there can no love be fixed; discord is reputed the mother of division, and in nature this is an unrefuted principle, that it falteth which faileth in uniformitie'.[49] At the end of the text, however, the word is used as part of the emotional reconciliation between Democles, Sephestia, and Maximus: 'he leapt from his seate, and imbraced them all with teares, crauing pardon of *Maximius* and *Sephestia:* and to shew that the outward object of his watrie eies, had a sympathie with the inward passion of his hart, he impald the head of his yong newev *Pleusidippus* with the crowne and diadem of *Arcadie*' (sig. L2v). This latter example uses 'sympathie' to describe the correspondence between Democles's tears and his 'inward passion', and associates the term with heightened (and shared) emotions.[50]

Greene also uses the familiar phrase 'sympathy of affections' in several other works; in *Ciceronis amor* (1589), for example, the Roman politician Lentulus notes the affinity between himself and Terentia: 'In that madame we are both novices in love, the simpler are our thoughts, and the neerer should be the simpathy of our affections'.[51] The phrase appears in

---

[49] Robert Greene, *Menaphon. Camillas alarum to slumbering Euphues, in his melancholie cell at Silexedra* (London, 1589), sig. D2r. *Menaphon* includes several verse interludes and is set in Arcadia (and indeed was reprinted as *Greenes Arcadia or Menaphon* after the author's death). See Gavin Alexander, *Writing after Sidney: The Literary Response to Sir Philip Sidney, 1586–1640* (Oxford University Press, 2006), pp. 263–4.
[50] John Rider's English-Latin dictionary *Bibliotheca scholastica* (London, 1589) contains the Latin *sympathia* under the entry for 'A Passion of the bodie, or minde', suggesting that the word was becoming more closely associated with the passions: '1 Passiuncula. *A natural passion of one to the other.* 1 sympathia, f. *A proper passion of a disease.* 1 Idiopathia, f.' (sig. Z2r).
[51] Greene, *Ciceronis amor. Tullies love* (London, 1589), p. 18.

other contemporaneous prose texts, including Anthony Munday's translation of Claude Colet's *Palladine of England* (1588), when the narrator describes the painful parting of Palladine and the young Duchess Brisalda: 'whereupon they parted, not without sufficient shewes on either side, that betweene them was a sympathie of affection. What severall afflictions they endured in absence, let them imagine, who have no comfort but in the presence of their favourite.'[52] Another translation by Munday printed the same year, *Palmerin D'Oliva* (1588), associates sympathy and 'afflictions' even more explicitly in its description of the Princess Polinarda's sorrowful words at Palmerin's departure: 'These words were delivered with such teares and reking sighes, as *Palmerin* might well perceive the vehemence of her greefes, and answering her heavines with as earnest oppression, said. Sweete Ladie bee perswaded, & temper your sorrow with patience, considering the union of our spirites makes a simpathie of afflictions' (p. 113). The union of Polinarda and Palmerin's spirits leads to a 'simpathie of afflictions'. This subtle but significant modification of a common formulation associates the term *simpathie* with a correspondence of woe, rather than a generalized sharing of emotions.[53]

We might suggest, then, that these prose works constitute a network of sympathetic texts, in which characters borrow and imitate each other's emotions using formulations that are themselves textual borrowings and imitations. And yet, as Munday's *Palmerin* demonstrates, subtle variations on these imitated phrases can give rise to literary and verbal creativity, and can modify the meanings of certain emotion words. We have also seen how several of these prose texts make explicit references to earlier texts, in particular Lyly's *Euphues* books; but there is also something decidedly self-reflexive about how characters within these texts conceive of and express their feelings. Indeed these works bear out Roland Barthes's suggestion that 'writing becomes the origin of emotion'.[54] This is certainly the case when we turn to Lodge's *Rosalynde*, which reworks aspects of the

---

[52] Claude Colet, *The famous, pleasant, and variable historie, of Palladine of England ... Translated out of French by A.M.* (London, 1588), p. 37. The phrase also appears in a letter by Brisalda that emphasizes their comparable status: 'our desires had then such a Simpathie of affection, as in all matters we were alike, having each others honor in equall commendation, our nobilitie, parentage, and what else beside, combined together in a rich procall knot' (p. 89).
[53] Munday's prose is a fairly creative adaptation of the French text, which does not include the term *sympathie*: 'ains temperer votre douleur, laquelle (pour l'union de noz esprit) je ne sens moindre que vous' ('so temper your pain, which (for the union of mind) I do not feel less than you'); quoted from *L'histoire de Palmerin d'Olive, filz du roy Florendos de Macedone, & de la belle Griane, fille de Remicius Empereur de Constantinople* (Antwerp, 1572), sig. K4r.
[54] Roland Barthes, *S/Z*, trans. Richard Miller (New York: Farrar, Straus and Giroux, 1974), p. 74.

Arcadia, as well as referring to Lyly's *Euphues* in its title.[55] This engaging romance, which is perhaps best known as the main source of Shakespeare's *As You Like It* (*c.* 1599–1600), draws upon the early modern discourse of friendship, although here Lodge explores the close relationship between two female friends: Rosalynde and Alinda.[56] While *Rosalynde* uses *sympathy* in this context, it also highlights the different ways in which the word could be employed at this time. Moreover, Lodge's text goes further than Sidney's *Arcadia* in reflecting upon the imitative and intertextual aspects of love and desire.

When the usurping King Torismond of France resolves to banish Rosalynde from the court, his daughter Alinda (the model for Celia in Shakespeare's play) offers an impassioned defence of her friend, reminding her father of their long-established friendship:

> Rosalynde and I have been fostered up from our infancies, and nursed under the harbour of our conversing together with such private familiarities, that custom had wrought a union of our nature, and the sympathy of our affections such a secret love, that we have two bodies and one soul.[57]

Alinda is at pains to emphasize the strength of their union, a sympathetic affinity that connects their souls in the manner of the other friendships that we have encountered. She invokes the paradox of unity, suggesting that their close upbringing – and similarity of temperament – means that they have separate bodies but one mind. This speech is reworked in Shakespeare's *As You Like It* as Celia's description of Rosalind: 'if she be a traitor, / Why, so am I. We still have slept together, / Rose at an instant, learned, play'd, eat together, / And wheresoe'er we went, like Juno's swans, / Still we went coupled and inseparable' (1.3.72–6). Shakespeare does not borrow the word *sympathy* from Lodge, but the term *coupled* in Celia's speech is suggestive, and implies that they are yoked together not only in the same harness (drawing Juno's chariot) but also in bonds of affection.[58] A similarly

---

[55] On the influence of Sidney on Lodge see Brian Gibbons 'Amorous Fiction and *As You Like It*', in *Shakespeare and Multiplicity* (Cambridge University Press, 1993), ch. 6; Clare R. Kinney, 'Feigning Female Faining: Spenser, Lodge, Shakespeare, and Rosalind', *Modern Philology*, 95 (1998), 291–315; and Katherine Wilson, *Fictions of Authorship in Late Elizabethan Narratives: Euphues in Arcadia* (Oxford University Press, 2006), ch. 5.
[56] Nathaniel Strout has discussed the idea of mutuality in the two texts in '*As You like It, Rosalynde*, and Mutuality', *Studies in English Literature, 1500–1900*, 41 (2001), 277–95, but he focuses on audience participation, not representations of emotional transference within the texts.
[57] *Lodge's 'Rosalynde': being the original of Shakespeare's 'As You Like It'*, ed. W. W. Greg (London: Chatto and Windus, 1907), p. 29.
[58] See Juliet Dusinberre's Arden 3 edition of *As You Like It* (London: Thomson Learning, 2006), note to 1.3.73.

impassioned description of female friendship features in Shakespeare's *A Midsummer Night's Dream* (c. 1595–6) when Helena describes her childhood friendship with Hermia. She likens the pair to 'artificial gods' who have together created 'one flower, / Both on one sampler, sitting on one cushion'. So complete was their interpersonal harmony that the two become indistinguishable:

> Both warbling of one song, both in one key,
> As if our hands, our sides, voices, and minds
> Had been incorporate. So we grew together,
> Like to a double cherry, seeming parted,
> But yet an union in partition,
> Two lovely berries moulded on one stem;
> So, with two seeming bodies, but one heart …   (3.2.206–12)

But while Celia's speech in *As You Like It* emphasizes the friends' affinity, in the *Dream* Helena's idealized description of unity – which allows for 'partition' within their union – is offered in the context of its dissolution: at this point in the play Helena believes that Hermia has joined with Lysander and Demetrius in order to mock her. She suggests that other women may share her indignation, but that only she experiences the emotional pain: 'Our sex, as well as I, may chide you for it, / Though I alone do feel the injury' (218–19). Helena's eloquent hymn to their lost friendship only serves to heighten her sense that she is a solitary individual feeling this emotional hurt.

While Lodge uses the word *sympathy* in the context of female friendship he also uses it to describe the bringing together of two seemingly contrasting or even opposing elements. At the start of *Rosalynde*, Torismond proposes a day of wrestling and tournament, and arranges for Alinda and Rosalynde to be present, along with various other beautiful damsels: 'Thus in that place did love and war triumph in a sympathy; for such as were martial might use their lance to be renowmed for the excellence of their chivalry, and such as were amorous might glut themselves with gazing on the beauties of most heavenly creatures' (p. 16). Love and war, two antithetical forces, are brought together and made to complement one another; this complementarity is reflected in Lodge's euphuistic prose, with the balancing of these two matching clauses describing the martial and amorous onlookers. *Sympathy* is used in a similar way to describe the possibility of love between two people from opposite ends of the social spectrum. Towards the end of the text, Alinda is still disguised as the rustic Aliena, and she converses with Saladyne (the model for Shakespeare's Oliver) after his redemption. She wonders whether a high-born gentleman could love a lowly shepherd such as herself:

> Saladyne is now in love with Aliena, he a gentleman of great parentage, she a shepherdess of mean parents; he honourable and she poor? Can love consist in contrarieties? Will the falcon perch with the kestrel, the lion harbour with the wolf? Will Venus join robes and rags together, or can there be sympathy between a king and a beggar? (p. 130)

Here, then, *sympathy* is used to suggest a harmony of feelings between individuals of different social classes – and thus recalls the comparison between Sephestia and Samela in Greene's *Menaphon*. Alinda's questions are somewhat disingenuous, however, given that she is of noble blood. Lodge's text might thus be regarded as fairly conservative, inasmuch as it implies that 'sympathy' is only possible between individuals from the same social estate. Yet it nevertheless raises the possibility of likeness, or even love, between a king and a beggar; in this way, the potential radicalism of Alinda's question points towards some of the ideological and ethical concerns explored in several Jacobean works (which will be discussed in Chapter 5), in particular Shakespeare's *King Lear*.

Lodge's conception of sympathy in other parts of the text goes beyond straightforward models of similarity and dissimilarity. The characters in *Rosalynde* also experience pity for others through listening to their verbal articulations of grief, recalling Sidney's interest in the aesthetics of compassion. There is a notable example of such sympathetic exchange later in the text, when Gerismond asks Rosader if he has any news of his banished daughter:

> At this Rosader fetched a deep sigh, and shedding many tears, could not answer: yet at last, gathering his spirits together, he revealed unto the king, how Rosalynde was banished, and how there was such a sympathy of affections between Alinda and her, that she chose rather to be a partaker of her exile, than to part fellowship; whereupon the king banished them both ... (p. 63)

Here the retelling of Rosalyde and Alinda's plight – once again emphasizing the 'sympathy of affections' between them – elicits pity and compassion from listeners. Indeed the king is so moved by this account that he retreats to a place of private grief: 'This news drave the king into a great melancholy, that presently he arose from all the company, and went into his privy chamber, so secret as the harbour of the woods would allow him' (p. 63). Even more suggestive in this regard is Salydyne's act of storytelling, in which he recounts his plight to his estranged brother. Rosader discovers Salydyne sleeping by a lion, and, after debating with himself what course of action to take, he decides to let his brother live: he slays the lion, receiving a wound in the process. Rosader realizes that Salydyne does not recognize him, and invites him to reveal the 'tragic cause of [his] estate' (p. 98). Salydyne acknowledges that, while retelling his sufferings will be painful, it is nonetheless necessary: 'Although the discourse of my fortunes be the renewing of my sorrows, and the rubbing of the scar will open a fresh wound, yet that I may not prove ingratefull to so courteous a Gentleman, I will rather sit down and sigh out my estate, than give any offence by smothering my grief with silence' (p. 98).

Saladyne suggests the almost physical pain involved in retelling his tale. He begins his attempt to 'sigh out' his bodily and mental state, recounting how he spurned 'such golden principles of brotherly concord' (pp. 98–9). And yet, at the point when he mentions Rosader's name, Saladyne breaks off his tale with weeping. Rosader suggests that tears are inappropriate and unhelpful under the circumstances: 'Nay, forward man … tears are the unfittest salve that any man can apply to cure sorows, and therefore cease from such feminine follies, as should drop out of a woman's eye to deceive, not out of a gentleman's look to discover his thoughts, and forward with thy discourse' (p. 99). For Rosader at least, grief is an inherently gendered process, and he enjoins Saladyne not to let tears – women's weapons, in his view – stain his man's cheeks.[59] More importantly, perhaps, this bodily expression of emotion prevents him from continuing with his tale. When Saladyne finally resumes his story we find that Rosader has been moved to compassion:

> Rosader, hearing the resolution of his brother Saladyne, began to compassionate his sorrowes, and not able to smother the sparks of nature with feigned secrecy, he burst into these loving speeches: 'Then know, Saladyne,' quoth he, 'that thou hast met with Rosader, who grieves as much to see thy distress, as thyself to feel the burden of thy miserie.' (p. 100)

As he listens to Saladyne's pitiful tale, Rosader begins to 'compassionate' his distress, employing an unusual verbal form of the word. It is a precursor to the term *sympathize*, which was not yet available, and arguably points to the need for an active verb to denote the process of commiserating another's suffering.[60] Here Rosader suggests that his own grief at

---

[59] I discuss King Lear's characterization of tears as 'women's weapons' in Chapter 5, below. The Lord in Shakespeare's *The Taming of the Shrew* describes 'a woman's gift / To rain a shower of commanded tears' (Induction 1.124–5).

[60] The *OED*'s first citation for this verbal usage of *compassionate* is John Marston's *The Metamorphosis of Pygmalion's Image* (1598): 'then pitty me, / Compassionate my true loves ardencie'. As we shall see in Chapter 3, below, the word *sympathize* first appears in print in 1594.

seeing his brother's misery is equal to the original misery; the transference of sorrow marks the restoration of their brotherly concord. The narrator suggests that nature has worked 'an union of their thoughts' (p. 101), while Adam describes their reunion in similar terms, suggesting that their reconciliation has made real 'the concord that old Sir John of Bordeaux wished betwixt you' (p. 102). But it is Saladyne's act of storytelling – the conversion of his suffering into narrative – that makes his reconciliation with his brother possible.

At the same time, however, *Rosalynde* suggests that verbal expressions of emotion are not always successful at eliciting compassion. This is particularly apparent in the Petrarchan situation of Montanus and his beloved Phoebe. When Alinda and Rosalynde encounter Montanus sitting by a fountain, we are told that his piteous looks and sighs 'would have made Diana herself to have been passionate' (p. 115), suggesting the now obsolete senses of infatuated (*OED*, 4) and pitiful (*OED*, 5a). Earlier in the text Rosalynde describes how Rosader has 'painted out' (p. 104) his passions in sonnets and roundelays. Now we find Montanus attempting to win Phoebe's affections through poetry:

> A turtle sate upon a leavelesse tree,
>   Mourning her absent fere
>   With sad and sorry cheer:
>   About her wondring stood
>   The citizens of wood,
>   And whilest her plumes she rents
>   And for her love laments,
>   The stately trees complain them,
>   The birdes with sorrow pain them.
>   Each one that doth her view
>   Her pain and sorrows rue;
>   But were the sorrows known
>   That me hath overthrown,
> Oh how would Phoebe sigh if she did looke on me! (p. 116)

In Montanus's sonnet of pain and sorrows, which is itself about emotional transference, the turtle's love laments are echoed by the trees, who join with her in a sympathetic complaint, while the birds similarly 'pain' her sorrows. In his idealized description of audience response, Montanus suggests that '[e]ach one' that looks upon the turtle will 'rue' her pain and sorrows. *Rue* is an older English term that could mean 'To regard with pity and compassion; to feel sorry for (a person, etc.)' (*OED*, 4c); we will return to this emotion word in Chapter 4. He goes on to suggest that his own sorrows outdo even those of the tragic turtle he describes. Hoping that the disdainful Phoebe might replicate these poetical images of pity, Montanus describes the sighs that Phoebe would exhale, if only she would look upon him. He suggests that his sorrows have affected not only the natural world, but also figures from classical mythology: 'my scalding sighes have made the air echo her pity conceived in my plaints: Philomele hearing my passions, hath left her mournful tunes to listen to the discourse of my miseries' (p. 120). Thus Montanus argues that his sorrows – and his attempts to articulate them – are equal to, or even surpass, those of the tragic Philomel. Yet Phoebe remains unmoved, even registering her amusement at Montanus's plight: 'But she, measuring all his passions with a coy disdain, and triumphing in the poor shepheard's pathetical humours, smiling at his martyrdom as though love had been no malady' (p. 117). We might wonder, then, why Montanus's attempts at moving Phoebe fail, when the other attempts to elicit sympathy in the text tend to succeed.

Lodge seems to be making a distinction between desire on the one hand and fellow-feeling on the other. At this point in the text Phoebe does not desire Montanus, but the fact that she has never felt love herself means that she is unable to feel pity for him either. However, when Phoebe falls for Rosalynde – in the attractive guise of Ganymede – Phoebe finds herself in an analogous position to that of Montanus, which increases her capacity for compassion. When Montanus visits the lovesick Phoebe, it turns out that she can now identify with his predicament: 'Where sitting by her bedside he began his exordium with so many tears and sighs, that she, perceiving the extremity of his sorrows, began now as a lover to pity them, although Ganymede held her from redressing them' (pp. 134–5). Because Phoebe is now herself a lover she is able to 'perceiev[e]' Montanus's pain. Yet Phoebe comes to resemble Montanus in other ways as well; she writes to Ganymede, enclosing a sonnet:

> My boat doth pass the straits
>   of seas incensed by fire,
> Filled with forgetfulness;
>   amidst the winter's night,
> A blind and careless boy,
>   brought up by fond desire,
> Doth guide me in the sea
>   of sorrow and despite.   (p. 137)

This poem – which goes on to describe Phoebe's 'mighty storm of tears' – is highly conventional, and recalls the language and imagery of Petrarch's

Rime 189.[61] It not only reminds us of the ways in which desire is often bound up with literary and poetic conventions, but also emphasizes the extent to which Phoebe's expression of her desires recalls that of Montanus. Lodge thus reminds us of the extent to which apparently 'natural' feelings and sensations are reliant upon imitation, and bound up with cultural constructions. Indeed the parallelism between Montanus and Phoebe is further highlighted when Ganymede receives Phoebe's sonnet and, as with Phoebe's reactions to Montanus's poetic efforts earlier, is amused rather than moved, falling into 'a great laughter' (p. 138). Montanus is himself aware of the overlap between their predicaments; when Rosalynde suggests that she might act with disdain towards Phoebe, Montanus is even more troubled, once again using the word *renew* to suggest a repetition of sorrows: 'Oh … that were to renew my griefs, and double my sorrows' (p. 141). Montanus implies that his grief will be doubled not only because of his pity for Phoebe but also, perhaps, because this imagined scenario will recall his own predicament. Rosalynde points this out to Phoebe when she tries to persuade her to love Montanus: 'I am glad … you look into your own faults, and see where your shoe wrings you, measuring now the pains of Montanus by your own passions' (p. 145).

As with Sidney's *Arcadia*, then, *Rosalynde* invites us to reflect upon the nature of fellow-feeling and the relationship between sets of suffering individuals. Phoebe herself is keen to underscore the similarity between her own situation and that of Montanus, using a series of metaphors to describe this likeness: 'Yet Venus, to add revenge, hath given me wine of the same grape, a sip of the same sauce, and firing me with the like passion, hath crossed me with as ill a penance; for I am in love with a shepherd's swain, as coy to me as I am cruel to Montanus, as peremptory in disdain as I was perverse in desire' (p. 156). Phoebe's metaphorical comparisons, which recall the style of Lyly's *Euphues*, suggest that the pair have experienced the same emotions. And yet, what we have seen throughout this chapter is that two characters' situations are never precisely the same. Indeed *Rosalynde* goes beyond a straightforward celebration of the sympathy of affections between Rosalynde and Alinda; it suggests the problems of repeating and articulating one's sorrows while simultaneously highlighting the necessity of doing so. Even though verbalizing one's grief may, metaphorically speaking, reopen a wound and bring painful memories to

---

[61] The poem thus recalls Wyatt's Sonnet XIX ('My galley charged with forgetfulness'), which is also based on Petrarch's *Rime* 189. See Sir Thomas Wyatt, *The Complete Poems*, ed. R. A. Rebholz (Harmondsworth: Penguin, 1978), p. 349, and Kinney, 'Feigning Female Faining', p. 298.

mind, that act nonetheless has the power to move listeners to compassion. In addition, the example of Phoebe and Montanus reveals the extent to which compassion for the other involves drawing upon one's own emotions. At the same time, however, Lodge suggests that those emotions may themselves already be copies or imitations.

The imitative nature of emotions is further emphasized through Lodge's use of the language of art and portraiture. On his deathbed, Sir John of Bordeaux has 'tears in his eyes to paint out the depth of his passions' (p. 2), while the melancholy Montanus's face is said to be 'the verie pourtraiture of discontent' (p. 40). *Rosalynde* thus reminds us of the ways in which emotional expression involves mimesis and representation, and points to the difficulty of 'locating the passions independent of the signs that may express and produce them'.[62] Lodge's later works also refer to the concept of sympathy in ways that recall *Rosalynde*'s interest in emotion. For example, at the close of *The famous, true and historicall life of Robert second Duke of Normandy* (1591), the narrator describes the title character's silent and sympathetic embrace with Editha following his conversion: '*Editha* devoured in joy, instead of reply, fell upon his neck in a sound, and with such entyre affection embraced him, that it was thought that both their bodyes were united together with a mutuall simpathie of affections'.[63] But while this example reproduces the familiar phrase 'a simpathie of affections', Lodge's poetic complaint *The Complaint of Elsted* (1593), which we will explore in Chapter 3, more explicitly associates *sympathy* with an exchange of sorrows. As we move into the 1590s, then, more writers use the term in the context of woe and grief, in addition to the more generalized sense of affinity and shared emotions.

'But a mutuall passion wrought, / In one sympathie of thought': Revising Sidney's *Arcadia*

One instructive case study here is the afterlife of Sidney's *Arcadia*, and how later adaptations and continuations of the text represent and articulate the concept of sympathy. Several of these creative responses use the

---

[62] See Miller, 'The Passion Signified', p. 414.
[63] Thomas Lodge, *The famous, true and historicall life of Robert second Duke of Normandy, surnamed for his monstrous birth and behaviour, Robin the Divell* (London, 1591), fol. 40r. Lodge's *Euphues shadow* (1592), another response to Lyly, uses *sympathy* in a more general sense of agreement and correspondence: it opens with a letter from 'Philautus, to his Sonnes living at the Courte', which describes how, 'by making a simpathie betweene Will and Wit, your rashness in youth might breede repentance in age' (*Euphues shadow, the battaile of the sences, Wherein youthfull folly is set downe in his right figure, and vaine fancies are prooved to produce many offences* (London, 1592), sig. A4v).

term *sympathy* in ways that extend the *Arcadia*'s concern with pity, compassion, and mutuality, while at the same time highlighting the shifting understanding of the term in the 1590s and early 1600s. John Dickenson's *Arisbas* (1594) refers to Lyly in its subtitle, *Euphues amidst his slumbers*, but is more specifically indebted to Sidney's *Arcadia*, or rather 'follows Sidney into an Arcadia that has become an intertextual dream space'.[64] When the narrator describes the attractive lad Hyalus, it appears that the gods are just as moved by his beauty as humans:

> if *Hyalus* by hap came by (as oft he did) they [the shepherds] would abruptly break off these discourses, and follow him greedily, gazing on so glorious an object. Nor was this uniformitie of affections only in humane hearts, for the rurall powers were touched with like simpathy: *Pan* sighed to see him, remembring by him his *Syrinx*, though of an other sexe.[65]

Simpathy is used here to describe a unity of affections between the shepherds, which is mirrored in the affections of the pastoral gods (hence the somewhat tautologous 'like sympathy'). They are 'touched' with sympathy, recalling Sidney's usages of the word *touch* that we considered earlier. There is another reference to sympathy later in the text that appears alongside a more explicit reference to Sidney, when Arisbas refers to the scene in the *Arcadia* in which Pyrocles watches while Philoclea bathes. In Dickenson's text we have two poems, 'The strife of Love and Beautie' and 'Cupids Palace', and in the latter Arisbas describes how two sympathetic hearts can help to reduce Cupid's workload: 'These serve when the god doth strike, / Both hearts with one shaft alike'. Arisbas continues:

> But a mutuall passion wrought,
> In one sympathie of thought:
> Or when hope of hap unproved,
> Plots the praise of things beloved.
> Pyrocles such fancie knew,
> Fancie giving Love his due,
> Which did on Philoclea looke,
> Bathing in a Christall brooke. (sig. G1r).

For Gavin Alexander, this reference to Sidney suggests that 'Dickenson has turned Arcadia into a place where texts meet' (p. 268). But it is striking that this intertextual moment also includes the term *sympathy*: it describes two people in one 'sympathie of thought'. We might also suggest that it enacts a kind of sympathy with Sidney's original text (which is itself

---

[64] Alexander, *Writing after Sidney*, p. 267.
[65] John Dickenson, *Arisbas, Euphues amidst his slumbers: or Cupids journey to hell* (London, 1594), sig. C3v.

preoccupied with various forms of 'mutuall passion'), using a word that did not appear in the original. Sympathy could almost be seen a figure for the relations between these two texts.

While Dickenson's text alludes to *Arcadia*, Gervase Markham's *The English Arcadia*, published in two parts in 1607 and 1613, was the first attempt to write a continuation of Sidney's work. Markham was a writer associated with the earl of Essex's faction; he composed plays, poems, and prose works, several of which use *sympathy* in relation to woe and grief.[66] In this passage from the first part of the *English Arcadia*, the son of Pyrocles, Pyrophilus, comes across a convocation of pitiful people:

> he mounted upon his horse againe, and ryding before the Coach, paced backe to that place where before hee had left the two unfortunately loving Shepheards, & now found convocated togither on that reserved Theather of the most worst expectations, an infinite number of all sorts of pitiful and unpitying people, some shedding teares of true sorrowe for the accident; some weeping to see others weepe, and some for fashion sake to be thought soft hearted, though they neither apprehended the terror, nor felt in themselves any sympathies of like misfortune ...[67]

This passage recalls the mixed responses to Gynecia's confession in the final book of Sidney's *Arcadia*. Some feel 'true sorrow' for the accident itself; some weep in spontaneous sympathy with others; while others weep for fashion's sake – in other words, they simply weep in order to appear soft-hearted. The word *sympathies* is used to describe the sharing of misfortune, but interestingly this is a moment when some individuals do not feel it. This relates to a moment earlier in the first book when the virgins lamenting the fate of the city of Phalautus sing an elegy that is said to produce universal mourning; those present judge the city 'a vaste, sadde and disconsolate *Trophonias*' (p. 27). Their song has the capacity to make all present weep, 'so that even to such (if such in such a place could be) as had no feeling of the cause of this felt woe, yet the touch thereof the effects of others participated a sympathized wayling to their rockie senselessness' (p. 27). As in Sidney, the conversion of sorrow into art leads to a sharing of grief; and Markham also uses the Sidnean word *touch* to describe this

---

[66] For example, Markham's poem *The most honorable tragedie of Sir Richard Grinvile, Knight* (London, 1595) describes Grinvile in explicitly emotional terms: 'In that faire vessell lives my garlands flower, / Grinvile, my harts immortall arterie; / Of him thy dietie had never power, / Nor hath hee had of griefe one simpathie' (sig. C2r).

[67] *The English Arcadia: alluding his beginning from Sir Philip Sydneys ending* (London, 1607), quoted from Marea Mitchell and Ann Lange (eds.), *Continuations to Sidney's Arcadia, 1607–1867*, gen. ed. Marea Mitchell, 4 vols (London: Pickering and Chatto, 2014), vol. 1, p. 35.

'felt woe'. But he also adds 'sympathized' to denote the 'wayling' in which these senseless folk participate. As we shall see in Chapter 3, *sympathized* first appears in print in the mid-1590s, and clearly Markham felt that this new emotion word was appropriately Sidnean for his extension of the *Arcadia*, as he extends its concern with compassion and shared feelings.

Clare Kinney has suggested that the provisional and incomplete form of the hybrid 1593 edition of the *Arcadia*, which brings together Sidney's new material and the unrevised 'old' version, 'offers its own provocation to textual supplementation'.[68] We might add that these reworkings also enact a kind of verbal supplementation, given how many of them employ the innovative words *sympathy* and *sympathize*. William Alexander's bridging passage, which was first inserted into editions of the *Arcadia* in 1613, is especially intriguing here because he uses *sympathy* in relation to both friendship and the exchange of sorrows.[69] The word first appears in Alexander's extravagant description of Pyrocles and Musidorus's reunion, in which Pyrocles discards his various swords so that 'nothing might hinder him from embracing the Image of his soule, which reflected his owne thoughts'. This moment thus recalls Sidney's description of friends as a mirror or 'lively picture' of each other. But Alexander extends this idea by describing the joining of their souls in sympathy:

> Their soules by a divine sympathie did first joyne, preventing the elementall masses of the bodies: but ah, whilest they were clasped in others armes (like two graffes graffed in one stocke) the high tide of over-flowing affection restraining their tongues with astonishment, as unable to express an unexpressable passion …[70]

This passage suggests a Neoplatonic understanding of the friends' souls conjoining in a 'divine sympathie' before their bodies do. They are also grafted together in a close embrace, 'like two graffes graffed in one stocke', recalling Helena's description of herself and Hermia as a 'double cherry'. Their embrace leads to an overflow of inexpressible passion, and Alexander uses the term *sympathie* to describe their reunion. In this way, Alexander

---

[68] Clare R. Kinney, 'Continuations and Imitations of the *Arcadia*', in Margaret P. Hannay, Michael G. Brennan, and Mary Ellen Lamb (eds.), *The Ashgate Research Companion to the Sidneys, 1500–1700*, 2 vols (Farnham: Ashgate, 2015), vol. 2, pp. 113–23 (p. 113). Natasha Simonova similarly suggests that 'the gaps apparent in [the *Arcadia*'s] printed form also seemed to invite, even require, some sort of continuation', in *Early Modern Authorship and Prose Continuations: Adaptation and Ownership from Sidney to Richardson* (Houndmills: Palgrave Macmillan, 2015), pp. 29–30. Simonova has a useful discussion of Markham's *English Arcadia* (pp. 81–8).

[69] It was printed separately in 1617 and then included in the 1621 and later editions; see Alexander, *Writing after Sidney*, p. 273.

[70] Quoted from Mitchell and Lange (eds.), *Continuations to Sidney's Arcadia, 1607–1867*, vol. 1, p. 160.

seeks to emulate yet extend the *Arcadia*'s conception of human relations by adding a word that does not appear in Sidney's descriptions of male friendship. It is even more suggestive, then, that the word is also used by Alexander to denote an exchange of sorrows. Pyrocles and Musidorus enter a castle and hear a piteous noise:

> As they were walking amongst a Gallerie, they heard ... a dolorous sound, but so heavily delivered with a disordered convoy, that choaked with sobbs else drowned with teares, the paines of the bearer had so spoiled the birth, that it could not be known: yet a secret sympathie by an unexpressable working did more wound the minde of *Pyrocles*, then it was wounded by all the wounds of his bodie, he pitying the complaint, though not knowing from whom, nor for what. O how the soule apt for all impressions transcending reason, can comprehend unapprehensible things! (p. 162)

This passage is also about the mysteries of emotion and the problems of expression. The cries are hard to interpret, but nevertheless lead to a 'secret sympathie' that affects Pyrocles. The term *secret* could suggest both hidden emotions (*OED*, 1f) and occult qualities (*OED*, 1g); but this moment seems more concerned with communication and the exchange of feeling than with sympathetic magic. Indeed it ends with an apostrophe to the soul and its capacity to feel 'unapprehensible things' external to the self. Alexander uses the word 'sympathie' to describe this wondrous process, in which the articulation of woe leads to sympathy. In this way, Alexander's creative attempt to bridge the gap between the two versions of the *Arcadia* leads to him using the term *sympathy* to describe the space – and emotional affinity – between individual selves.

Conclusion: 'a *Simpathy* of mindes from man to man'

We have seen, then, how the writers examined in this chapter used the word *sympathy* to describe a harmony or agreement between people, but we have also seen how this interest in sympathetic relationships is part of a larger fascination with emotional correspondence, and the ways in which sympathy often involves mirroring and imaginative projection. The various metaphors that these writers employ to describe sympathy and fellow-feeling – measuring, balancing, tuning, touching, and image-making – suggest the complex cognitive processes involved in comparing one's own sorrows with those of others. Thus while metaphysical and occult ideas of sympathy clearly persisted into the seventeenth century – as indicated by the 'secret sympathie' described in Alexander's addition to the *Arcadia* – we can also detect a simultaneous fascination with the imitative and intertextual aspects of sympathy. The specific phrase 'sympathy of affections', the most obvious and frequently used emotional trope here, hints at the ways in which emotional and textual imitation are intriguingly related.

We will return to such affective intertextuality in Chapter 3, which considers the links between various complaint poems in the 1590s. But I want to conclude the present chapter by emphasizing that the use of *sympathy* to refer to friends or lovers was not confined to the fictional or intertextual realms in this period; rather it was disseminated more widely across the culture in works that instructed readers how to write. For example, Angel Day's letter writing manual *The English secretorie* (1592) contains a discussion 'Of Epistles Amatorie'. Here he makes 'a distinction of love wherein a *Simpathy* of mindes from man to man as wel uniteth together by an indissoluble league of amitie their hearts in one, as betweene man and woman, and that for the most part in a farre more weighty league, and more inviolable discretion'.[71] As both types of love are different in quality, Day suggests, they have different titles: 'one termed by the name of *Friendship*, and this other changeling only to be deciphered by *Love*'. The advice about writing that follows is confined to letters of 'amours', but this example demonstrates that the word '*Simpathy*' (capitalized and italicized in Day's text) was increasingly available to early modern readers via a wide range of cultural texts. And yet, while such texts played an important role in introducing the word *sympathy* to English readers, as well as exploring and expanding the meanings of the term, they tend to focus on pairs of individuals. In the next chapter, we will consider how Protestant preachers used the term *sympathy* to describe the affective bonds between communities of people. As we shall see, however, the fact that such compassionate groups are increasingly regarded as a network of individuals means that the sympathy of affections between them is just as complex and multifaceted as that between pairs of siblings, lovers, or friends.

---

[71] Angel Day, *The English secretorie, or, Plaine and direct method, for the enditing of all manner of epistles or letters ... now corrected, refined & amended* (London, 1592), p. 137.

CHAPTER 2

'Compassion and mercie draw teares from the godlyfull often'
The Rhetoric of Sympathy in the Early Modern Sermon

John Prime's *An Exposition, and Observations upon Saint Paul to the Galathians* (1587) contains a powerful description of Christ's Passion and its effect upon the surrounding environment:

> When our Saviour suffered, we read that the sun was darkened, the earth moved, the powers of heaven and earth were shaken, the rock did rive asunder, the vaile was rent, and the graves were open, & al things felt a sympathy & a compassion at the passion of Christ.[1]

In Prime's account, both heaven and earth are shaken by Christ's suffering: the earth is literally 'moved' by the experience. This idea derives from Matthew 27, which describes how 'the vaile of the Temple was rent in twayne, from the top to the bottome, and the earth did quake, and the stones were cloven. And the graves did open them selves'.[2] Yet Prime's creative reworking of these biblical verses ascribes a certain degree of feeling to the landscape, describing how 'al things felt a sympathy & a compassion'. His use of the term *sympathy* might appear to suggest occult affinities between inanimate objects, but the fact that it is combined with an older emotion word – the Latinate *compassion* – suggests that it also refers to emotional affinities between individuals. In this passage, the term hovers between these two overlapping senses, suggesting both unseen forces at work and a compassionate response to Christ's death. Prime's *An Exposition* is based upon sermons that he had been preaching at Abingdon in Oxfordshire 'every other weeke', which makes his emphasis upon sympathetic transference even more suggestive.[3] Of course, it is difficult to say

---

[1] John Prime, *An Exposition, and Observations upon Saint Paul to the Galathians* (London, 1587), p. 308.
[2] Matthew 27:51–2. Unless otherwise stated, quotations from the Bible are taken from *The Geneva Bible: A Facsimile of the 1560 Edition*, with an introduction by Lloyd E. Berry (Madison: University of Wisconsin Press, 1969).
[3] See Prime's *Dedication to John Piers, Bishop of Salisbury* (sig. ¶2r). Prime became a fellow of New College, Oxford, in 1571, and gained a university preaching licence in 1581. See Julian Lock, 'Prime,

how closely the text reproduces the sermon on which it is based; nevertheless, this description of Christ's Passion is immediately followed by an exhortation to Prime's audience: 'and shal not man have a feeling of these sufferings, for whom onely hee suffered them? Shal he not, should hee not mourn for these sins, that caused the son of God to take upon him the shape of man, and the shame of the crosse?' (pp. 308–9). These rhetorical questions encourage Prime's listeners to emulate the sympathetic landscape he has just described, and to 'have a feeling' of Christ's Passion. This is an emotional and rhetorical performance, designed to stir up sympathy and compassion in Prime's listeners – and indeed readers.

The present chapter explores the ways in which sermons in the late sixteenth century are fascinated with ideas of sympathy and compassion, and often draw upon natural philosophical ideas to make analogies between the human body and the body of the church. These sermons also contain an intriguing performative and self-reflexive element whereby they invoke the concept of physiological agreement as a way of uniting a socially diverse community into a single compassionate body. At the same time, however, they implicitly question the assumption that early modern sympathy was a primarily automatic or humoral phenomenon, whereby individuals were easily affected by either sympathetic forces or powerful orators.[4] Rather, the materials I explore suggest a considerable degree of emotional agency and imagination, increasingly so as we move into the 1590s. My interest in the affective aspects of sermons corresponds with that of Arnold Hunt, who has argued that 'sermons were addressed to the emotions as well as to the intellect … and were designed not merely to impart doctrinal information but to elicit an affective response from the audience, with the help of voice, gesture and all the other rhetorical skills at the preacher's command'.[5] Hunt's emphasis on affect and rhetoric is certainly welcome; but

---

John (1549/50–1596)', *ODNB*. Lock suggests that Prime 'established a reputation for aggressively protestant preaching'.

[4] See the Introduction, above.

[5] Arnold Hunt, *The Art of Hearing: English Preachers and Their Audiences, 1590–1640* (Cambridge University Press, 2010), p. 11. He continues: 'Audiences were encouraged to develop techniques of listening that enabled them to form an emotional rapport with the preacher, even to put themselves in the preacher's place by appropriating the sermon for their own use and preaching it back to themselves and others' (p. 11). See also Kate Armstrong, 'Sermons in Performance', in Hugh Adlington, Peter McCullough, and Emma Rhatigan (eds.), *The Oxford Handbook of the Early Modern Sermon* (Oxford University Press, 2011), pp. 120–36; Daniel Derrin, 'Engaging the Passions in John Donne's Sermons', *English Studies*, 93 (2012), 452–68; Lori Anne Ferrell, 'Sermons', in Andy Kesson and Emma Smith (eds.), *The Elizabethan Top Ten: Defining Print Popularity in Early Modern England* (Aldershot: Ashgate, 2013), pp. 193–202; Alec Ryrie, 'The Experience of Worship', in *Being Protestant in Reformation Britain* (Oxford University Press, 2013), pp. 317–62; and Jennifer Clement, 'The Art of Feeling in Seventeenth-Century English Sermons', *English Studies*, 98 (2017), 675–88.

I want to make a more specific observation about the particular words and concepts that preachers used. I argue that late-Elizabethan sermons both reflect and help to facilitate a shift in the understanding of sympathy from the physical and physiological to the emotional and imaginative – a process that existed alongside similar developments taking place in literary and dramatic culture.

The chapter begins by exploring how metaphors and concepts involving the human and social body were appropriated by religious writers in the 1570s and 1580s, including Edwin Sandys, John Udall, and Christopher Hooke. It then explores a specific sermon by William James from 1589 that uses the term *sympathy* in a way that binds together the members of the church – and indeed his listeners – whilst excluding those of a different religious or political persuasion. The chapter goes on to argue that, by the mid-1590s, preachers such as Henry Holland were using the term to describe an active and imaginative engagement with the other, in ways that recall several contemporaneous dramatic works – including Shakespeare's *Romeo and Juliet*. Finally, it examines Thomas Wright's *The Passions of the Minde in Generall* (1604), which demonstrates how these questions about the performance and representation of sympathy recur across Protestant and Catholic cultures. As we shall see, there are some revealing tensions apparent in several of these texts, in the sense that sympathy is presented as a natural and automatic phenomenon, but simultaneously one that needs to be activated and encouraged. More broadly, religious writings about compassion suggest that sympathy could be an atomizing process rather than a homogenizing one. Such texts reflect certain cultural anxieties about early modern English society, whereby social groups began to recognize themselves as a gathering of individual selves rather than a unified or uniform body.[6]

'The members rejoice and suffer together': Sermons and the Social Body

In the previous chapter we saw how writers of Renaissance prose fiction were fascinated by concepts of pity and compassion, and how they used the word *sympathy* in its earlier senses of likeness and correspondence to

---

[6] On the shift from the idea of a homogenous social body to a greater emphasis upon the 'community-detached self as a locus of valued experience' see Davis, *Early Modern Writing and the Privatization of Experience* (p. 5), and the Introduction, above. Mullaney's *The Reformation of Emotions* is interested in the concept of 'cultural performances' and emphasizes the importance of the pulpit for delivering stories that shaped social practices (p. 23), although its primary focus is early modern drama.

describe love and friendship. Around the same time, other writers used the word to describe the interrelationship between the soul and the body. One such early usage appears in Thomas Newton's translation of Levinus Lemnius's *The touchstone of complexions* (1576), which describes 'both the partes of man, that is to saye, both Soule & Body (which by a certayne Sympathie or mutuall consent and conspyracie agree together) shal be in perfect state and soundnes withoute beinge wyth any Sicknesse, or greevous malady distempered'.[7] Here the idea of sickness is used to describe the 'Sympathie or mutuall consent' between body and soul; in other texts this relationship is described in terms that suggestively recall the discourse of early modern friendship. For example, in Richard Mulcaster's educational manual *Positions* (1581) he writes that:

> The soule and bodie being coparteners in good and ill, in sweete and sowre, in mirth and mourning, & having generally a common sympathie, & a mutuall feeling in all passions: how can they be, or rather why should they be severed in twaine? the one made stronge, and well qualified, the other left feeble, and a praye to infirmitie? will ye have the minde to obtaine those things, which be most proper unto her, and most profitable unto you, when they be obtained?[8]

For Mulcaster, the soul and body are like two friends or 'coparteners' who have a 'common sympathie' in all passions, including mirth and mourning. This idea of mutual suffering appears in a more explicitly religious context in Thomas Wilcox's *An exposition uppon the Booke of the Canticles* (1585), which describes the 'conjunction betwixt Christ & his church'. He writes that 'There is also a sympathy & fellowlike feeling, or suffering together as it were, Christe beeing seased with sadnesse (as a man would say) in the greefe of the church, and rejoycing again in the gladsomnesse and joy thereof'.[9] In this way, the concept of sympathy (here combined with the phrase 'fellowlike feeling') was a mutually illuminating way of describing human relationships, including the union between Christ and the Church, as well as the affinity between the soul and the body. These examples also emphasize the extent to which the soul and the body were thought to be closely related but ultimately distinct.[10]

---

[7] Levinus Lemnius, *The touchstone of complexions* (London, 1576), p. 60.
[8] Richard Mulcaster, *Positions wherin those primitive circumstances be examined, which are necessarie for the training up of children* (London, 1581), p. 40.
[9] Thomas Wilcox, *An exposition uppon the Booke of the Canticles, otherwise called Schelomons Song* (London, 1585), pp. 174–5.
[10] On the complexity of the relationship between the body and soul in the period see Angus Gowland, 'Melancholy, Passions and Identity in the Renaissance', in Cummings and Sierhuis (eds.), *Passions*

As we saw in the Introduction, such correspondences were regarded by some as part of a larger system of sympathies and antipathies, which included the cosmic order of the earth and the heavens, as well as the natural order of society. In William Lightfoot's *The complaint of England* (1587), a polemic against papists, he offers this rapturous celebration of unity: 'And therefore Nature in all her actions intending *unitie*, buildeth her whole frame upon the groundworke of sweete harmonie, and musicall concent: tempering the qualities in each severall body with such indifferent proportion, that albeit some one overrule the rest, yet it is not permitted to overthrow them: but they all by a secret *sympathie* & mutual agreement, indevour to support the one the others burden'.[11] Similarly, William Averell's *A mervailous combat of contrarieties* (1588), a political dialogue between parts of the body, uses *sympathy* to describe a kind of agreement between fellowships of men: 'In this order we knowe there is a continuall *Sympathie*, no shew of contrarietie, for if there were, it could be no order but a disorder, no *Sympathie* but an *Antipathie*, so ye whole course of natural things should either be dissolved or unnaturally be mervailously confounded'.[12] Averell's text was one of the sources for Menenius's fable of the belly in Shakespeare's *Coriolanus* (c. 1608), reminding us that metaphors involving the body had particular currency in the late sixteenth and early seventeenth centuries. As Averell suggests, we are all part of God's creation, and our bodies are not only part of a larger creation but also resemble it: man is a 'lesser world, in respect of the greater, participating both of the heavenly and terrestriall matter, and bearing also a similitude of the heavens and elements likewise'. He continues: 'what a natural agreement there should be among the fellowships of men, to the making up of a politique bodie, knit together in the unitie of mindes' (sig. D1r).

This desire for a 'unitie of mindes' clearly has a political dimension in Averell's text, which was printed in the year of the Armada crisis, and concludes with a plea for loyalty for Queen Elizabeth.[13] Yet this rhetorical strategy also relates to several late sixteenth-century sermons, which are also preoccupied with concepts of social and emotional unity. It is here that we can see the word *sympathy* being used to describe a mutual

---

    and Subjectivity, pp. 75–84. He writes that while the crucial connections between the soul and body 'were suggestive of a radical materialism … the two domains never collapsed into each other' (p. 83).

[11] William Lightfoot, *The complaint of England* (London, 1587), sig. A2r-v.
[12] William Averell, *A mervailous combat of contrarieties* (London, 1588), sig. D1r.
[13] See Jonathan Gil Harris, *Foreign Bodies and the Body Politic: Discourses of Social Pathology in Early Modern England* (Cambridge University Press, 1998), pp. 40–7, and Lobis, *The Virtue of Sympathy*, p. 21.

suffering between individuals. One sermon from the 1580s preached by Edwin Sandys, Archbishop of York and recorded in his *Sermons* (1585), takes as its text Philippians 2:2: '*Be like minded, having the same love, being of one accord and of one judgement*'.[14] One of the central concerns of this sermon is 'unitie and concord', and Sandys cites an analogy made by St Paul between three forms of unity: the mystical body of Christ, the company of men professing the Christian faith, and the parts and members of a natural body.[15] As Sandys writes, 'the bodie by nature is a thing whole and perfect, consisting of all his members; if any part be wanting or cut off, it is maimed' (pp. 83–4). It is the same with the mystical body of Christ, whereby the Church is regarded as a unified body of many members, of which Christ is the head:

> All the members and every one of them labour not for themselves onely, but for the use and preservation of the whole bodie. So are we borne not for our selves alone, but for others also, for whom we should travell as for our selves … The members rejoice and suffer together: Even so should wee bee kindely affected eche to other, mourning with them that mourne, and being glad with them that doe rejoice. That member which hath not this sympathie, this mutuall suffering, this feeling of other mens hurts is dead and rotten. (p. 84)

In Sandys's reworking of Paul's analogy he begins with the idea of the members of the 'whole bodie', and how they do not labour 'for themselves onely'. Similarly, he suggests, human beings do not exist in isolation but rather experience the same emotions as the other members of the church. In this way, the natural philosophical concept of bodily parts sympathizing with others develops into a discussion of emotional correspondence. More specifically, Sandys claims that any 'member' who does not experience this 'sympathie' with others – glossed as a 'mutuall suffering' – is dead and rotten. In other words, an essential aspect of being a human being is being part of a larger whole, and being affected by the suffering of others.

The penultimate sentence in this passage recalls Romans 12:15, an oft-cited verse describing compassion: 'Rejoyce with them that rejoyce, & wepe with them that wepe'. Sandys also explicitly cites Hebrews 13, which encourages his audience and readers to imagine themselves in the bodies of those who are suffering: '*Remember them* saith the Apostle, *that are in bonds, as though yee your selves were bound with them, and them that*

---

[14] *Sermons made by the most reverende Father in God, Edwin, Archbishop of Yorke* (London, 1585), p. 78.
[15] Cf. 1 Corinthians 12:12: 'For as the bodie is one, and hathe many membres, and all the membres of the bodie, which is one, thogh they be many, yet are but one bodie: even so is Christ'.

are in affliction as if yee your selves were afflicted in their bodies' (p. 84). This is a fairly accurate quotation of Hebrews 13:3, which asks people to imagine the bodily suffering and incarceration of others.[16] However, Sandys goes on to make a further analogy with the body politic: 'Even so in this resembled bodie, and civil societie there must be diversitie as of members so of functions. The prince is as the head, without whose discreete and wise governement the Lawes would cease, and the people being not ruled by order of Lawes, ruine and confusion would soone followe, eche contending and striving against other the end would be the utter subversion of all' (p. 84). The political import of this section is underscored by the fact that this sermon was preached before Queen Elizabeth herself. In this way, the knitting together of individual selves has political as well as ethical implications, and encourages the listeners to see themselves as part of a natural hierarchy: 'Men of lower degrees are set as inferior parts in the bodie, painefully to travel for the necessarie sustentation both of themselves and others. All these members are so necessarie that none can want without the ruine of the whole. For everie one hath need of other & by the help of the other is maintained' (p. 85). Here the rhetorical and political aspects of Sandys's argument are most explicit: individuals can – and indeed should – experience a mutual suffering of others' hurts, but should also remain in their appropriate place in the social hierarchy. The further implication is that they are part of a receptive and compliant audience – obeying the preacher, the monarch, and above that God.

Sandys's sermon thus serves as a fascinating example of a natural philosophical concept being imported into a religious context, and used as a way of describing social emotions and relationships. At a time when analogical thinking was widespread, the concept of sympathy appears to have been eminently translatable across a wide range of medical, political, and religious discourses.[17] And yet, while Sandys presents sympathy as a natural or physical process, some preachers went further by associating it with thinking and meditation. John Udall, a lecturer at Kingston upon Thames, printed several of his sermons in the 1580s and early 1590s.

---

[16] 'Remember them that are in bondes, as thogh ye were bonde with them: and them that are in affliction, as if ye were also afflicted in the bodie' (Hebrews 13:3). This verse is disussed in more detail in Chapter 6, below.

[17] For a discussion of 'the Renaissance habit of mind to think analogically' and how this related to ideas of societal order see Jonathan Goldberg, 'Fatherly Authority', in Margaret Ferguson, Maureen Quilligan, and Nancy Vickers (eds.), *Rewriting the Renaissance: The Discourses of Sexual Difference in Early Modern Europe* (University of Chicago Press, 1986), pp. 3–32 (p. 9).

'Compassion and mercie draw teares from the godlyfull often'   79

In one of the sermons reproduced in *The True Remedie against Famine and Warres* (1588), Udall describes the importance of reflecting on the sufferings of others:

> the consideration of them doe effect us in such manner, that it may woorke in us a sorrowing of heart, and mourning of soule … if our hearts be framed unto that sympathie and fellowe feeling that one member hath of anothers condition, then must the myseries of our brethren (yea though they bee onely brethren according to the flesh) so greeve us, as the meditation therof do leave that impression of the greefe in us, which maye inforce us in the fervencie of our spirites, to powre out our praiers unto the Lord in their behalfe.[18]

This is an intriguing description of 'sympathie and fellowe feeling' that encourages 'meditation' – thinking about other people's miseries – and is certainly more concerned with thought and consideration than humours. For Udall, this 'impression' of another's grief is not an automatic or physical copying but derives from meditating on their miseries; this process of emotional transference involves thinking about, and then praying on behalf of, others. He goes on: 'then much rather must wee take heede, that when those threatnings are uttered, whereof wee our selves are guiltie, that we be not senselesse, and (as the greatest number doe) carelesly lette it passe: for those men must needs be in a fearfull plight, who are not moved with those things whereat the very divelles do quake and tremble' (p. 52). The sermon makes it clear that being 'moved' – not 'senseless' – is an important part of being a good Christian.

The ethical value of being moved is also underscored by the Puritan physician Christopher Hooke in his *The child-birth or womans lecture* (1590). Hooke uses the metaphor of hard flint to describe individuals who are immune to the feelings of others:

> This their corruption appeareth manifestly hereby, for though they heare of never so great distresse of the Church of God beyonde the Seas, they are thereby no more affected to weepe *quam si dura silex, aut stet marpesia mutis:* than is the hardest flint, nor though they heare of never so good the successe thereof, are they at all more affected to rejoyce, than was *Timon* of *Athens*.[19]

Hooke quotes a line from book 6 of the *Aeneid*, which describes Dido's refusal to be moved by Aeneas's pleas, 'than if she had been a block of flint

---

[18] John Udall, *The True Remedie against Famine and Warres: five sermons … preached in the time of the dearth* (London, 1588?), pp. 51–2.
[19] Christopher Hooke, *The child-birth or womans lecture* (London, 1590), sig. C3r.

or Parian marble on Mount Marpessus'.²⁰ Early modern listeners would likely have recognized this reference to the affective world of the *Aeneid*, which we will discuss further in Chapter 4. The concept of hardheartedness was also familiar from both proverb lore and Protestant religious culture. As Alec Ryrie has written, '*Hardness* referred in general to the Biblical concept of hardness of heart, and more particularly to God's promise to the prophet Ezekiel that he would give his people hearts of flesh instead of hearts of stone. The sense of being stony-hearted, blankly indifferent to God, was one which many Protestants shared, and which – in very un-Stoic fashion – they deplored in themselves'.²¹ Ryrie is discussing the metaphors that were used to describe one's receptiveness to God; yet the term was also used in sermons to describe a lack of compassion. In this passage, Hooke invokes the concept of being stonyhearted as a rhetorical counterexample, which contrasts with the emotional receptivity of his implied audience.

Hooke also invokes the unfortunate figure of Timon of Athens, who was to be the subject of a play by Shakespeare in the early years of the seventeenth century. This reference might thus prompt us to reflect upon the similarities between the rhetorical strategies of both preachers and playwrights from this period, both of whom present hardheartedness as an undesirable quality.²² Hooke attempts to move his audience to compassion by suggesting that hardhearted individuals are

> not to be of the communion of Saints, nor members of the mystical bodie of Christ: betwixt whom is the like or greater *Sympathie*, than is betwixt the members of this our naturall bodie, wherein if one member suffer, all suffer with it, and if one member be had in honor, all the other members rejoyce with it. (sig. C3r)

Like Edwin Sandys, Hooke recalls 1 Corinthians 12, contrasting the proverbial and religious concept of hardheartedness with the sympathetic members of the mystical body of Christ.²³ And indeed Hooke employs

---

²⁰ *The Aeneid*, trans. David West (Harmondsworth: Penguin, 1990), 6:471 (p. 147). Thomas Phaer and Thomas Twyne's translation has 'Than sturres a standing stone, or mountaine rocke for blast of winde' (*The 'Aeneid' of Thomas Phaer and Thomas Twyne*, ed. Steven Lally (New York and London: Garland, 1987), 6:500).
²¹ Ryrie, *Being Protestant*, p. 20.
²² In the opening scene of Shakespeare's *Julius Caesar* (c. 1599), for example, Murellus castigates the commoners for celebrating Caesar's victory over Pompey: 'You blocks, you stones, you worse than senseless things! / O you hard hearts, you cruel men of Rome, / Knew you not Pompey?' (1.1.35–7). Clearly Murellus is addressing the onstage audience, but he is perhaps softening up the hearts of the offstage audience as well.
²³ Cf. 1 Corinthians 12:26: 'Therefore if one member suffer, all suffer with it: if one member be in honour, all the membres rejoyce with it'.

the innovative word *sympathy* – capitalized and italicized in the text – to describe this exchange of suffering and rejoicing. Clearly preachers like Hooke could have chosen the more conventional word *compassion*, but were drawn to this new term, perhaps in part because of its connotations of being affected or influenced by an unseen force – and which thus serves as an optimistic template for the effectiveness of their own rhetoric. The emotional transference described within Hooke's text offers a model for the emotional transference initiated by the text. Whether that process necessarily followed is, however, a more complex question that will be considered further below.

'Doeth thy brother suffer trouble or losse?' William James and the Limits of Sympathy

By the early 1590s, then, the word *sympathy* was being used by preachers as a term for describing both natural philosophical phenomena and emotional correspondence. While not strictly speaking an 'emotional practice', to borrow Monique Scheer's useful phrase, the use of *sympathy* as an emotion word can nevertheless be regarded as a new form for nurturing (as well as expressing) the capacity for compassion.[24] We can see this process at work in a sermon preached by William James at Paul's Cross on 9 November 1589.[25] This is the second of his published sermons, and it is a vigorous defence of episcopacy – the idea that bishops should retain their position at the top of the body of the church. The sermon takes as its text three verses from 1 Corinthians 12, including the same verse cited by Christopher Hooke in the lecture discussed above: '*25 Least there should be any division in the body, but that the members should have the same care one for another. 26 Therefore if one member suffer, all suffer with it: if one member be had in honour, all the members rejoyce with it. 27 Now yee are the body of Christ, and members for your part*' (sig. B1r). Mary Morrissey has discussed this sermon in relation to puritan controversies, suggesting that treatments of these verses 'are dominated by dissuasions from contentions within the Church'.[26] However, the sermon offers a wide-ranging discussion of the ethics of compassion that goes beyond these topical considerations.

---

[24] Monique Scheer, 'Are Emotions a Kind of Practice (and Is That What Makes Them Have a History)? A Bourdieuian Approach to Understanding Emotion', *History and Theory*, 51 (2012), 193–220.
[25] William James, *A sermon preached at Paules Crosse the IX. of November, 1589* (London, 1590).
[26] Mary Morrissey, *Politics and the Paul's Cross Sermons, 1558–1642* (Oxford University Press, 2011), p. 214.

Like some of the writers that we have already examined, James discusses various natural forms of discord and harmony. In the first part of the sermon, he describes Nature as 'the common parent of us all, who (as Philosophie teacheth) doth nothing in vaine, albeit that all her motions be by contraries'. He continues: 'in this great and wide world, wherein there is wonderful and strange variety, yet hath she [Nature] so tempered and mingled all things, that there is not onely not any division and discord, but (if we beleeve some Philosophers) such and so sweete a harmony, that, as he saith of vertue, if it might be seene with bodily eies, it would stirre up incredible love thereof' (sig. B3r). In other words, while there is 'division and discord' in the world, there is nevertheless a sweet harmony that joins everything together. The same idea applies to human bodies: 'In this little world, this tabernacle of our bodies, this *microcosmos*, albeit it consist altogether of contrarie elements, and of those whereof every one seeketh to destroy another, and that by most contrarie qualities, as the extremities of heate, colde, moisture, and drought: and albeit there be never any peace or rest, untill (as Aristotle teacheth) there be *elementum praedominans,* a predominant element that ruleth all the rest' (sigs B3r-v). Thus we move from nature, where there is variety and division, to the microcosm of the human body, which contains various contrary elements but a 'predominant element' that maintains order and 'ruleth' the rest. In this way, while this part of the sermon is ostensibly concerned with natural philosophical ideas, there is once again a political aspect to James's arguments.

These arguments are presented in a highly rhetorical form that seeks to bind the audience together in agreement; for example, in the following passage James uses various forms of repetition and alliteration, and concludes with a powerful rhetorical question:

> Seeing we all inhabite here one and the same vale of miserie, the valley of teares, having all one and the same sworne enemie, the olde malicious and canckred serpent: Seeing there is but one God, one faith, one baptisme: Seeing we are all branches of the same vine, drawing all juice & moisture alike from the same roote, all servants of the same master, children of the same father, and (as the Apostle saith) all members of the same body: why do we either contemne or contend one with another? (sig. B4v)

James's emphasis upon hierarchy and authority feeds into the rhetorical movement of the passage, unifying the listeners into a sympathetic and compliant body. Once again, the orator seeks to unify his audience in acceptance of an intellectual argument about unity. Division across various sections of society is presented as undesirable: 'Dissension, division, is a most miserable thing, whether you respect the church, Commonwealth, or private families' (sig. C1v). All individuals take their place within this respective hierarchy, and simply by listening to the speaker the audience's assent is implicit.

But as well as these political elements the sermon also focuses closely on ideas of compassion and care. The second part of the sermon considers verse 25, '*Let the members have the same care for another*'. Once again, James makes a powerful analogy between the members of the body and the members of the church. His description of the body recalls Galen's interest in sympathy and infection: 'if one [member in the body] perish or putrifie, it infecteth first the next, and so in time anoieth all: or if any one in a common calamitie deny helpe to another, all thereby are brought into danger'. This is the same amongst Christians: 'even so among Christians, let no man suppose, that his brethrens cause appertaineth not unto him, but as the members of the bodie, the inferior serve, the superior rule, every one careth for, and regardeth another: so in the Church, so in the common wealth, let the highest and lowest, and all agree, and consent to the good of all' (sig. F1r). Just as the body cannot function with one part that is ill, there must also be a mutual care between members of the Church: 'Let the members care. Let no man thinke his brothers matters not to appertaine unto him. Let the members not only have a care, but the same care, let the members have the same care, let there be no distraction or separation of mindes' (sigs F1r-v). Here James uses a similar formulation to William Averell, describing the unity of minds between members of the church, and implicitly between members of the audience listening at Paul's Cross. This example further highlights how preachers sought to knit together the minds of their congregations in order to convince them of the importance of compassionate behaviour. Indeed it is an effective rhetorical strategy to join listeners together in a unity of minds, especially when a preacher's primary aim is to persuade his audience of the need for societal and emotional harmony.

James spends a considerable amount of the sermon reflecting on mutual love, before realizing that he has not quite addressed the last verse of his main text, and what he calls 'the third part of mutuall compassion, and the application' (sig. G4r). In the suggestive final pages of the sermon he uses the term *sympathy* to describe the relationship between the different parts of the body and the members of the church:

> *Yee are the bodie of Christ, and members for your part*, to your Christian consideration. Onely this I wish you all consider, that as in the griefe of the bodie, the very heart sigheth, the eies shead teares, the head aketh, the stomacke refuseth foode, the whole bodie is made feeble, though it be but

> the griefe of a finger, or of a toe: so in the church there ought to be a sympathie, and fellowe feeling, to weepe with them that weepe, to rejoyce with them that rejoyce. (sig. G4r)

This is a striking example of the word *sympathy* in transition; it looks back to the earlier, physiological concept but it also points forward to the more modern emotional usages. James suggests that his audience should respond to the suffering of others in the same way that parts of the body respond to each other. But it is worth noting that James says that there 'ought' to be a sympathy with others, suggesting that it is not necessarily automatic. He combines the word with the more familiar phrase 'fellowe feeling' with a biblical verse on the same theme: Romans 12:15. We might also note that this important verse, which we have already seen quoted by Edwin Sandys, itself employs repetition and rhetorical mirroring to reflect the sharing of emotions – weeping and rejoicing – that it describes. In this way, the rhetorical strategies employed by the sermon might contradict, or at least complicate, its central proposition. James's argument that sympathy is a natural process is belied by the very form of the sermon itself, and its reliance upon rhetoric and biblical authority to persuade its listeners to feel compassion for one another.

James goes on to discuss Chrysostom's *Commentary on Matthew*, Homily 35: 'Doeth thy brother suffer trouble or losse? if thou be sorie for him, thou art placed as a member in the bodie of the Church: if thou sorow not, if thou suffer not, thou art cut off, and peradventure thou therefore sorowest not, because thou art cut off' (sig. G4v). As James suggests, feeling sorrow for one's brother effectively makes one a member in the body of the church. If a member is cut off, he will have no sorrow precisely because he is no longer part of this metaphorical body. This discussion leads on to a second usage of the word *sympathy*:

> This your Sympathie and commiseration should shewe it selfe in releeving your needie brethren, in helping and succouring the poore maimed souldiers, in aiding and assisting your afflicted brethren in Fraunce and Flaunders for the Gospels sake. (sig. G4v)

Here the argument moves from a general consideration of sympathy and commiseration to a specific political situation: the French wars of religion. Clearly there is a desire for sympathy and commiseration to be active processes, and for the listeners to relieve the sufferings of others. Of course, it is impossible to know whether James's original audience – or readers of the printed text – put these ideas into practice, but certainly this discussion was of considerable interest to at least one early modern reader, as we can see from the Huntington Library copy of James's sermon.²⁷ This reader seems to have been particularly interested in the Latin and biblical phrases used, which are highlighted and joined up by lines traced in the margin. However, the two usages of *sympathy* are also highlighted, suggesting that they were regarded as a notable part of the argument and attracted this reader's attention.

This case study thus reveals how the word *sympathy* was now being used in the public sphere as a way of describing commiseration – and for putting such feelings into practice. But it is also noteworthy that the unity James describes is bound up with the contemporary political situation; there is no sympathy for people from Rome or Spain, who 'seeke to displace your dread Soveraigne ... to conquere & subdue this nation to a forraine yoke, to spoile man, woman, and childe, and to make us all slaves to their Romish and Spanish crueltie' (sig. G4v). Thus sympathy is not an automatic response to human suffering but is mediated by religious and political considerations.²⁸ Rather than bringing about a deeper understanding of the 'other', then, James's conception of sympathy and compassion only extends to brethren who closely resemble his Protestant audience. His argument about sympathetic inclusivity leads to the exclusion of others, although it is worth noting that it is James himself who limits the kinds of people to whom compassion extends. As we will see below, other preachers and writers acknowledged the ways in which audiences were more diverse and discriminating in their views – and capable of sympathizing with the 'other' – than James suggests.

James's consideration of commiseration culminates in a description of our love of Jesus. He recalls the book of Acts, in which Christ claims that he is being persecuted along with the Christians:

> In the 9. of the Actes, Christ saith to Saule, Saule, Saule, why persecutest thou me? Saule persecuted the Christians, not Christ that was in heaven, yet (saith Christ) because he had a compassion with his members, his Church, that that might be verified which the Apostle here saith: *If one member suffer, all suffer with it* ... When thou persecutest the least of mine, for whom my name sake, thou persecutest me. (sig. H1r)

This is the culmination of James's argument, which presents his audience and readers with a remarkable expression of unity: the members all suffer

---

²⁷ Huntington Library shelf mark 20681. Some earlier pages are also highlighted, but the sermon's final pages contain the most concentrated and sustained markings.
²⁸ For further discussion of compassion (and its limits) during the Wars of Religion see Ibbett, *Compassion's Edge*, ch. 1.

with each other, but Christ suffers with them all. The sermon concludes with James beseeching God for his mercy, 'so to soften our hard hearts, that there be no strife or contention among us … And that, as members, we may all have a care, and the same care, that if one suffer, all may suffer with it' (sig. H2r). In this way, the sermon ends with a plea for soft hearts, but it is also a plea for unity: 'as we are the body of Christ and members for our part, so we may with one mind and one mouth, glorifie God the father of our Lord Jesus Christ'. James presents himself as effectively speaking for all members of the Protestant community – but once again this can be seen as part of the sermon's rhetorical design, whereby the speaker seeks to unify all the listeners into one mind, and to bring about agreement between them. Certainly James's sermon makes the affective understanding of *sympathy* available to listeners and prompts them to reflect upon their Christian duty to be compassionate. At the same time, however, his argument about the ethics of compassion is complicated by the political contexts that he invokes; some brethren are more compassionate – or worthy of compassion – than others.

'[C]onsider of them as if wee were in their case': Imagining the Other in Sermons and Plays

While James's sermon tends to figure the sympathetic 'other' as someone rather similar to the self, other preachers were beginning to explore the ways in which sympathy and compassion could involve putting oneself in another individual's situation. The bodily conception of early modern compassion invoked by James – in which members of the church are encouraged to see themselves as parts of a single body – becomes increasingly inadequate. Indeed by the mid-1590s there appears to be a notable shift, whereby *sympathy* is used by preachers to describe an imaginative engagement with the other, rather than straightforward affinity or self-recognition. Of course, the term could still be used to describe correspondence and agreement, but was also used to describe the process of putting oneself imaginatively into another's situation and attempting to understand and feel his or her suffering. As we saw in the Introduction, the *OED* suggests that this more complex understanding of *sympathy*, 'the fact or capacity of entering into or sharing the feelings of another or others' (*OED*, 3b), does not appear until the later seventeenth century. However, several preachers in the 1590s clearly use the term in this sense, providing us with further evidence that the term was used in an emotional context considerably earlier than has been thought.

'Compassion and mercie draw teares from the godlyfull often'   87

One important case study in this regard is Miles Mosse's *The arraignment and conviction of usurie* (1595). Mosse is perhaps best known for these lectures, which are based on a series of sermons preached in March–July 1594. The treatise is especially pertinent to my argument because it includes several different usages of the term *sympathy*. The word is used in the second sermon in a financial and legal sense:

> The Grecians call convenantes … for the commutation, exchange, or reciprocall passion, and sympathie or agreement, which is betweene them that covenant together. And therefore the lawyers doe thus define a covenant: *Pactum est quod inter aliquos convenit:* A bargaine is that whereof divers doe agree: Or thus: *Pactum est duorum pluriumue in idem placitum*, A covenant is the agreement or consent of two or moe, about the same thing.[29]

As this example suggests, it was possible for sympathy to be used to suggest a legal 'agreement' between two separate parties entering into a covenant.[30] But Mosse also uses the term in the sixth and final sermon to suggest the feeling of another's misery, as he rails against the hardheartedness of usury:

> He that is rich and needeth not to borow, if he be a man of a tender hart, and hath any sympathie of another mans miserie, will curse an usurer for pinching of the poore. Hee that is poore, (and therefore needeth to borow,) but cannot borow for want of sufficient securitie to put in, he curseth the usurer for the hardnesse of his hart. (p. 146)

Mosse here invites rich parishioners, and indeed readers, to imagine being of a 'tender hart', and feeling 'sympathie of another mans miserie'. This form of sympathy resembles pity and mercy, and thus implies a kind of hierarchy, as the rich pity the poor. Indeed the rich man will curse the usurer, not because of his own predicament, but because the usurer 'pinch[es]' the poor. These examples in Mosse's tract point to the interchange and coexistence of these two forms of 'sympathy' in the mid-1590s. His text is particularly concerned with finance and the language of credit, but this latter example speaks to a human capacity to sympathize with the miseries of another.[31]

---

[29] Miles Mosse, *The arraignment and conviction of usurie* (London, 1595), pp. 49–50.
[30] The first Latin phrase in this passage appears in Cicero's *De Inventione*: 'A covenant is an agreement between some persons' (2:162), quoted from *On Invention. The Best Kind of Orator. Topics*, trans. H. M. Hubbell (Cambridge, MA: Harvard Universtiy Press, 1949), pp. 329–31.
[31] For a discussion of how later models of sympathy related to social and economic ideas see Evelyn L. Forget, 'Evocations of Sympathy: Sympathetic Imagery in Eighteenth-Century Social Theory and Physiology', in Margaret Schabas and Neil De Marchi (eds.), *Oeconomies in the Age of Newton* (Durham and London: Duke University Press, 2003), pp. 282–308.

88   Sympathy in Early Modern Literature and Culture

Other religious writers in this period go even further than Mosse in linking sympathy with an imaginative compassion for others, and draw upon biblical narratives and exemplars as a way of exploring this form of fellow-feeling. One notable example of this creative (and emotive) use of biblical stories is to be found in the sermons of Henry Holland, a writer on witchcraft who was also a priest. Holland was made vicar of Orwell in Cambridgeshire in 1580, and moved to St Bride's, London, in 1594.[32] In *The Christian Exercise of Fasting* (1596), which was based on his sermons and written after his move to London, Holland discusses the causes of private fasting, the third of which is the cure and comfort of the sick: 'so also when their brethren were in like dangers, they prepared themselves to cry unto God for them, in a religious abstinence'.[33] Holland suggests that God commands us 'to cherish this Christian sympathie in our hearts', and – like several other writers during this period – cites Romans 12:15–16: '*Weepe with them that weep, be of like affection one towards another.* And the sicke wee bee commanded to have in speciall regard, and to consider of them as if wee were in their case, for the time present' (p. 22). In this description of 'Christian sympathie' Holland implies a degree of separateness between individuals. He describes how it is possible to reflect upon the sick and imagine oneself (temporarily) in their situation. The idea of imagining the other as if we were 'in their case' clearly draws upon and extends biblical ideas; yet it also anticipates eighteenth-century conceptions of sympathy. In *The Theory of Moral Sentiments* (1759), Adam Smith writes that 'Though our brother is upon the rack, as long as we ourselves are at our ease, our senses will never inform us of what he suffers … It is by the imagination only that we can form any conception of what are his sensations. Neither can that faculty help us to this any other way, then by representing to us what would be our own, if we were in his case'.[34] As I noted in the Introduction, Smith's text is usually regarded as one of the foundational philosophical treatments of sympathy, with its emphasis upon imaginative perspective-taking. Yet Holland's sermon provides further evidence that this form of sympathy only emerged in the Enlightenment, and suggests that it can be traced fruitfully back to the sixteenth century at least.

---

[32] See Clive Holmes, 'Holland, Henry (1555/6–1603)', *ODNB*. Most of Holland's published works were based on his sermons, including *David's Faith and Repentance* (London, 1589) and *Spirituall preservatives against the pestilence: Or a treatise containing sundrie questions* (London, 1593).
[33] Holland, *The Christian Exercise of Fasting* (London, 1596), p. 22.
[34] Smith, *The Theory of Moral Sentiments*, p. 11.

Holland continues his emphasis upon the imagination in his discussion of the love of Job's friends, who came to lament with Job, and to comfort him: 'when they came to that place, whether because of smell, or infection, or both, it is uncertaine, standing a farre off, they lift up their voyces and wept' (p. 23). At first glance, this formulation might suggest a form of emotional contagion, and confirm the sense that conceptions of sympathy in the period were primarily physiological or Galenic. Yet this idea is soon replaced by a focus on the men's ability to imagine themselves in Job's situation. Job's friends are said to exemplify the kind of Christian sympathy Holland has already referred to:

> I finde also in these men a christian sympathie, this appears in their weeping, and rending of their clothes: they felt in the beginning such passions in themselves, as if their soules had been in his soules stead: as Job after wisheth, chap. 16.4. that is, they mourned as if they had been in the same case: such men onely can minister comfort and pray effectually for the sicke. (p. 24)

Holland suggests that Job's friends felt his passions, as if their souls 'had been in his soules stead'. This is a paraphrase of Job 16:4, in which Job says, 'I colde also speak as ye do: (but wolde God your soule were in my soules stead) I colde keep you companie in speaking, and colde shake mine head at you'. Holland's reworking of this verse extends its emphasis upon emotional exchange, and suggests that Job's friends mourned as if they had been in his situation: 'in the same case'. This formulation proposes a sophisticated conception of sympathy, which involves role-playing and imaginative substitution. Holland argues that only those who can imagine themselves in the case of others can truly offer comfort and pray for the sick. Godliness, he implies, is dependent upon 'christian sympathie', which is presented as an imaginative inhabiting of another's sorrowful situation. The wider implication is that if Job's friends can imagine themselves in Job's situation, then the audience listening to the sermon can imagine themselves in the situation of Job's friends.

Holland's text also includes a catechism that includes the question '*What affections and causes move teares?*' (p. 54). The fourth answer is that 'Compassion and mercie draw teares from the godlyfull often, because of their sympathie and griefe they have in the miseries of their brethren'. Holland cites John 11:34–5, which describes Jesus's weeping at the death of Lazarus: 'When Jesus therefore sawe her wepe, & the Jewes *also* wepe which came with her, he groned in the spirit, & was troubled in himself, And said, Where have ye laid him? Thei said unto him, Lord, come, and se.

And Jesus wept' (John 11:33–5). Again, Jesus is taken to be an exemplar: his compassion for Lazarus's death is presented as an example for us to replicate. Jesus speaks to Lazarus's sisters and his friends, is moved by their emotional response, and weeps himself. The passage thus describes an instance of compassionate grief; Holland's listeners are, in turn, invited to admire this sympathetic chain reaction, and to imitate Jesus's emotional imitation. This amplification and citation of scripture further demonstrates that the recollection of biblical narratives and figures played a key role in shaping the understanding of compassion in the period – arguably a more important one than humoral or medical models.

Holland's fascination with perspective-taking and the imagination resonates with other treatments of sympathy that we find in dramatic texts from the 1590s. Unfortunately, however, it is unlikely that Henry Holland took much pleasure in such works when he moved to London; in his *Spirituall preservatives against the pestilence* (1593), Holland's dedication to the Mayor of London describes '*the divellish theaters, the nurceries of whoredome and uncleannesse: they are* Cupids *and* Venus *temples, they are* Bacchus *and Sathans pallaces, they corrupt the youth of your citie intollerabie*'.[35] But Holland was clearly missing out, because the supposedly devilish theatres were employing some of the same words and concepts that appear in his sermons, and several of the other religious texts we have explored in the present chapter. In Shakespeare's *Romeo and Juliet* (c. 1595; first printed 1597), for example, the distressed Romeo suggests to his friend Friar Laurence that it is impossible for someone to experience his feelings unless he is in the same predicament.[36] Friar Laurence offers to 'dispute with thee of thy estate' (3.3.63), but Romeo declines this offer:

> Thou canst not speak of that thou dost not feel.
> Wert thou as young as I, Juliet thy love,
> An hour but married, Tybalt murderèd,
> Doting like me, and like me banishèd,
> Then mightst thou speak, then mightst thou tear thy hair,
> And fall upon the ground as I do now,
> Taking the measure of an unmade grave.   (3.3.64–70)

Romeo claims that sympathy – the experience of feeling another person's sorrow – is impossible. Nevertheless, this speech offers a moving evocation of Romeo's emotions, and provides a summary of his plight and a description of his sorrowful actions. The emotional power of the

---

[35] Holland, *Spirituall preservatives against the pestilence, The Epistle Dedicatory*, sigs A5v–A6r.
[36] Quotations are taken from *Romeo and Juliet*, ed. Jill L. Levenson (Oxford University Press, 2000).

play surely depends upon the audience's ability to put themselves in the lovers' position.

In the same scene, we also find an important Shakespearean use of the word *sympathy*. Juliet's Nurse arrives, and identifies Romeo as being in the same state as Juliet:

> O, he is even in my mistress' case,
> Just in her case! O woeful sympathy,
> Piteous predicament! Even so lies she,
> Blubb'ring and weeping, weeping and blubb'ring. –
> Stand up, stand up, stand an you be a man;
> For Juliet's sake, for her sake, rise and stand.
> Why should you fall into so deep an O? (3.3.84–90)

As with several other Shakespearean works from the 1590s, the word *sympathy* is associated with woe and pity – and is used here in the context of two individuals being in the same 'case'.[37] According to the Nurse, Romeo is 'Just in [Juliet's] case!'; that is, in precisely the same situation. In her Oxford edition, Jill Levenson glosses *sympathy* as 'likeness in misery'.[38] And indeed the Nurse's speech is replete with repetition and doubling; her description of Juliet's weeping and blubbering is a striking example of the figure of *antimetabole*, in which the verbal repetition itself repeats and mirrors the emotional agreement of the two lovers.[39] The emotional effect of this passage is, however, complicated by the Nurse's unintentional double entendres, which arguably detract from the 'woeful sympathy' that the audience might experience for Romeo.[40] Nevertheless, this scene not only debates the complex relationship between the self and the other, but also further associates *sympathy* with grief and fellow-feeling. One would not want to suggest that Holland's sermon necessarily alludes to *Romeo and Juliet*; yet there is clearly a sympathetic parallelism of ideas between the two. Both sermon and play – two contemporaneous social performances within the early modern public sphere – employ the word *sympathy* and the same concept of being in another's 'case'.

While *Romeo and Juliet* presents sympathy as likeness in grief, other dramatic texts go further in emphasizing the imaginative aspects of compassion. In *Sir Thomas More* (c. 1601–4), a passage that appears to be in Shakespeare's hand has More addressing an anti-immigration riot in the

---

[37] See Chapter 4, below.
[38] Note to 3.3.85.
[39] See Eric Langley, *Narcissism and Suicide in Shakespeare and His Contemporaries* (Oxford University Press, 2009), p. 128.
[40] See Levenson's note to 3.3.88–90.

streets of London. He urges the rioters to imagine themselves banished to a land where the inhabitants

> Whet their detested knives against your throats,
> Spurn you like dogs, and like as if that God
> Owed not nor made not you, not that the elements
> Were not all appropriate to your comforts,
> But charter'd unto them? What would you think
> To be thus us'd? This is the strangers' case
> And this your mountainish inhumanity. (Addition II, 134–40)

Of course, there are significant differences between the social body of a theatre audience and a congregation listening to a sermon; but it is striking how several of the examples we have explored from the 1590s and early 1600s encourage listeners to imagine themselves in the circumstances of another. Indeed this passage from *Sir Thomas More* differs from William James's sermon by inviting the audience to extend their selves into 'the strangers' case'; that is, feeling compassion as a result of imagining oneself in the situation of someone from a different ethnic group. The passage thus raises complex questions about the relationship between the self and the other – and about the individual and the group. Does compassion stem from identification or from difference? Does being part of a collective make one more or less compassionate? Such questions are pertinent to both the pulpit and the playhouse during this period – not least because both are social performances that employ rhetoric and storytelling to move audiences. Holland's comments about the devilish theatres may suggest that preachers did not learn about sympathetic perspective-taking from Shakespeare, but it is plausible that Shakespeare and other playwrights drew upon the vocabulary and ideas contained in sermons, and indeed there is some evidence of cross-fertilization between these two cultural forms.[41] We shall return to the importance of dramatic works to the development of sympathy in subsequent chapters; but certainly there appears to have been a parallel exploration of ideas of correspondence and

---

[41] For an intriguing example of such cross-fertilization see Hunt, *The Art of Hearing*, pp. 171–2. As Hunt points out, the Wiltshire preacher John Andrewes includes an extract from Portia's speech about mercy from *The Merchant of Venice* in his *Christ his crosse or The most comfortable doctrine of Christ crucified and joyfull tidings of his passion* (London, 1614): 'The quantity of mercy is not strange, it droppeth as the gentle dew from heaven upon the place beneath, it is twise blest, it blesseth him that gives, & him that takes' (p. 34). This example demonstrates that preachers were aware of, and drew upon, dramatic representations of mercy and compassion. For further discussion of the links between sermons and plays in the period see Jeanne Shami, 'The Sermon', in Andrew Hiscock and Helen Wilcox (eds.), *The Oxford Handbook of Early Modern English Literature and Religion* (Oxford University Press, 2017), pp. 185–206 (esp. pp. 198–9).

harmony, and the social body, which gave rise to the term *sympathy* being redeployed from the natural philosophical realm to the imaginative and the ethical.

'[T]he Art of moving the affections': Thomas Wright's *The Passions of the Minde in Generall*

Thus far we have considered discussions of sympathy in the work of Protestant preachers; but it is worth emphasizing that such concerns were also of interest to, and shaped by, Catholic writers during the same period. The year after Holland's sermon was printed, Robert Southwell's epistle to the Earl of Arundel – a letter of consolation on the death of the Earl's half-sister, Lady Margaret Sackville – appeared in print as *The triumphs over death* (1595). Southwell was a Jesuit priest, and so was unlikely to have been influenced directly by the sermons and plays we have been exploring. Nevertheless, his epistle does point to the increasing usage and dissemination of the affective usage of the term *sympathy* in the 1590s, amongst Catholic as well as Protestant writers. The subtitle of Southwell's work, which was composed in 1591, is *A consolatorie epistle, for afflicted mindes, in the affects of dying friends*, and in the text itself Southwell reflects upon the processes of grief and mourning – in part preparing the Earl for his own death.[42] The year of publication, 1595, was also the year of Southwell's death, offering another proleptic and autobiographical dimension to his reflections. Like the Protestant writers we have encountered, Southwell suggests that sympathy for the other is an important part of being human, although he also suggests that one should not allow grief to become immoderate:

> For to be without remorse in the death of friends, is neither incident nor convenient to the nature of man, having too much affinitie to a savage temper, and overthrowing the ground of all pietie, which is a mutuall simpathie in each of others miseries: but as not to feele sorrow in sorrowfull chances, is to want sence, so not to beare it with moderation, is to want understanding, the one brutish, the other effeminate, and he hath cast his account best that hath brought his summe to the meane.[43]

Southwell thus encourages the Earl, and by extension his later readers, to think that the ground of all piety is 'a mutuall simpathie in each of others miseries'. His formulation recalls the emphasis upon mutual suffering

---

[42] See Nancy Pollard Brown, 'Southwell, Robert [St Robert Southwell] (1561–1595)', *ODNB*.
[43] Robert Southwell, *The triumphs over death: or, A consolatorie epistle, for afflicted mindes, in the affects of dying friends* (London, 1595), sig. B1r-v.

we have seen in other religious works from the period; and like several Protestant preachers he explicitly uses the word *simpathie* to refer to a sharing of misery. Not to feel sympathy, he suggests, 'is to want sence' and thus to be brutish; yet to feel too much is to lack understanding and thus effeminate. For Southwell, then, moderation is best when it comes to sympathy and compassion.

Another Catholic writer from this period who argued for the virtues of the passions, somewhat more fervently, was Thomas Wright. Wright was trained as a theologian and priest, but like Southwell he was a Jesuit, and thus held different views about the relationship between the passions and the soul from the Protestant writers explored in the present chapter.[44] Nevertheless, Wright's treatise *The Passions of the Minde in Generall* (1604), which is often cited in critical discussions of early modern emotions, explores some of the same questions about sympathy that William James and Henry Holland had considered in their sermons – in particular the question of whether sympathy is a natural or automatic response to the sufferings of others, or needs to be cultivated. As we shall see, Wright's emphasis upon the performance and imitation of sympathy belies his interest in the natural philosophical understanding of the concept. Wright's text begins with an extraordinary account of a performance by an Italian preacher who had a particular ability to manipulate the passions of his listeners:

> I remember a preacher in *Italy*, who had such power over his Auditors affections, that when it pleased him he could cause them shedd abundance of teares, yea and with teares dropping downe their cheekes, presently turne their sorrow into laughter: and the reason was, because hee himself being extremely passionate, knowing moreover the Art of moving the affections of those auditors, and besides that, the most part were women that heard him (whose passions are most vehement and mutable) therefore he might have perswaded them what hee listed.[45]

Wright describes this ability as a 'commoditie' that can be employed and exploited by other orators as well as preachers. As Wright puts it, if orators can 'stirre a Passion or Affection in their Hearers, then they have almost halfe perswaded them, for that the forces of strong Passions marvellously allure and draw the wit & will to judge and consent unto that they are moved' (p. 4). As we have already seen, various sixteenth-century

---

[44] See Erin Sullivan, 'The Passions of Thomas Wright: Renaissance Emotion across Body and Soul', in Meek and Sullivan (eds.), *The Renaissance of Emotion*, pp. 25–44 (pp. 26–7). Wright's treatise was written in the late 1590s, first printed in 1601, and then reprinted in an expanded version in 1604. I quote from the 1630 reprint of the 1604 text.
[45] Wright, *The Passions of the Minde in Generall*, p. 3.

preachers attempted to tap into this cultural commodity, and sought to stir the passions of their auditors, and thus draw their 'wit & will' to 'consent'.

However, this sense that listeners can be moved to a passion by a powerful orator coexists with Wright's sense that compassion is an innate quality. This is hinted at above in the suggestion that women's passions are 'most vehement and mutable', and thus more susceptible to rhetorical persuasion. In Chapter 3, 'How the Passions may be well directed and made profitable', Wright refers to his own capacity for compassion:

> By this Discourse may be gathered, that Passions, are not only, not wholy to be extinguished (as the Stoicks seemed to affirme) but sometimes to be moved, & stirred up for the service of vertue, as learnedly *Plutarch* teacheth: for mercie and compassion will move us often to pitty, as it did *Job* ... Compassion grew with me from my infancy, and it came with me out of my mothers womb: therefore he declareth what succour he gave to the poore, *Job*. 31.18. (p. 17)

Here Wright claims that compassion is an innate quality. At the same time, however, he notes that the passions sometimes need to be moved and stirred up for the service of virtue. This seems to be a contradiction that exists in several texts from this period: a simultaneous belief that sympathy and compassion are natural, but nevertheless need to be elicited by preachers and orators. Like some of the other texts that we have explored, Wright inserts a reference to a biblical narrative to justify and amplify his argument, in this case the story of Job. In this way, Wright's defence of the passions draws upon both classical and biblical sources, and encourages his readers to remember the story of Job as they reflect upon their own pity for others.

Wright's text does acknowledge the earlier concept of sympathy as natural correspondence, which, according to him, explains some aspects of human emotions. For example, he notes that music can cause both sorrow and sadness, and wonders 'How musicke stirreth up these passions, and moveth so mightily these affections?' (p. 168). One of the answers that Wright proposes is a natural affinity between our souls and music:

> The first is a certaine sympathie, correspondence, or proportion betwixt our soules & musicke: & no other cause can be yeelded. Who can give any other reason, why the loadstone draweth iron, but a sympathie of nature? Why the Needle, toucht with such a stone, should never leave looking toward the North Poale; who can render other reason, then sympathie of nature? (pp. 168–9)

However, in addition to this natural model of sympathy, Wright proposes a rhetorical and performative model of sympathetic transference. This is particularly the case in his key chapter on 'How Passions are moved by action', which cites several Roman authorities on rhetoric who argued that orators have to be moved themselves before trying to move their listeners: 'so *Cicero* expresly teacheth that it is almost impossible for an Orator to stirre up a Passion in his auditors, except he bee first affected with the same passion himselfe' (p. 172). Wright links this to Horace's idea of passionate contagion, citing the famous Latin tag from *The Art of Poetry* and offering his own translation:

> *Si vis me flere, dolendum est*
> *Primum tibi: tunc tua me infortunia laedent.*
> If thou wilt have me weepe, a dolefull brest
> First show: and then thy woes will me molest … (p. 173)

Wright's translation uses the word *molest* in the now rare sense of 'To cause trouble, grief, or vexation to' (*OED*, 1); he suggests that the orator must reveal his 'dolefull brest' in order to move others to grief.[46] This model of sympathy presupposes a kind of emotional contagion, in which the listeners are moved by the orator, providing he is moved in the first place. As we have seen in the present chapter, however, we need to be cautious about treating such passages as accurate descriptions of early modern emotional experience, and to acknowledge the diversity and complexity of views that existed about emotional transference. The sermons that we have already examined suggest that preachers were somewhat more equivocal about the emotional efficacy of their performances – and indeed the receptivity of their listeners.[47]

As he expands upon Horace's ideas Wright does seem to admit that the social diversity of audiences means that they may not respond as a unified body. He likens the transference of passion to the movement of the air: 'the passion which is in our brest, must be the fountaine and origen of al externall actions … for the passion in the perswader seemeth to me, to resemble the wind a trumpeter bloweth in at one end of the trumpet, & in what maner it proceedeth from him, so it issueth forth at the other end, & commeth to our ears' (p. 174). In this extended metaphor, the heart of the orator is figured as the point of origin, and is compared to the wind that a trumpeter blows, reinforcing the idea that sympathy is a natural process – albeit one harnessed and exploited by a skilful artist. But it also implies that

---

[46] For Ben Jonson's translation of Horace's lines see the Introduction, above.
[47] Shami comments that 'While sermons could convey grace, preachers sometimes found their audiences unruly, disengaged, and difficult receptacles' ('The Sermon', p. 195). See also John Craig, 'Sermon Reception', in Adlington et al. (eds.), *The Oxford Handbook of the Early Modern Sermon*, pp. 179–93.

listeners are passive receivers of the persuader's passions: they resemble inert materials influenced by the natural forces around them. This process works best on what Wright refers to as the 'common people', who, unlike 'wise men', need to see evidence of the orator's passions with their own eyes: 'the evidence & certainty of the passion, perswadeth much more effectually the common people, than a suspected reason: & the suspicion of sophistication is much more increased, when wee see it not worke that effect in the teacher, which he would stir up in the hearer' (p. 175). Thus, while Wright describes the efficacy of this process, he acknowledges that it works better for some audience members than others, and it implies a degree of performance and self-persuasion on the part of the orator. Indeed if the orator is not moved himself the audience may suspect 'sophistication'; that is, 'The use or employment of sophistry … falsification' (*OED*, 1). In this way, Wright raises the possibility that orators are capable of using spurious arguments, or not believing in their own rhetoric.

This is why action – such as hand gestures and other forms of body language – is important in conveying and transferring emotion to the audience. Yet such action constitutes another layer of performance and representation at a further remove from the original passion:

> For action is either a certaine visible eloquence, or an eloquence of the bodie, or a comely grace in delivering conceits, or an external image of an internall minde, or a shadow of affections, or three springs which flowe from one fountaine, called *vox, vultus, vita*, voice, countenance, life; that is, the affection poureth forth it selfe by all meanes possible, to discover unto the present beholders and auditors, how the actor is affected, and what affection such a case and cause requireth in them. (p. 176)

Wright once again makes the point that the orator (here referred to as 'the actor') must stir up strong emotions in himself in order to produce lively actions.[48] As Wright puts it, 'the more vehement the passion is, the more excellent action is like to ensue … therefore the vehement passion venteth forth, the livelier action' (p. 177). The word *livelier* here may simply mean 'With animation; actively, briskly, nimbly, vigorously' (*OED*, 3a), but it also recalls the language of the prose texts that we explored in Chapter 1, which describe the other as a 'lively image' of the self, in which the term *lively* suggests both intense feelings and vivid representation. The word

---

[48] Farah Karim-Cooper cites this passage in her study of *The Hand on the Shakespearean Stage* (London: Bloomsbury, 2016), suggesting that 'The sensation and expression of emotion was at the core of the early modern actor's process' (p. 77); but it seems to me that Wright is using the term *actor* here in the broader sense of 'person who performs or takes part in an action; a doer, an agent' (*OED*, 3a), rather than a stage actor per se.

98 Sympathy in Early Modern Literature and Culture

lively itself appears in Wright's later comment that the orator 'ought to endevour, that every part of action immitate as lively as may be the nature of the passion … the actions of the bodie should be, in a perfit perswader, an image of the passion in the mind' (pp. 178–9). Thus Wright describes a kind of emotional mimesis in which the action of the orator is an 'image' or 'shadow' of the original passion, which the listener, in turn, imitates. Yet Wright's vocabulary implicitly reminds us that those imitated signs of passion could be no more than representations, or what Hamlet calls 'actions that a man might play' (1.2.84). Wright's insistence that these actions must appear authentic raises the possibility that they might not refer to an inner emotional reality.[49]

It is especially suggestive, then, that Wright goes on to describe the affective performances of stage players, who 'act excellently; for as the perfection of their exercise consisteth in of others, so they that imitate best, act best' (p. 179). Despite this praise for the actor's art, however, Wright emphasises its inferiority to the art of oratory: 'And in the substance of externall action for most part oratours and stage plaiers agree: and only they differ in this, that these act fainedly, those really; these onely to delight, those to stirre up all sorts of passions according to the exigencie of the matter; these intermingle much levitie in their action to make men laugh, those use all gravitie, grace, and authoritie to perswade: wherefore these are accounted ridiculous, those esteemed prudent' (p. 179). This passage, with its careful rhetorical balancing, is at pains to demonstrate the levity and ridiculousness of stage acting in comparison to the gravity and authority of oratory; in this it recalls the antitheatricality of other religious writers such as Henry Holland. And yet, as we have already seen, there is more overlap between strategies of actors and orators than Holland and Wright would like to admit. Indeed Wright's advice for stirring up sadness and commiseration could be employed by tragic actors, as well as preachers:

> In sadness & commiseration, a grave, dolefull, plaine voice is best, without much varietie either of eye, face, or hand, for the orator must shew himselfe in soule and heart afflicted, oppressed, halfe dead; and therefore no more life ought to appeare without externall eyes and ears, than is necessary to deliver the force of our reasons, and the griefe of our mindes: our proofes may be urged and prosecuted but alwaies with a pitifull weeping eye and a fainting lamentable tune: yet notwithstanding, the voice sometimes ought to be

---

[49] See Matthew Potolsky's discussion of 'Theatre and Theatricality' in *Mimesis* (London: Routledge, 2006), ch. 4, especially pp. 81–6. As Potolsky notes, 'A real emotion and an effectively mimed emotion look exactly the same to the spectator' (p. 85).

interrupted with wofull exclamations and ruthfull repetitions, with alas, woe is me, &c. The eye also must be gravely elevated up to heaven, or abjected to earth, but it must be done seldome and marvelous soberly. (p. 181)

Arnold Hunt has suggested that Protestant handbooks on preaching advocated a dignified form of oratorical performance, and that certain histrionic gestures – such as waving the arms or rolling the eyes – were more associated with 'the more theatrical preaching style of the Jesuits and monastic orders'.[50] Perhaps, then, some Protestant preachers may have found Wright's emphasis upon body language and rolling eyes a little too flamboyant; at the same time, however, other Protestant writers advocated the use of appropriate actions by the orator to convey his emotions to listeners. For example, in his preaching manual *The arte of prophecying* (1592; translated into English 1607) the Protestant clergyman William Perkins describes the art of preaching in a way that draws upon classical rhetoric and natural philosophy: 'Wood, that is capable of fire, doth not burne, unles fire be put to it: and he must first be godly affected himselfe, who would stirre up godly affections in other men. Therefore what motions a sermon doth require, such the Preacher shall stirre up privately in his owne mind, that hee may kindle up the same in his hearers'.[51] Perkins's analogy recalls Wright's description of sympathetic transference in *The Passions of the Minde*: 'If my hand be hot for the fire, the fire must bee more hot it selfe' (p. 173). This example reminds us that the difference between Protestant and Jesuit concepts of sympathy – and styles of preaching – may not have been as great as some writers of the time suggested.[52] It also highlights the suggestive tension at play within Wright's conception of sympathy and compassion. On the one hand, Wright compares the transference of passions to natural properties, such as heat, light, and air, implying that sympathy is an automatic process that involves a straightforward movement from one person to the other. On the other hand, however, Wright concedes that the articulation and transmission of emotion involves rhetoric, persuasion, and performance, and thus can be simulated. Wright's division of listeners into 'wise men' and 'the common people' is a rather problematic explanation for the fact that the rhetorical processes he describes do not always work; it also suggests that preachers did not necessarily regard early modern audiences as a unified social body.

---

[50] Hunt, *The Art of Hearing*, p. 84.
[51] William Perkins, *The arte of prophecying, or, A treatise concerning the sacred and onely true manner and methode of preaching*, trans. Thomas Tuke (London, 1607), p. 140.
[52] For further discussion of the overlap between Catholic and Protestant discourses of compassion in the period see van Dijkhuizen, *Pain and Compassion*.

Conclusion: 'touched with compunction'

We have already seen how Wright uses the term *sympathy* in its earlier sense of magical correspondences to refer to the relationship between the soul and music; towards the end of *The Passions* he uses it again in its arcane sense to account for the attraction between beasts and human beings: 'When we see beasts fight, we commonly wish in our harts the victory shold happen to the one party than the other: If a reason of this desire were demanded, it were impossible divers times to be rendered, except we resolved it into a secret sympathy of nature'. This phenomenon also explains why, when 'meeting with a company of strangers ... presently one shall perceive a certaine more affectuall fancie inclined to love one then another' (p. 220). But, despite this invocation of the earlier occult model of sympathy, Wright's treatise as a whole acknowledges the complex cognitive and rhetorical processes at work when individuals are moved by an emotional performance by a preacher, or indeed an actor within a play. This awareness of the complexity of fellow-feeling is most apparent in the Protestant sermons we have explored, which use the term *sympathy* in a more innovative way to evoke this more sophisticated and 'modern' understanding of emotional correspondence. It seems ironic, however, that this shift in usage, whereby a concept from natural philosophy is used to refer to human relationships, goes hand-in-hand with an increasing sense of the separateness of individuals. An imaginative sympathy for the other involves an outward movement from and return to the self.

Early modern preachers seem to have been fascinated by this evolving conception of social relationships and emotional affinities. But we have also seen how they drew upon biblical models and narratives in order to move their audiences to sympathy and compassion. I want to conclude by exploring one further example of this affective strategy from the turn of the seventeenth century: Lewis Thomas's *Demegoriai: Certaine lectures upon sundry portions of Scripture* (1600). Thomas's text consists of eight sermons, again on diverse biblical passages. In the first lecture, which discusses Christ's riding to Jerusalem, Thomas extols the virtues of compassion, writing that

> Cyprian hath a sweet saying: *Uere patitur, qui compatitur:* He is most patient, that is most passionate. Or rather, he hath passion enough in him, that hath in him compassion. And it argueth a most Christianlike, and charitable affection, when we are in a pittifull remorse touched with our brethrens infirmities.[53]

---

[53] Lewis Thomas, *Demegoriai: Certaine lectures upon sundry portions of Scripture, in one volume* (London, 1600), sig. B6r.

The fact that Christ weeps proves that he is a man like another, albeit one without sin. But Christ's weeping also teaches us about our relationship with him: 'by Christes weeping we learne the sympathie and holie union that is betwixt Christ and us. Hee feeleth our sorrowes, and is touched with our infirmities' (sig. B7r). As Thomas suggests, Christ's weeping not only proves that he is human in the sense that he weeps like us; he also weeps *for* us, and is 'touched' with our sorrows. This 'sympathie' that Thomas describes is thus both an affinity and an emotional connection. Yet this form of sympathy is also used to describe fellow-feeling between humans, as Thomas reflects upon the Apostles' compassion for Peter's imprisonment: 'The other Apostles greeving at his troubles, and vexed in spirit at Herods cruelty, and his imprisonment, made earnest prayer unto God for him' (sig. P6r). This leads him to note 'the simpathy and mutual feeling that one member hath with another. Peters passions wrought compassion in the brethren, and therfore they both sorrowed for him, & prayed for him. It greeved them to see so notable an instrument of Gods glory lie in bonds'. This example, he suggests, teaches us 'to have a feeling each of others calamity, to bee touched with compunction, in beholding our brethrens distresses and miseries' (sig. P6r). Peter's passions lead to compassion amongst the brethren: the Apostles are grieved by his troubles and are touched with 'compunction' after regarding him in bonds.[54]

This complex understanding of sympathy, which involves a biblical narrative being used as an exemplar for the reader or listener's behaviour, further complicates the Renaissance commonplace that passions could be automatically transferred from orator to audience. The sermons discussed in the present chapter suggest that the reality was somewhat more complex, and that articulations and representations of sympathy presupposed an active – and participatory – audience. These materials allow us to question some of the rhetorical commonplaces of the period, as well as the broader critical assumption that sympathy in the Renaissance was a primarily physiological process. Ideas of sympathy and compassion in the late sixteenth century were bound up not only with wider political and religious debates, but also with shifting concepts of the social body and the self. In the next chapter we will see how these questions regarding intersubjectivity and the transmission of sympathy were explored in one of the most influential poetic genres of the 1590s: the female complaint. The picture of sympathy

---

[54] Thomas uses the now obsolete form of *compunction* to mean 'A feeling of sorrow for the suffering of another; pity, compassion' (*OED*, 1d).

that emerges as we explore these distinct but overlapping genres, including religious, dramatic and poetic texts, suggests that the very idea of a homogenous social body was beginning to seem outmoded. Perhaps this is one reason why preachers began to address audiences as a compassionate network of individual selves, and not simply – as William Averell might have it – a 'unitie of mindes'.

CHAPTER 3

'Grief best is pleased with grief's society'
Female Complaint and the Transmission of Sympathy

About halfway through Shakespeare's *The Rape of Lucrece* the narrator states that Lucrece is 'deepe drenched in a Sea of care', and that everything around her – including the birds' beautiful singing – seems to renew her suffering.[1] The narrator then alludes to the proverbial idea that grief is lessened by being in the company of other sorrowful individuals. I quote here from the 1594 Quarto:

> The little birds that tune their mornings joy,
> Make her mones mad, with their sweet melodie,
> "For mirth doth search the bottome of annoy,
> "Sad soules are slaine in merrie companie,
> "Griefe best is pleas'd with griefes societie;
> "True sorrow then is feelinglie suffiz'd,
> "When with like semblance it is simpathiz'd.   (sig. H3v)

This passage is one of several in the Quarto text marked with double quotation marks, suggesting that they are commonplaces, and thus ripe for reuse (see Figure 3).[2] And indeed, as we will see later in this chapter, several lines from this passage would be reproduced in some of the poetic miscellanies that appeared at the turn of the seventeenth century. It would appear, then, that this is a fairly straightforward instance of late Elizabethan textual transmission, with Shakespeare reworking some well-worn ideas, which were then appropriated and reproduced in later printed works. Yet this stanza concludes with the innovative word *sympathized*,

---

[1] William Shakespeare, *Lucrece* (London, 1594), sig. H3v.
[2] See Peter Stallybrass and Roger Chartier, 'Reading and Authorship: The Circulation of Shakespeare 1590–1619', in Andrew Murphy (ed.), *A Concise Companion to Shakespeare and the Text* (Oxford: Blackwell, 2010), pp. 35–56 (pp. 47–8), and Kate Rumbold, 'Shakespeare's Poems in Pieces: *Venus and Adonis* and *The Rape of Lucrece* Unanthlogized', *Shakespeare Survey*, 69 (2016), 92–105 (pp. 97–9). These lines also recall and expand upon the proverbial saying that we encountered in Lyly's *Euphues*: 'It is good to have company in misery' (Dent C571).

103

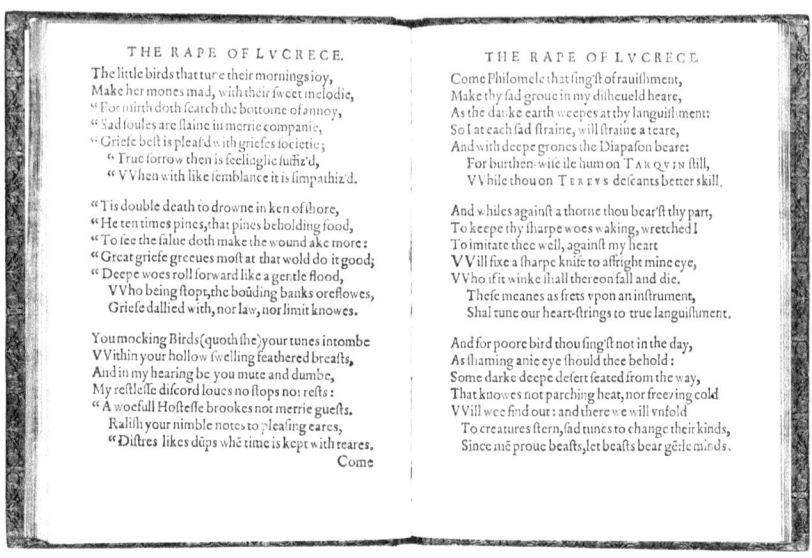

Figure 3 William Shakespeare, *Lucrece* (London, 1594), sigs. H3v–H4r. STC 22345 copy 1. Used by permission of the Folger Shakespeare Library.

which does not appear in print prior to 1594.[3] Did Shakespeare invent it? Did the conversion of *sympathy* into a verb offer Elizabethan readers a new term for describing the act of feeling the grief of others? What role did other writers play in this process of linguistic innovation – both those Shakespeare drew upon, and those who imitated Shakespeare's explorations of 'True sorrow' and 'griefes societie'?

In the last two chapters we have seen how prose writers used the word *sympathy* in the context of same-sex friendship and romantic love; and how preachers used the term as a way of constructing a community of sympathetic listeners, via biblical stories and exemplars. The present chapter extends these explorations of correspondence and community by considering the female complaint, a key literary mode that flourished in the 1590s. These narrative poems – which were frequently printed alongside sonnet sequences – typically featured a famous or legendary woman, who returns from the dead to tell her story in order to win posterity, fame, and pity.[4] Such poems not only depict women feeling sorrow for

[3] Shakespeare also begins to use the term in plays written around 1594–5, as we will see in the next chapter. *Lucrece*, however, contains the first Shakespearean usage of *sympathize* to appear in print.

[4] The best account of this tradition remains John Kerrigan, *Motives of Woe: Shakespeare and 'Female Complaint'* (Oxford: Clarendon Press, 1991). Kerrigan's anthology traces the tradition back to

each other, or comparing their sorrows, but also involve a considerable degree of intertextual borrowing and imitation. The chapter argues, then, that complaint poetry proved to be an especially fertile genre in which representations of emotional imitation and transmission were themselves imitated and transmitted. At the same time, however, some of the sympathetic encounters depicted within these texts turn out to be unsuccessful, or even duplicitous. These texts raise fundamental questions about gender, language, and intersubjectivity, and highlight the ways in which engaging with the other is an active process.[5] The word *sympathized* appears to have emerged from these poetic explorations of emotional and textual imitation.

The chapter begins by examining Samuel Daniel's *The Complaint of Rosamond* (1592), which paved the way for a number of complaint poems that employ the words *sympathy* and *sympathize*. *Rosamond* not only presents the reader with Rosamond's 'well-told tale' but also describes her desire for a compassionate reaction to her tale, along with various figured responses. The chapter goes on to discuss the complex representations of sympathy in Shakespeare's *Lucrece*, and focuses on Lucrece's emotional encounter with her maid, who, 'enforced by sympathy', begins to weep herself. The chapter then explores how this sympathetic encounter was itself imitated and reworked in several texts in the years that followed, including John Trussell's *The First Rape of Faire Hellen* (1595) and Samuel Nicholson's *Acolastus* (1600). The fact that several key passages from *Lucrece* were also reproduced in various poetic miscellanies around this time offers us further evidence of the poem's influence on the literary and emotional cultures of the late sixteenth century. The chapter thus explores two reciprocal forms of transmission in the 1590s: first, the transmission of sorrow and emotion between literary characters; and second, the transmission and exchange of these concepts between literary texts. These modes of transmission are intriguingly related: within particular complaint poems we find complex representations of emotional imitation and exchange – often involving classical and other intertextual influences – but this process is extended as other poets, in turn, are prompted to imitate such instances of emotional and intertextual transmission. As we shall see, this phenomenon

---

medieval lyrics, and forward into the eighteenth century. See also Anna Swärdh, '"Much augmented" and "somewhat beautified": Revisions in Three Female Complaints of the 1590s', *Modern Philology*, 113 (2016), 310–30.

[5] For a complex discussion of the 'projection and projective identification' involved in compassion see Teresa Brennan, *The Transmission of Affect* (Ithaca: Cornell University Press, 2001), pp. 29–33 and *passim*.

relates to my wider argument about the active dimensions of sympathy in the period, inasmuch as these textual reworkings are not merely passive imitations but rather creative and imaginative responses to the 'original' – which is itself often indebted to other texts and stories.

'No Muse suggests the pittie of my case': Authorizing Compassion in *The Complaint of Rosamond*

Samuel Daniel's *The Complaint of Rosamond* retells the story of Rosamond Clifford, mistress of Henry II, who committed suicide after being confronted by Henry's wife, Eleanor.[6] In the poem's opening stanzas, the ghost of Rosamond appears, and bemoans the fact that her soul has been denied transport to Elysium. Rosamond's soul, we are told, will only be allowed to pass the River Styx when 'Lovers sighes on earth' (14) deliver her.[7] From the outset, then, Rosamond aims to elicit an emotional reaction from those who hear her complaint. However, rather than attempting to move these lovers herself, Rosamond's ghost resolves to seek out the services of a ghost-writer. She thus recalls the complaints of the various tragic figures depicted in *The Mirror for Magistrates* – first printed in 1559 and expanded in 1563 – who ask for an auditor or spokesman to tell their tale. Indeed Rosamond explicitly refers to Thomas Churchyard's lament of Jane Shore, which appeared in the 1563 edition of the *Mirror*:

> No Muse suggests the pittie of my case,
> Each penne dooth overpasse my just complaint,
> Whilst others are preferd, though farre more base:
> *Shores* wife is grac'd, and passes for a Saint;
> Her Legend justifies her foule attaint;
>   Her well-told tale did such compassion finde,
>   That she is pass'd, and I am left behind.   (22–8)

Rosamond herself seems to have read the other complaint poems that were circulating in this period, and she also seems to have been cognizant of the

---

[6] Hallett Smith suggests that Rosamond's legend had become obscure by the early 1590s: he writes that '[Rosamond's] tomb at Gladstowe nunnery had been destroyed by a zealous bishop, and she now enjoyed no fame or compassion' (*Elizabethan Poetry: A Study in Conventions, Meaning, and Expression* (Cambridge, MA: Harvard University Press, 1952), p. 106). Yet the reality was somewhat more complex: Rosamond's story can be found in various ballads and histories of medieval England, even though she did not have quite the same degree of popular fame as Jane Shore; see Stephen Guy-Bray, 'Rosamond's Complaint: Daniel, Ovid, and the Purpose of Poetry', *Renaissance Studies*, 22 (2008), 338–50 (pp. 347–8).
[7] Quotations from *Rosamond* are taken from Arthur C. Sprague (ed.), *Samuel Daniel: Poems and A Defence of Ryme* (London: Routledge and Kegan Paul, 1950).

emotional effect that they had upon their readers. The example of Shore's wife has demonstrated to Rosamond the extent to which a 'well-told tale' can elicit 'pittie' and 'compassion', suggesting that she hopes that her own story will also be artfully constructed and will have a similar effect. Shore is pitied, suggests Rosamond, even though her case is 'farre more base'. Daniel thus creates a degree of competitiveness between these two suffering females, as if part of the meaning of Rosamond's plight is comparative, or even borrowed from another literary exemplar. One could say the same about Daniel's poem, of course, which can be read as an allegory of his own literary 'competition' with Churchyard.[8]

Rosamond imagines that this proposed poem will be a powerful piece of rhetorical persuasion, as well as a well-made work of literary art. Her ghost speaks directly to Daniel, stating that she 'Comes to sollicit thee, since others faile, / To take this taske, and in thy wofull Song / To forme my case, and register my wrong' (33–5). Rosamond thus invites Daniel to construct a legal case in her defence, offering a re-presentation of the facts that will present her in the best possible light.[9] Daniel thus presents himself as a mere scribe, or a kind of advocate who speaks on behalf of an actual historical figure come back from the dead – although it is worth emphasizing that he is 'mov'd with a tender care / And pittie' (57–8) by Rosamond's predicament.[10] Moreover, Rosamond herself seems to have read the sonnets that were printed alongside *The Complaint of Rosamond*, or at least to be familiar with their female protagonist: '*Delia* may happe to deygne to read our story, / And offer up her sigh among the rest' (43–4). Here the fictional Delia is also granted an independent life outside the pages of *Delia*, and becomes a potential reader of *The Complaint of Rosamond*. The poet, pitying Rosamond, will tell her story, and as a result Delia may in turn pity her. As Georgia Brown has written, Rosamond's complaint 'affects

---

[8] For a provocative account of the ways in which writing about female experience 'provided the structural ground for asserting poetic mastery' see Wendy Wall, *The Imprint of Gender: Authorship and Publication in the English Renaissance* (Ithaca and London: Cornell University Press, 1993), esp. pp. 250–78 (p. 252). Churchyard seems to have responded to Rosamond's concerns and published a revised and expanded version of 'the Tragedie of Shores wife' in *Churchyards Challenge* (London, 1593), pp. 127–44.

[9] On Daniel's use of legal language see Heather Dubrow, '"Lending soft audience to my sweet design": Shifting Roles and Shifting Readings of Shakespeare's "A Lover's Complaint"', *Shakespeare Survey*, 58 (2005), 23–33 (pp. 24–5). Shore's Wife uses a similar formulation in the *Mirror*: 'Yet geve me leave to pleade my case at large' (*The Mirror for Magistrates*, ed. Lily B. Campbell (Cambridge University Press, 1938), pp. 373–86, line 113 (p. 377)).

[10] Cf. Jason Lawrence, who comments that 'it is the emotional affect of the appeal itself rather than the justice of the case that persuades Daniel's poet … to retell Rosamond's story in her own words' ('Samuel Daniel's *The Complaint of Rosamond* and the arrival of Tasso's Armida in England', *Renaissance Studies*, 25 (2011), 648–65 (pp. 651–2)).

an exchange of pity through a series of substitutions'.[11] The exchange of pity, as we have already seen, is a recurrent concern in much early modern literature. Yet the network of compassion figured within *The Complaint of Rosamond* is especially complex and intricate, inasmuch as it centres on a character who not only recalls other exemplary figures but also addresses Daniel and his other fictional creations.

The reader is also drawn into this process of sympathetic borrowing and exchange, as the distinction between subject and object becomes increasingly blurred. For example, when Rosamond comes to describe her physical appearance she first likens it to the visual impact of a comet, and then to a tragic narrative: 'Looke how a Comet at the first appearing, / Drawes all mens eyes with wonder to behold it: / Or as the saddest tale at suddaine hearing, / Makes silent listning unto him that told it' (113–16). Rosamond describes the silent wonder that her beauty elicited; she states that her presence was as compelling as a sad tale, and assumes that such tales have the power to entirely absorb their listeners. Yet this passage also reflects upon Rosamond's hopes for the reader's response to *The Complaint of Rosamond*: she encourages the reader or listener to imagine the affective power of the 'saddest tale'; to recall other tragic narratives that they have heard; and to transpose these figured responses onto her own story.

However, while Rosamond claims that her story will reveal 'the simple truth' (66), her tale is necessarily a partial and subjective account, in which she seeks to win the reader's pity and exonerate herself. Rosamond decides to enter into an affair with Henry II, and gains materially from it, and as a result critics have disagreed over the extent to which she is culpable for her downfall.[12] Rosamond's position is further complicated by *The Complaint of Rosamond*'s self-consciousness about its status as a work of rhetorical persuasion. As part of her attempts to blame others for her downfall Rosamond even suggests that her own beauty was partly responsible, describing it as 'Sweet silent rethorique of perswading eyes: / Dombe eloquence, whose power doth move the blood, / More then the words' (121–3). Rosamond states that beauty is more affecting than language,

---

[11] Georgia Brown, *Redefining Elizabethan Literature* (Cambridge University Press, 2004), p. 199. Brown writes that the poem 'undermines stable definitions of internal and external, subject and object, as Rosamond, Delia and the poet see themselves reflected in each other' (p. 200).

[12] As Kelly A. Quinn has written, 'critical responses to Rosamond over the last century ... amply demonstrate, in their mix of approbation and castigation, the dubious position of the plainant who seeks fame and compassion by confessing to sin' ('Mastering Complaint: Michael Drayton's *Piers Gaveston* and the Royal Mistress Complaints', *English Literary Renaissance*, 38 (2008), 439–60 (p. 455)).

although this idea is expressed via a rhetorically ornate formulation.[13] She also presents rhetoric in a pejorative light in her description of the Matron, who is sent by the King to persuade Rosamond to yield to his desires. The Matron is presented as a woman who feels no sympathetic affinity with Rosamond:

> Shee set upon me with the smoothest speech,
> That Court and age could cunningly devise:
> Th'one authentique made her fit to teach,
> The other learn'd her how to subtelise.
> Both were enough to circumvent the wise.
>   A document that well might teach the sage,
>   That there's no trust in youth, nor hope in age.   (218–24)

Thus, on the surface at least, Rosamond seeks to warn others of the perils of rhetoric. The Matron's smooth speech has the capacity to beguile and seduce innocent listeners. She is not only fit to teach, but also to 'subtelise'; that is, 'To make subtle distinctions; to argue or reason in a subtle manner; to split hairs' (*OED*, 5a). Despite Rosamond's claim that she was 'wise' the Matron was nonetheless able to 'circumvent' her. Rosamond's presentation of the Matron thus alerts the reader to the speciousness of the Matron's arguments; yet it may also distract us from the ways in which Rosamond herself argues in a subtle manner to elicit pity from her readers.[14]

The ambiguities of Rosamond's position are further highlighted when she describes her own sympathetic engagement with a work of art. The King sends her a richly decorated casket; and this is arguably the poem's most explicit allegory of reading and interpretation. This episode not only highlights the power of art to resemble or outdo reality but also its ability to provoke viewers to compassion – and it thus anticipates Lucrece's encounter with the Troy painting in Shakespeare's *The Rape of Lucrece*.[15] The casket contains two depictions of mythological scenes that comment

---

[13] This formulation anticipates several Shakespearean texts and is reworked in Jonson's *Every Man Out of His Humour*. As Fastidious puts it, 'You shall see sweet silent rhetoric and dumb eloquence speaking in her eye' (Ben Jonson, *Every Man Out of His Humour* (1599), in David Bevington, Martin Butler, and Ian Donaldson (gen. eds), *The Cambridge Edition of the Works of Ben Jonson* (Cambridge University Press, 2012), 3.3.89–90). On the ironies of the 'dumb eloquence' trope in relation to *Lucrece* see my *Narrating the Visual in Shakespeare*, pp. 58–60.

[14] See Heather Dubrow, 'A Mirror for Complaints: Shakespeare's *Lucrece* and Generic Tradition', in Barbara Kiefer Lewalski (ed.), *Renaissance Genres: Essays on Theory, History, and Interpretation* (Cambridge, MA, and London: Harvard University Press, 1986), pp. 399–417 (p. 402).

[15] On the links between this section of *Rosamond* and Shakespeare's *Lucrece* see Kelly A. Quinn, 'Ecphrasis and Reading Practices in Elizabethan Narrative Verse', *Studies in English Literature, 1500–1900*, 44 (2004), 19–35.

upon and reflect Rosamond's own situation. The first that Rosamond describes is the tale of Amymone and Neptune:

> The day before the night of my defeature,
> He greets me with a Casket richly wrought:
> So rare, that arte did seeme to strive with nature,
> T'expresse the cunning work-mans curious thought;
> The mistery whereof I prying sought.
>   And found engraven on the lidde above,
>   *Amymone* how she with *Neptune* strove.
>
> *Amymone* old *Danaus* fayrest Daughter,
> As she was fetching water all alone
> At *Lerna*: whereas *Neptune* came and caught her,
> From whom she striv'd and strugled to be gone,
> Beating the aire with cryes and pittious mone.
>   But all in vaine, with him sh'is forc'd to go,
>   Tis shame that men should use poore maydens so.   (372–85)

The casket is the product of an artist, or 'cunning' work-man, which expresses his 'thought'; Rosamond assumes that works of art have a hidden message or 'mysterie' that is capable of being deciphered. In other versions of the tale, Amymone is sent to find water by her father, and a satyr attempts to rape her. Neptune then rescues her, and reveals to her the springs at Lerna, but only after he has slept with her – with Amymone's consent. In Rosamond's narrative retelling, which glosses over some of the complexities and ambiguities of the story, she simply suggests that Amymone was 'caught' and ravished by Neptune.[16] As she describes it, the story offers a warning to other young ladies, and she complains that men 'should use poore maydens so'. For Rosamond, then, the story depicted on the casket reflects and reinforces her own status as an innocent victim. It explores the conversion of suffering into art, and thus reflects upon the workings of *The Complaint of Rosamond* itself.

In her description of the casket Rosamond is particularly concerned to highlight Amymone's suffering and her capacity to generate pity:

> Wailing her heavie hap, cursing the day,
> In act so pittious to express despaire:

---

[16] Quinn notes that Rosamond's reading of Amymone 'is guided by her agenda of exonerating herself and thereby gaining the sympathy of her audience' ('Ecphrasis and Reading Practices', p. 21). For a very hostile interpretation of Rosamond, which views her as a 'self-centred, fame-seeking hedonist', see Ronald Primeau, 'Daniel and the Mirror Tradition: Dramatic Irony in *The Complaint of Rosamond*', *Studies in English Literature, 1500–1900*, 15 (1975), 21–36 (p. 23).

> And by how much more greev'd, so much more fayre;
> Her teares upon her cheekes poore carefull gerle,
> Did seeme against the sunne christall and pearle. (388–92)

According to Rosamond at least, Amymone's expressions of despair are 'pittious', but they also make her seem all the more beautiful. Her glistening tears come to resemble the very medium of the casket itself, and are described as being like 'christall and pearle'. Rosamond suggests that Amymone's tears are capable of moving others, 'Teaching afflicted eyes affects to move' (397). Rosamond thus becomes a figured reader within her own tale, and in doing so creates another exchange of sympathy: she sympathizes with Amymone, and hopes that the reader will, in turn, experience similar feelings of sympathy towards her. Having viewed the engraving of Amymone, Rosamond states that she was 'something moved' (400). She thus guides the reader's response to the poem, although the fact that Rosamond wants to read the artwork in relation to her own predicament leads to a kind of interpretative circularity. After all, readers cannot 'see' the casket, and have to rely upon Rosamond's interpretation of it. For Rosamond, the engravings are 'presidents presented to her view' (407), but we might suggest that they only become precedents retrospectively. This moment thus opens up wider questions about the ethics of sympathy, exposing Rosamund's empathetic encounter with the casket as a problematic form of self-centredness: while she emphasizes her affinity with, and compassion for, Amymone the particularities of the latter's situation are forgotten.[17]

Towards the end of the poem Rosamond describes the King's piteous and inarticulate response to her own death. She invites the reader to reflect upon the trials of all individuals who have suffered great losses:

> Judge those whom chaunce deprives of sweetest treasure,
> What tis to lose a thing we hold so deare:
> The best delight, wherein our soule takes pleasure,
> The sweet of life, that penetrates so neare.
> What passions feeles that hart, infor'd to beare
>   The deepe impression of so strange a sight?
> Tongue, pen, nor art, can never show aright.
>
> Amaz'd he standes, nor voyce nor body steares,
> Words had no passage, teares no issue found:
> For sorrow shut up words, wrath kept in teares,

---

[17] For a discussion of the negative reputation of empathy as a 'particularly invasive form of selfishness', in which one's feelings are imposed upon the other, see Suzanne Keen, 'A Theory of Narrative Empathy', *Narrative*, 14 (2006), 207–36 (p. 222).

> Confus'd affects each other doe confounde:
> Oppress'd with griefe his passions had no bounde:
>   Striving to tell his woes, wordes would not come;
>   For light cares speake, when mightie griefes are dombe.   (617–30)

The King's passions are presented as an automatic response to an external event. The sweet of life 'penetrates' his body, and his heart is 'infor'd' to bear the 'deepe impression' of the sight of Rosamond's corpse. These terms all suggest emotional passivity, in which feelings are imposed on the self from the outside. At the same time, however, Rosamond suggests that such losses are impossible to represent in spoken language, writing, or other forms of art. In the second of these two stanzas, the poem focuses on the King's boundless passions and his inability to communicate them outside the self. Indeed the line 'For light cares speake, when mightie griefes are dombe' (630) may suggest that eloquence is incompatible with extreme grief. This rhetorical strategy – in which a powerful emotion is said to be inexpressible – arguably makes these represented passions seem more powerful and real, and creates the illusion that they have an independent existence outside the text. The King's grief also provides a potential model for the reader's own sorrowful reaction to Rosamond's death. Such moments provide further evidence that compassion in *The Complaint of Rosamond* is a figured process of borrowing and exchange rather than a simple transference from text to reader.

This emphasis upon emotional transmission and comparability seems to have influenced contemporary responses to the poem. Francis Meres, commenting upon *Rosamond* in his *Palladis Tamia* (1598), makes a suggestive analogy as he describes the reader's compassion for Rosamond: 'As every one mourneth when hee heareth of the lamentable plangors of Thracian Orpheus for his dearest Euridice, so every one passionateth when he readeth the afflicted death of Daniel's distressed *Rosamond*.'[18] Meres does not use the words *sympathy* or *sympathize*, but uses the unusual verbal form of *passionate* to describe readers' emotional response to Rosamond's tragedy.[19] He also invites readers to compare their responses to Daniel's poem to their responses to the tragic tale of Orpheus, replicating *Rosamond*'s interest in emotional and intertextual comparisons. The fact that Meres alludes to the story of Orpheus is suggestive; in this period the tale was

---

[18] Francis Meres, 'Poetrie; Poets; and A Comparative discourse of our English Poets, with the Greeke, Latine, and Italian Poets', in *Palladis Tamia. Wits Treasury* (London, 1598), p. 280.
[19] See the *OED*, 'passionate', v. 1: 'To excite or imbue with passion, or with a particular emotion, as love, fear, anger, etc.', citing this passage.

frequently used as a metaphor for the capacity of music and poetry to elicit compassion.[20] But what is striking here is that Meres reaches for an innovative emotion verb in order to express both his active feelings of compassion for Rosamond – and those of the poem's community of readers – suggesting that Daniel's poem was particularly successful in eliciting such responses.[21]

The network of compassion dramatized within *Rosamond* – which Meres appears to have been affected by – also prompted other writers to participate in this emotional and intertextual process; and here we can see the word *sympathy* making its first appearances in the complaint tradition. In 1593 Thomas Lodge's *The Complaint of Elstred* was printed alongside his sonnet sequence *Phillis*. In the Induction, Lodge makes explicit reference to Daniel's *Delia* and her 'sweet Prophe[t]':

> Kisse *Delias* hand for her sweet Prophets sake,
> Whose not affected but well couched tears:
> Have power, have worth, a Marble mind to shake;
> Whose fame, no Iron-age or time out weares.
> Then lay you downe in *Phillis* lap and sleepe,
> Untill she weeping read, and reading weepe.[22]

As this intriguing intermingling of reading and weeping suggests, *The Complaint of Elstred* is also concerned with the representation and exchange of pity. *Elstred* features a narrator figure who, whilst lamenting his own misfortunes by the river Severn, has a vision of Elstred, mistress of Humber, and her daughter.[23] Elstred recounts her rise and fall, and how she was first won over by the Tamburlaine-like 'working words' of Humber (p. 62), and subsequently by Locrinus's 'sweet chains of honny speech' (p. 71).[24] Locrinus is forced to marry Guendolen, as he is betrothed to her, but persuades Elstred to embark upon an affair with him. Locrinus builds a 'Maze

---

[20] In *The Spanish Tragedy* Hieronimo recalls the myth of Orpheus in 3.13 when he states that he will descend to the underworld in search of justice; see Chapter 4, below.
[21] We should note, however, that some contemporaneous readers offered a more sceptical account of Daniel's heroine; Giles Fletcher the Elder, for example, appended a complaint to his sonnet sequence *Licia* (London, 1593) that castigates poets such as Daniel who 'write of women, and of womens falles, / Who are too light, for to be fortunes balles' (sig. L2v).
[22] Thomas Lodge, *Phillis: Honoured with Pastorall Sonnets, Elegies, and amorous delights. Where-unto is annexed, the tragicall complaynt of Elstred* (London, 1593), sig. A4v.
[23] As Wendy Wall has commented, *The Complaint of Elstred* 'opens with a series of doublings, as the speaker's complaints blend into those of the "woeful vision" he discovers. The fact that there are two women complaining within this already doubled frame creates a network of echoes and reverberations' (*Imprint of Gender*, p. 258).
[24] Quotations from the poem are from *The Complaint of Elstred*, in *The Complete Works of Thomas Lodge*, 4 vols (1883; rpt. New York: Russell and Russell, 1963), vol. 2, pp. 59–84.

and curious Cave' (p. 72) where he places Elstred in order to keep their relationship secret. Ultimately, however, despite Elstred's attempts to plead for her life and that of her daughter, they are both killed by Guendolen. Like Rosamond, then, Elstred – for all of her scepticism towards rhetoric – seeks to use her persuasive powers to elicit pity and compassion from others.

For our purposes, however, what is most striking about *Elstred* is the fact that it employs the term *sympathy* to describe the correspondence of emotions between Elstred and Locrinus:

> "For where there growes a simpathie of harts,
> "Each passion in the one, the other paineth,
> "And by each cariage of the outward parts,
> (Wherein the actuall worke of love remaineth)
>   The inward griefes, mislikes, and joyes are tought:
>   And every signe bewraies a secrete thought. (p. 68)

In Chapter 1 we saw how, three years earlier in *Rosalynde* (1590), Lodge had used the term *sympathy* to describe the 'sympathy of … affections' between Rosalynde and Alinda. In this stanza, Lodge describes the 'simpathie of harts' between Elstred and Locrinus.[25] Here the word is explicitly used to refer to a correspondence of emotion: each passion that one experiences is felt by and communicated to the other. By the time he wrote *Elstred*, then, Lodge's own conception of the term seems to have narrowed, and he uses *sympathy* to refer to a correspondence of various passions, including 'inward griefes'. Lodge's poem is clearly indebted to *The Complaint of Rosamond* in terms of its sympathetic protagonist and concern with pity, but it develops Daniel's poem by including the term *sympathy* to describe this efficacious exchange of feelings.

This process of linguistic innovation is extended in another female complaint printed in the same year: Anthony Chute's *Beawtie dishonoured* (1593).[26] Chute's poem retells the story of Jane Shore, and while it imitates Thomas Churchyard quite closely it does not acknowledge its debts to him.[27] Yet one significant development is that it joins Lodge in including the word *sympathy*, which does not appear in any of Churchyard's versions. The narrator describes Jane's private grief and turbulent passions:

> *Thus waking to her selfe and watching all:*
> *Discentious union in her selfe discording:*
> *Fearing the fortune worthie may be fall.*
> *Onel' in a divers* Sympathie *according.* (sig. B4r)

---

[25] *Rosalynde*, ed. Greg, p. 29.
[26] Anthony Chute, *Beawtie dishonoured written under the title of Shores wife* (London, 1593).
[27] See the *ODNB*, s.v. 'Anthony Chute'.

In the printed text the word is emphasized, which suggests that it was still considered to be a new or noteworthy loan word. Chute's protagonist also asks '*What* Sympathie *of love (quoth I) can be / Twixte crooked old, and excellently fayre*' (sig. C2v). Both Lodge and Chute thus anticipate Spenser's usage of the term in *An Hymne in Honour of Beautie* (1596), which describes love as 'a celestiall harmonie, / Of likely harts composd of starres concent, / Which joyne together in sweete sympathie'.[28] This is the *OED*'s first example of *sympathy* being used in the sense of 'Conformity of feelings, inclinations, or temperament, which makes persons agreeable to each other' (*OED*, 3a); but clearly the term was used by both Lodge and Chute in this sense several years earlier. Thus, while Daniel's *Rosamond* does not employ the terms *sympathy* or *sympathize*, it did initiate a poetic investigation into the workings of compassion in which these important emotion words start to emerge.

'Grieving themselves to guess at others' smarts': Shakespeare's *Lucrece*

As we noted at the start of this chapter, Shakespeare's *Lucrece* (1594) contains what may be the first appearance of the word *sympathized* in print. And, while not strictly speaking a complaint, *Lucrece* does contain several important features of the genre.[29] It is arguably Shakespeare's most direct response to Daniel's *The Complaint of Rosamond*: in particular, Lucrece's emotional encounter with a painting of the fall of Troy appears to be indebted to Rosamond's 'reading' of the mythological scenes on the casket.[30]

---

[28] Quoted from Richard A. McCabe (ed.), *Edmund Spenser: The Shorter Poems* (Harmondsworth: Penguin, 1999), lines 197–9. Here Spenser draws upon Marsilio Ficino's commentary on Plato's *Symposium*, in particular the notion that 'likeness generates love'. McCabe paraphrases: 'Those who are born under the same star, and are therefore endowed with similar virtues, have souls which are naturally sympathetic' (note to 190–203).

[29] William P. Weaver has suggested that, while influenced by the complaint genre, *Lucrece* is not a complaint, and that 'the differences between [Lucrece's] speeches and those in the complaints are as instructive as their similarities'; see '"O teach me how to make mine own excuse": Forensic Performance in *Lucrece*', *Shakespeare Quarterly*, 59 (2008), 421–49 (p. 422). However, this perhaps underestimates the poem's indebtedness to the tradition and Shakespeare's interest in the complaint genre more generally. See Elizabeth Scott-Baumann and Ben Burton, 'Shakespearean Stanzas? *Venus and Adonis*, *Lucrece*, and Complaint', *ELH*, 88 (2021), 1–26.

[30] Daniel's poem would also influence Shakespeare's *A Lover's Complaint*, which was probably written around 1600 and printed alongside his sonnets in 1609. However, Shakespeare's later poem does not include the terms *sympathy* or *sympathize*, and did not play as significant a role as *Lucrece* in the subsequent transmission of these concepts. For useful discussions of *A Lover's Complaint* see Dubrow, '"Lending soft audience to my sweet design"', and Katharine A. Craik, 'Poetry and Compassion in Shakespeare's "A Lover's Complaint"', in Jonathan Post (ed.), *The Oxford Handbook of Shakespeare's Poetry* (Oxford University Press, 2013), pp. 522–39.

Colin Burrow has written that *Lucrece* is 'partly *about* the different ways in which readers read, and the distinct ways in which different people and different sexes respond to material realities'.[31] We might make a more specific observation, however, and suggest that *Lucrece* is interested in the different ways in which men and women respond to each other's suffering. Indeed, *Lucrece* not only builds on Lodge and Chute by associating the word *sympathy* with ideas of emotional resemblance but also uses it to describe an exchange of sorrow between two women. As we shall see, Lucrece's maid experiences a passionate response to Lucrece's sorrow without the need for any verbal explanation or persuasion. Yet the poem also dramatizes Lucrece's unsuccessful attempts to dissuade Tarquin from raping her – an episode that does not appear in any of Shakespeare's sources – and thus implies a lack of pity between men and women.

Gazing on Tarquin with 'pity-pleading' (561) eyes, Lucrece first attempts to elicit his compassion. After likening her sighs to 'whirlwinds' that have the power to 'heave' Tarquin, she enjoins him to be moved by her protestations: 'If ever man were moved with woman's moans, / Be movèd with my tears, my sighs, my groans' (587–8). As she continues, Lucrece embarks upon an extended metaphor in which her tears and sighs are figured as water, while Tarquin's heart is likened to a rock:

> All which together like a troubled ocean
> Beat at thy rocky and wreck-threatening heart,
> To soften it with their continual motion;
> For stones dissolved to water do convert.
> O if no harder than a stone thou art,
>   Melt at my tears and be compassionate:
>   Soft pity enters at an iron gate. (589–95)

Lucrece's watery metaphor corresponds with the early modern idea that women were thought to be more 'liquid', and thus more compassionate, than men.[32] She asks Tarquin to be moved by her bodily effects, figuring

---

[31] Colin Burrow, 'Introduction' to *The Complete Sonnets and Poems*, p. 59. Subsequent quotations from *Lucrece* and the sonnets are taken from this edition.

[32] Ian Maclean summarises this view: 'The softer flesh of women predisposes her to psychological softness' (*The Renaissance Notion of Woman: A Study in the Fortune of Scholasticism and Medical Science in European Intellectual Life* (Cambridge University Press, 1980), p. 42). See also Fay Bound Alberti, 'Emotions in the Early Modern Medical Tradition', in Alberti (ed.), *Medicine, Emotion and Disease, 1700–1950* (Basingstoke: Palgrave, 2006), pp. 1–21. Alberti reminds us that humoral theory was 'inherently gendered'. Women tended towards 'a phlegmatic or cold and moist disposition, since their bodies were fleshier, softer and weaker than those of men ... The greater passivity of women (and later their wombs) also made them more subject to such emotional extremes as hysteria' (p. 4). For a discussion of the ways in which Shakespeare's works interrogate this view see my chapter

her tears and sighs as a troubled but powerful ocean. Lucrece proposes that Tarquin's hard heart will melt because of her tears, and will even 'convert' to water itself. She imagines, then, that Tarquin will not only share her feelings, but that there will be a kind of natural similitude – or even sympathy – between them, as Tarquin's impermeable self 'dissolve[s]' and he becomes constituted of tears himself. And indeed the poem as a whole uses tears and sighs as metaphors for the permeability of the self, and for the potential of such signs to enter another person's consciousness. Lucrece's description of her tears picks up on a metaphor already used by the narrator: 'his heart granteth / No penetrable entrance to her plaining: / Tears harden lust, though marble wear with raining' (558–60). In an uncomfortable irony, then, Lucrece asks Tarquin to be 'penetrated' by her attempts to move him.

When these arguments do not seem to work, Lucrece attempts another strategy. She moves beyond the physical model of sympathy proposed by her metaphor of tears-as-ocean, and appeals to Tarquin's imagination, asking him to see himself from the perspective of someone else:

> Think but how vile a spectacle it were
> To view thy present trespass in another:
> Men's faults do seldom to themselves appear;
> Their own transgressions partially they smother.
> This guilt would seem death-worthy in thy brother:
>   O, how are they wrapped in with infamies,
>   That from their own misdeeds askance their eyes?   (631–7)

Here Lucrece appeals to Tarquin's mental faculties in order that he might see the vileness of his proposed action. She commands him to use his imagination ('Think …') and to imagine how his 'present trespass' (632) would appear if he saw someone else committing it. By extension, Tarquin is being invited to leave the confines of his own body – and indeed mind – and to see himself from the outside, thus recognizing that his own perspective is but one among many.[33] Much of the imagery in this stanza is to do with seeing: Lucrece suggests that Tarquin is so 'wrapped in with infamies' – that is, enveloped within his own mental universe – that he

---

on 'Sympathy', in Katharine A. Craik (ed.), *Shakespeare and Emotion* (Cambridge University Press, 2020), pp. 224–37.

[33] Lucrece's description here anticipates what Evan Thompson has called 'reiterated empathy'; that is, when 'I do not merely experience myself as a sentient being "from within", nor grasp myself as also a physical thing in the world; I experience myself as recognizably sentient "from without", that is, from your perspective, the perspective of another' ('Empathy and Consciousness', *Journal of Consciousness Studies*, 8/5–7 (2001), 1–32(p. 19)).

fails to see his transgressions *as* transgressions. We might even say that Lucrece asks Tarquin to not only feel her pain but also develop a theory of mind. And yet, for all of Lucrece's sophistication and eloquence, Tarquin is unmoved and continues with his vile action. On the one hand, then, the poem may seem to confirm the commonplace notion that men are by nature less compassionate than women. On the other hand, Shakespeare presents Tarquin as an especially unsympathetic counterexample, and invites his readers to pity its protagonist rather than emulate Tarquin.

Lucrece's failed attempts to elicit Tarquin's compassion are contrasted with her encounter with her maid – an episode that appears to have been Shakespeare's invention.[34] This meeting takes place later in the poem after Lucrece has been raped, and is perhaps the poem's most explicit representation of sympathetic engagement between two individuals. The maid sees that Lucrece has been crying, but 'durst not ask her audaciously / Why her two suns were cloud-eclipsèd so' (1223–4); that is, the maid is not bold enough to ask why Lucrece is upset. Nonetheless, the maid begins to weep herself, and the narrator uses an elaborate meteorological metaphor to describe this exchange of emotion:

> But as the earth doth weep, the sun being set,
> Each flower moistened like a melting eye;
> Even so the maid with swelling drops gan wet
> Her circled eyne enforced by sympathy
> Of those fair suns set in her mistress' sky,
>   Who in a salt-waved ocean quench their light,
>   Which makes the maid weep like the dewy night. (1226–32)

This passage describes a cosmological or physical model of sympathetic correspondence; the maid imitates Lucrece's tears without knowing their cause, and responds to her mistress's grief in the same way that the earth appears to 'weep' at sunset. The stanza is replete with correspondences and analogies: flowers resemble melting eyes; Lucrece's eyes resemble suns; the maid's tears resemble the dewy night; the maid resembles Lucrece; and so on. The word *sympathy* is used in its physiological sense to suggest an automatic reaction to the outward signs of Lucrece's grief, rather than an imaginative or cognitive response. Indeed this passage recalls Gail Paster's suggestion that early modern passions were 'like liquid forces of nature'.[35]

---

[34] John Roe suggests that this episode recalls Rosamond's description of the casket: 'What both descriptions have in common is that they effect a moment of contemplative pathos centred on a female figure (or figures) or conveyed through a female sensibility' (Roe (ed.), *The Poems*, updated ed. (Cambridge University Press, 2006), pp. 40–1).

[35] Paster, *Humoring the Body*, p. 4.

Here passions are something that happen to the maid: she is 'enforced' by sympathy, while her grief 'makes' the maid weep. Certainly the imagery drawn from the natural world seems to emphasize the apparent naturalness of the maid's reaction, and may point to what Michael Schoenfeldt has called 'the contagious nature of powerful passion'.[36]

And yet, as the poem continues, we find that the maid's sympathy is more complex than the narrator's metaphorical schema suggests:

> A pretty while these pretty creatures stand,
> Like ivory conduits coral cisterns filling.
> One justly weeps; the other takes in hand
> No cause but company of her drops' spilling.
> Their gentle sex to weep are often willing,
>   Grieving themselves to guess at others' smarts,
>   And then they drown their eyes, or break their hearts.   (1233–39)

The narrator states that the maid has 'no cause but company' to weep, which might suggest that the maid weeps merely because she is *with* Lucrece. Yet the word *company* also connotes 'Companionship, fellowship, society' (*OED*, 1). Moreover, the formulation 'Grieving themselves to guess at others' smarts' (1238) suggests that the maid's sympathy for Lucrece is not simply automatic or 'enforced' but rather involves an act of imaginative speculation: an empathetic attempt to determine the reasons for Lucrece's suffering.[37] The narrator goes on to explain the maid's reaction in terms of gender difference: 'For men have marble, women waxen minds, / And therefore are they formed as marble will' (1240–41). By quoting this stereotypical concept the poem reinforces the contrast between Tarquin and the maid in terms of their respective impermeability and liquidity; Tarquin is 'harder than a stone' (593) while the maid is 'like the dewy night' (1232). And yet the narrator's suggestion that women 'guess at' the cause of each other's sorrows suggest that they are not simply the passive or 'waxen' creatures that these commonplace ideas describe.

---

[36] Michael Schoenfeldt, 'Shakespearean Pain', in Craik and Pollard (eds.), *Shakespearean Sensations*, pp. 191–207 (p. 196).

[37] Samuel Arkin has written that the maid's experience 'seems to happen at the border between an older cosmological definition of sympathy … and a newer psychological model where sympathy is registered as both an unconscious or involuntary response and as an impulse over which we might assume a degree of understanding' ('"That map which deep impression bears": Lucrece and the Anatomy of Shakespeare's Sympathy', *Shakespeare Quarterly*, 64 (2013), 349–71 (p. 367)). Arkin also suggests, however, that the narrator offers a 'false gloss' on what we have just read, and that this second stanza is a 'misrepresentation' of the maid's enforced sympathy (pp. 366–7). This account seems to miss the poem's ambivalent attitude towards emotional correspondence.

Lucrece's encounter with the maid, with its emphasis upon sympathy and society, recalls the narrator's reflections upon grief's society – quoted at the start of this chapter – which culminate in the word *sympathized*:

> Sad souls are slain in merry company.
> Grief best is pleased with grief's society:
>   True sorrow, then, is feelingly sufficed
>   When with like semblance it is sympathized.   (1110–13)

In this intriguing and intricate passage, sorrow itself is said to be 'feelingly sufficed' – that is, satisfied – by being compared with similar sorrows. We might also note, however, that this formulation contains what John Roe has called 'almost a surplus of words', inasmuch as several terms here refer to ideas of resemblance and likeness. Roe writes that *like*, *semblance*, and *sympathized* 'only marginally extend each other's meanings, existing rather for decorative symmetry'.[38] But perhaps Shakespeare's use of *sympathized* is less tautologous than Roe suggests. According to the *OED*, the word means 'To agree with, answer or correspond to, match' (*OED*, 'sympathize', 3, citing this passage). Yet the fact that the words *like* and *semblance* appear in the same phrase suggests that Shakespeare is expanding the meaning of *sympathy* to suggest something more active and complex, and expressive of emotional exchange. Indeed this repetition of comparable words and phrases enacts the emotional 'society' that the passage itself describes. By converting *sympathy* into a verb, and associating it with ideas of grief, sorrow, feeling, and resemblance, Shakespeare arguably fashions a new concept, which draws upon and combines these surrounding words and ideas.

It is thus tempting to propose that *sympathize* is an important Shakespearean coinage. However, we should note that the word also features in Samuel Daniel's closet drama *The Tragedie of Cleopatra*, which first appeared in the augmented 1594 edition of *Delia* and *Rosamond*. *Cleopatra* begins with an extended speech from its female protagonist in which she laments Antony's demise. As she resolves to follow him in death, Cleopatra suggests that they will continue to share each other's pain and sorrow:

> And next is my turne, now to sacrifize
> To Death, and thee, the life that doth reprove mee,
> Our like distresse I feele doth sympathize,
> And even afflicion makes me truly love thee.[39]

---

[38] See Roe (ed.), *The Poems*, note to 1113.
[39] Samuel Daniel, *Delia and Rosamond augmented. Cleopatra* (London, 1594), sig. I4v. *Cleopatra* was reprinted in *The Poeticall Essayes of Sam. Danyel. Newly corrected and augmented* (London, 1599), and then in the folio of Daniel's *Workes* in 1601.

This is the first appearance of the term *sympathize* in Daniel's works, and it recalls – or perhaps anticipates – Shakespeare's use of *sympathized* in *Lucrece*. Addressing Antony, Cleopatra describes their 'like distresse', apparently using the term *sympathize* in the sense of correspondence. Yet the fact that she is referring to the 'even afflicion' between herself and Antony means that *sympathize* denotes an imaginative equivalence of grief. Shakespeare and Daniel can thus be plausibly claimed as co-inventors of *sympathize* in its 'modern' sense.[40] But while it is possible that Shakespeare borrowed the term from Daniel, perhaps having read *Cleopatra* in manuscript form, it is worth emphasizing that Shakespeare often converts nouns into verbs – a linguistic process that David Crystal has wittily called 'verbing'.[41] Given that this process is a distinctively Shakespearean characteristic then *sympathize* seems more likely to be Shakespeare's coinage than Daniel's.[42] Certainly Shakespeare's usages of the term appear to have been more influential upon other poets, as we shall see below. Whichever poet invented the term, however, the appearance of the word *sympathize* in print in 1594 marks an important linguistic shift, whereby *sympathy* becomes available as a verb. It reflects a change in the understanding of sympathy: from an automatic process to an active experience.

Lucrece goes on to compare her sorrows to those of the mythical figure of Philomel, invoking the concept of musical sympathy. She offers to hum the diapason – the bass line – about Tarquin, while Philomel will sing the descant part about Tereus: 'These means, as frets upon an instrument, / Shall

---

[40] The word also appears in Sonnet 19 in the anonymous sonnet sequence *Zepheria*, although it is used in a more generalized sense to suggest a harmony between two lovers: 'And with thine heavens calme smiles mine heart imparadize: / Shine forth thy comforts sunne, my feares dismayer, / Oh well it fits lovers to simpathize'. See Sonnet 19 in *Zepheria* (London, 1594), lines 10–12, sig. D2r. The word is not glossed in Margaret Christian's critical edition of the poem: '*Zepheria* (1594; STC 26124): A Critical Edition', *Studies in Philology*, 100 (2003), 177–243 (p. 219). I have not been able to trace any other usages prior to 1594.

[41] See David Crystal, 'Verbing', *Around the Globe*, 7 (1998), 20–1. See also Terttu Nevalainen, 'Shakespeare's New Words', in Sylvia Adamson et al. (eds.), *Reading Shakespeare's Dramatic Language* (London: Thomson Learning, 2001), pp. 237–55, and Lynne Magnusson, 'Shakespearean Tragedy and the Language of Lament', in Michael Neill and David Schalkwyk (eds.), *The Oxford Handbook of Shakespearean Tragedy* (Oxford University Press, 2016), pp. 120–34 (pp. 126–7).

[42] This complex relationship between the works of Shakespeare and Daniel would continue; the word also appears in Daniel's epic poem *The First Fowre Bookes of the Civile Wars between the Two Houses of Lancaster and York* (London, 1595). Daniel's narrator uses the term to describe a moment of communication between King Richard II and Queen Isabel: 'For whether love in him did sympathize / Or chance so wrought to manifest her doubt, / Even just before, where she thus secret prize, / He staies and with cleare face lookes all about' (2.84). See my chapter on '*Richard II* and the Imitation of Sympathy', in Meek and Sullivan (eds.), *The Renaissance of Emotion*, pp. 130–52 (esp. pp. 132–5), for further discussion of the *Civile Wars* and its influence on Shakespeare's *Richard II*.

tune our heart-strings to true languishment' (1141).⁴³ A similar formulation occurs in Lucrece's response to the 'piece / Of skilful painting' (1366–7) that depicts the events of the fall of Troy. Here we find another example of active sympathy between two women, as Lucrece focuses her attention on the tragic figure of Hecuba: 'On this sad shadow Lucrece spends her eyes, / And shapes her sorrow to the beldam's woes' (1457–8). The narrator acknowledges that Hecuba is a 'shadow', in the sense of 'a portrait as contrasted with the original … an actor or a play in contrast with the reality represented' (*OED*, 6b). And yet, despite – or perhaps because of – the fact that this is merely a representation, Lucrece 'shapes' her woes to those of Hecuba. Indeed Lucrece becomes so entranced by the painting that she seems to forget the difference between life and art. She tears at the deceptive Sinon with her nails, because he reminds her of Tarquin, but then remembers that she is looking at a painting:

> Which all this time had overslipped her thought
> That she with painted images hath spent,
> Being from the feeling of her own grief brought
> By deep surmise of others' detriment,
> Losing her woes in shows of discontent:
>   It easeth some, though none it ever curèd,
>   To think their dolour others have endurèd.   (1576–82)

Here the narrator describes Lucrece's 'deep surmise of others' detriment' – suggesting the complexity of her emotional and cognitive engagement with the characters on the painting.⁴⁴ I have argued elsewhere that Lucrece's temporary absorption into the fictional world of the painting both comments upon and intensifies the way in which we respond to Shakespeare's poem. The poem warns us not to get too caught up in a work of art, as Lucrece does, but perhaps paradoxically this is what draws us further into the mimesis.⁴⁵ In this way, as well as being concerned with the capacity of words to depict visual images, this passage is about the representation and exchange of emotion. The fact that Lucrece is sympathizing with characters represented within a work of art offers further evidence that, for Shakespeare and his contemporaries, the emerging concept of sympathy was bound up with ideas of imitation. Lucrece's act of sympathizing with

---

⁴³ For useful discussions of *Lucrece* and Philomel see Lynn Enterline, *The Rhetoric of the Body from Ovid to Shakespeare* (Cambridge University Press, 2000), pp. 181–97, and Amy Greenstadt, *Rape and the Rise of the Author* (Farnham: Ashgate, 2009), pp. 68–9.

⁴⁴ The *OED* cites this passage under its fifth definition of *surmise*: 'The formation of an idea in the mind; conception, imagination' (*OED*, 5).

⁴⁵ See *Narrating the Visual in Shakespeare*, pp. 76–80.

Hecuba thus reflects upon, and complicates, the rhetorical and mimetic processes of *Lucrece* itself.

This fascination with concepts of mimesis and imitation also permeates the poem's language, and in particular its descriptions of its sympathizing characters. Lucrece states that she will 'imitate' the figure of Philomel (1137), and when the grieving Collatine lies next to the bleeding body of Lucrece at the end of the poem we are told that he 'counterfeits to die with her a space' (1776). Most suggestively of all, perhaps, the narrator describes Lucrece's sympathetic maid as a 'poor counterfeit' (1269) of her complaining. The term *counterfeit* might suggest that there is something inauthentic or second-hand about this form of emotional duplication, and that the sympathizer becomes a mere copy of the person whose emotions they replicate. And yet, as we have seen, Shakespeare suggests that the passions that sympathy produces can be 'real'. Indeed we should remember that, in sixteenth-century usage, the term *counterfeit* did not always have the pejorative associations that it has in modern usage. In the *Defence of Poesy*, for example, Sidney glosses the term *mimesis* as 'a representing, counterfeiting, or figuring forth'.[46] We might also note that in Sonnet 82, Shakespeare uses the word *sympathized* in the context of a discussion about language and representation:

> And do so, love; yet when they have devised
> What strainèd touches rhetoric can lend,
> Thou, truly fair, wert truly sympathized
> In true, plain words, by thy true-telling friend.
>   And their gross painting might be better used
>   Where cheeks need blood: in thee it is abused.   (9–14)

In this sonnet the term *sympathized* is contrasted with excessive literary or pictorial art, and thus suggests a kind of authentic or faithful mimetic resemblance.[47] In this way, it is far from clear that the phrase 'poor counterfeit' dismisses Lucrece's maid as an inadequate copy; the phrase might suggest, rather, that she is a piteous imitator, who is moved by the grief of her mistress, and whose emotional response comments upon that of the poem's readers.[48]

---

[46] Sidney, *The Defence of Poesy*, in Duncan-Jones (ed.), *The Oxford Authors: Sir Philip Sidney*, p. 217.
[47] See *OED*, 'sympathize', 3b: 'To represent or express by something corresponding or fitting; to apprehend mentally by the analogy of something else. *Obs.*'
[48] Samuel Daniel's *Musophilus: Containing a General Defence of Learning* (1599) also uses the word *sympathize* to reflect upon the capacity of poetry to survive the death of the body. As Musophilus ('lover of the muses') puts it, 'these lines are the vaines, the Arteries, / And undecaying life-strings of those harts / That still shall pant, and still shall exercise / The motion spirit and nature both imparts, / And shall, with those alive so sympathize / As nourisht with their powers injoy their parts' (Sprague (ed.), *Poems and A Defence of Ryme*, lines 183–8). Musophilus thus implies that dead poets will 'sympathize' with those still alive and will be nourished by the physical and mental energy of their readers.

There is another figured act of emotional exchange at the end of the poem, when Collatine and his companions return from Ardea to Rome, and Lucrece finds herself at the centre of an audience of men. There is much potential here for a sympathetic reaction to her plight, yet this encounter involves a failure of compassion. There is clear physical evidence that Lucrece has been crying, and the narrator expresses this in richly metaphorical language that recalls Lucrece's encounter with the maid: 'And round about her tear-disdainèd eye / Blue circles streamed, like rainbows in the sky' (1586–7). Yet Collatine's reaction is notably different from the maid's passionate response:

> Which when her sad-beholding husband saw
> Amazedly in her sad face he stares:
> Her eyes, though sod in tears, looked red and raw,
> Her lively colour killed with deadly cares.
> He hath no power to ask her how she fares.
>   Both stood like old acquaintance in a trance,
>   Met far from home, wond'ring each other's chance.   (1590–96)

Collatine 'guess[es] at' Lucrece's 'smarts', as her maid did earlier, yet he does not share in her physical emotional response. Rather, he is 'sad-beholding'; regarding her sorrow, but not necessarily participating in it. As the narrator expresses it, they resemble two old friends meeting by chance, speculating on each other's fortunes, rather than a loving couple instinctively sharing each other's passions. Eventually Collatine asks Lucrece the cause of her external misery: 'Unmask, dear dear, this moody heaviness, / And tell thy grief, that we may give redress' (1602–3). Thus Collatine stresses the positive effects that telling her story will lead to: decisive, mitigating actions. Lucrece hopes that this act of narration will bring about her husband's revenge upon Tarquin. Yet Collatine's reaction resembles that of the King in *The Complaint of Rosamond*, inasmuch as he cannot express or articulate his sorrow: 'But, wretched as he is, he strives in vain: / What he breathes out, his breath drinks up again' (1665–6). Lucrece notes Collatine's silent woe:

> Which speechless woe of his poor she attendeth,
> And his untimely frenzy thus awaketh:
> 'Dear lord, thy sorrow to my sorrow lendeth
> Another power: no flood by raining slaketh.
> My woe too sensible thy passion maketh,
>   More feeling-painful. Let it then suffice
>   To drown one woe, one pair of weeping eyes.'   (1674–80)

In this stanza we find Lucrece pitying Collatine's grief, when it should probably be the other way round. His sorrow, which Lucrece perceives, makes her own woe all the more 'feeling-painful'. She suggests that it will be enough if she cries; yet one might argue that Lucrece is making excuses for Collatine's inarticulacy. Shakespeare implies that female woe is more capable of feeling, and sensitive to the pain of others, than male grief, and thus conforms to the period's commonplace ideas about male and female pity. Yet elsewhere the poem suggests the capacity of art to question – and even change – such stereotypes. When Lucrece addresses Philomel she states that their shared story has the potential to alter people's natures: 'there we will unfold, / To creatures stern, sad tunes to change their kinds: / Since men prove beasts, let beasts bear gentle minds' (1146–8).

Shakespeare's representations of emotional transference in *Lucrece*, then, not only explore gendered conceptions of sympathy and compassion but also work to destabilise our sense of the original and the 'counterfeit'. Such representations thus prompt us to reflect upon our own aesthetic and affective engagement with *Lucrece*. The poem does not necessarily provide evidence of how early moderns read, but it does offer us several potential models of reader response, including Tarquin's hard-heartedness; the maid's 'enforced' sympathy; Lucrece's 'deep surmise' of a represented character's sorrow; and Collatine's 'sad-beholding' grief. Shakespeare acknowledges the complexities involved in emotional identification, and implies that a reader's response to a work of art does not simply involve the passive imitation of the emotions represented but rather involves an intricate combination of imagination, judgement, and feeling. As Lucrece shapes her sorrow to Hecuba's woes, Shakespeare reveals the potential for representations of sympathy – whether pictorial or poetic – to collapse the distinction between art and life. Certainly this interest in emotional imitation, and in exploring innovative emotion words, caught the imagination of other poets in the period. Interestingly, however, it seems to have been Lucrece's encounter with her maid, rather than the encounter with Hecuba, that became the subject of poetic imitation by several of Shakespeare's contemporaries in the 1590s.

'Thus in our teares there was a simpathie': Reading and Rewriting *Lucrece*

We have seen how it is difficult to determine whether Daniel's *Cleopatra* was influenced by *Lucrece* or vice versa. Yet there are several other works that appeared in the second half of the decade where it is clear that *Lucrece* is the source text. Some especially striking parallels are to be found in John Trussell's *The First Rape of Faire Hellen* (1595), a complaint poem in

Figure 4 John Trussell, *Raptus I. Helenae. The First Rape of Faire Hellen* (London, 1595), title page. STC 24296. Used by permission of the Folger Shakespeare Library.

which Helen's ghost recites her woeful tale to the poet (Figure 4). And while it has a happy ending, in which Helen marries Menelaus, the poem centres on Helen's account of her rape by Theseus, aligning it with other works such as *Lucrece*, *The Complaint of Rosamond*, and *The Complaint of Elstred*.[49] It thus recalls and develops these poems' concern with sympathy, or the lack of it, between men and women. There are four instances of the term *sympathy* in Trussell's poem. The first two usages are concerned with Helen's grief, and in the first of these Helen's arteries 'signifie' their sympathy with her sorrows:

> Thus actuallie my actuall Arteries,
>   did signifie my sorrowes simpathie:
> My head, handes, haires, voice-mooving tongue & eyes

---

[49] *Raptus I. Helenae. The First Rape of Faire Hellen. Done into poeme, by J. T.* (London, 1595). See M. A. Shaaber, '*The First Rape of Faire Hellen* by John Trussell', *Shakespeare Quarterly*, 8 (1957), 407–48 (pp. 414–15). The poem survives in only two printed copies: one in the Folger Shakespeare Library, which is imperfect, and one in the Rosenbach Museum and Library, Philadelphia. I quote from Shaaber's transcription of the latter, although I have consulted the Folger copy (STC 24296).

> do manifest their mutuall miserie.
> Making the wind a witnesse of my woe,
> Which Eccho-like when that I sigh'd did blowe. (199–204)

Here sympathy is presented as an affinity between different bodily parts but nonetheless associated with Helen's 'sorrowes': the various parts of her body have a 'mutuall miserie'. More interesting still is Helen's encounter with her maid:

> I wept to thinke upon my wofull fall, and
>   she weeps to see her Mistresse malecontent.
> Sighes flie from me: teares from her eies doe fall,
>   yet neither knoweth th'others languishment.
> Thus in our teares there was a simpathie,
> Yet neither knew th'others reason why … (379–84)

This stanza is clearly an imitation of the corresponding passage from *Lucrece*. As well as borrowing the situation from Shakespeare's poem, Trussell uses the term *simpathie* to describe the exchange of grief between his protagonist and her maid.[50] And, like *Lucrece*, Trussell's poem explores what takes place in the minds of these two women, rather than focusing solely on their spontaneous sharing of sorrow: 'Yet neither knew th'others reason why' (384).

We should note, however, that the passage is not simply a passive borrowing of the characters and situation that Trussel found in Shakespeare.[51] Rather, Trussell extends and complicates the situation depicted in Shakespeare's poem by having Helen speculate on the cause of the maid's woe:

> At length I sighing might perceive her Eccho,
>   and in her ecchoing to give two for one:
> Which made me mervaille at her sudden sorrow,
>   and to demaund of her her cause of mone.
> She soone replide: you know the reason why
> Your selfe doe weepe, for that same cause weep I.
>
> Then I supposed, hearing her say so,
>   that *These-us* had harm'd both her and me:
> And so to both had geven one cause of woe,
>   and not that one had causde boths misery.

---

[50] The word is also used later in the poem to refer to the loving sympathy between Helen and Menalaus: 'He is my comfort, I am his delight, / thus in our actions seem'd a simpathie' (813–14); 'Our copulation made us mutually, / Proove in our mirths a perfect simpathy' (863–4).

[51] Shaaber also notes this allusion, but he does not comment upon it in any detail, or upon the echoing of the term *sympathie*, simply stating that 'Helen's maid does the same thing' as Lucrece's (p. 416).

>   Which so afresh did gall my fore galde wound,
>   That in a traunce I suncke unto the ground.   (385–96)

In this passage Helen becomes aware of the fact that the maid is weeping, and partakes in her sorrow. Helen misinterprets the maid's remarks, thinking that the maid, too, has been raped by Theseus, and that he has 'to both had geven one cause of woe' (393). The maid's grief, then, does not offer Helen comfort, but rather increases her woe, in the sense that Theseus's crime appears to have been doubled. This moment of misunderstanding is both curious and fascinating: it is almost as if Helen is caught in the older understanding of sympathy as straightforward correspondence, and does not realize that it can involve imaginative projection. This passage might even be read as a moment when this shift in understanding of sympathy is being staged, or when Trussell acknowledges the term's imaginative aspects. In this complex encounter Helen invokes the figure of echo; and yet the poem reveals that sympathy is about far more than echoing or imitation, and is bound up with cognition and (mis)interpretation. We might even suggest that, in an analogous way, Trussell's poem itself emerges as more than a passive echo of the Shakespearean original. In other words, the issues about sympathy that Trussell explores also pertain to the larger questions about literary imitation that his apparent 'plagiarism' of *Lucrece* provokes.[52]

These questions of imitation and intertextuality are even more pertinent in Samuel Nicholson's *Acolastus his after-witte* (1600).[53] At first glance, this is a very different poem from works such as *Lucrece* and *Faire Hellen*, and centres on a young shepherd named Acolastus, who has been rejected by the lady of his choice because of his poverty. It thus returns us to the Petrarchan mode of various Elizabethan sonnet sequences, and recalls the difficult relationships of literary couples such as Montanus and Phoebe from Lodge's *Rosalynde*.[54] At the same time, however, the language of the poem is highly indebted to the complaint poems that we have examined thus far, especially *Lucrece*, and to several other Shakespearean works.[55]

---

[52] See the report on the poem in the *Times Literary Supplement*, 9 July 1931, and Shaaber's summary (pp. 408–9).
[53] Samuel Nicholson, *Acolastus his after-witte* (London, 1600). I follow the line numbers given in Alexander B. Grosart's edition of the poem (Blackburn, Lancashire: Printed for the Subscribers [by Charles E. Simms, Manchester], 1876).
[54] See Chapter 1, above. On the relationship between these different forms of complaint see Burrow's 'Introduction', p. 143.
[55] In one of the few critical accounts of the poem, J. M. Bemrose usefully discusses some of *Acolastus*'s Shakespearean allusions, but overall he is rather too concerned to demonstrate the discrepancy between 'Shakespearian force and Nicholsonian vapidity' ('A Critical Examination of the Borrowings from *Venus and Adonis* and *Lucrece* in Samuel Nicholson's *Acolastus*', *Shakespeare*

For example, Acolastus's description of his disdainful lady, 'O woolvish heart wrapt in a womans hyde' (265), recalls the celebrated line, parodied in *Greenes Groats-worth of Witte*, from *3 Henry VI*: 'O tiger's heart wrapt in woman's hyde' (1.4.137).[56] At another point, Acolastus becomes disillusioned with the language that he uses: 'Hence idle words, servants to shallow braines, / Unfruitfull sounds, wind-wasting arbitrators' (560–61). This passage closely echoes *Lucrece*'s 'Out idle words, servants to shallow fools, / Unprofitable sounds, weak arbitrators' (1016–17).[57] This reworking of Shakespearean language can also be detected in the poem's representations of sympathy and male-female relationships. In addition, the poem raises wider questions about the authenticity of grief and pity, which recall some of the preoccupations of Daniel's *Rosamond*.

In the first part of the poem, Acolastus confesses his woes to Eubulus, an old shepherd, whose name ('the well-advised') recalls the councillor figure at the start of Lyly's *Euphues*. Acolastus describes his dejection and bitterness, and there are various moralistic digressions, in which he criticizes Faithlessness, Lust, and Avarice. In the course of these musings he refers to a type of natural 'sympathy' as a way of expressing the relationship between the heart and desire: 'As is the sympathie twixt flaxe and fire, / Such is the heart compar'd to hot desire' (221–2). Using the older meaning of the term, Acolastus suggests that the heart has a natural affinity with or tendency towards strong desire. But then, as the poem continues, he uses 'sympathize' to describe the exchange of misery:

> Who right conceits the miseries of *Job*,
> His children, servants, goods, and cattell lost,
> His bodie botched, basest ragges his robe,
> His mind with millions of temptations tost:
>   Can fittest deeme their griefes true qualitie,
>   And sympathize poore Souldiers miserie. (451–6)

This stanza is concerned with the relationship between grief, analogy, and comparability. As Acolastus suggests, it is through the 'concei[t]' of Job's miseries that people are able to judge or estimate the 'true qualitie' of their own grief. Once again, then, we have a literary text suggesting that the act

---

Quarterly, 15 (1964), 85–96 (p. 92)). Grosart suggests that the poem's interest is 'the witness it bears to the popularity of Shakespeare' at this early stage, and he points to Nicholson's 'prescient discernment of the genius of Shakespeare in his felicities of word-painting' (*Acolastus*, ed. Grosart, p. v).

[56] The parody, which describes 'an upstart Crow … with his Tygers hart wrapt in a Players hyde', appeared in *Greenes Groats-worth of Witte* (London, 1592), sig. F1v. See Michael Hattaway's New Cambridge edition of *The Third Part of Henry VI* (Cambridge University Press, 1993), p. 53.

[57] One reader has noted this in pencil in the British Library copy (shelf mark C.40.e.69).

of sympathizing with a mythical (or in this case biblical) exemplar enables us to conceptualise our own grief more effectively, and to sympathize with the misery of others. According to the *OED*, Nicholson's use of *sympathize* here means 'To represent or express by something corresponding or fitting' (*OED*, 3b, citing this passage), recalling the usage in Shakespeare's Sonnet 82. But while the emphasis of this stanza is on correspondence and analogy, it specifically points to the ways in which such comparisons are an important aspect of understanding and indeed sharing grief. This instance of the word *sympathize* thus points towards, and arguably already carries, the sense of 'To feel sympathy; to have a fellow-feeling; to share the feelings of another or others' (*OED*, 4a; first cited usage 1607).

As Acolastus continues to articulate his own emotional state and the disdain of his lady, he contrasts her lack of pity with the sympathy of the natural world. Even marble and the 'dum creatures' are moved by his plight:

> The senseles marble movèd with my plaining,
> Wets his pale cheekes and seemes to weepe with me;
> The showres which daily from mine eyes are raining,
> Draw the dum creatures to a sympathie;
>   Poore *Philomele* that sings of ravishment,
>   Forgets her tune to list to my complaint. (481–6)

This passage contains the *OED*'s first example of *sympathy* in the sense of 'compassion or commiseration' (3a). The irony, however, is that this is a highly intertextual moment. The metaphor of hard marble succumbing to tears recalls various other texts, including *Lucrece*'s 'Tears harden lust, though marble wear with raining' (560). The stanza also contains a more explicit allusion to *Lucrece*, and Lucrece's command that Philomel should sing for her: 'Come, Philomel, that sing'st of ravishment: / Make thy sad grove in my dishevelled hair' (1128–29).[58] Here the intertextuality invites us to compare two sets of comparisons: Lucrece compares herself to Philomel, while Acolastus does the same, implicitly comparing himself to Lucrece in the process. In addition, the idea that Philomel will forget her troubles when she hears the complaints of the speaker recalls the love-sick Montanus, who makes a similar claim in *Rosalynde*: 'Philomele hearing my passions, hath left her mournful tunes to listen to the discourse of my miseries'.[59] What these allusions suggest, then, is

---

[58] See *Acolastus*, ed. Grosart, p. xv. This echo is noted in Malone's copy in the Bodleian Library (shelf mark Mal. 332 (4)).
[59] *Rosalynde*, ed. Greg, p. 120.

that Nicholson's use of the term *sympathy* is not a point of origin, but rather a moment rich in echoes and allusions, which refers back to other texts that use the word in a similar context, and which themselves allude to the Philomel myth.

Yet, while the poem contains some unequivocal allusions to *Lucrece*, it is clear that it has a very different perspective on male-female relations, in the sense that it presents men as more sympathetic than women. For example, when Acolastus mistakes Eubulus for a Satyr in disguise, or his beloved lady pretending to be piteous, his friend assures him that he is not a disdainful woman: 'I am no flint-hart female, bloody minded' (709). The poem contains an allusion to the most explicit moment of female sympathy in *Lucrece*, but the situation in *Acolastus* is markedly different. In the second part of the poem, Acolastus describes his first meeting with his beloved during a shepherd's revel. She is described as 'wanton youngling' (843) who slips away from her fellows. She strikes his eyes 'like a Comet' (844) – perhaps recalling Daniel's *Rosamond* – and they stand before each other:

> A prettie while this prettie creature stoode,
> Before the engin of her thoughts began,
> Seeming to sympathize my heavie moode,
> Pittying my prone lookes, and my colour wan:
>   Till blushing forth a pure vermillion dye,
>   With low-tun'd voice she made me this replie. (853–8)

Here Nicholson borrows the language of Shakespeare's encounter between Lucrece and her maid ('A pretty while these pretty creatures stand' (*Lucrece*, 1233)) and uses it to describe a meeting between a man and a woman ('A prettie while this prettie creature stoode' (847)). It is thus striking that Nicholson, like Trussell, must have been particularly drawn to Shakespeare's representation of sympathetic engagement, and chose to rework it.[60] Now it is the lady who appears to 'sympathize' with Acolastus's 'heavie mood'. This stanza thus recalls Shakespeare's use of the phrase 'enforced by sympathy'; yet this is not the compassionate sympathy that we find in *Lucrece*. Nicholson borrows Shakespeare's language but transplants it into a conventionally Petrarchan situation; the sympathy here is short lived and the lady soon rejects Acolastus's offer of marriage.

---

[60] See Bemrose, 'A Critical Examination', p. 92. Later in the poem we find the phrase 'Greiving your selfe to gesse at others fate' (1119), which closely echoes a key line that describes Lucrece's encounter with her maid: 'Grieving themselves to guess at others' smarts' (*Lucrece*, 1238).

Towards the end of the poem, when Acolastus has returned to his melancholy mood once again, he declaims a Latin passage expressing his sorrow, and looks around to see if anyone else is listening:

> I lookt about if any would replie,
> (Griefe best is pleasde with partners in his plaining)
> The Damsell gone, I saw no creature nye,
> Save trees and stones which could not know my meaning:
>   To whom shrill Eccho in pittie of my paine,
>   Records my woes, and tels them o're againe. (1455–60)

Acolastus thus recalls the line from *Lucrece*, 'Grief best is pleased with grief's society' (1112). The landscape echoes his complaints, yet he is aware that the trees and stones cannot possibly sympathize as they do not understand his 'meaning'. The poem seems to suggest, then, that the automatic 'pittie' of the natural world coexists with a more complex conception of *sympathy* in which the sympathizer does 'know [the] meaning' of the sufferer. Indeed the invocation of 'Eccho' – who also appears in Trussell's *The First Rape of Faire Hellen* – again emphasizes the extent to which complaint poems from this period present sympathy as something far more complex than a mere echo of another's feelings. Moreover, *Acolastus*'s various allusions to Shakespeare do not simply expose Nicholson's shortcomings as a writer, but rather emphasize the extent to which sympathy is a complex intertextual process bound up with our knowledge and understanding of other literary texts, and how such texts might, in turn, shape our understanding of the grief of others.

As well as modifying the vocabulary and understanding of sympathy, then, these reworkings of *Lucrece* raise wider questions regarding the nature of representation and the power of art to elicit emotional responses. John Lane's *Tom Tel-Troths message, and his pens complaint* (1600), which was printed in the same year as Nicholson's *Acolastus*, also adapts some of the vocabulary of *Lucrece*. Lane's poem offers an account of the vices of England and the unfortunate state of the two universities.[61] The speaker describes how he sees 'the ghost of *Conscience*', whose cheeks are 'with teares made wet', and 'with sighs made dry' as she views the world from where she has been banished. He goes on to describe a shared grief between Conscience, himself, and his pen:

> She wept, I saw her weepe, and wept to see
> The salt teares trickling from her aged eyes,

---

[61] See Verne M. Underwood, 'Lane, John (*fl.* 1600–1630)', *ODNB*.

> Yea and my pen copartner needs would bee,
> With black-inke teares, our teares to simpathize:
> So long wee wept that all our eyes were drie,
> And then our tongues began aloud to crie.[62]

Upon seeing Conscience's weeping, the speaker himself begins to weep. Yet his pen also becomes a 'copartner' with his own pain – and indeed with his own feelings of sympathy. But there is another form of sharing at work here; Shakespeare's Lucrece articulates her desire for 'co-partners in [her] pain', and for 'fellowship in woe' (789–90). Lane's pen is thus a figure for poetic composition, and indeed his borrowing from other writers, rather than a vehicle for transcribing his tears or the 'gall' contained in his body.[63] Such moments highlight the ways in which the act of sympathizing in the period taps into a fascination with imitation and transmission of various kinds: emotional, mimetic, and intertextual. But this particular example also dramatizes a successful act of sympathizing between a male poet and a tragic female figure, which is both figured in and expressed through the act of writing.

Conclusion: 'Of Griefe, &c.'

What we have seen in this chapter, then, is that poetic works from the 1590s present us with a range of perspectives regarding the relationships between men and women, and their capacity to feel pity. We have also seen how several writers seem to have picked up on *Lucrece*'s interest in sympathy and Shakespeare's innovative use of emotion words. This process of textual reproduction and transmission is further extended at the turn of the seventeenth century, when fragments of the texts I have been discussing began to circulate in various printed commonplace books, in particular Robert Allot's *Englands Parnassus: or The choysest flowers of our moderne poets*, and John Bodenham and Anthony Munday's *Bel-vedére, or, The Garden of the muses*, both printed in 1600. Both of these collections reproduce material from several of the texts explored in the present chapter, demonstrating that such miscellanies played an important role in further disseminating the terms *sympathy* and *sympathize*.

Robert Allot's *Parnassus* contains approximately two thousand literary extracts under general subject headings, arranged alphabetically. The

---

[62] John Lane, *Tom Tel-Troths message, and his pens complaint* (London, 1600), p. 8.
[63] As the title suggests, the speaker's pen is almost a character in the poem, and is addressed as 'the hearts true secretarie, / Imbath'd in sable liquor mixt with gall' (p. 7).

twenty-page section entitled 'Love' includes three examples of the word *sympathy*, including Spenser's *An Hymne in Honour of Beautie*.[64] We also find this passage from Lodge's *Elstred*:

> — Where there growes a sympathy of harts,
> Each passion in the one, the other paineth:
> And by even carryage of the outward parts,
> (Wherein the actuall worke of love remaineth.)
> The inward griefes, mislikes and joyes are taught,
> And every signe bewraies a secret thought.
> D. Lodge. (p. 181)

The inclusion of these passages (the latter misattributed to '*D. Lodge*', rather than Thomas) suggests that Allot was struck by their use of the term *sympathy*; although their appearance under the rubric of 'Love' might be taken as evidence that the term was still understood in its earlier sense of affinity between individuals. However, the word also appears in a section entitled 'Sorrow', which concludes with this key passage from Thomas Hudson's 1584 translation of *Judith*, which we explored in the Introduction:

> — As a stroke given on the righter eye
> Offends the left, even so by simpathy
> Her husbands dolours made her hart unglad,
> And *Judiths* sorrowes made her husband sad.
> T. Hudson. (p. 428)

The appearance of this passage suggests that Allot – and by implication his readers – was aware that 'simpathy' could be used to describe not only an affinity between lovers but also a exchange of sorrows. It is also worth emphasizing that these examples from Lodge and Hudson do not endorse the commonplace notion of gendered sympathy, in which women are more sympathetic than men, but rather represent a form of gendered intimacy in which both sexes feel each other's sorrows. Along with the other texts we have considered in this chapter, these passages remind us that representations of the passions – and sympathy in particular – offered early modern writers a way to investigate and conceptualize the workings of gender itself.

Allot also includes a variety of quotations from Shakespeare's plays, although his poems are especially well represented, with twenty-six quotations from *Venus and Adonis* and thirty-nine from *Lucrece*. Two quotations from *Lucrece* appear under the subject heading 'Of Sorrow' (pp. 278–81),

---

[64] See *Englands Parnassus: or The choysest flowers of our moderne poets, with their poeticall comparisons* (London, 1600), pp. 170–92. The Spenser quotation appears on p. 171.

which also includes extracts from Samuel Daniel, Michael Drayton, and Edmund Spenser. The Daniel passage reproduces the narrator's comment on the King's grief from *Rosamond*: 'Sighes are the ease calamitie affoords, / Which serve for speech when sorrow wanteth words' (p. 280). The first short passage from *Lucrece* describes Lucrece's emotional response to the Troy painting: 'Sad sorrow like a heavie ringing bell, / Once set in ringing, with his owne weight goes, / Then little strength rings out the dolefull knel' (p. 279). The second is this longer quotation:

> — Mirth doth search the bottom of annoy,
> Sad soules are slaine in mirthie companie,
> Greefe best is pleasde with griefes societie:
> True sorrow then is feelingly suffizde,
> When with like sorrow it is sympathizde.
> True sorrow hath not ever a wet eye.
> *Th. Dekker.* (pp. 280–1)

The passage is slightly mangled and misattributed to Thomas Dekker, but nevertheless demonstrates that the word *sympathized* was being presented in this literary and emotional context, alongside other poetic expressions of sorrow and grief. The inclusion of this passage in *Englands Parnassus* suggests that *Lucrece* had become a sourcebook of feeling by the early seventeenth century, and that its impact went beyond the confines of narrative verse and complaint poetry into people's lived emotional experience.

Something similar happens in the case of John Bodenham and Anthony Munday's *Bel-vedére*. The extracts in *Bel-vedére* are all individual 'sentences' (of ten or twenty syllables), organized under topical headings. These extracts are presented anonymously, although the writers included are named in the introductory epistle.[65] The collection includes eighty-eight quotations from Shakespeare's plays, but ninety-one quotations from *Lucrece*. Especially relevant here is a section entitled 'Of Griefe, &c.':

> Distresse likes dumps, when time is kept with teares.
> Woe is most tedious when her words are briefe.
> Though woe be heavie, yet it seldome sleepes.
> *Kind fellowship in woe, doth woe asswage,*
> *As Palmers chat makes short their pilgrimage.*

---

[65] As with Allot's *Parnassus*, we have a section entitled 'Of Love', which also includes the same couplet from Lodge's *Elstred* quoted earlier: '*Where growes a perfect sympathie of hearts, / Ech passion in the one, the other paineth*' (sig. D1r; p. 33).

> Love ne're so loyall, is not free from care.
> Weepe ne're so long, yet griefe must have an end.
> Of sorrow, comes but fancies and fond dreames.
> *True sorrow then is feelingly suffis'd,*
> *When with like semblance it is sympathiz'd.*[66]

Bodenham takes his cue from Shakespeare, or from the printer Richard Field, and includes several couplets that are annotated with commonplace markers in the Quarto.[67] In this set of extracts, we find the passage from *Lucrece* with which we began this chapter – albeit interwoven with other passages from the poem and other texts – including the innovative word '*sympathiz'd*'. Indeed there is arguably something curiously self-reflexive about the fact that this resonant phrase is placed alongside several other literary expressions of grief and sorrow (see Figure 5). We might even say that this italicized couplet – which is itself concerned with grief and resemblance – is itself 'sympathizing' with these other similar poetic descriptions of woe.

These examples from *Parnassus* and *Bel-vedére* thus provide clear evidence that early modern readers were encouraged to recall and utilise the terms *sympathy* and *sympathize* as they expressed and experienced specific emotions. They also reveal how poetic miscellanies continued the process of textual borrowing and transmission that has been the focus of this chapter. Certainly complaint literature written in the 1590s was a rich and provocative place for debating – as well as complicating – early modern conceptions of gender and compassion. Works by Lodge, Shakespeare, Daniel, Trussell, and Nicholson demonstrate that *sympathy* and its cognate terms were increasingly used in this period to describe a correspondence of sorrows. Shakespeare seems to have played a particularly important part in this linguistic and conceptual shift, prompting other writers to borrow situations and vocabulary found in *Lucrece*. At the same time, however, these early poetic responses to Shakespeare should not be regarded as straightforward or passive imitations, but rather a set of creative reflections on the issues raised by the encounter between Lucrece and her maid.[68] This is where we can see most clearly the suggestive correspondence between

---

[66] *Bel-vedére, or, The Garden of the muses* (London, 1600), p. 142.
[67] See Stallybrass and Chartier, 'Reading and Authorship', pp. 46–7.
[68] The echoes of the encounter between Lucrece and her maid can also be traced into the Jacobean period. William Webster's *The most pleasant and delightful historie of Curan* (London, 1617) describes a sympathetic encounter between Prince Curan and Princess Argentile in terms that recall and echo Shakespeare's *Lucrece*: 'His wonder was, to see her wonder so / His sorrow was to see her sorrow such … Thus they doe now each others harmes condole, / And sympathize as both had but one soule' (sig. G4r).

Figure 5 *Bel-vedére, or, The Garden of the muses* (London, 1600), sigs. K7v-K8r (pp. 142–3). STC 3189. Used by permission of the Folger Shakespeare Library.

the forms of subjectivity and emotional transmission explored within the texts, and the forms of imitation and transmission enacted by the texts themselves.

My final example in this chapter is taken from another poetic miscellany: *Englands Helicon*, a collection of lyrical and pastoral poetry published by John Flasket in 1600.[69] It also contains various examples of female complaint. Typical of the genre we find in *Englands Helicon* is 'Oenones complaint' by George Peele, the penultimate poem in the collection, which features a female speaker lamenting her woes in a pastoral setting. Oenone describes her rejection by Paris, her husband, and calls upon Melpomene – 'the Muse of tragicke songs' – for help with the singing of her tragic tale:

> This lucklesse wreathe becomes not me to weare,
> The Poplar tree for tryumph of my love,
> Then as my joy, my pride of love is left;
> Be thou uncloathed of thy lovely greene.

[69] See Kerrigan, *Motives of Woe*, p. 19.

> And in thy leaves my fortunes written be,
> And then some gentle winde let blow abroad,
> That all the world may see, how false of love,
> False *Paris* hath to his *Oenone* beene.[70]

As with the other female complaints we have explored in this chapter, we have an exemplary figure bemoaning her fate and asking for poetic inspiration from a muse. Oenone's apostrophe to the poplar tree may imply that she conceives of her emotions in relation to the wider environment; yet Oenone's description of her fortunes being written on 'leaves' that 'blow abroade' also serves as a metaphor for textual inscription and dissemination. Indeed it is curiously apt that this poem was itself reproduced in *Englands Helicon*, thus enacting the very process of writing and transmission that Oenone craves. This complaint, with its focus on emotion, pity, and compassion, appears immediately after another poem by Peele, 'Colin the enamoured Sheepheard, singeth this passion of love', in which Colin describes another transferral of affect, in which he hopes that his feelings of love will transfer to his beloved: 'Too faire that fortune were, nor never I / shall be so blest, / among the rest: / That love shal ceaze on her by simpathy' (sig. 2B4r). This is another moment when the term *sympathy* – used in its earlier sense of correspondence and agreement – appears near a description of deep sorrow and fellow-feeling.

This moment, then, might be seen as further evidence that Elizabethan poetry played a key role in evolution of the word *sympathy* in the period. But the situation is more complex, as both poems are extracted from a single dramatic work: George Peele's *The Araygnment of Paris* (1584). This play, which was first performed in front of Elizabeth I, tells the story of Paris's declaration that he loves Venus more than his own wife.[71] It is also the first example that I have found of the word *sympathy* appearing in a dramatic text, and thus points to the equally important role that drama played in associating sympathy with the transmission of emotion. In the next chapter, we shall see how Shakespeare – along with playwrights such as Thomas Kyd, Christopher Marlowe, and Samuel Brandon – offered a series of theatrical meditations on sympathy and fellow-feeling, and continued this process of offering early moderns a new vocabulary for understanding and describing their passionate responses to others.

---

[70] *Englands Helicon* (London, 1600), sig. 2B4r-v.
[71] George Peele, *The Araygnment of Paris: A Pastorall. Presented before the Queenes Majestie, by the Children of her Chappell* (London, 1584).

CHAPTER 4

'*O, what a sympathy of woe is this*'
Passionate Sympathy in Late Elizabethan Drama

In *The Two Gentlemen of Verona* (c. 1590), which may be Shakespeare's first work for the stage, the resourceful Julia – who has been abandoned by Proteus – disguises herself as a page named 'Sebastian'. In Act 4 Shakespeare complicates things further by having Sebastian describe another, virtual instance of cross-dressing. Sebastian recounts to Sylvia how he once borrowed his mistress's clothes in a pageant and performed to her the tragic role of Ariadne:

> And at that time I made her weep agood,
> For I did play a lamentable part.
> Madam, 'twas Ariadne passioning
> For Theseus' perjury and unjust flight;
> Which I so lively acted with my tears
> That my poor mistress, moved therewithal,
> Wept bitterly; and would I might be dead
> If I in thought felt not her very sorrow. (4.4.165–72)

Here Shakespeare appears to be highlighting the emotional power and immediacy of theatrical performance, implying that a 'lively' representation of grief has the power to elicit tears from spectators. And yet the performance that 'Sebastian' describes is an entirely fictional one, which figures not only Julia's emotional state but also the audience's imaginative engagement with Shakespeare's characters. This elaborate theatrical metaphor enables Julia to articulate her identification with the classical figure of Ariadne, the archetypal abandoned woman.[1] The passage thus recalls the pedagogical practices of the Elizabethan grammar school, in which (male) students were instructed to imagine themselves in the role of tragic

---

[1] Ariadne's tale is recounted in book 10 of Ovid's *Heroides* and book 8 of the *Metamorphoses*. Ariadne helped Theseus kill the Minotaur; however, he abandoned her on the island of Naxos. See *The Two Gentlemen of Verona*, ed. Roger Warren (Oxford University Press, 2008), note to 4.4.164–5, and T. W. Baldwin, *William Shakspere's Smalle Latine and Lesse Greeke*, 2 vols (Urbana: University of Illinois Press, 1944), vol. 2, p. 424.

women from classical texts.² By importing this rhetorical method into a theatrical context Shakespeare creates a remarkably complex meditation on the relationship between the self and the other. His emphasis upon the theatricality and two-way spectatorship involved in fellow-feeling anticipates Adam Smith's *The Theory of Moral Sentiments* (1759) by more than one and a half centuries.³ In this vivid description of an imaginary performance, Sebastian makes his mistress weep and comes to feel her sorrow 'in thought' (4.4.170). The irony, of course, is that the mistress described here is Julia: the supposed 'other' with whom Sebastian weeps turns out to be a projected version of the self.

This speech reminds us that early modern dramatists were often fascinated by the relativity or comparability of sorrows – and sought out new words and metaphors for expressing such feelings. Shakespeare was not yet using the word *sympathize*, but here we see him exploring, and trying to find words for, related concepts. The term *passioning* – an innovative verbal form of *passion* – appears to be a Shakespearean coinage, and suggests that Ariadne (and implicitly Julia) is not simply affected by grief, but chooses to communicate and perform it.⁴ Such reflections upon theatrical performance would intersect with Shakespeare's writing of female complaint, making him especially well-placed to articulate a more active theory of the passions. Recent critics of early modern drama have argued that playwrights 'identified emotional experience firmly with the body', and have tended to focus their attention on the 'feeling bodies of early modern theatregoers'.⁵ But this passage from *The Two Gentlemen of Verona*, which makes considerable demands on the audience's imagination, offers a model of emotional experience that is more performative and rhetorical than bodily or humoral.⁶ The present chapter examines this

---

² Enterline writes that 'Hecuba, Niobe, Philomela, Lucrece, Venus, Adonis, Actaeon, Apollo, Daphne, Narcissus, Dido, Aeneas, Sinon, and Medea (among others) provide the Latin mythographic template from which [Shakespeare's] scenes of overpowering feeling derive their force' (*Shakespeare's Schoolroom*, p. 27). Enterline does not discuss the figure of Ariadne, however, nor this particular example from *The Two Gentlemen of Verona*.

³ Smith writes: 'As they [the spectators] are constantly considering what they themselves would feel, if they actually were the sufferers, so he [the sufferer] is as constantly led to imagine in what manner he would be affected if he was only one of the spectators of his own situation' (*The Theory of Moral Sentiments*, pp. 27–8). See David Marshall's 'Adam Smith and the Theatricality of Moral Sentiments', *Critical Inquiry*, 10 (1984), 592–613, and his *The Surprising Effects of Sympathy*.

⁴ See *OED*, 'passion', v. 3, citing this passage: 'To show, express, or be affected by passion or deep feeling. Formerly *esp.*: to grieve. ... Now *rare*'.

⁵ Craik and Pollard (eds.), *Shakespearean Sensations*, p. 3; Hobgood, *Passionate Playgoing*, p. 8.

⁶ For an account of early modern drama that emphasizes 'contagious or infectious sympathies' rather than moral philosophy see Floyd-Wilson, *Occult Knowledge* (p. 9). Floyd-Wilson offers a brief

fascination with the imaginative aspects of fellow-feeling, and the part that Elizabethan dramatic works played in the development of the term *sympathy*. As we have seen in previous chapters, the word was in transition during the late sixteenth century, and there appears to have been a particular shift in its meaning in the mid-1590s. At this time, playwrights start to use the word to describe an exchange of woe, as well as associating it with communication, understanding, and the imagination. *Sympathy* initially coexists with – but soon begins to displace – earlier terms for emotional correspondence such as *rue* and *ruth*. By the end of the decade the term *sympathize* had appeared in several dramatic texts; I argue that this new word reflected and enabled a more active conception of sympathy as a practice of individual choice and agency.

The chapter begins by considering two dramatic works by Marlowe and Kyd from the late 1580s: *Dido, Queen of Carthage* (c. 1585–6) and *The Spanish Tragedy* (c. 1587). These plays centralise ideas of emotional comparability, receptivity and resistance that fed into the subsequent emergence of the term *sympathy*. The chapter goes on to examine Shakespeare's *Titus Andronicus* (c. 1593), which not only offers a complex exploration of pity and compassion but also contains an important early example of the word *sympathy* being used to describe a harmony of woe. Finally, the chapter explores the development of the verbal form *sympathize* in Shakespeare's *The Comedy of Errors* and *Troilus and Cressida*, and in Samuel Brandon's 1598 closet drama *The Vertuous Octavia*. The fact that the terms *sympathy* and *sympathize* are in flux during this period has created particular challenges for editors and critics, who tend to gloss these words – when they are explained at all – by way of earlier concepts of physical harmony and correspondence. As we shall see, however, these usages become increasingly metaphorical or contested within early modern dramatic works, and when read within a broader set of cultural contexts these terms implicitly question the predominance of humoral or physiological models of the passions.

'I die with melting ruth': Marlowe's *Dido, Queen of Carthage*

Marlowe's highly influential play *Dido, Queen of Carthage* reworks material from the first four books of Virgil's *Aeneid* – in particular books 2 and 4 – into an extraordinary meditation on pity and fellow-feeling, and

discussion of Adam Smith, but suggests that the distance between audience and theatrical spectacle that Smith describes 'did not exist for theater-goers in Shakespeare's London, who were subject to less predictable and more contagious sympathies' (p. 21). See also Langley, *Shakespeare's Contagious Sympathies*.

the capacity of storytelling to move listeners.[7] Like other contemporaneous works, the play contributed to the cultural process by which the fall of Troy – and specifically Aeneas' retelling of it to Dido – became one of the archetypal tragic narratives of the period.[8] This act of storytelling relates to the play's wider interest in relationships between men and women, and the extent to which both sexes are capable of compassion – a question that we have already considered in the previous chapter in relation to the female complaint. When Dido first encounters Aeneas in Act 2, she is surprised by his humility, thinking it not befitting of a soldier, and desires to know the cause of his sadness. Dido has heard stories of Troy's fall, but demands an authoritative account from Aeneas:

> DIDO May I entreat thee to discourse at large,
>   And truly too, how Troy was overcome?
>   For many tales go of that city's fall,
>   And scarcely do agree upon one point.
>   Some say Antenor did betray the town;
>   Others report 'twas Sinon's perjury;
>   But all in this, that Troy is overcome,
>   And Priam dead; yet how, we hear no news.
> AENEAS A woeful tale bids Dido to unfold,
>   Whose memory like pale Death's stony mace,
>   Beats forth my senses from this troubled soul,
>   And makes Aeneas sink at Dido's feet.[9]

Aeneas likens the memory of these events to pale Death's stony mace, as if the memory itself has a profound physical effect on him, as well as hinting at the painfulness of the narration that is to follow. This speech is a close reworking of the corresponding passage in the *Aeneid* – well known in the early modern period from grammar school syllabi.[10] In Thomas Phaer and Thomas Twyne's widely read translation, Aeneas states that to articulate

---

[7] Sheldon Brammall has argued that by removing Virgil's sympathetic narrator, Marlowe creates a 'truly pessimistic' response to the *Aeneid* ('"Sound this Angrie Message in Thine Eares": Sympathy and the Translations of the *Aeneid* in Marlowe's *Dido Queene of Carthage*', *Review of English Studies*, 65 (2013), 383–402 (p. 383)). He concludes that Marlowe's reworking of Virgilian elements 'without the sympathetic narrative-voice ... presents them even more poignantly than they appear in the original' (p. 20), but does not consider the representation of sympathy within the play itself.

[8] See James, 'Dido's Ear', and Abigail Heald, 'Tears for Dido: A Renaissance Poetics of Feeling', unpublished PhD thesis, Princeton University (2009).

[9] Christopher Marlowe, *Dido, Queen of Carthage*, in *Complete Plays and Poems*, ed. E. D. Pendry and J. C. Maxwell (London: J. M. Dent, 1976), 2.1.106–17.

[10] See Peter Mack, *Elizabethan Rhetoric: Theory and Practice* (Cambridge University Press, 2002), p. 13, and Burrow, *Shakespeare and Classical Antiquity*, ch. 2 (esp. p. 56).

his sufferings will be painful and problematic, as the repetition of his experience will be almost as bad as the real thing:

> A doleful worke me to renew (O Queene) yu doost costrain,
> To tel how Greekes ye Troian welth, & lametable raigne
> Did overthrow, which I my selfe have seene and been a part
> No small thereof, but to declare the stories all: what hart
> Can of the Greekes or soldiour one of all Ulisses rout
> Refraine to weepe?[11]

To 'renew' the story – in the sense of 'To go over again, to repeat, relate afresh' (*OED*, 5a), but also, perhaps, in the sense of 'To reopen (a wound)' (*OED*, 1d) – will be, for Aeneas, a 'doleful worke'. But while Virgil's Aeneas suggests that his tale will move all listeners to compassion, Marlowe's reworking has Aeneas voicing his concerns about the effect of the story:

> Then speak, Aeneas, with Achilles tongue;
> And, Dido, and you Carthaginian peers,
> Hear me; but yet with Myrmidons' harsh ears,
> Daily inur'd to broils and massacres,
> Lest you be mov'd too much with my sad tale.   (2.1.121–5)

Here Aeneas describes the capacity of his tale to move its audience. As Timothy Crowley has written, Aeneas 'expresses the grief he feels in describing his own people's destruction by counter-intuitively requiring that he imagine himself as Achilles, premier enemy of Troy'.[12] But Aeneas also suggests that Dido listens with the 'harsh ears' of the Myrmidons, who were notorious for their fierceness, and whose cruelty is mentioned within the tale itself.[13] Paradoxically, then, Aeneas elicits a pitiful response to his tale by enjoining his listeners not to be moved excessively by it.

Aeneas offers a powerful account of Troy's fall, and how Priam's court was seduced by the duplicitous Sinon: 'To whom he us'd action so pitiful, / Looks so remorseful, vows so forcible, / As therewithal the old man overcome' (155–7). In this way, Aeneas warns his listeners about the dangerous effects of pity, and being overcome by passion, even as he draws their

---

[11] *The 'Aeneid' of Thomas Phaer and Thomas Twyne*, 6:500. See Burrow's discussion of Phaer's translation (pp. 67–9).
[12] Timothy D. Crowley, 'Arms and the Boy: Marlowe's Aeneas and the Parody of Imitation in *Dido, Queen of Carthage*', *English Literary Renaissance*, 38 (2008), 408–38.
[13] H. J. Oliver writes that the 'harshness of the Myrmidons ... was proverbial and is best illustrated by their part in the murder of the unarmed Hector' (Oliver (ed.), *Dido, Queen of Carthage and The Massacre at Paris* (London: Methuen, 1968), note to 2.1.123). Katharine Eisaman Maus describes them as 'the notoriously remorseless followers of Achilles' (Maus (ed.), *Four Revenge Tragedies* (Oxford University Press, 1995), note to *The Spanish Tragedy*, 1.1.49).

attention to the emotional power of his tale. Marlowe's self-conscious handling of this act of tragic storytelling is further evidenced by Dido's various interjections, in which she encourages Aeneas to continue, or articulates her emotional state. For example, when Aeneas mentions Hector's ghost, Dido says, 'O Hector, who weeps not to hear thy name?' (209). These interruptions are Marlowe's invention: as Colin Burrow puts it, Virgil's idiom 'is that of the set-piece declamation, the performance of rhetorical artistry rather than of exchanges between people'.[14] Dido's interjections not only describe her responses but also offer a potential model for the audience's feelings. In contrast, the tale itself contains a description of another unmoved listener. Aeneas recounts how Pyrrhus discovered Priam and Hecuba, and how Priam pleaded for his life:

> Achilles son, remember what I was,
> Father of fifty sons, but they are slain;
> Lord of my fortune, but my fortune's turn'd,
> King of this city, but my Troy is fir'd;
> And now am neither father, lord, nor king:
> Yet who so wretched but desires to live?
> O let me live, great Neoptolemus.   (233–9)

Pyrrhus is unaffected by Priam's speech: 'Not mov'd at all, but smiling at his tears, / This butcher, whilst his hands were yet held up, / Treading upon his breast, struck off his hands' (240–2). Aeneas thus presents his listeners with a pitiless 'butcher', a kind of cruel counterexample. This would appear to be an important rhetorical strategy employed in *Dido* and several other tragedies from this period: describing the unsympathetic response of a character within the text as a way of eliciting compassion from both the onstage and offstage audiences.

This strategy works on Dido herself: she is, of course, another figured listener within the text, and her reaction is highly emotional. She associates herself, and her pity, with liquidity: 'I die with melting ruth; Aeneas, leave' (289). *Ruth* was a term derived from Old and Middle English that could mean both 'The quality of being compassionate; the feeling of sorrow for another; compassion, pity' (*OED*, 1a) and 'Sorrow, grief, distress; lamentation. Obs.' (*OED*, 4). In Dido's formulation, *ruth* is used in conjunction with *melting* to describe a physical tenderness or softening. It thus implies a degree of passivity and loss of self: a combination of compassion and sorrow that causes her to dissolve in tears. *Ruth* appears six times in *Dido*,

---

[14] Burrow, *Shakespeare and Classical Antiquity*, p. 55.

reminding us that the term and its cognates were in common usage in the late sixteenth century.[15] The play also contains the term *ruthful* ('That excites compassion or pity; lamentable, piteous' (*OED*, 2)). It appears in Dido's description of Aeneas's tale, which Achates steps in to complete: 'Trojan, thy ruthful tale hath made me sad' (301). This formulation again suggests a degree of passivity, and is somewhat tautologous: Dido is *made* sad by Aeneas's ruthful tale. Collapsing the distinction between grief and compassion, and relying upon a conception of emotion as a force that acts upon the passive subject, such terms were becoming increasingly outmoded.

The unhelpful imprecision of *ruth* is also evident in Act 4 when Iarbus – Dido's rejected suitor – makes a speech addressed to Jove. Iarbus resembles other literary complainers we have encountered, as he attempts to elicit pity from the landscape after being rejected by his beloved Dido, here referred to by her original name Elissa: 'Hear, hear, O hear Iarbas' plaining prayers, / Whose hideous echoes make the welkin howl, / And all the woods "Eliza" to resound' (4.2.8–10). Iarbus appeals directly to Jove:

> Now, if thou be'st a pitying god of power,
> On whom ruth and compassion ever waits,
> Redress these wrongs, and warn him to his ships
> That now afflicts me with his flattering eyes. (4.2.19–22)

Iarbus's use of the phrase 'ruth and compassion' is suggestive. Are *ruth* and *compassion* synonymous here? Or is Iarbus using *ruth* in a narrower sense to suggest sorrow and grief? If the latter, this may suggest that Marlowe is making a distinction between the two terms, and that the newer *compassion* – its only appearance in the play – is being presented as the more useful word for describing interpersonal and participatory suffering. After all, the term derives from the French *compassion* and late Latin *compassiōn-em*, meaning 'to suffer together with, feel pity'.[16] As the *OED* reminds us, *ruth* is archaic in later use, although interestingly it survives in modern English in the form of *ruthless*.[17] These earlier terms struggle to do justice to the complex

---

[15] The word is similarly associated with melting in a contemporaneous poem, suggestively entitled 'They soonest yeelde remedy, that have felt lyke extremetie', which appears in Thomas Howell's collection *H. His devises, for his owne exercise, and his friends pleasure* (London, 1581): 'So should perhaps thy frozen hart, now harde as Flintie stone, / Within thy brest with melting teares, take ruth on this my mone' (sig. D2r).

[16] See the *OED*'s etymology for *compassion*. The word's primary meanings in the period also imply an action or activity: 'Suffering together with another, participation in suffering' (*OED*, 1), and 'The feeling or emotion, when a person is moved by the suffering or distress of another, and by the desire to relieve it' (*OED*, 2).

[17] See Robert Stockwell and Donka Minkova, *English Words: History and Structure* (Cambridge University Press, 2001), p. 62.

emotional exchanges that Marlowe's play represents, hence such attempts to inflect them with additional shades of meaning.

Such passages also reflect the play's concern with contemporary conceptions of the relationship between gender and emotion. When Iarbus goes on to refer to his own sorrows, and Dido's lack of feeling for him, he resorts to the earlier term *ruth*:

> Mine eye is fix't where fancy cannot start;
> O leave me, leave me to my silent thoughts,
> That register the numbers of my ruth,
> And I will either move the thoughtless flint,
> Or drop out both mine eyes in drizzling tears,
> Before my sorrow's tide have any stint. (37–42)

There is a certain reflexivity in Iarbus's formulation, inasmuch as 'numbers of my ruth' refers to the poetic 'numbers' (that is, lines or verses) that describe his emotions. He invokes a 'thoughtless' object – the proverbially unsympathetic flint – as a way of articulating the force of his grief. He hopes that his 'ruth' will move the flint to tears, but even in using this metaphor Iarbus implies Dido's hardheartedness: he might be able to move flint, but he cannot move her.

The play thus not only utilises current metaphors of soft and hardheartedness, but also complicates their gendered associations.[18] Women were often figured as water or tears, and men often as stone or flint. This cultural commonplace is referred to by Thomas Wright: 'Women, by nature, are enclined more to mercie and pitie than men, because the tendernesse of their complexion moveth them more to compassion'.[19] As Wright suggests, the 'tendernesse' of women could be understood literally as well as metaphorically, as he offers a physiological explanation for their compassionate nature. *Dido* largely subscribes to this gendered stereotype, but the fact that Iarbus finds himself in a typically Petrarchan situation ('wronged with disdain' (3.3.69)) reminds us that men could find themselves struggling to elicit pity from hardhearted women (as we have already seen in the case of Montanus in Lodge's *Rosalynde*). The notion of flint-heartedness is applied to Iarbus himself when Anna – who is in love with him and hears his complaint – states that she will not leave him in this 'delight of dying pensiveness' (4.2.44). Iarbus rejects Anna, and she accuses him of lacking pity: 'Hard-hearted, wilt not deign to hear me speak?' (54). On the one

---

[18] The dangers of being hardhearted would also have been familiar to playgoers from Protestant teachings (see Chapter 2, above).
[19] Wright, *The Passions of the Minde in Generall*, p. 40.

hand, then, Anna's comment might seem to confirm the hardheartedness of Iarbus and men more generally; on the other hand, however, the fact that Dido remains impervious to Iarbus's advances implicitly questions the fixity of these gendered metaphors – a process that Shakespeare would continue in his early dramatic works.[20]

While Iarbus is unable to win Dido's pity, at the close of the play Dido finds herself unable to elicit pity from Aeneas. Recalling Aeneas's earlier description of the Trojans being taken in by Sinon, she likens Aeneas to a serpent who seduced his way into her heart: 'O serpent, that came creeping from the shore, / And I for pity harbour'd in my bosom, / Wilt thou now slay me with thy venomed sting, / And hiss at Dido for preserving thee?' (5.1.165–8). Ultimately, however, Dido realises that her words do not have the same effect upon Aeneas: 'I have not power to stay thee' (5.1.183). Nevertheless, Marlowe implies that words do have the power to elicit pity from his audience, not least when Anna recounts to Dido her own attempts to move Aeneas:

> Then gan they drive into the ocean,
> Which when I view'd, I cried, 'Aeneas, stay!
> Dido, fair Dido wills Aeneas stay!'
> Yet he, whose heart of adamant or flint
> My tears nor plaints could mollify a whit.
> Then carelessly I rent my hair for grief,
> Which seen to all, though he beheld me not,
> They gan to move him to redress my ruth,
> And stay a while to hear what I could say;
> But he, clapp'd under hatches, sail'd away.   (5.1.231–40)

As we saw with Aeneas's tale to Dido, a story about the failure of pity can be moving in spite of – or perhaps because of – its content. Indeed this narrative account is all the more powerful because it places the audience in Dido's situation, as they have to imagine Anna's (offstage) renting of her hair. It is also noteworthy that Aeneas's men do appear to be moved by Anna's plight: 'They gan to move him to redress my ruth'. The reason that Aeneas himself is impervious to her pleas is that he hides himself away – 'clapp'd under hatches' – and refuses to listen.

Anna's own suicide, which follows that of her mistress, is by her own admission a demand for pity: 'this shall I do, / That Gods and men may pity this my death, / And rue our ends, senseless of life or breath' (325–9).

---

[20] In Shakespeare's *3 Henry VI* the Duke of York makes it clear that the murderous Queen Margaret does not live up to the stereotype of a soft and compassionate woman: 'Women are soft, mild, pitiful, and flexible; / Thou stern, obdurate, flinty, rough, remorseless' (1.4.141–2).

Like *ruth*, *rue* is an archaic term that denoted both grief and compassion, and in its verbal form could mean 'To affect with sorrow or regret; to distress, grieve' (*OED*, v. 1, 1a) and 'To regard with pity and compassion; to feel sorry for (a person, etc.)' (4c). Here the word's combination with 'pity' recalls Iarbus's earlier combination of *ruth* and *compassion*, and may similarly imply that *rue* is the less useful term. In this way, several of the older emotion words that Marlowe employs in *Dido* – especially *ruth*, *ruthful*, and *rue* – are revealed to be increasingly redundant and outmoded, not least because they fail to distinguish between a generalized feeling of grief, and the more specific sense of feeling another individual's sorrow. This may explain why the terms began to fall out of favour during this period: they became inadequate as ways of describing the complex emotional interactions between distinct individuals. And while *Dido* ends on an apparently conservative note by depicting the hardheartedness of Aeneas, we have seen how his lack of pity is the result of a conscious choice rather than a physical or physiological quality. Moreover, we have also seen some of the sophisticated ways in which *Dido* attempts to move its audience by encouraging it to feel the pity that Aeneas lacks.

'The lively portrait of my dying self': Kyd's *The Spanish Tragedy*

Thomas Kyd's *The Spanish Tragedy* shares *Dido*'s interest in grief and emotional agency, and in implicitly reflecting upon the responses of its audiences and readers. Like *Dido*, the play explores the limitations of certain emotion words such as *rue* and *ruth*.[21] However, *The Spanish Tragedy* goes further by acknowledging the ways in which emotional comparability often involves a degree of projection and self-recognition. In 3.13, the grieving Hieronimo encounters some poor petitioners who wish him to 'plead their cases to the king' (3.13.48). One of the poor citizens is Don Bazulto, who introduces himself in terms that recall Marlowe's descriptions of grief and pity in *Dido*: 'O worthy sir, my cause, but slightly known, / May move the hearts of warlike Myrmidons / And melt the Corsic rocks with

---

[21] In 2.1, for example, Lorenzo encourages Balthazar to ignore Bel-Imperia's coyness, and to trust that patience and persistence will be rewarded: 'And she in time will fall from her disdain, / And rue the sufferance of your friendly pain' (Thomas Kyd, *The Spanish Tragedy*, ed. J. R. Mulryne (London: A & C Black, 1989), 2.1.7–8). Kyd thus associates the verbal form of *rue* with a clichéd concept of female weakness and submission, and with a speaker whose opinions are not to be trusted. The play as a whole, of course, shows the limitations of this conception. Quotations from the play are taken from Mulryne's edition.

ruthful tears' (70–2).²² As we have seen, the term *ruthful* is used by Dido to describe her reaction to Aeneas's tale, while Bazulto's reference to the pitiless Myrmidons echoes Aeneas's suggestion that Dido listen to his tale 'with Myrmidons harsh ears' (2.1.123). Like Dido, Hieronimo is a highly sympathetic listener, although he emphasizes the ways in which Bazulto's plight closely resembles his own:

> HIERONIMO What's here? 'The humble supplication
>   Of Don Bazulto for his murdered son'.
> SENEX Ay, sir.
> HIERONIMO No, sir, it was my murdered son,
>   O my son, my son, O my son Horatio!
>   But mine or thine, Bazulto, be content.
>   Here, take my handkercher, and wipe thine eyes,
>   Whiles wretched I in thy mishaps may see
>   The lively portrait of my dying self.   (3.13.78–85)

Bazulto's tale causes Hieronimo to recall his grief at his own son's death. Indeed Hieronimo's sharing of his handkerchief acts as a metonym for their shared grief, as the pair wipe their tears with the same object.²³ He also uses the same pictorial metaphor that we saw in the prose works discussed in Chapter 1, such as Euphues's description of Philautus as his 'lively image', or the idea expressed in Sidney's *Arcadia* that a friend offers us a 'lively picture' of our own emotional state. Bazulto becomes a 'lively portrait' of Hieronimo's grief. On the one hand, this phrase suggests the ways in which contemplating the suffering of another can offer both consolation and a means of understanding one's own grief. On the other hand, however, it also implies that Hieronimo regards Bazulto as no more than a mirror or self-reflection, and erases the uniqueness of Bazulto's situation even as he draws our attention to it.

Hieronimo goes on to describe Bazulto's sorrows by articulating his shame at not having yet revenged his son's death. This prompts him to embark upon an extraordinary oceanic metaphor:

> See, see, O see thy shame, Hieronimo,
> See here a loving father to his son!
> Behold the sorrows and the sad laments
> That he delivereth for his son's decease!

---

²² Mulryne points out that Seneca's *Octavia* has a reference to the 'craggy corsicke rockes' where Seneca lived in exile (note to 3.13.72).

²³ On the significance of the handkerchief see Andrew Sofer, 'Absorbing Interests: Kyd's Bloody Handkerchief as Palimpsest', *Comparative Drama*, 34 (2000), 127–53, and Hobgood, *Passionate Playgoing*, esp. p. 74.

> If love's effects so strives in lesser things,
> If love enforce such moods in meaner wits,
> If love express such power in poor estates –
> Hieronimo, whenas a raging sea,
> Tossed with the wind and tide, o'erturneth then
> The upper billows, course of waves to keep,
> Whilst lesser waters labour in the deep,
> Then sham'st thou not, Hieronimo, to neglect
> The sweet revenge of thy Horatio?   (95–107)

Even though Hieronimo regards Bazulto as a 'lesser thin[g]' in social terms, and he suggests that his own reaction to Horatio's death should be equal to Bazulto's 'sad laments'. Critics of the play are uncertain of the precise meaning of Hieronimo's metaphorical scheme; but one possible interpretation is that individuals from both poorer and richer 'estates' – represented by the 'upper billows' and 'lesser waters' of the sea – suffer the same emotional turmoil if they suffer great losses, even if one is more obviously visible.[24] Despite their social differences, Hieronimo acknowledges that Bazulto is also 'a loving father to his son' (96). This speech is thus significant in social, ethical, and aesthetic terms: Hieronimo's recognition that he and Bazulto share a sense of loss apparently breaks down the social distinctions between them. At the same time, however, this apparent emphasis on equivalence and comparability is complicated by the fact that the central focus of Hieronimo's speech is on the self rather than the other.

In the previous chapter we saw how Shakespeare's Lucrece tunes her suffering to that of the figure of Philomel, thus creating a form of sympathetic harmony: 'So I at each sad strain will strain a tear, / And with deep groans the diapason bear: / For burden-wise I'll hum on Tarquin still, / While thou on Tereus descants better still' (*Lucrece*, 1131–4). *The Spanish Tragedy* employs a similar musical metaphor to describe the emotional harmony between Hieronimo and Bazulto, suggesting that Shakespeare may have had *The Spanish Tragedy* in mind when he composed *Lucrece*. Hieronimo states that he will descend to the underworld in search of justice, and that Bazulto should assist him by emulating Orpheus:

> Yet lest the triple-headed porter should
> Deny my passage to the slimy strond,
> The Thracian poet thou shalt counterfeit:
> Come on, old father, be my Orpheus,

---

[24] For the alternative reading see Philip Edwards (ed.), *The Spanish Tragedy* (Manchester University Press, 1959), note to 3.13.102–7.

> And if thou canst no notes upon the harp,
> Then sound the burden of thy sore heart's grief,
> Till we do gain that Proserpine may grant
> Revenge on them that murdered my son.
> Then will I rent and tear them thus and thus,
> Shivering their limbs in pieces with my teeth. (3.13.114–23)

Hieronimo enjoins Bazulto to 'counterfeit' – that is, to assume the character of – Orpheus, and 'sound the burden' of Hieronimo's grief.[25] Such was the power of Orpheus's music that it had the capacity to move the natural world; it also moved Proserpine and Pluto to pity, and they allowed him entrance into the underworld.[26] Hieronimo thus articulates his own emotional state by recalling a classical narrative about the sympathetic power of music and poetry, and asks another suffering individual – Bazulto – to emulate Orpheus on his behalf. The word *burden*, which also appears in *Lucrece*, suggests not only Bazulto's 'burdensome or heavy lot or fate' (*OED*, 8) but also 'The bass, "undersong", or accompaniment' (*OED*, 9) of a piece of music. This musical analogy, like Hieronimo's sea metaphor, further suggests that Bazulto is a character whose grief is metaphorically beneath that of Hieronimo, and yet who nonetheless accompanies Hieronimo in sorrow.

This sense of equivalence is further complicated, however, by the fact that Hieronimo mistakes Bazulto for Horatio's ghost: 'Had Proserpine no pity on thy youth, / But suffered thy fair crimson-coloured spring / With withered winter to be blasted thus? / Horatio, thou art older than thy father; / Ah ruthless fate, that favour thus transforms!' (146–8). In Hieronimo's imagination, Proserpine's lack of pity has resulted in Horatio being denied entry to the underworld, and transformed into an old man. For Hieronimo, this is another example of the 'ruthless' nature of fate. Bazulto then reminds Hieronimo who he is, and Hieronimo reverts to his former conception of Bazulto as a reflection of his own suffering:

---

[25] See the *OED*, 'To assume the character of (a person, etc.); to pretend to be; to pass oneself off as; to personate' ('counterfeit', v. 5a). For further discussion of the play's interest in the term *counterfeit*, and in emotional and aesthetic comparisons, see my chapter '"Fabulously Counterfeit": Ekphrastic Encounters in *The Spanish Tragedy*', in David Kennedy and Richard Meek (eds.), *Ekphrastic Encounters: New Interdisciplinary Essays on Literature and the Visual Arts* (Manchester University Press, 2019), pp. 48–69.
[26] Ovid describes the sympathetic power of Orpheus's music in book 10 of the *Metamorphoses*: 'Then first by that sad singing overwhelmed, / The Furies' cheeks, it's said, were wet with tears; / And Hades' queen and he whose sceptre rules / The underworld could not deny the prayer, / And called Eurydice' (Ovid, *Metamorphoses*, trans. A. D. Melville (Oxford University Press, 1986), book 10, p. 226).

> Ay, now I know thee, now thou nam'st thy son;
> Thou art the lively image of my grief:
> Within thy face my sorrows I may see.
> The eyes are gummed with tears, thy cheeks are wan,
> Thy forehead troubled, and thy muttering lips
> Murmur sad words abruptly broken off
> By force of windy sighs thy spirit breathes;
> And all this sorrow riseth for thy son:
> And selfsame sorrow feel I for my son. (161–8)

According to Hieronimo at least, the two men feel the 'selfsame sorrow' (168). Certainly Hieronimo does seem to derive a degree of comfort from this catalogue of Bazulto's external symptoms of grief. And yet, the fact that Hieronimo had mistaken Bazulto for Horatio suggests that Bazulto may be less a piteous fellow sufferer and more a blank canvas for Hieronimo's imaginative projections.[27]

Hieronimo suggests that they meet with Isabella in order that the three of them might console each other through song – and in the process creates another musical metaphor to describe their shared sorrow:

> Come in old man, thou shalt to Isabel;
> Lean on my arm: I thee, thou me shalt stay,
> And thou, and I, and she, will sing a song,
> Three parts in one, but all of discords framed – (170–3)

'Three parts in one' is a well-known musical term from the period, and refers to a common sixteenth-century contrapuntal texture.[28] It is thus a suggestive metaphor for the harmony of woe that Hieronimo describes. Yet Hieronimo also implies that this harmony will derive from disharmony; that is, the three singers share an inner emotional discord, which will result in a form of discordant affinity with one another.[29] Indeed the word *discord* reminds Hieronimo of the precise means of his son's murder – a memory that is particular to his situation: 'Talk not of cords, but let us now be gone, / For with a cord Horatio was slain' (174–5). This important exchange suggests that Hieronimo, and by extension Kyd, has found a way to articulate a model of fellow-feeling that takes into account

---

[27] This moment might thus be regarded as an instance of what Suzanne Keen has called 'empathetic inaccuracy': see 'A Theory of Narrative Empathy' (pp. 222–3), and 'Empathic Inaccuracy in Narrative Fiction', *Topoi*, 39 (2020), 819–25.

[28] See Maus (ed.), *Four Revenge Tragedies*, note to 3.13.172.

[29] See Carla Mazzio, *The Inarticulate Renaissance: Language Trouble in an Age of Eloquence* (Philadelphia: University of Pennsylvania Press, 2009), pp. 108–9. Mazzio is not interested in sympathy *per se* but she does comment on how 'even apparently "plain terms" become complicit with frustrations of communication that become … engines of dramatic affect' (p. 109).

both identity and dissimilarity: it involves finding a way of harmonizing discord through art and metaphor.

In the late 1580s, then, theatregoers had various opportunities to see compassion and pity being represented – and to some degree theorised – on stage. This fascination with grief and fellow-feeling had not yet coincided with the term *sympathy*, which was still being used in its earlier sense of agreement and correspondence. In Kyd's contemporaneous *Soliman and Perseda* (?1588–9), for example, Ferdinando describes his feelings towards Lucina: 'As fits the time, so now well fits the place, / To coole affection with our woords and lookes / If in our thoughts be semblance simpathie'.[30] Here Kyd uses the term *simpathie* to describe a harmony of thoughts between two people. As we have seen, however, *The Spanish Tragedy* demonstrates that correspondence between individuals is always more complex than mere 'semblance'. Moreover, the handling of earlier emotion words such as *rue* and *ruth* in both *Dido, Queen of Carthage* and *The Spanish Tragedy* suggests that these terms were becoming increasingly inadequate for describing the period's complex conceptions of pity. Arguably, then, both of these plays highlighted the need for a new word for describing concepts of pity and compassion, and certainly played an important role in stimulating Shakespeare's literary and linguistic imagination.

'Grief has so wrought on him / He takes false shadows for true substances': Shakespeare's *Titus Andronicus*

Shakespeare's first dramatic tragedy, *Titus Andronicus*, both draws upon and extends the concern with fellow-feeling that we have noted in plays from the 1580s and early 1590s. Steven Mullaney has offered a brief comparison of *Titus* and *The Spanish Tragedy*, suggesting that 'Kyd's affective intelligence is fully absorbed into the play as a whole'. Mullaney is especially concerned with the audience's conflicted response to Marcus' lengthy and highly poetic description of Lavinia's mutilated body: 'Sympathy or empathy for Lavinia becomes entirely and ironically different from what Marcus embodies and expresses'.[31] Mullaney rightly emphasizes the play's

---

[30] Thomas Kyd, *The tragedye of Solyman and Perseda* (London, 1592), sig. C3v. Lukas Erne suggests that the play was written in 1588 or 1589 (see *Beyond 'The Spanish Tragedy': A Study of the Works of Thomas Kyd* (Manchester University Press, 2001), p. 160).

[31] Mullaney, *The Reformation of Emotions*, pp. 69, 74. See also Marion A. Wells's discussion of the speech in 'Philomela's Marks: Ekphrasis and Gender in Shakespeare's Poems and Plays', in Jonathan Post (ed.), *The Oxford Handbook of Shakespeare's Poetry* (Oxford University Press, 2013), pp. 204–24 (pp. 210–12).

interest in the complex relationship between the audience's emotional responses and the emotions represented on stage. I want to make a more specific observation about *Titus*, however, and suggest that it is the first Elizabethan play to use the term *sympathy* to mean a community of feeling. The play's ambivalent fascination with pity and compassion – and with the words and metaphors used to describe such feelings – grows out of the theatrical context that I have been sketching thus far; but *Titus* goes further by offering audiences and readers a new word for an exchange of woe. The appearance of the term *sympathy* in the play highlights a shift in the understanding of the concept from a quasi-scientific phenomenon to a process of social and emotional engagement. Moreover, the play as a whole explores the extent to which pity and compassion are bound up with language, narrative, and the imagination.

There are certainly moments in *Titus* that allude to the earlier idea of sympathy as a physical or occult process. In 3.1, for example, Titus pleads for the lives of Quintus and Martius by attempting to elicit pity from the tribunes. He claims that he has 'never wept before' (3.1.25), because in the past his other sons have been killed in battle, and thus died a noble death.[32] When Lucius points out that no one is listening, Titus states that he has to go on talking, even if only the stones at his feet can hear him:

> Why, 'tis no matter man: if they did hear,
> They would not mark me, or if they did mark,
> They would not pity me; yet plead I must,
> And bootless unto them.
> Therefore I tell my sorrows to the stones,
> Who, though they cannot answer my distress,
> Yet in some sort they are better then the tribunes
> For that they will not intercept my tale.
> When I do weep, they humbly at my feet
> Receive my tears and seem to weep with me,
> And were they but attired in grave weeds
> Rome could afford no tribunes like to these.
> A stone is soft as wax, tribunes more hard than stones;
> A stone is silent and offendeth not,
> And tribunes with their tongues doom men to death. (3.1.33–47)

Titus suggests that the stones are a better audience than the Tribunes, as they will not 'intercept' – that is, interrupt – his tale. The senseless stones '[r]eceive' his tears and thus appear to weep with him. Joseph Ortiz has

---

[32] Quotations from *Titus Andronicus* are taken from Jonathan Bate's Arden 3 edition (London: Routledge, 1995).

considered this moment in relation to the double meaning of the word *moving* in Ovid's *Metamorphoses*. He suggests that the Ovidian sense of *movere* – which could refer to the literal moving of inanimate objects such as stones and musical strings – corresponds with the early modern occult notion of sympathy. However, Ortiz argues that the occult model is being ironized here: 'Titus's confusion of the literal and metaphorical senses of "move" … invokes the doctrine of sympathy in a way which appears ridiculous'. For Ortiz, occult sympathy 'is merely an empty conceit in the universe of the play'.[33] But perhaps Titus is not quite as confused as Ortiz suggests. Titus's desire to move the stones can be read as a metaphorical expression of his desire to move others: as Titus himself notes, the stones only 'seem' to weep with him. The image of weeping stones is a way for Titus to express his disdain for the unsympathetic tribunes, and his desire for a more sympathetic hearing. Shakespeare does not simply offer a critique of occult sympathy, but rather has Titus use it as a powerful metaphor for the emotional receptivity he seeks.

Titus's ability to express his grief is tested even further later in the same scene when his daughter is brought on with her tongue cut out and her hands removed. Titus's hand is then cut off by Aaron in what turns out to be a futile gesture to save the life of his sons. Titus asks the heavens to pity him: 'If any power pities wretched tears, / To that I call' (3.1.209–10). His language becomes increasingly metaphorical, as he describes how his sighs will 'breathe the welkin dim / And stain the sun with fog' (212–13). The stoical Marcus tries to get Titus to tone down these outlandish images, and to temper his passions with reason: 'do not break into these deep extremes' (216). Yet Titus suggests that, because his sorrows are bottomless, his 'passions' should be likewise (218), using the word in the relatively new, but now obsolete, sense of 'A literary composition or passage marked by deep or strong emotion; a passionate speech or outburst' (*OED*, 'passion', 6b). Titus allows himself another passionate outburst in which he compares the exchange of grief between himself and Lavinia to the processes of the natural world:

> When heaven doth weep, doth not the earth o'erflow?
> If the winds rage, doth not the sea wax mad,
> Threatening the welkin with his big-swollen face?
> And wilt thou have a reason for this coil?

---

[33] Joseph M. Ortiz, '"Martyred Signs": *Titus Andronicus* and the Production of Musical Sympathy', *Shakespeare*, 1/1&2 (June/December 2005), 53–74 (p. 69). The influence of Ovid on the emotional world of *Titus* is also considered by Cora Fox in 'Grief and the Ovidian Politics of Revenge in *Titus Andronicus*', in *Ovid and the Politics of Emotion*, pp. 105–24.

> I am the sea. Hark how her sighs doth blow.
> She is the weeping welkin, I the earth.
> Then must my sea be moved with her sighs,
> Then must my earth with her continual tears
> Become a deluge, overflowed and drowned,
> For why my bowels cannot hide her woes,
> But like a drunkard must I vomit them. (3.1.222–32)

In this complex metaphorical schema, Titus is both the earth and the sea, while Lavinia is the sky, acting upon him. The metaphor develops into a description of the physiological nature of his emotions. The bowels were seen as the seat of the tender and sympathetic passions, and could actually mean 'Pity, compassion, feeling, "heart"' (*OED*, 'bowels', 3a). In addition, the 'her' in line 231 is ambiguous, and could refer to the woes of Titus's bowels, or to Lavinia's woes, further blurring the distinction between Titus's body and Lavinia's grief. This speech might thus be seen as evidence that 'the passions of the early modern subject have an elemental character more literal than metaphoric in force'.[34] Titus's woes have a physiological basis, and have to be literally vomited out. And yet – as with Hieronimo's description of the sympathetic environment that we examined earlier – using the term *literal* in the context of an explicitly poetical speech about the passions is problematic. Should we regard this speech as a metaphorical evocation of feeling, rather than an attempt to offer an accurate or quasi-scientific description of Titus's emotions?

The idea of bodily or automatic sympathy is further complicated in the play by its juxtaposition with a cognitive and imaginative conception of emotional correspondence. Immediately after Titus's meteorological speech we have a Messenger who feels the woes of Titus and his family, but not due to any kind of automatic sympathy:

> Worthy Andronicus, ill art thou repaid
> For that good hand thou sent'st the emperor.
> Here are the heads of thy two noble sons,
> And here's thy hand in scorn to thee sent back:
> Thy grief their sports, thy resolution mocked,
> That woe is me to think upon thy woes
> More than remembrance of my father's death. (235–41)

The Messenger remembers his father's death as he 'think[s] upon' Titus's woes: his pity for Titus is thus bound up with his own emotional experiences. Here emotional correspondence is the product of thought and

---

[34] Paster, *Humoring the Body*, p. 19.

memory, rather than a process of bodily contagion or straightforward 'identification'. Indeed the Messenger suggests that Titus's grief is actually worse than his own grief, but nonetheless invokes his father's death as he attempts to express and conceptualize his response to Titus's predicament. We might also suggest that the Messenger's speech implicitly reflects upon the audience's responses as well: Titus's losses will, one hopes, be far more violent and extreme than anything that members of the audience will have experienced; yet they may nevertheless recall their own losses as they too 'think upon [Titus's] woes'. In this way the Messenger can be seen as an example of what Alastair Fowler has called an 'involved spectator'. Fowler notes the 'intense participation' of such spectator figures in Renaissance art and literature, and suggests that they 'illustrate how far the Renaissance viewer's role was from passive observation'.[35] As the Messenger compares his woes to those of Titus, the audience may, in turn, compare their responses to those of the Messenger. This speech thus highlights the extent to which there is often a comparative aspect to our sorrows, or perhaps to all our emotional responses.

The play's treatment of sympathy is even more complex, however, because Shakespeare also demonstrates that such comparisons do not always elicit pity or compassion. In the opening scene Tamora offers a passionate plea for the life of her son Alarbus. Tamora asks Titus to imagine what he would feel if one of his own sons were executed:

> Stay, Roman brethren, gracious conqueror,
> Victorious Titus, rue the tears I shed,
> A mother's tears in passion for her son!
> And if thy sons were ever dear to thee,
> O, think my son to be as dear to me.   (1.1.107–11)

Tamora uses the verbal form of *rue* to invite Titus to imagine her feelings for her son.[36] She asks him to be merciful, like the gods: 'Wilt thou draw near the nature of the gods? / Draw near them then in being merciful. / Sweet mercy is nobility's true badge' (1.1.120–22). As Tamora suggests, *mercy* was

---

[35] See Fowler, *Renaissance Realism*, pp. 66–84 (p. 76). This relates to an analogous concept in art criticism: 'the idea that the painter should include an *Assistenzfigur*, advice first formulated in the Italian tradition, directly to ideas stemming from Aristotle's theory of tragedy' (Thijs Weststeijn, 'Between Mind and Body: Painting the Inner Movements According to Samuel van Hoogstraten and Franciscus Junius', in Stephanie S. Dickey and Herman Roodenburg (eds.), *The Passions in the Arts of the Early Modern Netherlands* (Zwolle: Waanders, 2009), pp. 261–81 (pp. 272–3).

[36] Her words echo Hieronimo's comparison between his own losses and those of the Viceroy and Castile at the close of *The Spanish Tragedy*: 'O good words! / As dear to me was my Horatio / As yours, or yours, or yours, my lord, to you' (4.4.168–70).

a quality associated with nobility, and implied a power structure in which the merciful individual was positioned above the poor wretch asking for pity.[37] In *A table of humane passions* (1621), Nicholas Coeffeteau writes that '*Mercy is a* Griefe *or feeling which we have of another mans miseries, who we hold worthy of a better fortune*'. He continues: 'it is most certaine that such as feele their hearts touch't with pitty, must bee in that estate as they thinke that either themselves or their friends may fall into the like accident, and runne into the same misfortune that he hath done, whose misery doth move them to this commiseration'.[38] Yet Tamora's attempts to make Titus imagine experiencing the same losses, and thus move him to compassion, are ineffective. Titus suggests – in a mathematical, business-like way – that Alarbus needs to be killed in order to pay for the deaths of others.

In 2.2, however, Tamora faces the piteous pleas of another woman: Lavinia. Demetrius enjoins his mother not to feel pity: 'let it be your glory / To see her tears, but be your heart to them / As unrelenting flint to drops of rain' (2.2.139–41). We have already seen how stones and flint could serve as metaphors denoting a lack of compassion, sometimes with a gendered dimension. However, *Titus Andronicus* reminds us that this seductive set of metaphors does not necessarily describe intrinsic differences between men and women. Lavinia attempts to invoke the stereotypical idea of compassionate femininity, and asks Chiron to entreat his mother to 'show a woman's pity' (2.2.147). Lavinia hopes that, even if her sons may be pitiless, Tamora may nonetheless show mercy:

> 'Tis true, the raven doth not hatch a lark.
> Yet I have heard – O, could I find it now –
> The lion, moved with pity, did endure
> To have his princely paws pared all away.
> Some say that ravens foster forlorn children
> The whilst their own birds famish in their nests.
> O be to me, though thy hard heart say no,
> Nothing so kind, but something pitiful. (149–56)

Lavinia uses a proverbial fable as a kind of exemplary narrative to encourage Tamora to show pity.[39] Yet Tamora states that she will remain 'pitiless' in imitation of Lavinia's father: 'Remember, boys, I poured forth tears in

---

[37] For a valuable account of the ways in which mercy was discussed in the period – as a virtuous act, or a kind of 'contagion' – see John Staines, 'Compassion in the Public Sphere of Milton and King Charles', in Paster et al. (eds.), *Reading the Early Modern Passions*, pp. 89–110 (esp. pp. 99–100).
[38] Nicolas Coeffeteau, *A table of humane passions. With their causes and effects*, trans. Edward Grimeston (London, 1621), pp. 357–8.
[39] See Bate's note to 2.2.151–2 and his 'Introduction', p. 93.

vain / To save your brother from the sacrifice, / But fierce Andronicus would not relent' (162–5). Tamora's description of Titus recalls the 'unrelenting' flint invoked by Demetrius, and she thus resists the stereotype of soft or passive female compassion. Tamora's emotional state is presented as a deliberate choice in which she imitates Titus's lack of feeling rather than responding to Lavinia's pleas.

The absence of pity or compassion is a key feature of the play, and part of its insistence that passions involve a considerable degree of choice, thought, and judgement. Marcus's address to the heavens at the end of 4.1 also bemoans a lack of pity, but here amongst the gods: 'O heavens, can you hear a good man groan / And not relent or not compassion him' (4.1.123–4). This striking and unusual use of *compassion* as a verb – which resembles Julia's use of *passioning* in *The Two Gentlemen of Verona* – again implies that passions are active processes.[40] But while the play represents various instances of compassion being withheld or suppressed it also explores the attempts of Titus and Marcus to communicate with the silenced Lavinia, and to imagine and articulate her feelings; and it is here that we find one of Shakespeare's most important usages of the term *sympathy*. This moment in the play provides further evidence that Shakespeare was exploring the need for a new set of terms to describe a more active conception of emotional engagement.

We saw in Chapter 2 that the word appears in *Romeo and Juliet*, which was probably written shortly after *Titus*, to describe the 'woeful sympathy' (3.3.85) between the two protagonists.[41] The word's appearance in *Titus* is even more suggestive, however, because it is not only used in conjunction with woe but also associated with an imaginative and emotional engagement with the other. Towards the start of 3.1, Marcus offers to dry Titus's eyes, but Titus suggests that Marcus's napkin has lost its absorbency as it is already 'drowned' (3.1.142) with Marcus's tears. Lucius then offers to dry Lavinia's cheeks, and Titus suggests that he might have the same problem. There is thus a curious double-mirroring here: Marcus's grief matches that of Titus, while Lucius's grief matches that of Lavinia. In other words,

---

[40] The *OED* cites this passage as one of the few examples of *compassion* used as a verb, and notes that this usage was short lived: 'To have compassion on, to pity. ("A word scarcely used", Johnson)'.

[41] The word *sympathy* also appears in several of Shakespeare's other early dramatic works in its earlier sense of correspondence and agreement. In *2 Henry VI*, for example, King Henry uses the term as he welcomes Margaret to the court: 'thou hast given me in this beauteous face / A world of earthly blessings to my soul, / If sympathy of love unite our thoughts' (1.1.21–3). There is a similar usage in *A Midsummer Night's Dream*, when Lysander comments on the various scenarios in which love has failed to run smoothly: 'Or if there were a sympathy in choice, / War, death, or sickness did lay siege to it' (1.1.141–2).

there is a correspondence between these two examples of matching grief. And when Lavinia makes a non-verbal attempt to communicate, Titus attempts to imagine her thoughts, and what Lavinia would say if she still had the facility of speech:

> Mark, Marcus, mark! I understand her signs:
> Had she a tongue to speak, now would she say
> That to her brother which I said to thee.
> His napkin with his true tears all bewet
> Can do no service on her sorrowful cheeks.
> O, what a sympathy of woe is this;
> As far from help as limbo is from bliss. (3.1.144–50)

The word *sympathy* is not glossed in Jonathan Bate's Arden 3 edition, while the *Riverside* simply has 'sharing'.[42] Alan Hughes suggests 'likeness in suffering' in his New Cambridge edition.[43] Yet these attempts at glossing the term do not do justice to its significance and complexity. In this speech, Titus imagines what Lavinia would say, and tries to communicate what she feels. He uses the term *sympathy* to describe not only this community of feeling but also the process of imagining, sharing, and articulating Lavinia's grief. It is striking that *sympathy* is used in this emotional and imaginative context, and not in the passage later in 3.1 in which – as we have already seen – Titus employs a set of meteorological metaphors to describe his bodily passions. Titus's speech about a 'sympathy of woe' thus represents an important moment in the history of the word *sympathy* and offers further evidence that Shakespeare's early dramatic and poetic works played an important role in associating the term with a correspondence of sorrows.

In addition to this complex exploration of emotion words, the play raises wider questions about the ways in which grief might impede our ability to tell the difference between representation and reality. In 3.2 – the so-called fly scene, first printed in the Folio – the Boy asks Titus to break off his sorrowful speech, and instead to make Lavinia merry 'with some pleasing tale' (3.2.47). Marcus notes the extent to which the Boy is moved by Titus's pain: 'Alas, the tender boy in passion moved / Doth weep to see his grandsire's heaviness' (48–9). Yet their discussion of the Boy's passion is broken off when Marcus stabs at a fly with his knife. Titus berates Marcus for his murderous act, and when Marcus responds

---

[42] *The Riverside Shakespeare*, ed. Evans, note to 3.1.148.
[43] Alan Hughes (ed.), *Titus Andronicus*, updated ed. (Cambridge University Press, 2006), note to 3.1.148.

that he has 'but killed a fly' (59), Titus invites him to consider the grieving parents the fly has left behind:

> 'But'?
> How if that fly had a father and a mother?
> How would he hang his slender gilded wings
> And buzz lamenting doings in the air.
> Poor harmless fly,
> That with his pretty buzzing melody
> Came here to make us merry, and thou hast killed him. (3.2.60–6)

Here Titus's powers of sympathy are extended as he projects his own paternal grief for Lavinia's plight onto the newly deceased fly. Yet the scene also suggests that Titus's sympathy for the fly is excessive, or even arbitrary. Indeed the instability of Titus's interpretation of the fly is revealed when Marcus states that he killed the 'black ill-favoured fly' (67) because it reminded him of Aaron the Moor. Titus immediately accepts Marcus's suggestion that the fly is a figure for Aaron, and he asks Marcus's forgiveness, repeatedly stabbing the fly with Marcus's knife. It is at this point that Marcus points to the fragility of Titus's mind, in terms that are particularly germane to the present discussion: 'Alas, poor man! Grief has so wrought on him / He takes false shadows for true substances' (80–1). On one level, this comment suggests that Titus has lost the ability to tell the difference between fantasy and reality. For Bate the scene represents 'a glorious comic parody of tragic empathy'.[44] But rather than simply being a parody, we might also see Marcus's comment as reflecting upon the audience's engagement with the fictional world of *Titus Andronicus*. After all, the word *shadow* is often used by Shakespeare to refer to actors, or to artistic representation more generally.[45] As we saw in Chapter 3, the phrase 'sad shadow' is used to describe the tragic Hecuba in *Lucrece*, in the context of Lucrece's passionate reaction to her plight (1457). These passages from *Titus* and *Lucrece* implicitly explore the ways in which audiences and readers might respond to 'false shadows' – the fictional personages who inhabit Shakespeare's plays and poems – as though they were 'true substances'. Both texts suggest that powerful representations

---

[44] Bate, 'Introduction', p. 121. Charlotte Scott has also written about this scene in 'Still Life? Anthropocentrism and the Fly in *Titus Andronicus* and *Volpone*', *Shakespeare Survey*, 61 (2008), 256–68. Scott writes that 'This scene uses shadow to find its way to substance … the shadow or flattery of distraction leads Titus into action' (p. 264), but she does not tease out fully the metadramatic implications of Titus's comment.

[45] Cf. Theseus's comments in *A Midsummer Night's Dream*: 'The best in this kind are but shadows, and the worst are no worse if imagination amend them' (5.1.210–11).

of grief can work to blur any simple dichotomy between 'real' and 'imagined' emotions.

Certainly *Titus Andronicus* is interested in the ability of fictional narratives – including, implicitly, the play itself – to elicit an emotional reaction from audiences and readers. This concern with the complex interplay between art and life is made more explicit at the end of the fly-scene. We find that Titus is still attempting to make sense of unspeakable events by returning to other texts. He seems to want to replace emotion with narrative, and proposes a retreat to Lavinia's closet in order to read old sorrowful tales:

> Come, take away. Lavinia, go with me;
> I'll to thy closet and go read with thee
> Sad stories chanced in the times of old.
> Come, boy, and go with me; thy sight is young,
> And thou shalt read when mine begin to dazzle. (3.2.82–6)

On one level, this recourse to other sad stories could be seen as a denial of reality. Yet Titus's remarks also point to the consolations that such tales can offer. In the following scene Titus suggests further ways in which fictional narratives can offer a welcome distraction from suffering: 'Come and take choice of all my library, / And so beguile thy sorrow till the heavens / Reveal the damned contriver of this deed' (4.1.34–6). For Cora Fox, this is a problematic moment for Titus, in the sense that he is deluded about the ability of literature to make sense of one's sorrows: 'Titus tries to instruct Lavinia about literature's place in social life – that it can entertain her, or distract her from the "real" sorrows occurring around her – but literature in this play, and especially Ovid's poetry, does not function in the way Titus describes'. Fox goes on to suggest that 'Titus appears to be spouting a useless and escapist aesthetic theory'.[46] Yet the fact that Titus encourages Lavinia to compare her sorrows to those described within other texts does not necessarily suggest that Titus's aesthetic theory is useless: the play suggests, rather, that we need narratives to make sense of our lives, and to contemplate others' suffering. This is perhaps analogous to the way in which Titus uses the concept of occult sympathies as a way of expressing and making sense of his passions, despite his apparent awareness that the concept may be more fanciful than real.

The use of fictional or mythical narratives as a way of articulating extreme passions is also a focus of the play's final scene. The Roman Lord

---

[46] Fox, *Ovid and the Politics of Emotion*, pp. 113–14.

seeks an explanation for why the body of Rome – in a metaphorical sense – has been dismembered like Lavinia's body:

> Speak, Rome's dear friend, as erst our ancestor
> When with his solemn tongue he did discourse
> To lovesick Dido's sad-attending ear
> The story of that baleful burning night
> When subtle Greeks surprised King Priam's Troy.
> Tell us what Sinon hath bewitched our ears,
> Or who hath brought the fatal engine in
> That gives our Troy, our Rome, the civil wound.   (5.3.79–86)

The Roman Lord here attempts to pre-empt the story he is about to hear by placing it in the context of other sad stories. He explicitly alludes to Aeneas's tale to Dido, and thus implicitly recalls both Virgil's *Aeneid* and Marlowe's *Dido*. This moment may hint at the influence of Marlowe's play on Shakespeare's dramatic thinking, particularly in its concern with the affective power of Aeneas's narrative.[47] But what is interesting here is that the events of *Titus* are so dreadful that Marcus struggles to put them into words or translate them into a story. Nonetheless he is able to say that he cannot speak, and he tells us (rhetorically) what the effects of his narrative would have been:

> My heart is not compact of flint nor steel,
> Nor can I utter all our bitter grief,
> But floods of tears will drown my oratory
> And break my utterance even in the time
> When it should move ye to attend me most,
> And force you to commiseration.   (87–92)

Again, the audience's response is anticipated, but in a highly self-conscious manner. Marcus claims that he does not conform to the conventional male stereotype of being flint-hearted and is thus incapable of articulating his grief without being overwhelmed by tears. Yet he goes on to suggest the emotional power that such a speech would have, echoing Philip Sidney's claims that tragedy 'stir[s] the affects of admiration and commiseration'.[48] On the one hand, then, this passage seems to confirm the idea – described by Horace, Quintilian, and many Renaissance commentators on acting

---

[47] On the influence of *Dido* on Shakespeare's works see Laurie McGuire and Emma Smith, 'What Is a Source? Or, How Shakespeare Read his Marlowe', *Shakespeare Survey*, 68 (2015), 15–31. They write: 'when the Shakespeare canon refers to Dido, one has to suspect a source in Marlowe as much as a source in Virgil' (pp. 28–9).
[48] Sidney, *The Defence of Poesy*, in Duncan-Jones (ed.), *The Oxford Authors: Sir Philip Sidney*, p. 230. See also Bate's note to 5.3.92.

and oratory – that an actor's tears could provoke spontaneous tears in their audience, and 'force [us] to commiseration'. On the other hand, however, it is worth emphasizing that this is a description of Marcus's story, rather than the thing itself. It is Lucius who offers a partial account of the play's events, after which Marcus finally begins his own narrative. The passage cited above invites the audience to *imagine* a scene of tragic storytelling, and perhaps it is all the more powerful for the fact that Marcus's tale is temporarily withheld from us. Like Julia in *The Two Gentlemen of Verona*, Marcus invokes the idea of emotional contagion and spontaneous sympathy, but it features here primarily as a rhetorical trope. This moment further highlights the extent to which sympathy in early modern texts is often relational, comparative, and intertextual – and bound up with the reader or spectator's imagination.

Perhaps, then, what is most striking about the emotional landscape of *Titus Andronicus* is that various early modern conceptions of the passions – such as occult sympathies and correspondence, humoral theory, and rhetorical affect – are employed in ways that highlight their metaphorical or imaginary status. This is not to say that the play is incapable of producing spontaneous tears in its audiences, nor that Shakespeare is dismissing humoral theory in any simple sense, but rather to suggest that *Titus* reflects upon the multiple ways in which early moderns understood and experienced the grief of others. Along with several other early Shakespearean works – *Lucrece* in particular – the play dramatizes and thereby facilitates the redeployment of *sympathy* as a new term for expressing a highly complex emotional and cognitive process.

'And let me share in sympathie of griefe': From *Sympathy* to *Sympathize*

We have seen how *Titus Andronicus* played a key role in the development of the term *sympathy* in the 1590s, not least in its description of a 'sympathy of woe' between individuals. In the latter part of the decade, Shakespeare and his contemporaries continued this process of associating the word *sympathy* with sorrow and grief. The striking formulation we find in *Titus* was echoed by two poets familiar with Shakespeare's works. Thomas Edwards's 'Cephalus & Procris', which was printed alongside his poem 'Narcissus' in 1595, uses the phrase 'Sympathy of sorrows' to denote a sharing of grief:

> To post foorth gan another *Phaeton,*
> And swore once more, he should the world uppon,
> Or as tis thought to trie th'adventrous boy.

> Yet some suppose, he meant upon this day,
> A Sympathy of sorrowes to advaunce.⁴⁹

Both 'Cephalus & Procris' and 'Narcissus' are Ovidian epyllia, written in the style of Marlowe's *Hero and Leander* and Shakespeare's *Venus and Adonis*.⁵⁰ It is thus tempting to see Edwards's 'Cephalus & Procris' as a response to Shakespeare's narrative poems, both of which contain the term *sympathy*. However, the phrase 'Sympathy of sorrowes' more closely resembles Titus's 'sympathy of woe'. In Chapter 1 we saw how the phrase 'sympathy of affections' appeared in various prose works in the 1580s and 1590s. This example from Edwards suggests that *Titus* initiated an important variation on that theme, and encouraged other writers to use the term to refer to a correspondence of grief, rather than 'affections' more generally.

Titus's formulation also appears to have caught the poetic ear of John Weever, author of the earliest complete poem in praise of Shakespeare, 'Ad Gulielmum Shakespear', which appears in his 1599 *Epigrammes*.⁵¹ Weever's poem reveals his knowledge of *Venus and Adonis* and *The Rape of Lucrece*, and perhaps *Richard II* and *Romeo and Juliet* as well. This familiarity with Shakespeare's early dramatic and poetic works is particularly suggestive, given that one of Weever's other poems uses the term *sympathy* to suggest a sharing of woe. This poem, 'The Pilgrims Story', appears in the anonymous pamphlet *The whipping of the satyre* (1601), which was almost certainly written by Weever. On his pilgrimage the speaker sees two discontented sisters who turn out to be 'the Sacred Church' and 'the Commonwealth'.⁵² Keeping out of their sight at first, he listens to their conversation, and notes the shared sorrow between them:

> But at the last (for long I lent mine eare,)
> I heard the younger say with heavy heart,
> Sister, more crosses I am borne to beare,
> Then tongue can speake, or speaches can impart;
> Yet none hath heapt such sorrowes in my brest,
> As those which now; and sighed out the rest.

---

⁴⁹ Thomas Edwards, *Cephalus & Procris* (London, 1595), sig. A4r.
⁵⁰ See Matthew Steggle, 'Edwards, Thomas (*fl.* 1587–1595)', *ODNB*.
⁵¹ John Weever, 'Epigram 22, Ad Gulielmum Shakespeare', in C. M. Ingleby et al. (eds.), *The Shakespeare Allusion Book: A Collection of Allusions to Shakespeare from 1591 to 1700*, 2 vols (London: Oxford University Press, 1932), vol. 1, p. 24.
⁵² See E. A. J. Honigmann, *John Weever: A Biography of a Literary Associate of Shakespeare and Jonson, Together with a Photographic Facsimile of Weever's Epigrammes (1599)* (Manchester University Press, 1987), p. 38.

> Nay, said her sister, do not smother't so,
> Impart it soone, if it import releefe:
> I prithee (sweete) communicate thy woe,
> And let me share in sympathie of griefe:
> Seeme not to be what it beseemes not thee,
> So miserable of thy miserie.[53]

The second stanza is especially concerned with the communication and sharing of woe, and contains the phrase 'sympathie of griefe', again recalling the 'sympathy of woe' between Titus and Lavinia.[54] It also echoes the meeting between Lucrece and her maid in *Lucrece*, not least because Weever's poem also represents a sympathetic encounter between two women. Whether Weever is directly responding to *Titus*, or *Lucrece*, or both, he further associates the noun *sympathy* with woe – and places the term in the mouth of the character who is trying to imagine and understand the sorrows of another. Furthermore, this allegorical text also points to the ways in which the word was beginning to be used to explore political concerns at the start of the seventeenth century – a process that, as we shall see in the next chapter, would continue into the Jacobean period.

While Weever's poem points to the development of *sympathy* in the late 1590s it also hints at the need for the verbal form of the word. After all, the older sister in Weever's poem desires to 'share in sympathie of griefe'. We might suggest that, in the late Elizabethan period, there was a desire not only to 'share' in another's grief but also to find a new word for this active process of communicating and participating. Shakespeare's early dramatic works played an important part in exploring and popularizing the verbal form of *sympathy*. In the previous chapter we saw how the term *sympathize* appears in three poetic works in 1594: Shakespeare's *Lucrece*, Daniel's *Cleopatra*, and the anonymous sonnet sequence *Zepheria*. At around the same time, the word appears in Shakespeare's *The Comedy of Errors* (*c.* 1594) and *Love's Labour's Lost* (*c.* 1594–5).[55] The latter contains Moth's sarcastic response to Armado's request for the swain to carry a letter for him: 'A message well sympathiz'd – a horse to be embassador

---

[53] *The whipping of the satyre* (London, 1601), sig. B4r-v.
[54] Aside from Shakespeare's *Titus*, these examples from Edwards and Weever are the only two instances I have located of the specific formulation 'sympathy of …' used in conjunction with the words *grief*, *woe*, or *sorrow* in the late sixteenth and early seventeenth centuries.
[55] *The Comedy of Errors* may have been written around 1594 (as proposed by the Oxford editors), although R. A. Foakes suggests that links with other works suggest it was written between 1590 and 1593, just before or just after the theatres were closed because of the plague; see his Arden 2 edition (London: Methuen, 1962), p. xxiii.

for an ass' (3.1.51–2).⁵⁶ However, the usage of the word in *Errors* is more complex, as it describes the capacity of narrative to bring about a sharing of emotions.

In the play's final scene, the Abbess, who has revealed herself to be Egeon's lost wife Emilia, suggests that the other characters congregate in the abbey in order to hear a narrative account of the play's events. Intriguingly, she uses the term *sympathized* as a way of describing this shared experience:

> Renowned duke, vouchsafe to take the pains
> To go with us into the abbey here,
> And here at large discoursed all our fortunes;
> And all that are assembled in this place,
> That by this sympathized one day's error
> Have suffer'd wrong, go keep us company,
> And we shall make full satisfaction.   (5.1.394–400)

In his Arden 2 edition, R. A. Foakes glosses this usage of *sympathized* as 'shared by in all equally'. However, the precise meaning of the term is unclear, and Foakes admits that this is 'an odd use of the word'.⁵⁷ The *OED* is also uncertain, even as to whether the word is being used as an adjective or a verb: this passage is cited as an example of both 'Compounded of corresponding parts or elements, complicated' (*OED*, adj. a), and 'To make up or compound of corresponding parts or elements; to form or contrive harmoniously or consistently. Obs.' (*OED*, v. 3c). In other words, it is unclear whether the word describes the *complexity* of the day's errors, or suggests that everyone *shares in* these errors.

Martine van Elk has likened this example to other early Shakespearean usages of *sympathize*, and argues that the term is more complex than Foakes's gloss suggests: 'its primary meaning, at least within the frame of romance, is closest to the usage in *The Rape of Lucrece*. There, it points to similarity and profound emotion as well as decorum'. However, she goes on to suggest that 'The early modern understanding of sympathy differs from our modern definition in highlighting a mystical affinity leading to a correspondence of experience, as well as a natural fellowship'.⁵⁸ In this way, while van Elk acknowledges the interest and complexity of the word,

---

⁵⁶ H. R. Woudhuysen glosses Moth's 'sympathized' as 'fittingly contrived' (see his Arden 3 edition of *Love's Labour's Lost* (London: Thomas Nelson, 1998), note to 3.1.48).
⁵⁷ See Foakes's note to 5.1.397.
⁵⁸ Martine van Elk, "'This sympathizèd one day's error': Genre, Representation, and Subjectivity in *The Comedy of Errors*', *Shakespeare Quarterly*, 60 (2009), 47–72.

she still adheres to the commonplace critical view that early modern sympathy was understood as a kind of occult affinity.[59] I would argue that there is a sense of active participation in the Abbess's formulation, rather than a generalized sense of affinity or agreement. It is also significant that, according to the Abbess, everyone has 'suffered wrong', suggesting that the term *sympathized* is being used here to describe a correspondence of suffering that recalls Titus's 'sympathy of woe'. The fact that this shared emotion is experienced through a figured act of storytelling makes this example even more suggestive. The Abbess's formulation 'all that are assembled in this place' ostensibly refers to the characters on stage, but it also implies that the audience – who are also 'assembled' in the theatre – are included in this shared experience, and indeed sharing of affect.

This newer affective conception of sympathy – together with the appearance of the word *sympathize* – had considerable implications for the understanding of subjectivity and emotional agency at the end of the sixteenth century. Some of these implications are explored in Samuel Brandon's closet drama *The Tragicomoedi of The Vertuous Octavia* (1598), which dramatizes the plight of Octavia following her abandonment by Mark Antony.[60] While Octavia is the play's central focus, one of its most suggestive scenes involves Octavia's two waiting women – Julia and Camilla – discussing Antony's apparently irrational love for Cleopatra. In 5.1 Julia describes love as a 'deepe affection' that is 'Wrought by th'instinct of natures hidden might'. She suggests that it comes about through chance and mysterious forces of nature: 'When such a beautie we do chaunce to see: / As with our nature best doth simpathize, / Which nature, faultie is, and not poore we'.[61] In Julia's formulation, human beings have little emotional agency; nature is to blame for causing beauty to 'simpathize' with human natures – she thus uses the term in its more general senses of 'to be

---

[59] Kent Cartwright, in his Arden 3 edition (London: Bloomsbury, 2016), follows van Elk by suggesting that the term 'has a strong connection with magic and denotes a capacity to work long-distance magical effects on a person' (note to 5.1.397).

[60] Andrew Hadfield has written that the play 'undoubtedly deserves to be better known than it currently is as it reveals its author to be an often subtle and thoughtful reader of other writers, as well as a decent poet' in 'Edmund Spenser and Samuel Brandon', *Notes and Queries*, 56 (2009), 536–8 (p. 537). Hadfield is mainly concerned with the influence of Spenser, but the play is also indebted to Samuel Daniel's *Cleopatra*; see the Malone Society reprint of *The Tragicomoedi of The Vertuous Octavia*, prepared by Ronald B. McKerrow (Oxford University Press, 1909), p. v. Yvonne Bruce discusses the play's emotional complexity in '"That which Marreth All": Constancy and Gender in *The Virtuous Octavia*', *Medieval and Renaissance Drama in England*, 22 (2009), 42–59, although she is more concerned with Stoicism and Senecanism than sympathy.

[61] *The Tragicomoedi of The Vertuous Octavia*, 5.1 (TLN 1983–5). Quotations are taken from McKerrow's edition, which gives Through Line Numbers.

similarly or correspondingly affected; to respond sympathetically to some influence' (*OED*, 1) and 'To agree with, answer or correspond to' (*OED*, 3a). She goes on to offer an intricate description of occult sympathies as a further explanation for this idea:

> Look how the Loadstone draws nought els but steele,
> Though mettals far more pretious are about it:
> Yet this as his fit subject seemes to feele
> His power attractive, and mooves not without it,
> Or as in diverse instruments we see,
> When any one doth strike a tuned string:
> The rest which with the same in concord be,
> Will shew a motion to that sencelesse thing;
> When all the other neither stirre nor playe,
> Although perhaps more musicall then they:
> So are our minds, in spight of reasons nay,
> Strain'd with the bent of natures sympathie:
> Whose powerfull force, no wit, no arte, can stay. (2019–31)

Here Julia turns to the earlier notion of magical sympathy to explain Antony's feelings of love. In spite of reason, individuals are 'bent of natures sympathie'; a 'powerfull force' that affects them from without. Taken out of context, this speech might well confirm the thesis that the notion of occult sympathies continued to be the primary explanation for human feelings and emotions in the late sixteenth century. However, Julia's interlocutor, Camilla, is rather more sceptical about Julia's quasi-scientific explanations for Antony's behaviour: 'But Lord how willing are we to invent, / And finde out coverts to obscure our sinne' (2069–70). She states that God gave humans reason, and that we should use it to govern our passions: 'Our trouping thoughts should marshall in such wise, / That no affect from reason should decline, / Nor rebell passion in our hearts arise' (2082–4). In this way, the text itself invites its audience to debate the relationship between reason and passion – and, more specifically, the question of whether or not sympathy should be regarded as an automatic process or a matter of choice.

At the start of 5.2, Octavia enters with her children, describing them as 'poore companions of [her] misery' (2098). Octavia bemoans Antony's lack of pity, contrasting his cruelty with the senseless stones at her feet:

> O *Antony,* borne of no gentle Syre,
> Some cruell *Caucasus* did thee beget:
> Even scencelesse things thy scencelesnesse admire,
> And seeme to feele, what thou seemst to forget.

> Oft have I seene these stones with pitty moved,
> Sheed dropping teares, lamenting my disgrace:
> When in thy heart where most it most behoved,
> No kinde remorse could ever finde a place. (2118–25)

This speech recalls various passages that we have already explored in the present chapter, including Titus's moving lament about the tribunes in 3.1 of *Titus Andronicus*, and behind that the ideas of hard-heartedness explored in Marlowe's *Dido*. These senseless stones are said to be more pitiful than a human being; in this case inanimate objects actually admire Antony's senselessness. Octavia claims that she has seen these stones moved with pity and 'Sheed dropping teares'. Once again, however, rather than seeing this speech as an endorsement of the older idea of occult sympathies, we should perhaps regard it as evidence that this notion came to have particular currency as a poetic trope during the 1590s. Like Titus, Octavia offers a powerful image of senseless objects being moved to tears as a means of expressing her dismay at Antony's lack of pity, as well as articulating her own feelings of grief.

Moreover, when Octavia herself uses the term *sympathize* its meaning is rather more complex than Julia's conception of human beings affected passively by external forces. In 3.1 Octavia describes how the populace emulate her and attempt to imagine her thoughts: 'When that I see the vulgar peoples eyes, / Make my designes the patterne of their deeds: / How with my thoughts they strive to simpathize, / And how my misse their certaine errour breedes' (1274–7). In this speech, the term is used to denote something that people do; it involves them striving to 'sympathize' with Octavia's thoughts. The word appears in an even more suggestive context in the verse epistles that appear at the end of the text, in Octavia's letter to Antony:

> Thou borne by nature to advance
> Thy thoughts to honors height;
> Dost carelesly stoope unto shame,
> And fall with thine owne waight.
> Then never thinke, I thinke it strange
> That thou art fled from mee:
> The heavens forbid my lowest thoughts,
> Should simpathize with thee. (370–7)

In this remarkably sceptical and self-possessed speech, Octavia invokes the possibility that she might 'simpathize' with her husband; however, she makes it clear that she is capable of resisting such emotional forces. The emphasis in this speech is very much on Octavia's thoughts, rather than her bodily passions. She commands the heavens *not* to allow her 'lowest thoughts' to 'simpathize' with Antony. The play thus demonstrates the range of meanings that the term *sympathize* carried during this period. Certainly the more general senses of 'to be similarly or correspondingly affected' (*OED*, 1) and 'To have an affinity; to agree in nature, disposition, qualities, or fortunes' (*OED*, 2a) were still available at the end of the sixteenth century, but these definitions clearly existed alongside other senses, as 'sympathizing' was increasingly understood as an active process that involved individuals imagining and participating in the suffering of another. At the same time, however, this last example from *The Vertuous Octavia* also emphasizes the fact that sympathizing was already regarded as an emotional response that individuals could resist. In this way, the play implicitly questions the notion of occult sympathies as an explanation or excuse for human behaviour. Brandon presents his readers with a decidedly dialogic work, in which the earlier concept of sympathy is interrogated and tested, and its poetic and ethical possibilities are further highlighted.

Of course, ideas of cosmic or meteorological sympathy continued to appear in dramatic works as we move into the early seventeenth century. Criticus in Ben Jonson's *Cynthia's Revels* (1600) uses the term *sympathize* in this sense, as he responds to Arete's command that he stages a masque for Cynthia's pleasure: 'Better and sooner durst I undertake / To make the different seasons of the year, / The winds, or elements to sympathize, / Than their unmeasurable vanity / Dance truly in a measure'.[62] Similarly, in Shakespeare's *Troilus and Cressida* (c. 1602), Nestor uses the term in an elaborate speech that describes how show and valour 'divide / In storms of fortune' – and can be affected by the 'splitting wind' (1.3.46–9). He continues:

> why then the thing of courage,
> As rous'd with rage, with rage doth sympathize,
> And with an accent tun'd in self-same key
> Retires to chiding fortune.   (1.3.51–4)

In Nestor's formulation, the 'thing of courage' – any courageous creature – that is roused to rage sympathizes with the natural rage of the storm, and

---

[62] Quoted from *The Cambridge Edition of the Works of Ben Jonson*, 4.6.2–6. We find an analogous use of the term in Shakespeare's *1 Henry IV* (c. 1596), in which King Henry associates the blustery weather with the rebels: 'Then with the losers let it sympathize, / For nothing can seem foul to those that win' (5.1.7–8). He goes on to make a suggestive analogy between the celestial and social order, asking the defiant Worcester whether he will 'unknit / This churlish knot of all-abhorred war? / And move in that obedient orb again / Where you did give a fair natural light, / And be no more an exhal'd meteor, / A prodigy of fear …?' (5.1.15–20). Henry is invoking Ptolemaic cosmology, but using this concept in a metaphorical way, perhaps suggesting that his use of the term *sympathize* should be understood in a figurative sense as well.

with a voice 'tuned' to the same wrathful key answers back to fortune.[63] This speech thus implies that human beings can be affected by the natural environment, suggesting that sympathizing is something that happens *to* people. It is worth noting, however, that Nestor is using the idea of a storm as part of an extended metaphor that describes the ups and downs of fortune's wheel.

The word appears again in 4.1 during an exchange between Diomedes and Aeneas. When Aeneas says, 'No man alive can love in such a sort / The thing he means to kill more excellently', Diomedes responds thus:

> We sympathize. Jove, let Aeneas live,
> If to my sword his fate be not the glory,
> A thousand complete courses of the sun!
> But, in mine emulous honour, let him die,
> With every joint a wound, and that to-morrow! (4.1.26–30)

In this way, two discrete but related forms of the word *sympathize* coexist in Shakespeare's final Elizabethan play. In this scene, Diomedes uses the word to describe his feelings of agreement with Aeneas. The latter responds 'We know each other well' (4.1.31). But of course the relationship between these two characters is highly ambiguous; as Paris suggests, 'This is the most despiteful gentle greeting, / The noblest hateful love, that e'er I heard of' (33–4). Nevertheless, Diomedes's formulation makes the word available as a term for describing the active process of understanding and articulating the feelings of others.[64]

Conclusion: 'There was but one sole man, in all the world, / With whom I ere could sympathize'

As we have seen, then, dramatic texts in the final decade of the sixteenth century took a particular interest in exploring affinities between sorrowful individuals, as well as creating a new vocabulary for describing the 'sympathy of woe' between them. But we have also seen the ways in which compassionate relationships between individuals represented onstage, as

---

[63] The *Riverside* glosses the key phrase here as 'being itself roused to rage reacts sympathetically with the rage of the elements' (note to 1.3.52).
[64] For a stimulating discussion of *Troilus and Cressida*, and how Shakespearean drama 'repeatedly emphasizes selfhood's position as something called into being dialogically, in association with others', see Tilmouth, 'Passion and Intersubjectivity', pp. 19–20. Tilmouth is not concerned with the development of sympathy in the period, although his interest in intersubjectivity does chime with the concerns of the present chapter. See also Tilmouth's *Passion's Triumph over Reason: A History of the Moral Imagination from Spenser to Rochester* (Oxford University Press, 2007).

well as those between actors and audience, are not necessarily depicted as bodily or physical processes; rather, conceptions of sympathy in the period were bound up with thinking as well as feeling. The dramatic works we have explored in this chapter, together with other poetic and religious works in the period, imply that pity and compassion involve a considerable degree of choice, judgement, and agency. Moreover, the appearance of the word *sympathize* in several plays from the 1590s points to a fascination with individual characters expressing and exploring the extent of their emotional agency, and to the increasing understanding of sympathy as an active process. Earlier terms such as *rue* and *ruth* were beginning to appear outmoded, or required explanations or intensifiers as the conception of fellow-feeling shifted.

By 1603, we find an adaptation of the term *ruth* in Florio's translation of Montaigne's essay 'Of diverting and diversions', as part of a moving description of 'poore creatures we see on scaffolds': 'their eares attentive to such instructions as Preachers give them, their hands and eies lit up towardes heaven; their voice uttering loud and earnest praiers; all with an eager and continual ruth-mooving motion'.[65] The use of the obscure compound word 'ruth-mooving' – which is combined with the word *motion* – provides further evidence that the term *ruth*, with its connotations of melting and passivity, was starting to appear inadequate on its own for the articulation of this newer, active sense of fellow-feeling. The word *motion* also seems to anticipate the outward movement implicit in the newer term for the passions – *emotions* – that would become current in the later seventeenth century.[66] At the start of the century the act of pitying another individual could be expressed by the verb *to sympathize*. And indeed Florio does adopt the word in his translation of Montaigne's 'Of Vanitie': 'Besides the profit I reape by writing of my selfe, I have hoped for this other, that if ever it might happen my humours should please or sympathize with some honest man, he would before my death seeke to be acquainted with me, or to overtake mee'.[67]

In 1607 the word appears as a fashionable term to be scoffed at in Ben Jonson's *Volpone*. In 3.4, Lady Politic Would-Be is mocked for her excessive verbiage and clumsy use of fashionable phrases. As Volpone puts it in an aside, tiring of Lady Would-Be's florid speech, 'Another flood of words!

---

[65] *Essays written in French by Michael Lord of Montaigne*, p. 467.
[66] On the significance of this semantic shift see Dixon, *From Passions to Emotions*, and Thorley, 'Towards a History of Emotion, 1562–1660'.
[67] *Essays written in French by Michael Lord of Montaigne*, p. 553. The French verb *sympathizer* does not appear in the original passage.

A very torrent!'.⁶⁸ In this scene, Lady Would-Be emphasizes her up-to-date medical knowledge as well as her classical learning, and claims to have read Petrarch, Tasso, Dante, and Guarini. She also acknowledges the importance of Montaigne's essays, noting that 'All our English writers … Will deign to steal out of [Guarini] … Almost as much as from Montagnié'. She continues: 'He has so modern and facile a vein, / Fitting the time, and catching the court ear' (3.4.87–92). On the one hand, then, Jonson implies that Montaigne is 'facile', in the sense of undemanding. At the same time, however, this scene dramatizes the ways in which new English words were finding their way into the everyday vocabulary of English speakers. When Volpone states that he is perturbed, Lady Would-Be tells him that he can be cured: 'Why, in such cases, we must cure our selves, / Make use of our philosophy' (3.4.99–100). She continues:

> And as we find our passions do rebel,
> Encounter 'em with reason, or divert 'em
> By giving scope unto some other humour
> Of lesser danger, as in politic bodies
> There's nothing more doth overwhelm the judgement
> And clouds the understanding than too much
> Settling and fixing and, as 'twere, subsiding
> Upon one object. For the incorporating
> Of these same outward things into that part
> Which we call mental, leaves some certain faeces
> That stop the organs and, as Plato says,
> Assassinates our knowledge.   (3.4.101–12)

Richard Dutton describes the opening lines of this speech as 'trite commonplaces of the era', reproducing the arguments of Thomas Wright's *Passions of the Minde*.⁶⁹ But what is also striking about this discussion of reason and the passions is the vocabulary that Lady Would-Be employs. *Settling*, *fixing*, and *subsiding* are all innovative chemical terms, here used to describe actions of judgement and understanding; *assassinates* is another new word, which may have carried particular significance in the light of the Gunpowder Plot. Lady Would-Be goes on to use another innovative verb, stating that 'There was but one sole man, in all the world, / With whom I ere could sympathize' (3.4.116–17).

The word *sympathize* is not glossed in Dutton's Cambridge edition; but it seems clear that this is another modish term being used by Lady

---

⁶⁸ Quotations are taken from Richard Dutton's edition of *Volpone*, in *The Cambridge Edition of the Works of Ben Jonson*, 3.4.64.
⁶⁹ See Dutton's note to 3.4.101–4.

Would-Be. Indeed it is possible that she herself has 'stolen' the word from Montaigne – or rather Florio's Montaigne. Her usage of *sympathize* is the *OED*'s first citation of the modern sense of 'To feel sympathy; to have a fellow-feeling; to share the feelings of another or others' (*OED*, 4a). As we have seen, however, *sympathize* did not appear suddenly in English via Florio; rather, the term emerged through a complex process of literary imitation and borrowing, in which Shakespeare played a particularly significant part.[70] The imaginative processes of depicting sorrowful characters on stage – and their interactions with each other – required a new word for an active exchange of sorrows. Together with the poems we explored in the previous chapter, plays such as *The Comedy of Errors*, *Troilus and Cressida* and *The Vertuous Octavia* were exemplary works in this process.

My final example from *Volpone*, then, needs to be read in a broader cultural and literary context in order to appreciate its resonances. Perhaps Jonson borrowed the term from Montaigne in order to satirize Lady Would-Be's facile borrowings from foreign authors – although, if so, it is clear that he is borrowing from Florio rather than returning to the French original; or perhaps Jonson was borrowing from and mocking those fellow playwrights who had begun to use the term. Either way, in this instance Jonson was swimming against the linguistic current of his day. His satirical usage of *sympathize* inadvertently extends the process whereby the term is made available a verb – and continues to shed its associations with sympathetic magic. As we shall see in the next chapter, this newer conceptualization of sympathy became increasingly available in the public sphere, and was used as a way of debating larger questions regarding the relationship between scientific, emotional, and political forms of correspondence.

---

[70] In his *Worlde of Wordes*, Florio translates *simpathia* as 'a sympathie or naturall combination of things naturall in the operation of the powers, nature and qualities, as water in coldnes doth participate with the earth, in moisture with the aire, a natruall passion of one to the other'. Meanwhile *simpathizzare* is glossed as 'to sympathize or agree in nature or disposition' (*A Worlde of Wordes, or Most Copious, and Exact Dictionarie in Italian and English, Collected by John Florio* (London, 1598), p. 372). As we have seen, however, the term *sympathize* was already current in English by 1598, suggesting that the term was an English coinage and not necessarily an Italian or French import.

CHAPTER 5

'Soveraignes have a sympathie with subjects'
The Politics of Sympathy in Jacobean England

We saw in the previous chapter how, by the end of the sixteenth century, the term *sympathy* could be used to describe compassion and fellow-feeling, without explicitly invoking earlier scientific and medical concepts. We also saw how the public theatres played an important role in making the term available to audiences and readers. As we move into the seventeenth century, the concepts of pity and compassion continue to be explored and debated, while the word *sympathy* is increasingly co-opted into political discourse. As well as denoting ideas of societal unity and natural order, the term is used in the context of the accession of King James to describe the emotional union of his subjects. In *The time triumphant* (1604), for example, Gilbert Dugdale offers a remarkable description of James's arrival into England:

> let me tell you by the way the joy was not so great in *England,* by the English to fetch him, as the sorrowe was in *Scotland* of the Scots to leave him, and that was more confounding to their Joyes then the rest, the parting betwixt his Queene and him in the open streete, in the full eye of all his subjects, who spent teares in aboundance to behold it, heare English and Scottish in one simpathy: Joyned first in hartie affected love, in signe whereof the flouds of their eyes drawne from their kind harts, conjoyned there Amitie, and no doubt they that in kindnes being possessed with one joy: can weepe togither, they wil now and at all times live and die together.[1]

Dugdale presents his readers with a moving account of a public event: the King and his Queen parting in the open street. The subjects watching this scene are universally affected by it, with 'English and Scottish in one simpathy'. Here sympathy suggests their 'hartie affected love', which is indicated by their tears of joy. Of course, this is a piece of political mythmaking and not necessarily an accurate account of the event, but it

---

[1] Gilbert Dugdale, *The time triumphant declaring in briefe, the arival of our soveraigne liedge Lord, King James into England, his coronation at Westminster* (London, 1604), sig. A2v.

is highly suggestive that Dugdale describes a figured audience within the text – ordinary subjects who are moved by what they see – that channels and prefigures the reader's response. While this is 'simpathy' as shared joy rather than sorrow, it is nevertheless an instance of emotional correspondence being used in an ideological way, bringing English and Scottish citizens together in a form of emotional unity.

The present chapter considers how the concept of sympathy figured in Jacobean writings regarding political and social relations within the commonwealth, and between the monarch and his subjects. I argue that there is a particular concern in this period with the possibility of sympathy between individuals from different social groups, and a renewed interest in the question of whether there could be 'sympathie betweene a King and a begger'.[2] George Abbot, who preached at Oxford and later became Archbishop of Canterbury, stated in one of his sermons (printed in 1600) that

> There should be a fellow-feeling, and sympathy in mens minds, a compassion in a ruler, wishing that there were no cause of punishment to be suffered. And this not for a fashion, and because they are words of course, but in sincerity and simplicity; not with the teares of a Crocodile, or with the sighs of an hypocrite, but truly and in heart.[3]

Abbot suggests that the monarch should not only display sympathy and compassion towards his or her subjects but also feel those emotions – rather than simply conjuring up crocodile tears. This represents a significant shift from the well-established tradition that rulers should be merciful; sympathy implies greater equality and identification than the more hierarchical model implied by mercy.[4] And yet if kings and beggars are sympathetically

---

[2] John Hind, *The most excellent historie of Lysimachus and Varrona* (London, 1604). Varrona's musings on her love for *Lysimachus* are a reworking of Alinda's corresponding speech in Lodge's *Rosalynde*: 'Can love consist of contrarieties? ... Will *Venus* joyne roabes and rags together? or can there be a simpathie betweene a King and a begger? Then *Lysimachus*, how can I beleeve that love should unite our thoughts, when fortune hath set such difference betweene our degrees?' (sig. F1v). See my discussion of *Rosalynde* in Chapter 1, above.
[3] George Abbot, *An exposition upon the prophet Jonah* (London, 1600), p. 143.
[4] For a wide-ranging history of mercy in public discourse see Alex Tuckness and John M. Parrish, *The Decline of Mercy in Public Life* (Cambridge University Press, 2014). John Staines has written about these concepts in relation to Milton and Charles I in 'Compassion in the Public Sphere of Milton and King Charles', in Paster et al. (eds.), *Reading the Early Modern Passions*, pp. 89–110. He suggests that compassion 'served as an ideal for political order and political debate' (p. 92) during the mid-seventeenth century, but does not trace this history back to the earlier part of the seventeenth century. Similarly, Thomas Dixon's *Weeping Britannia: Portrait of a Nation in Tears* (Oxford University Press, 2015) leaps over the period from Shakespeare and Elizabethan drama to the Civil War (pp. 53–9).

compatible then certain social and political hierarchies threaten to collapse. Moreover, several writers in the early seventeenth century suggest that sympathy is never automatic or absolute; we have seen evidence of such scepticism in previous chapters, but this view is powerfully articulated during this period, perhaps even as a response to the optimistic and ideologically inflected views presented by writers such as Dugdale. Indeed political deployment of the term is often troubled or anxious, witnessing the failure of sympathy in groups or individuals.

The chapter begins by exploring the role of sympathy in early Jacobean political discourse, focusing on responses to the crises of succession and the plague. We will see how *sympathy* is used in various political and cultural texts to describe the emotional link that binds social groups as well as the state and the commonwealth – including the monarch and his subjects. But while some texts, such as William Alexander's closet drama *The Tragedy of Croesus*, offered an optimistic representation of sympathy, other works – such as William Muggins's *Londons Mourning garment* – worried about a lack of sympathy between people. The chapter goes on to consider Shakespeare's *The History of King Lear* as a work emerging from and responding to such debates. Situating the play in relation to these cultural materials highlights its particular interest in the moments when sympathy fails. The chapter then turns to royal elegies from the 1610s and 1620s, including poetic responses to the deaths of Prince Henry and Queen Anne. While such texts imagine a kind of collective sympathy between English subjects and the King, and seek to unify the nation in grief, some writers from the same period acknowledge the ways in which sympathy could also unite individuals in opposition to the monarch. As we shall see, the historical and cultural events of this period prompted a reassessment of the role of sympathy in public life, whereby a more realized form of individuality enabled people to identify with certain groups while pushing back against others.

'Symphathie betweene the common wealth and her members': Sympathy and the Body Politic

The idea that there was an affinity or sympathy between the commonwealth and her members appears in various political texts in the late sixteenth and early seventeenth centuries. One of the most influential was Jean Bodin's *Les six livres de la Republique* (1576), which gained additional currency when it was translated into English by Richard Knolles as *The six bookes of a common-weale* (1606). Ioannis Evrigenis has recently highlighted the importance of Bodin's work to political thought in early modern England, including its influence upon King James, who owned a copy of the French text.[5] Knolles's translation employs the term *sympathie* – borrowed from the French original – in the context of the body politic, and describes 'the nations betwixt both the qualitie of *Jupiter* and *Mercurie,* fit for politike governments: the which hath a straunge sympathie in mans bodie, which is the image of the universall world, and of a well ordered Commonweale'.[6] We also find a musical analogy at the close of the text, which is used to illustrate its arguments about societal harmony:

> Wherefore as of Treble and as well as Base voyces is made a most sweet and melodious Harmonie, so also of vices and vertues, of the different qualities of the elements, of the contrarie motions of the celestiall Spheres, and of the Sympathies and Antipathies of things, by indissoluble meanes bound together, is composed the Harmonie of the whole world, and of all the parts thereof: So also a well ordered Commonweale is composed of good and bad, of the rich and of the poore, of wisemen and of fools, of the strong and of the weake, allied by them which are in the meane betwixt both. (pp. 793–4)

While Bodin offers a hymn to order and harmony, he simultaneously acknowledges that a well-ordered society is made up of disharmonious elements, or what he calls 'the Sympathies and Antipathies of things'.[7] The musical analogy offers a means of understanding the elements of the celestial spheres, which are bound together by cosmological sympathy. Yet his suggestion that a well-ordered commonwealth is composed of contradictory elements – and seemingly incompatible individuals – arguably points to its potential instability. Thus, in order to describe the sympathetic harmony between parts of the nation one has to acknowledge the multiplicity of those different elements.

Legal texts from this period also extolled the virtues of a sympathetic commonwealth. The English attorney William West includes a discussion

---

[5] Ioannis D. Evrigenis, 'Sovereignty, mercy, and natural law: King James VI/I and Jean Bodin', *History of European Ideas*, 45 (2019), 1073–88. See also Jane Rickard, *Authorship and Authority: The Writings of James VI and I* (Manchester University Press, 2007), p. 36.

[6] Jean Bodin, *The six bookes of a common-weale*, trans. Richard Knolles (London, 1606), p. 561. Knolles's first published work, *The generall historie of the Turks* (London, 1603), contains a notable usage of the term *sympathy* in its description of Peter, a French hermit, who recounts the sufferings of 'the poor oppressed Christians at Jerusalem' to a council at Claremont in France. The letters that he reads out are so 'lively represented' that they 'mooved the whole assembly with the like simpathie of heavinesse and greife' (pp. 13–14).

[7] The terms *sympathies* and *antipathies* are borrowed directly from the original French text, which describes 'des elemens, des mouvemens contraires, & des sympathies, & antipathies, liees par moyens inviolables, se compose l'harmonie de ce monde' (Jean Bodin, *Les six livres de la Republique* (Paris, 1576), p. 759).

of '*Symphathie betweene the common wealth and her members*' in the second part of his *Symboleography* (first printed 1590), a compendium of legal documents and precedents: 'For certes, when a private person is offended, it cannot lightly be devised, but that the common wealth is thereby also offended, and againe, the common wealth being endammaged, howe can it be chosen but everie Subject thereof is also affected, as being a member of the same'. He goes on to describe this process in terms of sympathy: 'So great a Sympathie and mutuall suffering being in them, as betweene the head and members of a naturall bodie'.[8] West's description of societal unity resembles William Averell's account of the 'politique bodie' in *A mervailous combat of contrarieties* (1588), which we encountered in Chapter 2. We saw there how preachers in the late Elizabethan period drew upon this discourse in order to describe the relationship between members of the church. However, in the early seventeenth century such descriptions of the sympathetic commonwealth had a renewed applicability, not least because of the issue of the union between England and Scotland. This is the first royal succession when the term *sympathy* was available, and it is very early in James's reign that the concept was appropriated and employed by political writers to describe the relationship between Scotland and England, the sympathy between church and state, and social and political unity more generally.

Francis Bacon's early Jacobean works are particularly interesting in this regard because he uses *sympathy* not only in its earlier sense of natural affinity and correspondence but also in relation to current political concerns.[9] In *A briefe discourse, touching the happie union of the kingdomes of England, and Scotland* (1603), which was dedicated to James, Bacon writes that there is 'a great affinity and consent between the Rules of Nature, and the true Rules of Policy'.[10] While various elements in nature might have their 'private particular affection and appetite', they nevertheless 'forsake their own particularities and proprieties, and attend and conspire to uphold the publike'. Bacon illustrates this idea by making an analogy with the process of natural sympathy: 'we see the Yron in small quantitie will ascend and approach to the Load-stone, upon a particular Sympathie. But, if it bee any quantitie of moment, it leaves his appetite of amity with the

---

[8] William West, *The second part of Symboleography, newly corrected and amended, and very much enlarged in all the foure severall treatises* (London, 1601), p. 86.
[9] See Joel J. Epstein, 'Francis Bacon and the Issue of Union, 1603–1608', *Huntington Library Quarterly*, 33 (1970), 121–32.
[10] Francis Bacon, *A briefe discourse, touching the happie union of the kingdomes of England, and Scotland* (London, 1603), sig. A3v.

Load-stone, and like a good Patriott, falleth to the earth, which is the place and region, of massy bodies' (sig. A5r).[11] The iron is naturally attracted to the loadstone, Bacon suggests, but this attraction is only temporary and it will return to the greater whole: thus the rules of nature and the rules of policy are the same. Like Dugdale, Bacon notes all the 'great consent of harts' amongst the people, and goes on to present the King with a discourse on 'the grounds of Nature, touching the Union and commixture of bodies; & the correspondence which they have with the grounds of Policy, in the conjunction of states and kingdomes' (sig. A8r). Natural unions, he argues, are superior to violent ones; and the perfect fermentation and incorporation of bodies 'must be left to *Nature* and *Time*' (sig. C3v). In this way, while Bacon supports James's desire for union he also cautions against the unnatural forcing through of the project.

King James himself borrowed from and participated in this discourse of the sympathetic commonwealth, and played a part in authorizing and disseminating the term *sympathy* in his own writings. Evrigenis has noted the influence of Bodin upon *Basilikon Doron* (1599), in which James draws upon some of the same classical examples to advise his son on the relationship between justice and mercy.[12] But it is also worth emphasizing that the term *sympathy* appears in *Basilikon Doron* – in its earlier sense of correspondence – to refer to Prince Henry's easy acceptance of the book's instructions: '*Thus hoping in the goodnes of God, that your naturall inclination shal have a happie sympathie with these precepts*'.[13] A more explicitly political usage of the term appears in *A counterblast to tobacco* (1604), when James makes an analogy between the body and the state, describing how 'a strong enemie, that invades a towne or fortresse' is able to make his breach or entry at the weakest point. He continues:

> so sickenesse doth make her particular assault, upon such part or parts of our bodie, as are weakest and easiest to be overcome by that sort of disease, which then doth assaile us, although all the rest of the body by Sympathie feele it selfe, to be as it were belaied, and pity besieged by the affliction of that speciall part, the griefe and smart thereof being by the sence of feeling dispersed through all the rest of our members.[14]

---

[11] Bacon reuses this formulation in *The advancement of learning* (London, 1605), p. 246. Elsewhere in the same book, Bacon makes a distinction between natural philosophy and what he terms 'Natural Magic', criticizing the 'credulous and superstitious conceits and observations of Sympathies and Antipathies and hidden properties, and some frivolous experiments, strange rather by disguisement than in themselves' (p. 201). For further discussion of Bacon's explorations of sympathy see Chapter 6, below.

[12] See Evrigenis, 'Sovereignty, mercy, and natural law', p. 1082.

[13] James I, *Basilikon Doron: Devided into three bookes* (Edinburgh, 1599), p. 157.

[14] *A counterblast to tobacco* (London, 1604), sigs C2v-C3r.

In this way, James demonstrates an awareness of the physiological understanding of the concept, and the extent to which sympathy could refer to a correspondence of 'griefe and smart' between parts of the body. In the same year, Robert Cawdry's *A table alphabeticall* (1604) defines *sympathie* as 'fellowelike feeling', which emphasizes the continuing prevalence of the affective understanding of term.[15] James's discussion does present sympathy as a 'sence of feeling' dispersed through the members of the state; yet his emphasis is political rather than emotional, and he uses the term to suggest a perfect sympathy and union between individual members of a healthy state.

And yet what James had encountered in the first year of his English reign was a rather more literal form of bodily disease and societal contagion. The year 1603 was undoubtedly one of mixed emotions in the country: James arrived in London on 7 May, but that summer London's citizens suffered a deadly attack of the plague. This outbreak was commemorated in William Muggins's *Londons Mourning garment, or Funerall Teares* (1603), a brief 'plague epic' that mourns the loss of nearly 40,000 citizens.[16] What is striking about this text is its emphasis upon the absence of sympathy and fellow-feeling between members of the commonwealth. It opens with an account of James's accession and his arrival in the city ('this day of joy'), but goes on to describe the coming of the plague and the populace's lack of pity.[17] London, personified as a woman, seeks out mourners to share in her sorrow:

> Drown'd in deepe seas (poore Lady) thus I lye,
> Unlesse some speedie helpe a comfort yeeld:
> Is there no wife nor widdow that will hye,
> And reach a hand that hath some sorrowes felt,
> My griefes are more then I my selfe can welde,
>   Helpe some good woman with your soules-sigh deepe,
>   For you are tender hearted and can weepe.   (sig. B1v)

And yet despite women being more 'tender hearted' than men there is no pity forthcoming. The narrator suggests that this proves the old proverb 'The widowes care is studious where to love' (sig. B2r). Death is likened

---

[15] Robert Cawdry, *A table alphabeticall conteyning and teaching the true writing, and understanding of hard usuall English wordes, borrowed from the Hebrew, Greeke, Latine, or French, &c.* (London, 1604), s.v. 'sympathie'.

[16] See Ernest B. Gilman, *Plague Writing in Early Modern England* (University of Chicago Press, 2009), Rebecca Totaro and Ernest B. Gilman, *Representing the Plague in Early Modern England* (London: Routledge, 2011), and Rebecca Totaro, *The Plague Epic in Early Modern England: Heroic Measures, 1603–1721* (Farnham: Ashgate, 2012).

[17] William Muggins, *Londons Mourning garment, or Funerall Teares* (London, 1603), sig. B1v.

to 'a greedy Wolf' who robs lambs from 'harmless Ewes', and 'no compassion shows' (sig. B3r); and compassion is in short supply across the city. One widow describes the deaths of her two daughters, and the reader is enjoined to imagine her pain: 'With lamentations, and with Teares good store, / Ymmagin now, you heare a Mothers griefe' (sig. C2r). However, the narrator can only present a sample of London's sorrows: 'Many more sorrowes might I here repeat, / Of grieved mothers for their children dear' (sig. C2v). Such losses are not confined to the poor citizens of the city but affect the rich as well: 'Shall they escape? No, the Plague will them not spare'. Moreover, there appears to be a lack of understanding between these different social ranks:

> If rich men dye, and poorer people stay,
> They will exclame with hate and deadly ire,
> Saying with surfets they consume the day,
> Wallowing in ease like dirtie Swyne in myre,
> Judging their scarcitie and their thinne atyre
>   The onely Phisicke, poysons to with stand,
>   But they like others have given death their hand.   (sig. C3v)

While this stanza suggests a division between rich and poor, other writers attempted to join readers together in a community of sorrow. As Thomas Dekker writes in *The wonderfull yeare* (1603), 'Joyne all your hands together, and with your bodies cast a ring about me: let me behold your ghastly vizages, that my paper may receive their true pictures: *Eccho* forth your grones through the hollow truncke of my pen, and raine downe your gummy teares into mine Incke, that even marble bosomes may be shaken with terrour, and hearts of Adamant melt into compassion'.[18] In this way, Dekker offers a more optimistic view of the capacity of his text to capture and channel people's suffering, and to move his readers in compassion in the process.

Such emotional and readerly unity is conspicuous by its absence in *Londons Mourning garment*. Most critics who have written about the text focus on the elegiac poem that forms its main body.[19] But the prayer addressed to God that is printed at the end of the text ('A godly and zealous Prayer unto God, for the surceasing of his irefull Plague, and grievous

---

[18] Thomas Dekker, 1603. *The wonderfull yeare. Wherein is shewed the picture of London lying sicke of the Plague* (London, 1603), sig. C3v.
[19] See Totaro, *The Plague Epic in Early Modern England*, pp. 15–25; see also Patricia Phillipy, 'London's Mourning Garment: Maternity, Mourning and Royal Succession in Shakespeare's *Richard III*', in *Women, Death, and Literature in Post-Reformation England* (Cambridge University Press, 2002), pp. 109–38.

Pestilence') is also of considerable interest. The speaker bemoans the lack of sympathy and compassion between the citizens:

> Where are our solemne meetings, and frequent assemblies: men stand a farre off: the Streates and high wayes mourne: trafficke ceaseth: marchandize decayeth: the craftes-man and cunning artificer is ashamed of his povertie … we have not comforted the weake and feeble knees, we have not wept with them that weepe. We have not had that sympathy, and fellow-feeling of each others miserie, which ought to bee in the members of Christ. (sig. D3v)

Sympathy is specifically used to refer to 'fellow-feeling of each others miserie'; yet this text laments a decline in sympathy, which 'ought' to exist between members of the Christian community. The picture painted here of Jacobean lockdown – a lack of community, meetings, and physical closeness – leads into a lament about the absence of sympathy and collective emotional response. Muggins reworks Romans 12:15, a biblical verse which, as we have already seen in previous chapters, was often cited in sermons from this period: 'Rejoice with them that rejoice, and weep with them that weep'. Muggins's anxiety about a lack of sympathy in society had existed previously; for example, the Church of Scotland minister Robert Rollock (1555–99) offers a despairing disquisition on the lack of people who feel this emotion:

> It is the sense of misery that makes any bodie to weepe: No doubt when one weepes sore, the heart hath a sense of misery: and this sense is either of a mans owne misery, or for a sympathie of the miserie of another. They who have a sense of the miserie of others, they will mourne. I see fewe of this sort in these dayes. There are few now that will weepe for the misery of another. All sympathie is out of the world, and the pleasure of men is in the pleasure of others. Indeede I thinke that Jesus condemned not this compassion.[20]

Like Muggins, Rollock is pessimistic about the idea that such sympathy, which he describes so eloquently, is actually put into practice. All sympathy, he suggests, is 'out of the world'. This does appear to be a recurrent trope in early modern religious writings on compassion, which may be explained in part by reference to the Reformation, and what Kristine Steenbergh has called 'the disappearance of traditional habits of charitable giving and compassionate meditation'.[21] We might also, however, suggest that there

---

[20] Robert Rollock, *Lectures, upon the history of the Passion, Resurrection, and Ascension of our Lord Jesus Christ* (Edinburgh, 1616), p. 172.
[21] Kristine Steenbergh, 'Mollified Hearts and Enlarged Bowels: Practising Compassion in Reformation England', in Kristine Steenbergh and Katherine Ibbett (eds.), *Compassion in Early Modern Literature and Culture: Feeling and Practice* (Cambridge University Press, 2021), pp. 121–38 (p. 122).

is a perennially nostalgic element in all discussions of sympathy, whereby writers invariably tend to feel that the age before their own was more compassionate. Yet this feeling must have intensified during the plague of 1603, when public meetings were cancelled and infected citizens were confined to their homes, potentially increasing the sense of atomization described by Muggins.[22] On the one hand, then, sympathy in this period is increasingly regarded as an active process, which offers individuals a greater degree of agency in their emotional lives. On the other hand, however, individuals are not necessarily as compassionate as they should be: sympathy turns out to be optional rather than automatic.

This awareness of the elective aspects of sympathy is reflected in other works that advised the monarch to feel compassion for his subjects – although once again there is some ambiguity as to whether such feelings were part of natural law or required cultivation and instruction. William Thorne's *Esoptron basilikon. Or A kenning-glasse for a Christian king* (1603) is an English sermon addressed to the King, which offers an extended interpretation of Pontius Pilate's words 'behold the man' (John 19:5):

> Now againe by way of exhortation, *Behold the man*. And that the eye of our faith may have some certaine object, wheron to fixe and setle it selfe; Behold him first *in his life and actions;* Secondly in his *death and passion;* Thirdly in *his session* at the right hand of God his father, & *intercession*. In the actions of his life behold him with a zealous, yet *sober eye* of *imitation;* In his death and passion, behold him with the eye of *Sympathie and compassion;* In his session, and intercession, beholde him with the eye of *affiance* and *consolation*.[23]

We should imitate Christ; as Thorne puts it, '*The actions* of Christ (say the Fathers in generall) are a Christians imitations: *The summe of Christian* Religion (saith *Augustine*) is to *imitate* Christ'. Such sentiments are addressed to both monarch and subjects: individuals should feel sympathy for Christ, but he, in turn, teaches us to be sympathetic. The idea that the ruler should feel sympathy and compassion for his subjects is made more explicit in Edward Forset's *A comparative discourse of the bodies natural and politique* (1606). Like Bacon and other political writers of the period, Forset invokes the idea of the body politic, using it here as a way of reflecting upon, and advising, the compassionate monarch:

---

[22] F. P. Wilson notes that 'All public meetings, feasts, and assemblies were now being postponed ... Ceremonies not absolutely necessary to the coronation were deferred on 6 July' (*The Plague in Shakespeare's London* (Oxford University Press, 1963), p. 92).

[23] William Thorne, *Esoptron basilikon. Or A kenning-glasse for a Christian king* (London, 1603), p. 26.

> We see the head naturally endued with a fellow feeling of any the griefes in the whole bodie, in so much as there is scant any disease so weake or small in any part, as doth not affect and disturbe the head also; yea, it holdeth such a sympathie with the verie foot, as that a little wet or cold taken in that remotest place, hath forthwith a readie passage to the head. Gracious Soveraignes have the like compassions and compunctions in the distresses of their subjects, and be in the same sort deeply peirced & perplexed with any wrong or distemperatures, hapning to the meanest of their people.[24]

This passage is summarised in a succinct marginal note: 'Soveraignes have a sympathie with subjects'. Forset thus presents the monarch's sympathy as part of natural law; he feels a sensitive sympathy for the suffering or injustice afflicting his subjects, including the most lowly.[25] But this analogy also offers the sovereign a convenient get-out clause, inasmuch as doctors have, according to Forset, proposed that diseases of the mind arise from the body: 'I have learned of the Phisitions, that most of the diseases of the head, are originally arising and caused from the bodie: and I think that I may thus thereof infer; That many the escapes of Soveraignes by omission or comission, may thus far by this excuse be extenuated, as more imputable to the people than to them' (p. 28). In this way, the workings of sympathy are usefully ambiguous in Forset's account; he uses the concept as a way of exonerating sovereigns by proposing that their 'escapes' – that is, their errors or transgressions – can be blamed on a disease caught from their subjects.

The figure of the compassionate ruler is imagined and represented in several plays from the period, including William Alexander's closet drama *The Tragedy of Croesus*, one of *The monarchick tragedies* (1604), which was dedicated to the King. This play reflects James's advice back at him, inasmuch as the wisdom of the counsellor Solon recalls some of the ideas in *Basilikon Doron*.[26] Yet *Croesus* also considers the monarch's emotional

---

[24] Edward Forset, *A comparative discourse of the bodies natural and politique* (London, 1606), p. 27. The tract also makes the case for union with Scotland, again employing a bodily analogy: 'Have we not had within this one land of England, the hideous Heptarchie of seven heads at once? nay hath not the whole Iland of *Britania*, being a bodie perfectly shaped, rounded, and bounded with an invironing sea, beene a long time thus dissevered, and disfigured by that unluckie dualitie the authour of division?' (p. 58).

[25] See Lobis, *The Virtue of Sympathy*, p. 21; and Amanda Bailey, 'Speak What We Feel: Sympathy and Statecraft', in Amanda Bailey and Mario DiGangi (eds.), *Affect Theory and Early Modern Texts: Politics, Ecologies, and Form* (New York: Palgrave Macmillan, 2017), pp. 27–46 (p. 37). On the limitations of such bodily analogies see J. P. Somerville, *Royalists and Patriots: Politics and Ideology in England, 1603–1640*, 2nd ed. (London and New York: Routledge, 1999), pp. 52–3.

[26] See Rickard, *Authorship and Authority*, p. 35; and Astrid Stilma, *A King Translated: The Writings of King James VI & I and Their Interpretation in the Low Countries, 1593–1603* (Farnham: Ashgate, 2012), pp. 244–5.

state and his sympathy with his subjects. In Act 3, Adrastus attempts to decipher the 'mighty passion' written on Croesus' face:

> Whence (mighty Soveraigne) can this change proceede,
> That doth obscure the rayes of princely grace?
> Those that are school'd in wo may clearly reede
> A mighty passion written in your face;
>   And if a stranger may presume so farre,
> I would the copie of your passions borrow,
> I else conjecture in what state you are,
> Taught by secret sympathie in sorrow.
>   Two strings in divers Lutes set in accord,
> (Although th'one be but toucht) together found,
> Even so souls tun'd to griefe the like afford,
> And other with a mutuall motion wound.[27]

Having noted the change in Croesus's demeanour, Adrastus attempts to 'conjecture' his emotional state. Invoking the idea of 'secret sympathie', Adrastus likens their shared grief to the sympathetic vibrations caused when the strings of different lutes resonate with each other. While it may be presumptuous for a subject to enquire after the monarch's innermost thoughts and feelings, Croesus admits that such sympathy 'disburdens much the mind' and describes Adrastus as 'A Secretarie in distress' (sig. E1r). Croesus states that he has had a disturbing dream in which his son, Atys, is killed. Adrastus then reveals that he has a sad story to tell, which 'may move stones to teares' (sig. E2r). It transpires that he was banished from Phrygia after accidentally killing his brother, having mistaken him for a man who poisoned his lover. Croesus suggests that such 'rare mischances / Would force compassion from your greatest foe, / Where all the griefe-begetting circumstances / Doe joyne to make a harmony in woe' (sig. E4r). Yet, despite this sympathy of grief, Croesus resolves to prevent his son's death rather than dwell on past miseries. In this way, the play explores and acknowledges the ways in which there can be a 'harmony in woe' between the monarch and his subjects, especially if their situations are comparable.

Even more suggestive, perhaps, is the play's treatment of compassion in the following scene (3.2), when Croesus encounters a chorus of countrymen. These figures admit their poverty, but suggest they are nevertheless part of the commonwealth, and thus have a connection with the monarch: 'As vile as our estate is thought of now / You are our head, and we are of your members, / And you must care for us, we care for you' (sig. E4v). Croesus is happy to hear their complaint, in spite of their baseness:

[27] William Alexander, *The monarchick tragedies* (London, 1604), sig. D4r.

> Be not discourag'd by your base estate,
> Yee are my people, and I'le heare your plaint,
> A King must care for all, both small and great,
> And for to helpe th'afflicted never faint.
>   The Scepter such as these should chiefely shrowd,
> Not cotages, but Castles spoile the Land,
> T'advance the humble and t'abate the prowd;
> This is a Vertue that makes Kings to stand.   (sig. F1r)

This speech may read like thinly veiled advice directed at James; it implies that it is the monarch's duty to care for all his subjects, and to help the afflicted. This is, of course, familiar advice to monarchs from the classical period onwards.[28] Yet the juxtaposition of such advice with the emotional bond between Croesus and Adrastus offers a potentially radical picture of monarchical sympathy. This is not simple mercy, in which the monarch feels pity for subjects lower down the social ladder; rather the play posits a bond of compassion and care between the monarch, state, and people. It implies an emotional equivalence between the monarch and his subjects, which is expressed in the parallel phrases of their language ('you must care for us, we care for you'). Such a bond works both ways; when Atys is indeed killed later in the play, Croesus's counsellor Sandanis states that the country grieves with him: 'This crosse with you alike your Countrie beares' (sig. H2r). Croesus must put aside his grief for the good of the nation: 'Have pitie of your people, spare your selfe, / If not to your owne use, yet unto ours' (sig. H2v). It is a tragic irony that James himself would later find himself in a similar predicament, mourning the loss of his son Prince Henry, while the nation was encouraged to participate in his grief. Croesus seeks relief in terms that recall Shakespeare's *Lucrece*: 'make me to forgoe sad thoughts content, / Or els acquire copartners in my griefe, / If not for me, yet with me to lament' (sig. H2v). Whether or not this is a conscious echo of Shakespeare's *Lucrece*, there is no doubt that Alexander's play – with its interest in the emotional bonds between monarchs and subjects, and the politics of compassion – shares several key concerns with Shakespeare's other works, in particular his most significant dramatic tragedy from this period.[29]

---

[28] See Tuckness and Parrish, *The Decline of Mercy in Public Life*, esp. ch. 4. The phrase 'T'advance the humble and t'abate the prowd' is an allusion to a passage from Virgil's *Aeneid*, which is also quoted on the final page of *Basilicon Doron* (p. 154). See Rickard, *Writing the Monarch in Jacobean England: Jonson, Donne, Shakespeare and the Works of King James* (Cambridge University Press, 2015), pp. 62–3.

[29] As Lucrece puts it, 'So should I have co-partners in my pain' (789). See also Theophilus Field, *An Italians dead bodie, stucke with English flowers elegies, on the death of Sir Oratio Pallauicino* (London, 1600), which addresses the dead man's 'much honoured Lady, the Lady *Pallauicino*', stating that the book itself is a 'perfect mourner' and 'will be copartner of your griefe' (sig. B3r).

'[T]he art of known and feeling sorrows':
Shakespeare's *The History of King Lear*

The political aspects of sympathy described above are explored and extended in Shakespeare's *The History of King Lear* (1608), which was likely performed in front of the King in 1606. According to the title page of the 1608 quarto, this performance took place at Whitehall upon St Stephen's Day, which was 'the holiday most associated with the granting of traditional hospitality', when 'the high were to look out in pity upon the tribulations of the low'.[30] The play thus raises further questions about the role of compassion in the public sphere, and in particular whether there could be 'sympathy' between kings and beggars. For some recent critics, the play's interest in sympathy is evidence of an early modern preoccupation with cosmology. Gail Paster has argued that, in the world of *King Lear*, 'the question of how the cosmological bonds of sympathy and antipathy, desire and aversion, express themselves socially preoccupies everyone'.[31] Similarly, Leah Marcus has reconsidered the play as 'an investigation of vitalism – of the connections among things, the energy surging through things and people alike, thereby creating complex networks of sympathy and causality that can both sustain and destroy'.[32] It seems to me, however, that the play offers a rather more sceptical exploration of cosmological sympathies than these critics have suggested, and that Shakespeare presents us with a society in which human nature is increasingly understood as separate from 'Nature'. As with the political texts that we have already examined, the play does not simply present sympathy in terms of cosmology or magic but rather as a productive way of exploring the relationships between individuals in a commonwealth. But while the play's characters

---

[30] See Leah S. Marcus, *Puzzling Shakespeare: Local Reading and Its Discontents* (Berkeley: University of California Press, 1988), pp. 148–59 (p. 154). Marcus's new historicist account of the play argues that both Quarto and Folio versions 'can easily be interpreted as a dramatization of the perils of division' (p. 148), and 'an extended political exemplum promoting charity towards the Scots' (p. 154). See also Philip Schwyzer, 'The Jacobean Union Controversy and *King Lear*', in Glenn Burgess, Rowland Wymer, and Jason Lawrence (eds.), *The Accession of James I: Historical and Cultural Consequences* (London: Palgrave Macmillan, 2006), pp. 34–47, and Marie Theresa O'Connor, 'Why redistribute? The Jacobean Union Issue and *King Lear*', *Early Modern Literary Studies*, 91/1 (2016).

[31] Gail Kern Paster, 'Minded Like the Weather: The Tragic Body and Its Passions', in Neill and Schalkwyk (eds.), *The Oxford Handbook of Shakespearean Tragedy*, pp. 202–17 (p. 208). Drawing upon Timothy Reiss's term *passibility*, which suggests being both embedded in and acted upon, Paster suggests that 'The image of the cosmos and the passible self as its centre are never distant from the action of *King Lear*' (p. 208). This is part of her wider argument that 'early modern emotions belonged fully and seamlessly to the natural order' (p. 206).

[32] Leah S. Marcus, '*King Lear* and the Death of the World', in Neill and Schalkwyk (eds.), *The Oxford Handbook of Shakespearean Tragedy*, pp. 421–36 (p. 423).

constantly attempt to assume the emotional position or perspective of others they often fail to do so, suggesting that *King Lear* can be read as an essay on the problems and limitations of sympathy.

This anxiety regarding a lack of affinity between individuals is reflected in Edmund's description of 'unnaturalness between the child and the parent, death, dearth, dissolutions of ancient amities, divisions in state, menaces and maledictions against king and nobles, needless diffidences, banishment of friends, dissipation of cohorts, nuptial breaches, and I know not what' (2.134–9).[33] Admittedly, this is Edmund's cynical caricature of his father's astronomical beliefs; but it is nevertheless presented as plausible within the harsh world of the play. It is perhaps apt, then, that *King Lear* does not contain the word *sympathy*, but it does contain its opposite: *antipathy*.[34] In scene 7, Kent describes his disdain for Oswald, Goneril's steward, with whom he has just had an altercation: 'No contraries hold more antipathy / Than I and such a knave' (7.83–4). This is the only appearance of the word *antipathy* in Shakespeare's works, suggesting that *King Lear* is especially interested in 'Contrariety of feeling, disposition, or nature (between persons or things); natural contrariety or incompatibility' (*OED*, 1a). The word was relatively new at the time of the play's composition, and in early usages often appeared alongside *sympathy*.[35] The word could also suggest 'That which is contrary in nature' (*OED*, 3a), an especially suggestive meaning in the context of *King Lear*, which presents us with individuals whose belief in natural sympathies and antipathies is contrasted with those who resist such deterministic models of human nature.[36]

These contrasting philosophies are represented most starkly in the encounter between Gloucester and Edmund in scene 2. Gloucester describes

---

[33] Quotations are taken from Stanley Wells (ed.), *The History of King Lear* (Oxford University Press, 2000).

[34] See Seth Lobis, 'Sympathy and Antipathy in *King Lear*', in Roman Alexander Barton, Alexander Klaudies, and Thomas Micklich (eds.), *Sympathy in Transformation: Dynamics between Rhetorics, Poetics and Ethics* (Berlin and Boston: De Gruyter, 2018), pp. 89–107 (p. 89). Lobis pushes against recent ecologically inflected readings by arguing that, while the play 'suggests a naturalistic account of tragedy in terms of an ascendant, rogue antipathy, it also unsettles the assumption underlying it that sympathy and antipathy are objectively real, universally active principles' (p. 90).

[35] The *OED*'s first cited usage of *antipathy* is from 1601; yet John Bridges's *A defence of the government established in the Church of Englande for ecclesiasticall matters* (London, 1587) mentions both sympathy and antipathy in relation to the Greek physician and philosopher Empedocles: 'Empedocles among the heathen Philosophers, beholding the sympathie and antipathie that is in naturall creatures, and being moved with the admiration therof, concluded, that all things were done and undone, by concord and discord' (sigs ¶2v–¶3r).

[36] For an earlier study of the concept of 'Nature' in the play see John Danby, *Shakespeare's Doctrine of Nature: A Study of 'King Lear'* (London: Faber and Faber, 1948). Danby suggests that '*King Lear* can be regarded as a play dramatizing the meanings of the single word "Nature"' (p. 15).

the intimate relationship between self and the physical environment, and provides a cosmological explanation for current social antipathies:

> These late eclipses in the sun and moon portend no good to us. Though the wisdom of nature can reason thus and thus, yet nature finds itself scourged by the sequent effects. Love cools, friendship falls off, brothers divide; in cities mutinies, in countries discords, palaces treason, the bond cracked between son and father. (2.101–7)

According to Gloucester, while we might use human reason ('wisdom of nature') to explain these natural events scientifically, the natural world ('nature finds itself scourged'), which includes human beings, is nevertheless affected.[37] His sentiments express a common theme, derived from Matthew 10:21: 'And the brother shall betray the brother to death, and the father the son, and the children shall rise against *their* parents, and shall cause them to die'. But such concerns were given new urgency in the early 1600s in the light of the political upheavals and factionalism of Jacobean England, as well as the cultural and emotional responses to the plague. Like William Muggins and others who worried about a lack of sympathy, Gloucester laments a bygone age of unity and strong emotional bonds; he goes further by suggesting that these current divisions were predicted or even caused by the eclipses of the sun and moon.

At the same time, however, the play is highly sceptical about such explanations for human behaviour. Indeed it seems ironic that some recent critics of the play are adamant that *King Lear* represents sympathetic affinities between people and the world given that such beliefs are interrogated and ironised within the play itself.[38] Edmund in particular ridicules the idea that individuals are fiends or treacherous by 'spherical predominance' or an 'enforced obedience of planetary influence' (2.115–17). Thus, *pace* Gloucester, the play implies that whether we sympathize with others is a conscious choice. And yet, if we take the more sceptical view that a belief in magical sympathies is an 'admirable evasion of whoremaster man' (118–19) then we find ourselves aligned with the cynical and manipulative Edmund, a character notable for his lack of pity and compassion. As is often the case with Shakespeare, he displays an ironic scepticism regarding earlier models and theories of nature – including human nature – while simultaneously cautioning against the 'modern' alternative.

---

[37] See Jay L. Halio (ed.), *The Tragedy of King Lear* (Cambridge University Press, 1992), note to 1.2.92–3.
[38] See especially Paster, 'Minded Like the Weather'.

The most important filial bond cracked within the play is that between King Lear and Cordelia, which is not only its emotional centre but also the trigger for its subsequent plot. Lear invokes 'all the operation of the orbs, / From whom we do exist and cease to be' (1.103–4) when he disclaims his paternal care towards Cordelia, suggesting that he, like Gloucester, has considerable faith in the power of celestial bodies to determine human lives. Yet he soon discovers that an excessive faith in essential nature is misplaced. Having fallen out with Goneril following a disagreement regarding his retinue, Lear hopes that Regan will be generous and tender-hearted: 'No, Regan. Thou shalt never have my curse. / Thy tender-hested nature shall not give / Thee o'er to harshness. Her eyes are fierce, but thine / Do comfort and not burn' (7.327–30). Lear's unusual adjectival formulation ('tender-hested') suggests that Regan has a delicate frame or bodily nature.[39] He states optimistically that Regan, unlike Goneril, better knows 'The offices of nature, bond of childhood, / Effects of courtesy, dues of gratitude' (334–6). Unfortunately for Lear, however, his assumption that Regan has a particular 'nature' that respects these courteous bonds, does not apply to her – or necessarily to women more generally.

Regan declines Lear's request to remain with her, along with his hundred knights, suggesting that he listen to Goneril: 'For those that mingle reason with your passion / Must be content to think that you are old, and so – / But she knows what she does' (391–3). Here Regan recommends that Lear reign in his emotions, setting up a distinction between his passionate appeals and the rationality of his daughters. This results in Lear's highly emotional speech in which he enjoins his daughters to 'reason not the need', arguing that even 'basest beggars / Are in the poorest thing superfluous' (423–4). Subjugated by his daughters, the monarch implicitly compares himself to the lowest citizens of the kingdom. His best argument is to present himself as 'a poor old fellow, / As full of grief as age, wretchèd in both' (430–1). He suggests that, if the gods have stirred his daughters' hearts 'Against their father', they should touch him with 'noble anger' rather than tears, which he dismisses as 'women's weapons' that would stain his 'man's cheeks' (434–6). Thus, as Lear's belief in his daughters' compassionate nature is shaken, his sense of his own authority and masculinity is similarly undermined.

For both the play's characters and some of its critics the storm not only reflects but also interacts with Lear's emotional state.[40] The First Gentleman

---

[39] The *OED* suggests 'set in a delicate "haft" or bodily frame; hence, womanly, gentle' (*OED*, 'tender', adj., C2, citing this passage).

[40] Wells, for example, writes that the storm 'is also within Lear himself: the external tempest figures that which rages in Lear's mind' (note to 7.441.1).

who appears at the start of scene 8 in the Quarto makes an explicit analogy between microcosm and macrocosm: Lear, he suggests, 'Strives in his little world of man to outscorn / The to-and-fro-conflicting wind and rain' (8.9–10). And, for Leah Marcus, 'King Lear's madness and the contest of the elements are best understood as a fragile, temporary mutually reinforcing system of vibrating sympathies: the king rages along with the storm and the storm rages along with the king; they are communicating with each other'.[41] I would suggest, however, that the play is also interested in the extent to which human beings project their passions onto the surrounding environment – including other people. The Fool suggests that the night, like Lear's daughters, is devoid of pity: 'Good nuncle, in, and ask thy daughters blessing. Here's a night pities neither wise man nor fool' (9.11–13). Lear continues with this analogy but acknowledges that the elements are not the same as his daughters: 'I task not you, you elements, with unkindness. / I never gave you kingdom, called you children' (16–17). Clearly there are limits to this sort of analogical thinking. And yet, even as Lear's sense of self starts to collapse he sees his predicament in relation to that of the other – in this case the Fool: 'My wits begin to turn. / (*To Fool*) Come on, my boy. How dost, my boy? Art cold? / I am cold myself. – Where is this straw, my fellow?' (68–70). He enquires after the Fool's temperature, then notes that he is cold himself, referring to the Fool as his 'fellow'.[42] Whether or not this moment marks the point when Lear becomes aware of the sufferings of others, as some critics have suggested, it does seem to suggest Lear's concern and fellow-feeling for the other rather than a preoccupation with the self.[43]

These questions are heightened in scene 11, in which Lear and his companions take shelter in a hovel. This scene may recall the moment in Alexander's *Croesus* when the King hears the complaints of his poverty-stricken subjects; although here King Lear is prompted to imagine the sufferings of wretches rather than encountering them directly:

> Poor naked wretches, whereso'er you are,
> That bide the pelting of this pitiless storm,
> How shall your houseless heads and unfed sides,
> Your looped and windowed raggedness, defend you
> From seasons such as these? O, I have ta'en

---

[41] Marcus, '*King Lear* and the Death of the World', p. 426.
[42] Lear seems to be using the term in the obsolete sense of 'A person who partakes *of* a specified action, condition, etc.; a participant, a contributor; a sharer' (*OED*, 'fellow', 1c).
[43] Halio quotes the New Shakespeare editors, who suggest that 'From this point he [Lear] becomes aware of the sufferings of others' (note to 3.2.65).

> Too little care of this. Take physic, pomp,
> Expose thyself to feel what wretches feel,
> That thou mayst shake the superflux to them
> And show the heavens more just. (11.25–33)

The term *physic* suggests a medical treatment such as a purge, although even in the early seventeenth century the term could be understood in a figurative as well as a literal sense.[44] What Lear prescribes for himself – and implicitly other monarchs as well – is experiencing the sufferings of the poor. Feeling what wretches feel means that he is able to give them his unnecessary possessions: 'shake the superflux to them' (32). Such an action will demonstrate that the heavens are more just than we realise. It is tempting, then, to interpret this speech as a celebration of compassion, and the ways in which experiencing suffering can lead to sympathy for others. Sarah Skwire has offered an optimistic reading of the play along these lines:

> Shakespeare's *King Lear* suggests that what is needed in order for some individuals to learn to sympathize is a radical course of 'physic' in the form of directly experiencing the sufferings of others for oneself. For Lear, the practice of sympathy is such a difficult exercise that only the loss of everything – kingdom, family, servants, and wealth – can force him to learn it.[45]

Arguably, however, the play's presentation of sympathy is rather more ambiguous and complex than Skwire suggests. Her reading recalls the twentieth-century critical commonplace that Lear learns to be a better person by going through a terrible ordeal.[46] What is particularly ironic about this speech is that, immediately afterwards, Lear is confronted with a 'beggar' – in the form of Edgar, disguised as Poor Tom. We might expect Lear to have a newfound understanding of a beggar's state:

> EDGAR Away, the foul fiend follows me. Through the sharp
>   hawthorn blows the cold wind. Go to thy cold bed and warm thee.
> LEAR
>   Hast thou given all to thy two daughters?
>   And art thou come to this? (11.40–44)

---

[44] The term could suggest 'A medicinal substance; *spec*. a cathartic, a purgative' (*OED*, 1), as well as a 'Mental, moral, or spiritual remedy; an instance of this' (*OED*, 2b).
[45] Sarah Skwire, '"Take Physic, Pomp": King Lear Learns Sympathy', in Schliesser (ed.), *Sympathy: A History*, pp. 139–45 (p. 145).
[46] As Kenneth Muir writes in his Arden 2 edition, 'His prolonged agony and his utter loss of everything free his heart from the bondage of the self hood … He loses the world and gains his soul' ('Introduction' to *King Lear* (London: Methuen, 1972), p. l).

Poor Tom states that he is afflicted by a 'foul fiend' and the weather; but Lear assumes that Tom's situation is the result of giving away all of his possessions to his daughters. This exchange would appear to be an example of self-recognition, in which Lear projects his own predicament onto this unfortunate wretch.

In this way, the play exposes the ethical and philosophical problems involved in emotional perspective-taking. Lear's encounter with Poor Tom involves what Jason Kerr has recently described as a 'quandary of over-identification'.[47] This moment thus raises the larger philosophical question of how much sympathizers can or should identify with others, and the extent to which they retain their own identity in the process. This question is also addressed by Terry Eagleton, who notes that some philosophers have argued that an empiricist form of sympathy – in which we copy or reflect others' emotions – 'can be no sound basis for morality, since it is always bound to betray a self-regarding subtext'. But, despite this potential for self-recognition or self-interest, Eagleton prefers sympathy (which he characterises as 'feeling *for*') over empathy ('feeling'). He suggests that, while empathy involves becoming the other 'by an act of imaginative identification', and thus suspends the self that is seeking to exercise compassion, sympathy implies 'the existence of distinct identities'.[48] Yet Shakespeare's play demonstrates the difficulty of sympathizing with the other – particularly when it is across class boundaries – and suggests that some degree of imaginative identification or perspective-taking is necessary. As we have seen, King Lear expresses his desire to feel what others feel but is unable to escape his own identity and perspective. At the same time, however, the play queries the very notion of 'distinct identities' inasmuch as Edgar is an individual of high status pretending to be a man of low birth. Shakespeare implies that practising sympathy without either losing one's own identity or projecting it upon the other can be challenging – especially if the other is performing a role. In other words, this episode seems concerned to dramatize the limits of compassion and the problems of intersubjectivity.

Like other early seventeenth-century texts, then, *King Lear* acknowledges the possibility of sympathy between kings and beggars but falls short

---

[47] Jason A. Kerr, 'The Tragedy of Kindness in *King Lear*', *Studies in English Literature, 1500–1900*, 61 (2021), 45–64 (p. 54).

[48] Terry Eagleton, *Sweet Violence: The Idea of the Tragic* (Oxford: Blackwell, 2003), p. 156. See also Eagleton's more recent study, *Tragedy* (New Haven and London: Yale University Press, 2020). For further discussion of the ethics of sympathy and empathy see Neil Roughley and Thomas Schramme (eds.), *Forms of Fellow Feeling: Empathy, Sympathy, Concern and Moral Agency* (Cambridge University Press, 2018).

of representing Lear sympathizing with an 'actual' beggar. The question of whether a monarch can sympathize with his subjects is also reversed in the play. In scene 13, Edgar describes the importance of feeling pity for those further up the social ladder:

> When we our betters see bearing our woes,
> We scarcely think our miseries our foes.
> Who alone suffers suffers most i'th' mind,
> Leaving free things and happy shows behind:
> But then the mind much sufferance doth o'erskip,
> When grief hath mates, and bearing fellowship.
> How light and portable my pain seems now,
> When that which makes me bend makes the King bow.
> He childed as I fathered. (13.95–103)

Edgar's speech offers a fairly optimistic reading of sympathy and suffering: when we see our betters suffering similar affliction we no longer see our miseries as foes, and endure them more easily.[49] Fellowship in woe, Edgar suggests, makes one's pain seem 'portable' or endurable. Edgar's formulation – 'He childed as I fathered' – emphasizes the similarity between his situation and that of Lear: the King has been mistreated by his daughters, and Edgar by his father. Once again, however, this speech is somewhat misleading in finding equivalence between their situation – after all, Gloucester is not Goneril or Regan. Even if the subplot comments upon the main plot the two stories are not precisely the same. As Kent puts it to Lear, 'He hath no daughters, sir' (11.62).

Shakespeare's interest in the relationship between sympathy and social hierarchy is further explored in scene 15, when Edgar encounters the blinded Gloucester. Gloucester is addressed by Edgar in disguise; but it is striking that it is Gloucester who feels pity for Edgar-Tom. He even finds solace in the fact that his unfortunate predicament may offer Poor Tom some consolation – that is, he imagines seeing himself from Tom's perspective – and this moves Gloucester to an act of charity:

> Here, take this purse, thou whom the heavens' plagues
> Have humbled to all stroke. That I am wretched
> Makes thee the happier. Heavens deal so still.
> Let the superfluous and lust-dieted man
> That slaves your ordinance, that will not see
> Because he doth not feel, feel your power quickly.
> So distribution should undo excess,
> And each man have enough. (15.62–9)

[49] See Wells's note to 13.95–6.

This speech recalls Lear's earlier speech regarding 'physic'. We thus have two sympathetic speeches that mirror each other: we are encouraged to equate Lear's sympathy for the poor with Gloucester's sympathy for Edgar.[50] This speech has a more explicitly religious aspect, inasmuch as Gloucester hopes that the heavens will feel the justice of God. It also echoes the parable of Dives and Lazarus in its concern with the rich helping the poor.[51] Men that have too much and are living on a diet of lust, or have ignored God's ordinance, are also those that do not experience sympathy or compassion. The man who does not 'feel' – usually glossed by editors as 'sympathize' – will feel God's power. The radical argument here is that possessions should be redistributed so that each man has enough.[52] This proposed exchange of wealth and possessions can thus be seen as a metaphor for, or an extension of, the transferral of emotion and sympathy between people of different social groups. Once again, however, this speech is undercut by the fact that Edgar is not the poverty-stricken individual that he appears to be; once again, the sympathy represented here is imaginary or misplaced.

Nevertheless, such compassionate comparability and transference is powerfully articulated elsewhere in the play, such as the First Gentleman's description of King Lear's madness as 'A sight most pitiful in the meanest wretch, / Past speaking in a king' (20.193–4). Thus, due to his kingly status, Lear's plight – which would be bad enough for the lowliest subject – is practically unspeakable. And yet, as with other statements in the play regarding the limits of language, the Gentleman is still able to articulate such sentiments.[53] In the same scene, in which Gloucester falls from an imagined cliff, Edgar takes on another disguise, and presents himself as

> A most poor man, made tame to fortune's blows,
> Who, by the art of known and feeling sorrows
> Am pregnant to good pity.   (20.213–15)

Edgar's statement further extends the play's interest in imaginative identification and class-based sympathy: is it necessary to experience the

---

[50] Lobis has also noted the similarity between the two speeches ('Sympathy and Antipathy in *King Lear*', p. 99).

[51] As Halio points out (note to 4.2.63), the marginal gloss in the Geneva Bible offers readers a summary of the tale's moral instruction: 'By this storie is declared what punishment thei shal have, which live deliciously & neglect the poor' (Luke 16:19).

[52] On the political implications of this speech see Peter Holbrook, 'The Left and *King Lear*', *Textual Practice*, 14 (2000), 343–62 (p. 353). Holbrook quotes A. C. Swinburne's comment that *Lear* reveals 'a sympathy with the mass of social misery more wide and deep and direct and bitter than Shakespeare has shown elsewhere' (p. 353).

[53] On this aspect of the play see, for example, Anne Barton, 'Shakespeare and the Limits of Language', rpt. in *Essays, Mainly Shakespearean* (Cambridge University Press, 1994), pp. 51–69.

afflictions of others in order to experience pity? Is this combination of knowledge and feeling – suggesting both sympathy and empathy – part of human nature or an 'art' that needs to be cultivated? Edgar's metaphor here involves pregnancy, suggesting that he is receptive to pity, or perhaps ready to give birth to pity. Danielle St Hilaire suggests that 'This pity is articulated through identification, where Edgar is "pregnant to good pity" because he recognizes in Gloucester the same suffering he has experienced'.[54] And yet, as I have been arguing, the play demonstrates that individuals never experience exactly the same suffering, and implies that a certain amount of imaginative work is necessary to bridge the gap between the self and the other. Indeed the fact that Edgar has taken on another fictional persona at this point further emphasizes the extent to which his 'known and feeling sorrows' are bound up with role-play and the imagination. Edgar's speech recalls the sentiments of Henry Holland, whose sermons describe the value of 'afflictions experience', which 'both worketh in me a Christian sympathie & compassion towards other men in their miseries, and teacheth mee how to comfort them as I have beene comforted of the Lorde'.[55] At the same time, however, the play suggests that simply erasing the difference between the self and the other is problematic. At the close of the scene Gloucester bemoans the fact that his 'vile sense' still offers him 'ingenious feeling / Of [his] huge sorrows!' (272–3). Better, he suggests, to be distraught, so that his thoughts 'be fencèd from my griefs', and his woes 'by wrong imaginations' should lose the 'knowledge of themselves' (274–6). But, by simply becoming mad, like the King, Gloucester would lose not only his ability to feel and comprehend his own woes but also his capacity to engage sympathetically with others.

Certainly the wronged Cordelia feels a considerable amount of pity and compassion for her father, despite his harsh treatment of her. Her forgiveness may skew our sense of Lear's culpability and blameworthiness; in a highly affecting recognition scene Cordelia shifts the blame onto her two sisters and suggests that it was precisely because he was their father that they did not pity him: 'Had you not been their father, these white flakes / Had challenged pity of them' (21.28–9). Interestingly, however, Cordelia does not seem to share Lear's sympathy for the poor, but rather pities Lear for having had to associate with them: 'And wast thou fain, poor father, /

---

[54] Danielle A. St Hilaire, 'Pity and the Failures of Justice in Shakespeare's *King Lear*', *Modern Philology*, 113 (2016), 482–506 (p. 503).

[55] Holland, *Spirituall preservatives against the pestilence* (London, 1603), sigs F3v-F4r. For further discussion of Holland see Chapter 2, above.

To hovel thee with swine and rogues forlorn / In short and musty straw?' (36–8). Cordelia even expresses surprise that this dreadful experience did not destroy Lear's 'life and wits at once' (39). What is also striking here is the way in which Lear perceives himself, and his plight, from the outside: 'Where have I been? Where am I? Fair daylight? / I am mightily abused. I should e'en die with pity, / To see another thus' (50–2). On the one hand, this utterance could be read as an expression of Lear's new-found sympathy for the other, suggesting that he would feel an inordinate amount of pity if he saw 'another' in his tragic position. On the other hand, however, Lear's statement could be read as an example of self-pity, focusing on his own predicament seen from the perspective of the other.[56]

This pity for Lear – which the play works hard to encourage in its concluding movement – is contrasted with the lack of pity for Goneril and Regan. In the final scene their bodies are brought out, and Albany describes how there is no sympathy or compassion for them: 'The justice of the heavens, that makes us tremble, / Touches us not with pity' (24.226–7). Thus Albany links the feelings of the characters on stage to heavenly justice, even implying that pity – and emotions more generally – derive from an external source. Alternatively, this may simply be Albany's suggestion that the judgement meted out to Goneril and Regan does not, or should not, produce pity in the onlookers.[57] The lack of pity for the two sisters is contrasted with Lear's demand for an emotional response to Cordelia's death: 'O, you are men of stones. / Had I your tongues and eyes, I would use them so / That heaven's vault should crack' (253–5). The play's editors generally suggest that Lear is describing the men as being 'like statues'.[58] But this moment also recalls Shakespeare's earlier tragedy, *Titus Andronicus*, when Titus suggests that he might as well 'tell [his] sorrows to the stones' (3.1.37), which are a better audience than the unsympathetic Tribunes.[59] This comparison of men to senseless stones is taken further in *King Lear*, not least because there is a metadramatic aspect to

---

[56] For an important exploration of 'acknowledgement' in the play, and the way in which such acknowledgement involves recognition of the other's relation to the self, see Stanley Cavell, 'The Avoidance of Love: A Reading of *King Lear*', in *Disowning Knowledge in Seven Plays of Shakespeare*, updated ed. (Cambridge University Press, 2003), pp. 39–124. See also Stephen Mulhall, *Stanley Cavell: Philosophy's Recounting of the Ordinary* (Oxford University Press, 1994), p. 132.
[57] Wells suggests that this is Shakespeare invoking the Aristotelian notion of catharsis, and pity and fear (note to 24.226–7). But see Stephen Halliwell's chapter on 'Tragic Pity: Aristotle and Beyond', in which he notes that Aristotle 'provides no definition of these emotions, still less of their peculiarly tragic combination' (*The Aesthetic of Mimesis*, ch. 7 (p. 217)).
[58] See Wells's note to 24.253 and Halio's note to 5.3.231.
[59] See Chapter 3, above.

Figure 6 Print made by James Barry, *King Lear and Cordelia* (1776), Etching and aquatint with India ink, published state, Yale Center for British Art, Paul Mellon Collection, B1977.14.11064.

Lear's comment: on one level he is addressing the onstage audience but his comments could also refer to the offstage audience watching the play itself. Lear describes an emotional response that he thinks is not forthcoming; we might say that there is a disjunction, or even antipathy, between how Lear feels, and the apparent reaction of those around him. Lear expresses the extent of his own grief through imagining himself watching this scene as a spectator.

The responses of the onstage audience are depicted in one of the most celebrated visual responses to the play: James Barry's *King Lear Weeping over the Dead Body of Cordelia* (1786–88). What is interesting for our purposes is that Barry was responding to Lear's address to the onlookers, quoted above. In an etching based on the smaller 1774 version of the painting (Figure 6) these lines are included underneath the image, indicating the specific moment of the play being represented. But while Lear emphasizes the lack of compassion for his plight, Barry depicts Kent (flanked by two other soldiers), looking directly at Lear and partaking in his grief. Barry thus implies that Lear's statement does not necessarily describe the responses of those around him – and may even work to elicit their sympathy. Barry's later (and much larger) painting depicts a greater number of figures and diversity of responses: for example, it includes another older man – depicted alongside the compassionate Kent – who is clearly weeping.[60] It also features Albany and Edgar, placed in the centre of this larger composition, who appear more confounded than compassionate. Scott Paul Gordon has argued that the larger painting celebrates the Grecian style and stoical response of these younger men over the 'sentimental politics' of Lear and Kent.[61] It seems to me, however, that even this version does not necessarily prioritise stoicism over sentiment. Rather it offers an ambivalent response to the play's ending and acknowledges the potentially disparate emotional responses of those watching this tragic scene. It highlights the complexity of Lear's statement, and the ways in which his pessimistic characterization of the spectators' response might shape that response in different ways.

King Lear ends, then, with another act of imaginative substitution: if Lear was in the position of an onlooker he would make such a sorrowful noise that it would crack the vault of heaven. Lear's statement thus recollects Hamlet's extraordinary response to the Player's speech, in which he imagines the Player's passionate reaction were he to find himself in Hamlet's situation: 'He would drown the stage with tears, / And cleave the general ear with horrid speech'.[62] But while Hamlet imagines an idealised performance of his own part, Lear imagines an idealised audience responding to his tragedy. Lear imaginatively changes places not only with his subjects within the fiction but also with the audience members watching Shakespeare's play. Yet the fact that he describes a lack of pity on the part of the audience – whether onstage or offstage – taps into the questions of class and status I have been tracing, and points to the ways in which wider cultural anxieties regarding the practice of sympathy underlie Shakespeare's representation of the King. As we shall see below, the Folio text of the play is even more pessimistic than the Quarto regarding the possibility of emotional engagement across social boundaries.

---

[60] See the cover image.
[61] Scott Paul Gordon, 'Reading Patriot Art: James Barry's *King Lear*', *Eighteenth-Century Studies*, 36 (2003), 491–509 (p. 505).
[62] *Hamlet*, 2.2.514–15. See my discussion of the soliloquy in '*Hamlet* and the Imitation of Emotion', pp. 90–94.

'Heart, tongue, and eyes, and ev'rie sense did joine, / In equall simpathie': Constructing Sympathy in the Public Sphere

If Shakespeare's *King Lear* explores the problems faced by a monarch trying to imagine himself in the position of his subjects, another momentous political event in this period prompted an outpouring of sympathy from the subjects to the monarch. In November 1612, King James's eldest son and great hope of the nation, Prince Henry, died of typhoid fever. This was an event with considerable political and emotional significance; as Adrian Streete puts it, 'Henry had been the focus of militant Protestant expectations' and was 'everything that his pacific father was not, particularly in his apparent willingness to assert Britain's authority abroad'.[63] Yet he was also something of a blank space onto which Jacobean subjects could project their own fantasies for the nation. It is thus understandable that the various elegies that were printed to commemorate his death reflect upon, and give voice to, its emotional impact. Indeed for our purposes it is especially striking that several of these works invoke the concept of sympathy to describe the transference of compassion from subjects – not only the writer of the elegy but also the nation as a whole – to the King. In this way, these texts enact and explore the hierarchical and political forms of sympathy addressed in other Jacobean texts.

Christopher Brooke's *Two elegies* is particularly concerned to invoke the idea of Nature in its description of the 'publique Miserie' following Henry's death.[64] Brooke emphasizes the extremity of this tragedy: 'so DEATH (prepostrously) / To snatch a Kingdomes hope, gainst *Natures* Lawes / So Deare, so Young; begets extremitie / Beyond Loves ordinary course of teares, / Such Passion swallowes Pitie up in Feares' (sig. B1v). Henry's death is thus so preposterous and against the laws of nature that 'Pitie' itself is swallowed up. Brooke goes on to extol Henry's virtues in terms of delightful harmony:

> His LIFE, and LIVES delight, was harmonie;
> Whose Organs and whose Instruments were found
> Upon his PARTS in contrarietie,
> To make sweete Musique upon NATURES ground:

---

[63] See Adrian Streete, 'Elegy, Prophecy, and Politics: Literary Responses to the Death of Prince Henry Stuart, 1612–1614', *Renaissance Studies*, 31 (2017), 87–106 (pp. 87–8). See also Dennis Kay, *Melodious Tears: The English Funeral Elegy from Spenser to Milton* (Oxford: Clarendon Press, 1990), ch. 5.

[64] Christopher Brooke, *Two elegies: consecrated to the never-dying memorie of the most worthily admyred; most hartily loved; and generally bewayled prince; Henry Prince of Wales* (London, 1612), sig. B1r.

> But TIME too timelesse in this Sympathie,
> Hasting his Cloze, this heav'nly SPIRIT hath wound
> Up to the Spheres, and Orbs Celestiall,
> HEE was in NATURE so Angelicall. (sig. B3v)

Here Brooke invokes the two ideas of Nature we saw in *King Lear*: nature as one's constitution and the natural world. Henry's life, he suggests, was characterised by a kind of perfect harmony between his organs and contrary parts; now that his untimely death has occurred he has returned to the heavenly spheres above where he belongs. This stanza thus uses the term *Sympathie* to refer to the blissful harmony generated by Henry while still alive. The concept is also invoked later in the context of people's love for him: 'To him all IRON harts began to turne; / For he was Load-stone to all Harts desire' (sig. C2r). Henry is thus figured as a kind of loadstone that naturally attracted the iron hearts of the people. Similarly, they will all unite in mourning his demise: 'For HIM all Sexes and Degrees doe mourne; / And ever shall we (till our Breathes expire) / Embalme his VERTUES' (sig. C2r). In this way, men and women of all degrees mourn Henry and will continue to do so – at least until their breath expires. Brooke proposes that his readers are also united in communal mourning, which is both figured in and prompted by the poem itself.

The idea of a national shared sorrow is also invoked in Thomas Rogers's *Gloucesters myte* (1612), which describes the woe of the King and Queen, their children, and the populace at large: 'A King most humbly su'd, with teares of woe, / A Queen deepe plung'd in flouds of equal strife, / A Prince and Princesse (and a Million moe) / Made supplication for a Peerelesse life'.[65] In this way, the shared grief extends from the Royal family to the whole nation. The poem then describes the shared mourning that followed Henry's death:

> Heart, tongue, and eyes, and ev'rie sense did joine,
> In equall simpathie, of equall sorrow:
> And with one stampe, their equall grief did coine,
> Each one of other, equally did borrow.
>   And (as th' Apothecary) they were found,
>   Of manies sorrow, to make one compound. (sig. B3r)

The usage here is more explicitly emotional than in Brooke's elegy; it describes the 'equall simpathie' and 'equall sorrow' between the mourners

---

[65] Thomas Rogers, *Gloucesters myte* (London, 1612), sig. B2v. Like Brooke, Rogers describes Henry's magnetic powers: 'Loves zeale commands, we shal not leave thee yet / Thou like the *Loadstone*, doest draw the mind' (sig. B4r).

at Henry's funeral. Through the repetition of the term *equall* the poem associates the people's 'sympathie' with sorrow and grief. Using metaphors of coinage and medicine, Rogers describes how their equal grief comes together to make a single coin, and a single compound made up of many elements. But what is also striking in Rogers's elegy is the emphasis upon death as a leveler, whereby proud majesty is made a subject:

> The greatest Monarchs that doe breath alive,
> Who for their high degree, the rest excell
> And in the field of *Mars,* as chiefe do thrive,
> And by the Mines of gold and treasure dwell.
> They all are subjects, though they raign as kings
> They must obey, when *Death* his message brings. (sig. B3v)

This stanza reminds us of the undeniable truth that the 'greatest Monarchs', despite their 'high degree', are nevertheless subjects who 'must obey' the message of an even greater power. There are of course political implications here, inasmuch as this section of the poem implicitly questions the specialness of kings and princes, asking provocatively: 'What is their birth when he doth Summons give … Who can against the hand of God prevaile?' (sig. B3r). But it also enables a kind of shared sympathy between monarchs and subjects that is stronger than any individual grief.

The fact that there were a number of elegies printed around the same time, which echo and recall each other, adds to this sense of shared sympathy. George Wither wrote a sequence of 'Mournefull elegies' upon Henry's death that was printed alongside a 'supposed inter-locution' between Henry's ghost and Great Britain itself.[66] The first elegiac sonnet makes shared distress its subject: it acknowledges that it is good to have company in misery, but wishes that there was no cause for such misery in the first place: 'For if it be a comfort in distresse, / (As some thinke) to have sharers in our woes, / Then I desire to be comfortles' (sig. A3r), The speaker states that his soul knows no pleasure in 'publike greefe'. As the closing couplet puts it, 'Yea, I could wish, and for that wish would die, / That there were none had cause to greeve, but I'. The second sonnet extends this theme, wishing that it was only the speaker who had a reason to be miserable: 'And I should moane but for ones misery, / Where now for thousands, my poore heart doth ake' (sig. A3v). In this way, the speaker takes on, and indeed speaks for, the heartache of many others. The most explicit articulation of this shared grief appears in the fourth sonnet, which is addressed to this 'poore world-divided Ile':

---

[66] George Wither, *Prince Henries obsequies or Mournefull elegies upon his death: with a supposed inter-locution betweene the ghost of Prince Henrie and Great Brittaine* (London, 1612).

> I saw, how happie thou wert but of late
> In thy sweet *Henries* hopes, yea I saw too,
> How thou didst glory in thy blessed state:
> Which thou indeed hadst cause enough to doe.
> But, when I saw thee place all thy delight
> Upon his worth; and then, when thou didst place it,
> (And thy Joy almost mounted to her height)
> His haples end so suddainely deface it;
> Me thought, I felt it goe so neere thy heart,
> Mine ake't too, with a sympathizing smart.   (sig. B1r)

This sonnet thus describes the speaker's shared happiness in the nation's delight in Henry, followed by its rapid defacement upon the Prince's 'haples end' – the term *hapless* finding a tragic semantic affinity with 'happie', highlighting the fact that the people's happiness was itself the result of good chance that might change at any time.[67] The final couplet describes the shared pain between the speaker and the populace: the speaker feels the grief near Britain's heart, as his own heart aches with a 'sympathizing smart'. This emotional mirroring is itself mirrored and underlined by the rhyming of the island's 'heart' and the speaker's 'smart'. We have seen in previous chapters how the term *sympathize* was used by poets and playwrights to describe a correspondence of sorrows; and this usage is recorded in some early seventeenth-century dictionaries.[68] Wither's poem uses the term to suggest a sharing of affect, with the specific suggestion that the speaker shares the feelings of multiple others rather than an individualised other – although the elegy uses the personified 'Ile' to represent the whole of the nation and its feelings.[69]

But, as well as feeling the pain of the nation, the speaker feels the anguish of the King: 'For thee, great *James,* my spouts of sorrow runne, / For thee

---

[67] The term *happy* was, of course, originally associated with luck and good fortune: 'Of a person: favoured by good fortune; lucky, fortunate; successful' (*OED*, 1); 'Of an event or period: marked by good fortune; fortunate, lucky, auspicious; prosperous; favourable, propitious' (*OED*, 2). For discussion of the history of the word see Richard Chamberlain, 'What's Happiness in *Hamlet*?', in Meek and Sullivan (eds.), *The Renaissance of Emotion*, pp. 153–74. *Hapless* suggests 'Esp. of a person: destitute of or lacking good fortune; unfortunate, unlucky' (*OED*); it is used later in the seventeenth century by John Milton to describe 'hapless Eve' (*Paradise Lost*, ed. Alastair Fowler (London: Longman, 1968), 9.404).

[68] In Randle Cotgrave's *A Dictionarie of the French and English Tongues* (London, 1611) the French word *condouloir* Is translated as 'To sorrow, or moane with, to sympathize with the griefe, or paine of', while *sympathiser* is translated as 'To sympathize, or have a fellow-feeling of, to jumpe with in passion, consent with in affection, agree with in disposition' (s.v. 'condouloir' and 'sympathiser').

[69] Wither also uses *sympathize* in a similarly emotional context in *Faire-virtue, the mistresse of Phil'arete* (London, 1622): 'When I have reacht so high a straine, / Of passion in my Song; / That they, have seene the teares toraine / And trill my cheeke along: / Insteed of sigh, or weeping eye, / To sympathize with me' (sig. E7v).

my Muse a heavy song doth sing' (sig. B1r). This fifth elegy is especially self-reflexive in its concern with writing and emotion; the speaker feels sorrow for James, but this pain enables him to write. He also uses the idea of the body politic we have seen employed by other writers in the period: 'Needes must the paines, that doe disturb the head, / Disease the body throughout every part; / And therefore I might have bene lopt as dead, / If I had had no feeling of this smart' (sig. B1r). The pain that disturbs the head can cause sickness throughout every part of the body politic. As the poet is a living part of this body he feels the 'smart' of the King.[70] And yet, in addition to this interest in the politics of sympathy, and the capacity of the speaker to feel the pain of another or others, Wither's poetic sequence – like Shakespeare's *King Lear* – acknowledges that sympathy can involve projection and is not straightforwardly reciprocal. In elegy 33 the poet suggests that it is little wonder that creatures of 'weakest substance' should melt in 'tender passion' for the Prince's 'timeles end', 'Since (as it seem'd) the purer bodies felt / Some griefe, for this their sweet departed friend'. Thus nature and the heavens felt grief too, or at least 'seem'd' to do so:

> The Sunne wrapt up in clouds of mournfull black,
> Frown'd as displeas'd, with such a hainous deed,
> And would have staid, or turn'd his horses back,
> If Nature had not forc't him on with speed:
> Yea and the Heavens wept a pearly dewe,
> Like very teares, not so as if it rain'd.
> His Grand-sires tombes as if the stones did rue
> Our wofull losses; were with moisture stain'd:
>   Yea (either 'twas my easie mind's beliefe)
>   Or all things were disposed unto griefe. (sig. C4r)

This sonnet offers a powerful description of the natural world's grief for Henry's loss. The frowning sun is wrapped in mournful clouds, and has to be forced by nature to continue on his course. Meanwhile, the rain is said to be tears of the heavens, which in turn makes it seem that the tombs are also weeping, and 'did rue / Our wofull losses'. It appears to the speaker that 'all things were disposed unto griefe'; but he also recognizes the possibility that this may be the result of his 'easie mind's beliefe'. As with other similar articulations of an emotional natural world from the period, we find that the speaker's poetic description of the environment bestows upon it an emotional life – but he simultaneously acknowledges

---

[70] Interestingly this formulation echoes Julia's artful description of her mistress's grief in Shakespeare's *The Two Gentlemen of Verona*: 'and would I might be dead / If I in thought felt not her very sorrow' (4.4.168–9); see Chapter 4, above.

that this extended form of sympathy may be the product of metaphor and the imagination.

The idea of sympathy between the heavens and the earth was also employed several years later to describe another royal death – that of Queen Anne in 1619. The first of Patrick Hannay's *Two elegies, on the late death of our soveraigne Queene Anne* recalls Wither's elegy 33 by suggesting that the Queen's death – like that of Prince Henry – has caused the disappearance of the sun:

> The *Skies* of *Clowds* now make them mourning weeds,
> And generall *darknesse* all the *world* ore spreads:
> What? hath the *Sunne* for a new *Phaeton*
> Abandoned the *Heavens,* and beamy *throne?*
> Is the *cause* theirs? or doth it touch *us* nie?
> (Since with *their sorrow we* so sympathie:)
> No, its because our *Cynthia* left this *spheare,*
> The *world* wears blacke, because *she* moves not here,
> *Her* influence that made *it* freshly flourish,
> Leaves *it* to fade, and will no more *it* nourish.[71]

The speaker asks whether the cause of the cloudy darkness is the sorrow of the heavens, which earthly inhabitants also feel ('with *their sorrow we* so sympathie'). Yet the real reason is the loss of 'our *Cynthia*', whose influence made the world flourish. Not only does the earth sympathize with the heavens, but the whole world is also affected by the Queen's death: '*Griefes* Character on every *brow* is read. / Our *eyes* so drop (wer't not God frees those *fears*) / The *world* might dread a new *deludge* of *teares*' (sig. B1r). Hannay's second elegy continues this theme by describing how the Thames has been turned into brine by this tearful deluge, and is even joined by the weepy waters of Scotland: 'How weari'd is thy sister famous *Forth,* / Bringing sad *Scotland*'s sorrowes from the North' (sig. C1r). The union of the rivers figures the joining of the two nations in mourning, which leads to a hymn to national unity:

> In love so straight, they cannot be untwinde,
> *They* seeme both *one,* in *body* and in *minde.*
> O happy *union!* labour'd long in vaine,
> Reserv'd by *God* to *James* his joyfull *raigne* … (sig. C2r)

The poem recalls Gilbert Dugdale's description of 'English and Scottish in one simpathy'; but while Dugdale's account of emotional unity offered

---

[71] Patrick Hannay, *Two elegies, on the late death of our soveraigne Queene Anne With epitaphes* (London, 1619), sig. A4v.

an optimistic account of the succession, Hannay paints a moving picture of a nation united in grief. As the speaker suggests, however, this unhappy event has led to the long-laboured-for happy union that has been the aim of James's 'joyfull *raigne*'. The poem thus offers another politicized account of sympathy and compassion, which is felt by the grieving subjects of England and Scotland, and even implies that political union has finally been achieved through emotional affinity.

Yet, while such royal elegies describe subjects sympathizing with each other, and with the monarch, there are other texts from this period that describe a continuing, perhaps increasing, anxiety about a diminishment of sympathy. This is particularly the case in religious writings and sermons; in the same year that Queen Anne died, Nicholas Byfield lists sympathy as an important aspect of mercy in *The rules of a holy life* (1619), describing it as 'Pitie, a Fellow-feeling of the distresses of others, *being like affectioned* and laying their miseries to heart … There should be *bowels in our mercy*'.[72] Thus sympathy was understood to mean a fellow-feeling for the misery of others, and feeling their distress in one's heart; yet Byfield – like other religious writers we have considered – suggests that there should be bowels in our mercy, implying that sympathy must be cultivated and is not necessarily automatic. Thomas Medley's *Misericors, mikrokosmos* (1619) is even more realistic, or pessimistic, regarding the absence of sympathy. The whole text is an injunction to mercy, and consists of a reflection upon Romans 12:15, which is quoted on the title page and throughout the text:

> For even as charity maketh an others good her owne, and so gaineth much so mercy maketh also anothers evill her owne, by a fellow feeling of others miseries, according to this of the Apostle *Rejoyce with them that rejoyce, weepe, with them that weepe, and be of like affection one towards another*. But oh this iron and flinty age of the world; where are now become the bowels of mercy & loving kindnes? This simpathy *of affection one towards another*, which was amongst the Christians of ancient time *which were of one heart and one soule.* in what angle of the world (almost) shall we find them.[73]

Medley describes this as 'an iron and flinty age'. As we have seen in earlier chapters, flint was usually associated with a lack of compassion. But here we find a lament for an earlier age when people were more compassionate, and more like the Christians of ancient times, '*which were of one heart and*

---

[72] Nicholas Byfield, *The rules of a holy life* (London, 1619), p. 242.
[73] Thomas Medeley, *Misericors, mikrokosmos, or, Medeleys offices containing an injunction to all duties of mercy belonging to the whole man* (London, 1619), pp. 104–5.

one soule.⁷⁴ In this way, Medley laments the lack of sympathy in society, and imagines people as distinct individuals rather than interconnected parts of the body. Like Robert Rollock, who had argued that all sympathy is 'out of the world', Medley describes a society far more atomized and unsympathetic than the optimistic vision of unity articulated in royal elegies and some contemporary political works. He also, we might suggest, harkens back to a more unified pre-Reformation age; his sentiments might thus remind us of the continuing political and religious divisions of this period.

Even as Protestant preachers enjoined their listeners to sympathize with each other, the prospect of Catholics sympathizing together was a cause of alarm for some writers. John Vicars's *Mischeefes mysterie* (1617), which was based upon Francis Herring's anti-Catholic polemic *Pietas pontificia* (1606) is particularly suggestive in this respect. Herring's Latin poem, which describes the gunpowder plot, was reprinted in 1609 with minor corrections, together with a sequel describing the Midlands revolt of 1607.⁷⁵ Vicars's expanded translation includes a striking description of the joining together of Catholics:

> They surely thought that what they had begun
> In this one part of *England,* would incite
> All *Catholiques* to sympathize and run
> To armes, with them to joyne their power and might:
> Which also though their lying *Jesuites* sought,
> Yet heaven their hellish hopes did bring to nought.⁷⁶

This text offers further evidence that the word *sympathize* was being used in the political sphere, but here to describe a political affiliation or agreement with a particular cause; one could even argue that this usage anticipates the later term *sympathizer*, 'One who or that which sympathizes; *esp.* one disposed to agree with or approve a party, cause, etc.' (*OED*; first cited usage 1816). What seems clear, then, is that there was a particular

---

⁷⁴ Medeley quotes Acts 4:32: 'And the multitude of them that believed, were of one heart, and of one soul: neither any of them said, that anything of that which he possessed, was his own, but they had all things common'.

⁷⁵ Francis Herring, *Pietas pontificia* (London, 1609). See Anne James, *Poets, Players, and Preachers: Remembering the Gunpowder Plot in Seventeenth-Century England* (University of Toronto Press, 2016), pp. 161–4. As James points out, Vicars's dilated version introduces new material relevant to the current political situation, including the introduction of the Jesuits and altering the interpretation of the gunpowder plot to suggest it was 'merely one episode in an ongoing war between true and false religions' (p. 162).

⁷⁶ John Vicars, *Mischeefes mysterie: or, Treasons master-peece, the Powder plot Invented by hellish malice, prevented by heavenly mercy: truely related* (London, 1617), p. 75.

ambivalence about sympathy in the Jacobean period, which is reflected in these differing usages. As we have seen, *sympathy* could be used to describe 'A likenesse in quantitie; or a like disposition or affection of one thing to another', or a 'Mutuall affection' between individuals – definitions that circulated in contemporary dictionaries.[77] And yet, as this example from Vicars suggests, it could also involve a form of ideological sympathy between undesirable elements of society. This is an extension of the religious anxieties we saw expressed by preachers in Chapter 2: if Protestants are bound together through sympathetic bonds there are others who are excluded, and might form themselves into a group united against the monarch.

The limits and potential dangers of sympathy are also reflected in James's own writings, which further complicate the question of whether there can be sympathy between the King and his subjects. We have already seen how James used the term *sympathy* to refer to the shared feeling between parts of body. But he also uses the term *sympathize* in his reflections upon the assassination of King Henry of France in *A remonstrance of the most gratious King James I* (1616). In the Preface, James describes his

> late entire affection to K. Henrie IV. of happy memorie, my most honoured brother, and my exceeding sorrow for the most detestable parricide acted upon the sacred person of a King, so complete in all heroicall and Princely vertues; as also the remembrance of my owne dangers, incurred by the practise of conspiracies flowing from the same source, hath wrought me to sympathize with my friends in their grievous occurrents: no doubt so much more daungerous, as they are lesse apprehended and felt of Kings themselves, even when the danger hangeth over their owne heads.[78]

Henry was assassinated by a Catholic in 1610, and James fears that the forces that killed Henry might similarly destroy him. Such conspiracies at home and abroad have caused him '*to sympathize with* [his] *friends in their grievous occurrents*'. He implies that such fears are sensible, and indeed dangerous when they are ignored by kings. In this way, when James describes himself sympathizing with another it is with another Protestant monarch. That is, he sympathizes with an equal, not his subjects, as other texts from the period – such as Alexander's *Croesus* – had imagined. Moreover, James's sympathy for Henry IV inevitably prompts him to reflect upon his

---

[77] These definitions are taken, respectively, from John Bullokar's *An English expositor teaching the interpretation of the hardest words used in our language* (London, 1616), and Henry Cockeram's *The English dictionarie, or, An interpreter of hard English words* (London, 1623) s.v. 'sympathie'. Cockeram defines *sympathize* as 'Mutually to embrace each other'.

[78] *A remonstrance of the most gratious King James I* (Cambridge, 1616), sig. A1r-v.

own situation ('*the remembrance of my owne dangers*'), reminding us that sympathy for the other often involves a return to the self.

This awareness of the limits of sympathy is reflected and extended in the 1623 Folio text of Shakespeare's *King Lear*. Lear's final utterance in the Quarto, 'Break, heart, I prithee break' (24.306), which suggests that he dies in a state of grief, is given to Kent in the Folio. The monarch's self-pity thus becomes Kent's pity for the monarch – which, as we have already noted, is depicted in James Barry's visual responses to the final scene. This change makes Lear's death in the Folio more ambiguous; it also figures the sympathetic response of readers and audiences, who may follow Kent in mourning the King's demise. But other changes to the Folio make the later text more pessimistic about the practice of compassion. Gloucester's speech in the second scene about the weakening of familial bonds is extended in the Folio: 'This villain of mine comes under the prediction: there's son against father. The king falls from bias of nature, there's father against child. We have seen the best of our time. Machinations, hollowness, treachery, and all ruinous disorders follow us disquietly to our graves' (1.2.96–100).[79] Gloucester's sentiments here resonate powerfully with the gloomy nostalgia of writers such as Thomas Medley. Other scenes that involve the generation of sympathy are cut – such as the account of Cordelia's piteous response to Lear's predicament in scene 17, denying readers and audiences this counterexample to Goneril's cruelty.[80] Another moving moment in the Quarto text involves three low status characters caring for the recently blinded Gloucester. Members of the audience are encouraged to feel pity for Gloucester – and, by extension, King Lear – as the play depicts compassion being directed up the social ladder:

> SECOND SERVANT Let's follow the old Earl and get the bedlam
> To lead him where he would. His roguish madness
> Allows itself to any thing.
> THIRD SERVANT Go thou. I'll fetch some flax and whites of eggs
> To apply to his bleeding face. Now heaven help him!   (14.101–5)

This exchange is omitted from the Folio, indicating a degree of uncertainty about whether it is desirable – or necessary – to represent lowly characters

---

[79] Quotations are taken from Halio's New Cambridge edition.
[80] Albany's speech in scene 16, in which he admonishes Goneril for her ruthlessness (lines 37–46), is also omitted from the Folio. He describes Goneril and Regan as tigers, recalling other Shakespearean references to pitiless women: 'What have you done? / Tigers, not daughters, what have you performed?' (38–9). See R. A. Foakes, *Hamlet versus Lear: Cultural Politics and Shakespeare's Art* (Cambridge University Press, 1993), pp. 107–8. Foakes suggests that these scenes 'may have been omitted in revision because they are emotionally coercive in a way the play generally is not' (p. 108).

sympathizing with a high-status character. One could argue that the Folio simply trusts audience members to sympathize with Gloucester's plight without such prompting, but this omission nevertheless suggests that the later text is bleaker and less sympathetic than the Quarto. It would be simplistic to argue that such revisions were prompted or influenced by the more pessimistic cultural voices that I have been exploring in this chapter, particularly given that we cannot be certain when the Folio text was written.[81] And yet, for readers of the Folio in 1623, the revised text of *King Lear* would have offered another significant contribution to the Jacobean discourse of sympathy and compassion. It extends the debates regarding cross-class sympathy that I have been tracing in this chapter; in particular the question of whether there can be sympathy between high and low status individuals, and the form and nature of such emotional comparability. But we have also seen how the differences between the Quarto and Folio texts of *Lear* open up wider aesthetic questions about how to elicit sympathy from audiences and readers. Should sympathy be figured and represented within the text, or should the text draw attention to its absence? The two versions of *King Lear* – which offer contrasting perspectives on this question – may not reveal whether this was an especially compassionate or ruthless age, but they do highlight and exemplify the different rhetorical and emotive strategies employed by early seventeenth-century writers to generate sympathetic responses.

Conclusion: 'a fellow-feeling in mens minds'

We have seen throughout this chapter, then, that writers during the Jacobean period were especially concerned to explore the politics of sympathy, and the extent to which compassion and fellow-feeling could extend across social boundaries, or even between the monarch and his subjects. But we have also seen how this Jacobean fascination with political, emotional, and interpersonal union exists alongside a certain disillusionment about the workings and possibilities of sympathy. We might even argue that the optimistic articulations of national unity found in succession literature and royal elegies may have inadvertently highlighted the political and religious divisions in Jacobean society, and prompted some writers to comment upon a perceived lack of pity and compassion. But, whether they sought to encourage sympathy by describing its presence

---

[81] Stylistic evidence points to 1610; see Wells's 'Introduction', p. 5. But, as Halio points out, the evidence here is 'admittedly sensitive to editorial predisposition' (p. 70).

or its absence, Jacobean writers recognized the vital role that it plays in public and political life. This makes the period a significant stage in the history of sympathy, whereby the concept is absorbed into political discourse and used to reconsider the relationship between individual members of the commonwealth. Yet this recognition of sympathy's importance also means that there is correspondingly more anxiety about its absence, limitations, and potential misuse. This development thus contributes to the wider cultural transformation that I have been tracing in this book, whereby individuals are regarded as distinct entities able to resist the forces of sympathetic magic, and each other's emotions. The downside of this shift is the acknowledgment that individuals are not necessarily as compassionate as they should be. In a potentially fragmented society made up of individual selves, sympathy is both necessary and contingent.

Those texts that do represent instances of sympathetic exchange implicitly encourage citizens – and indeed the monarch – to imitate the acts of compassion depicted. This is certainly the case with poetic and dramatic articulations of sympathy; but we have also seen how religious writers reminded their readers and audiences that one of the aims of Christianity is, as William Thorne puts it, 'to *imitate* Christ'. The idea that Christ was the ultimate model or authority for the practice of compassion is made explicit in a sermon by John Lawrence, preached at Paul's Cross towards the end of James's reign in April 1624. Lawrence's sermon is addressed to magistrates and rulers, reminding them that they govern on behalf of God. In the dedicatory Epistle he writes that 'The *Common-wealth* is compared to a *Musicall Instrument, the strings whereof are the people, & you are the Musitioners*'.[82] Once again, then, the idea of musical and societal concord is invoked, with the commonwealth conceived of as a collection of sympathetic and harmonious parts. Yet in the main text Lawrence uses the term *sympathy* in the more specific sense of compassion: 'There ought to be a sympathy, and a fellow-feeling in mens minds, especially in a Ruler great compassion, wishing from the bottome of their hearts there were no such cause of punishment so to be suffered' (p. 97). The first part of this quotation appears to be a reworking of George Abbot's *An exposition upon the prophet Jonah* (1600), which we considered at the start of this chapter. But, while Abbot goes on to reflect upon the authenticity of a ruler's tears, Lawrence links these sentiments to Christ's passion:

[82] John Lawrence, *A golden trumpet, to rowse up a drowsie magistrate: or, A patterne for a governors practise drawne from Christs comming to, beholding of, and weeping over Hierusalem* (London, 1624), sig. A3r.

> For a Magistrate ought not to be like the proud *Pharises,* and insolent *Priests,* who when they had taken our Saviour, delighted not in any thing so much, as in *mocking, spitting, buffeting, railing, reviling, scourging, scorning, crowning* him with *thornes,* and *crucifying him betweene two Theeves.* (p. 97)

Such biblical counterexamples are invoked, with the implication that magistrates and rulers should not emulate the proud Pharisees described in the account of Christ's Passion but Christ himself: 'For this doing beseemeth not a King or Magistrate, they should rather with Christ here, grieve that any should grow to that extremity, as to deserve such judgement' (p. 98). This advice involves a levelling effect, recalling some of the radical implications that we noted in Thomas Rogers's elegy for Prince Henry, whereby even the 'greatest Monarchs' are subjects of Death. In this passage from Lawrence, kings and subjects are not only encouraged to feel compassion for one another – with all of the attendant political consequences – but also reminded that both are subject to the greater authority of Christ, particularly in terms of his passionate sympathy for humans. In the next chapter we will chart the continuing development of the emotional and affective understandings of sympathy into the Caroline period, and the extent to which religious models of compassion were inextricably linked to – or even superseded – natural philosophical ones.

CHAPTER 6

'As God loves Sympathy, God loves Symphony'
Sympathy at a Distance in Caroline England

John Donne's Christmas Day sermon of 1627, which was preached at St Paul's, is based on Exodus 4:13 ('O my Lord, send I pray thee, by the hand of him whom thou wilt send') and contains a lengthy meditation on God's relationship with Moses. Towards the end of the sermon Donne slips in an arresting digression regarding the godliness of sympathetic harmony between individuals:

> Slide wee in this note by the way; God loves not singularity: God bindes us to nothing, that was never said but by one: As God loves Sympathy, God loves Symphony; God loves a compassion and fellow-feeling of others miseries, that is Sympathy, and God loves Harmony, and fellow-beleeving of others Doctrines, that is Symphony: No one man alone makes a Church; no one Church alone makes a Catholique Church. Christ sent his owne Disciples by couples, two and two: And *Aquinas* says out of his observation, *Monachus solus est Daemon solitarius*: Though naturally a Monk must love retirednesse, yet a single Monk, a Monk alwaies alone, saies he, is plotting some singular mischiefe.[1]

As Donne suggests, God does not value separateness or solitariness; rather he loves sympathy – which Donne explicitly defines as 'a compassion and fellow-feeling of others miseries'. This emphasis upon the value of fellow-feeling and pairing up with others is further expressed through the rhetorical balancing and repetition in Donne's prose. God's love for sympathy matches his love for symphony, and the phonetic resemblance between these two words further underscores their similarity. *Symphony* could be used to suggest 'Harmony of sound, esp. of musical sounds; concord, consonance' (*OED*, 2), or in a more general sense to mean 'agreement, accord, concord, congruity' (*OED*, 3), which recalls earlier meanings of *sympathy*. George Puttenham had used *symphony* in *The Art of English Poesy* to

---

[1] Sermon V, 'Preached at Pauls, upon Christmas Day, 1627', in *LXXX sermons preached by that learned and reverend divine, John Donne, Dr in Divinity, late Deane of the cathedrall church of S. Pauls London* (London, 1640), p. 51.

suggest the affinity between rhyming words.² Here Donne goes further and finds a verbal counterpart for *symphony* itself. But this witty pairing and comparison of words is also used to make a specific point about religious doctrine – symphony or harmony is 'fellow-beleeving of others Doctrines', a formulation that echoes Donne's definition of sympathy. Donne states that no man alone makes a Church, and that no single Church makes a Catholic Church – 'Catholique' here referring to the church universal, or whole body of Christians. In this way, the sermon recalls the strategies of preachers that we examined in Chapter 2, inasmuch as Donne tries to convert his listeners into a unified Church, which is itself one among many. This emphasis on expansion and doubling is also replicated in Donne's reference to the disciples, who were sent forth in pairs ('two and two'). Aquinas's example of a mischievous singular monk adds a touch of irony and humour to this part of the sermon, and may even have united some of Donne's listeners in wry amusement.

Donne's sermon demonstrates that the affective meanings of *sympathy* and *sympathize*, which had recently emerged, persisted into the 1620s and 1630s. This is worth emphasizing, because the Caroline period sees a considerable amount of interest in the weapon-salve – a magical unguent that could allegedly cure wounds at a distance by sympathetic action. Attributed to Paracelsus, the cure was described in detail in 1608 by Rudolph Goclenius the Younger in his *De vita proroganda* and by Oswald Croll in his *Basilica Chymica* (1609).³ But the salve was also criticized by several continental and English authors, often on religious grounds, and presented as a mountebank application of natural sympathy, or even as a diabolical device.⁴ For cultural historians, this controversy – which peaked

---

² As Puttenham writes, comparing classical and English writers of verse, 'we have instead thereof twenty other curious points in that skill more than they ever had, by reason of our rhyme and tunable concords or symphony, which they never observed' (*The Art of English Poesy* (1589), in Alexander (ed.), *Selected Renaissance Literary Criticism*, p. 60).
³ See Rudolph Goclenius the Younger, *De vita proroganda* (Mainz, 1608), and Oswald Croll, *Basilica chymica* (Frankfurt, 1609). Croll's treatise was later translated into English as *Bazilica chymica, & Praxis chymiatricae, or, Royal and practical chymistry* (London, 1670); the recipe for the salve can be found on pp. 173–8.
⁴ For useful discussions of these debates see Allen G. Debus, 'Robert Fludd and the Use of Gilbert's *De Magnete* in the Weapon-Salve Controversy', *Journal of the History of Medicine and Allied Sciences*, 19 (1964), 389–417; Debus, *The Chemical Philosophy: Paracelsian Science and Medicine in the Sixteenth and Seventeenth Centuries*, 2 vols (New York: Science History Publications, 1977), vol. 1, pp. 279–92; Carlos Ziller Camenietzki, 'Jesuits and Alchemy in the Early Seventeenth Century: Father Johannes Roberti and the Weapon-Salve Controversy', *Ambix*, 48 (2001), 83–101; Lauren Kassell, 'Magic, Alchemy and the Medical Economy in Early Modern England: The Case of Robert Fludd's Magnetical Medicine', in *Medicine and the Market in England and Its Colonies, c.1450–c.1850*, ed. Mark S. R. Jenner and Patrick Wallis (Basingstoke: Palgrave Macmillan, 2007), pp. 88–107, and Mark A. Waddell, *Jesuit Science and the End of Nature's Secrets* (Farnham: Ashgate, 2015), pp. 38–42.

in England in the 1630s – appears to have reinforced the idea that sympathy in this period was predominantly understood in occult or scientific terms. For example, Christia Mercer writes that the seventeenth century 'begins with debates about "occult" sympathetic powers in nature ... By the end of the century, sympathy is a moral force to be reckoned with'.[5] Seth Lobis has similarly asserted that the affective meaning of *sympathy* 'does not become part of a wider cultural vocabulary ... until after the Restoration'.[6] In the present chapter, however, I argue that the Caroline fascination with natural sympathy does not diminish or displace the affective model – which was already part of the cultural vocabulary – but rather increases its complexity. As we shall see, the emotional understanding of the term is reasserted, sometimes in relation or contradistinction to the natural philosophical concept. Certainly the weapon-salve 'served as the locus of heated debates about the nature and theological legitimacy of actions at a distance in the early seventeenth century'.[7] But what is also striking is the way in which literary and religious writers drew upon these debates in order to explore and articulate the emotional, interpersonal, and imaginative aspects of sympathy.

The chapter begins with a discussion of Francis Bacon's *Sylva sylvarum* (1627) and other works that disputed the origin and nature of the weapon-salve, and the power and limitations of natural sympathy, including William Foster's *Hoplocrisma-spongus* (1631) and Robert Fludd's response, *Doctor Fludds answer unto M. Foster* (1631). It then explores dramatic texts from this period that engage with this debate, in particular Henry Glapthorne's *The Hollander* (written 1635–6; printed 1640). Glapthorne's play reminds us that the belief in magical sympathies was neither straightforward nor universal, and was the subject of parody as well as debate in the period. The chapter goes on to consider Charles Fitzgeffry's *Compassion towards captives* (1637), which not only invokes the concept of natural sympathy but also describes the '*Sympathy* or *Compassion*' that should be felt for fellow Christians in bondage. As we shall see, religious writers like Fitzgeffry continued to be fascinated by concepts of compassion and fellow-feeling,

---

[5] Christia Mercer, 'Seventeenth-Century Universal Sympathy', in Schliesser (ed.), *Sympathy: A History*, pp. 107–38 (p. 138). Andrew Cunningham writes that sympathy in this period 'became a principle of nascent "science" ... employed in accounts of action at a distance and particularly of magnetic effects' ('Was Eighteenth-Century Sentimentalism Unprecedented?', p. 384).
[6] Lobis, *The Virtue of Sympathy*, p. 4.
[7] Elizabeth Hendrick, 'Romancing the Salve: Sir Kenelm Digby and the Powder of Sympathy', *The British Journal for the History of Science*, 41 (2008), 161–85 (p. 161). Hendrick usefully distinguishes between the 'salve' (a wet preparation) and Digby's dry compound – a vitriol that was 'dissolved in water for use' (p. 162).

and used the term *sympathy* to refer to Christ's compassion for others and Christian compassion more generally. I argue that this religious conception of sympathy – involving an imaginative compassion for the other, as opposed to magical and medical models – emerges as the ultimate form of action at a distance.

'Where is then the sympathy?': Debating the Weapon-Salve

One of the most extraordinary texts printed in the 1620s was Francis Bacon's *Sylva sylvarum* (1627), which was originally dedicated to Prince Charles; the dedication to the new king was completed by William Rawley, who published the text after the deaths of King James and Bacon himself (Figure 7). The work is dedicated to 'Mighty Prince Charles … King of Great Britain'.[8] As the title suggests, the text is a compendium of experiments and recycled knowledge – including classical works, such as Pliny's *Natural History*, as well as works of Renaissance magic, such as Della Porta's *Magia naturalis*.[9] What is striking for our purposes is the sheer number of references to sympathy, which is generally understood in the natural philosophical sense – although precisely what Bacon himself thought about these sometimes conflicting models of sympathy can be hard to discern. The text opens with a discussion of the sympathy that exists between bodily parts, and between the soul and music. Recalling Wright's *Passions of the Minde*, Bacon notes the effect of music on people's 'manners': '*Tunes* and *Aires*, even in their owne Nature, have in themselves some Affinity with the *Affections*; As there be *Merry Tunes*, *Dolefull Tunes*, *Solemne Tunes*; *Tunes inclining Mens mindes to Pitty*; *Warlike Tunes*; &c. So as it is no Marvell, if they alter the *Spirits*; considering that *Tunes* have a Predisposition to the *Motion* of the *Spirits* in themselves' (114). As Bacon suggests, men's minds can be moved to pity through music, although he acknowledges that music cannot change people's passions entirely and merely 'feedeth that disposition of the *Spirits* which it findeth' (114).

---

[8] Francis Bacon, *Sylva sylvarum, or, A naturall history in ten centuries* (London, 1627), sig. ¶r. Further references will be given in the text by paragraph number. The ESTC notes that *Sylva sylvarum* was entered in the Stationers' Register on 4 July 1626 but gives the date as 1627 (as per the engraved title page; see Figure 7).

[9] See Doina-Cristina Rusu, 'Rethinking *Sylva sylvarum*: Francis Bacon's Use of Giambattista Della Porta's *Magia naturalis*', *Perspectives on Science*, 25 (2017), 1–35. See also Doina-Cristina Rusu and Christoph Lüthy, 'Extracts from a Paper Laboratory: The Nature of Francis Bacon's *Sylva sylvarum*', *Intellectual History Review*, 27 (2017), 171–202. Lobis notes that Della Porta included Paracelsus's recipe for the weapon-salve (*The Virtue of Sympathy*, p. 41).

Figure 7   Francis Bacon, *Sylva sylvarum, or, A naturall history in ten centuries* (London, 1627), title page. STC 1169 copy 1. Used by permission of the Folger Shakespeare Library.

This discussion feeds into a more extended treatment of sympathy and antipathy in music, including the 'Common Observation', which we have seen discussed elsewhere, 'that if a *Lute*, or *Viall*, be layed upon the Backe, with a small Straw upon one of the *Strings;* And another *Lute* or *Viall* be laid by it; And in the other *Lute* or *Viall*, the *Unison* to that *String* be strucken; it will make the *String*, move'. This phenomenon 'will appeare both to the Eye, and by the *Strawes* Falling off' (279), suggesting that it has been confirmed to Bacon by observation and experience. But when he moves on to the 'sympathy and antipathy of plants' (479), and why some plants grow well near others, Bacon sounds rather more sceptical: 'But these are Idle and Ignorant Conceits; And forsake the true *Indication* of the *Causes*; As the most Part of *Experiments*, that concerne *Sympathies* and *Antipathies* doe'. He suggests an alternative explanation: 'Wheresoever one *Plant* draweth such a particular Juyce out of the Earth; as it qualifieth the Earth; So as that Juyce which remaineth is fit for the other Plant, there the Neighbourhood doth good' (479). This phenomenon is explained by the fact of different plants making use of leftover nourishment, rather than an unseen affinity. Similarly, Bacon notes how 'Some of the Ancients, and likewise divers of the Moderne Writers, that have laboured in *Natural Magicke*, have noted a *Sympathy*, between the *Sunne, Moone*, and some Principall *Starres*; And certaine *Herbs*, and *Plants*' (493). He proposes that 'it is Nothing else, but a little Loading of the Leaves, and Swelling them at the Bottome, with the Moisture of the Aire … And they make it a Peece of the wonder, that *Garden Claver* will hide the *Stalke*, when the *Sunne* sheweth bright; Which is Nothing, but a full Expansion of the leaves' (493). Bacon thus queries the idea of sympathy and antipathy as a key to explaining all natural phenomena, and favours more complex analyses based upon careful observation and induction.[10] As Bacon wryly notes, 'Men favour Wonders' (495).

This scepticism is also apparent in his treatment of 'the Severall Kindes of the *Operations*, by *Transmission* of *Spirits*, and *Imagination*' (904), which includes a reference to the weapon-salve. Bacon points to the '*Emission* of *Spirits*, and *Immateriate Powers* and *Vertues*, in those Things, which worke by the *Universall Configuration*, and *Sympathy* of the *World*' (907). Interestingly, Bacon suggests that these immaterial forces work, 'Not by *Formes*, or *Celestiall Influxes*, (as is vainly caught and received,) but by the *Primitive Nature* of *Matter*, and the *Seeds* of *Things*' (907). This explains the workings of the loadstone and gravity, 'which is by *Consent* of *Dense Bodies*, with the *Globe* of the *Earth*'. The eighth type of transmission is the '*Emission of Immateriate Vertues*', or the '*Sympathy* of *Individuals*' (911). Bacon states that he will not dismiss such phenomena out of hand, but rather give them due examination: 'For as there is a *Sympathy* of *Species*; So, (it may be) there is a *Sympathy* of *Individuals*: That is, that in *Things*, or the *Parts* of *Things*, that have beene once *Contiguous*, or *Entire*, there should remaine a *Transmission* of *Vertue*, from the One to the Other: As betweene the *Weapon*, and the *Wound*' (911).[11] Bacon does sound less sceptical when he writes about the virtues of precious stones, and how 'There be many *Things* that worke upon the *Spirits* of *Man*, by *Secret Sympathy*, and *Antipathy*' (960). But there are limits to such beliefs: 'The *Writers* of *Naturall Magick*, commend the Wearing of the *Spoile* of a *Snake*, for

---

[10] See Brian Copenhaver's discussion of Bacon in *Magic in Western Culture*, pp. 351–62. He writes that 'The claims made by the ancients are idle because the old authors did not do the work of looking closely and systematically' (p. 356). But he also notes that Bacon's incredulity is somewhat contradictory: 'Bacon's criticism of philosophy as a chronicle of degeneracy leaves him tied to that philosophy, and nowhere more than in his views on magic' (p. 356). See also Stephen Gaukroger, *Francis Bacon and the Transformation of Early-Modern Philosophy* (Cambridge University Press, 2001).

[11] This is the sense of 'virtue' as 'Power, efficacy, worth … With reference to a precious stone: magical power, esp. for healing or protection; (in later use also) great worth or value' (*OED*, 8a).

Preserving of *Health*; I doubt it is but a *Conceit*; For that the Snake is thought to renue her *Touth*, by Casting her *Spoile*. They might as well take the *Beake* of an *Eagle*, or a Peece of a *Harts-Horne*, because those Renue' (969). In this way, Bacon's position is somewhat contradictory, accepting the possibility of a transmission of 'vertue' between objects and people, but dismissing some 'natural' remedies as mere imagination or fanciful.

Such debates are thus tied to wider philosophical questions of evidence, belief, and superstition; this is particularly apparent when Bacon discusses the possibility of 'Secret Passages of *Sympathy*, betweene *Persons* of *neare Blood*' (986). There are many reports, he says, that men have an 'inward feeling' when someone they know dies. Bacon recalls an instance of this that he has experienced:

> I my Selfe remember, that being in *Paris*, and my *Father* dying in *London*, two or three dayes before my *Fathers* death, I had a *Dreame*, which I told to divers *English Gentlemen*; That my *Fathers House*, in the *Countrey*, was *Plastered* all over with *Blacke Mortar*. (986)

For Bacon, this experience suggests that there was a secret passage of sympathy between himself and his father, which prompted him to have this premonition of his father's death, denoted through black mortar. But if there is force and imagination between individuals, Bacon writes, it is probable that 'the *Force* is much more in the *Joynt Imaginations* and *Affections* of *Multitudes*' (988). Here sympathy is understood as a transference of emotion. For example, if there is a battle some distance away, does the joy or grief of the soldiers transmit to the people at home? Bacon gives the example of the battle of the Lepanto: '*Pius Quintus,* at the very time, when that Memorable *Victorie* was won, by the *Christians,* against the *Turks*, at the *Navall Battell* of *Lepanto*, being then hearing of *Causes* in *Consistorie,* brake off suddenly, and said to those about him; *It is now more time, we should give thanks to God, for the great Victorie he hath granted us, against the Turks*' (988). The explanation is that '*Victorie* had a *Sympathie* with his *Spirit*', suggesting that the emotions of a multitude can affect an individual at a distance. Once again, however, Bacon's fascination with such phenomena is combined with an awareness that they may be a matter of perception, and the result of superstition or even confirmation bias: 'It is true, that that may hold in these Things, which is the generall *Root* of *Superstition*; Namely, that *Men* observe when *Things Hit*, and not when they *Misse*: And commit to Memory the one, And forget and passe over the other' (988).

It seems particularly suggestive, then, that the text concludes with a discussion of the weapon-salve. One might even suggest that this alleged cure is something of an exemplary test case for much of the evidence and debates gathered within *Sylva sylvarum*. As Bacon writes, 'It is constantly Received, and touched, that the *Anointing* of the *Weapon*, than maketh the *Wound*, will heale the *Wound* it selfe. In this *Experiment*, upon the Relation of *Men* of *Credit*, (though my selfe, as yet, am not fully inclined to beleeve it,) you shall note the *Points* following' (998). Bacon helpfully describes the recipe and directions for using the salve, which involves a bizarre concoction of ingredients being applied to the weapon (or one resembling it) that caused the original wound. The list of ingredients is long and somewhat challenging to obtain, and includes 'the *Mosse* upon the *Skull* of a *dead Men*, *Unburied*; And the *Fats* of a *Beare*, and a *Beare*, killed in the *Act* of *Generation*' (998). The specificity of such items seems almost designed to make the salve impossible to make, and must have deterred all but the most enthusiastic of natural philosophers and experimenters. Indeed Bacon suggests that there is a certain laziness in ascribing the causes of things to '*Secret* and *Hidden Vertues*, and *Proprieties*', because 'this hath arrested, and laid asleepe, all true *Enquiry*, and *Indications*'. And yet, he continues, 'I doe not understand, but in the *Practicall Part* of *Knowledge*, much will be left to *Experience*, and *Probation*, whereunto *Indication* cannot so fully reach' (999). In this way, Bacon indicates a certain ambivalence regarding natural magic in general and the weapon-salve in particular, suggesting that experience and examination is required when dealing with such uncertain phenomena.

Bacon's ambivalence was noted by William Foster in his *Hiplocrisma-spongus, or, A Sponge to Wipe Away the Weapon-Salve* (1631). Foster notes that 'the learned Sir *Francis Bacon* is not at all for this cure. He professeth himself not resolved whether it be affected or no'.[12] Foster's treatise represents most sustained and rigorous attack on the weapon-salve printed in England; he does not deny that it works, but rather that it is '*Magicall and Diabolicall*' (p. 4). The primary target is the London physician Robert Fludd's *Anatomiae amphitheatrum* (1623; Figure 8), which contained a brief defence of the salve as part of a digression on mystical properties of blood.[13] Indeed the title page of Foster's text was nailed to Fludd's door in

---

[12] William Foster, *Hiplocrisma-spongus, or, A Sponge to Wipe Away the Weapon-Salve* (London, 1631), p. 37.
[13] Robert Fludd, *Anatomiae amphitheatrum effigie triplici* (Frankfurt, 1623), pp. 236–39. See Debus, 'Robert Fludd and the Use of Gilbert's *De Magnete*', p. 393; and Kassell, 'Magic, Alchemy and the Medical Economy', p. 91. For a contemporaneous defence of the salve, which attributed its workings to magnetism rather than magical sympathy, see Jan Baptist Van Helmont's *De magnetica vulnerum curatione* (On the Magnetic Cure of Wounds) (Paris, 1621).

'As God loves Sympathy, God loves Symphony' 223

Figure 8 Robert Fludd, *Anatomiae amphitheatrum effigie triplici* (Frankfurt, 1623), title page. Wellcome Collection, London.

the year of its publication. As this pointedly Lutheran act might suggest, Foster was a Church of England clergyman, and his religious position is bound up with his intellectual objections to the salve. After listing various biblical example of cures, including Naaman washing himself in the River Jordan to cure his leprosy, Foster makes it clear that the weapon-salve is in a different category: 'But this *Weapon-Salve* worketh neither of these wayes; *Ergo*, the cures done by it are not lawfull, but prestigious, magicall and diabolicall' (p. 5). Foster offers a logical discussion of the theories behind the weapon-salve, and that fact it works 'not by corporall contact' because 'the bodies are disjoined' (p. 5). The very idea that the weapon-salve works across all distances, unencumbered by intervening objects, seems to Foster absurd, and his argument reaches a grand rhetorical crescendo:

> Now then shall terrestriall agents by distance and interposition bee totally, and celestiall partly hindred; and shall this *Weapon-Salve* worke from the weapon to the wound at all distances? Shall the interposition of neither ayre, woods, fire, waters, walles, houses, Castles, Cities, mountaines, heate, cold, nothing stay or hinder the derivation of the virtue of it, to the body

of the party wounded? O Agent beyond all Agents! Certainly the Angels of heaven cannot worke at such a distance. Onely God whose Essence is infinite, and is *Omnia in omnibus*, all in all, can worke thus: because from him nothing is distant at all. (p. 7).

In this way, the weapon-salve is an affront to God and his authority; for Foster, the salve is an opportunity to remind his readers of God's infinite essence and presence. He begins the second part of the text by claiming that the salve 'is the new invention of the divell, an old impostor' (p. 9). He also likens its working to the practices of witches, 'who make pictures of men in waxe, and pricking them, the party for whose picture it is made, is tormented' (p. 12). This is likened to the description of Medea in book 6 of Ovid's *Heroides*: 'Medea *curseth those which absent are, | And with her charmes she wounds mens hearts from farre; | Of waxe she images doth make of men, | And placeth needles in their bosomes then*' (p. 12). The speaker in this passage – which appears to be Foster's own translation – is Hypsipyle, who is writing to Jason, having learned that he has abandoned her for Medea. Hypsipyle thus emphasizes Medea's foreignness and occult powers, and especially the unsettling possibility that Medea can control men from afar.[14] In this way, Foster draws upon literary and mythical sources for his critique of the weapon-salve, and associates its workings with other dangerous forms of action at a distance.

Foster does include an objection, or defence of the salve, noting that there are 'naturall and lawfull cures which are wrought by Sympathies'. He continues: 'this unguent consisting of mans-mosse, blood and fat, hath in it a naturall Balsame. This naturall Balsame by the influence of the Starres, causeth a sympathy betwixt the weapon and the wound: and so the application of the Medicine to the one, effects the cure upon the other. Therefore this cure is naturall and lawfull' (p. 20). But for Foster it is false that this balsam can cause sympathy between the wound and the weapon, not least because the weapon is a 'is an hard insensible substance voyd of all affection and pathy' – that is, a feeling (*OED*, 'pathy', 1). This lack of 'pathy', combined with the sheer distance between the wound and the weapon, makes the idea of sympathy between them even less likely, and prompts an ironic apostrophe from Foster: 'O inchanting Salve!' (p. 21). Foster also denies that substances such as the loadstone or blood have agency or life that exists separately from the human body; he thus argues that the body and soul are separate: 'When we say the blood is the

---

[14] See Katherine Heavey, *The Early Modern Medea: Medea in English Literature, 1558–1688* (London: Palgrave Macmillan, 2015), p. 45.

life, it is a figurative speech' (p. 27). He continues with a discussion of the relationship between the soul the blood that reflects upon the workings of the affections:

> And for the boyling of the blood in anger, palenesse and flight of the blood in feare, rednesse of the face and blushing in shame, &c. These come not by reason of life and motion in the blood: but because the blood is moved according to the affections of the soule: and the soule is in the blood. (p. 30)

As Foster suggests, the soul resides in the blood while the body is alive, but the blood is moved according to the affections and not vice versa. His comments offer clear evidence that early moderns had a sense of the distinction between literal and metaphorical articulations of the body. Moreover, his reflections upon the workings of the blood implicitly question the critical commonplace that, for early moderns, the passions were primarily a bodily experience.

Having established this separation of the body and soul, Foster goes on to query the possibility of 'sympathy' between the substances smeared on the weapon, and those residing in the living human. He rehearses the argument that there is a likeness between sunbeams and the healing power of the balsam: 'For as the *radij* or Sun-beames are a messenger betwixt heaven and earth: So this vitall beame or invisible line is a messenger and conductor (by a kinde of Magneticall attraction) of the healing virtue of the balsame, residing in the unguent, to the body of the wounded party: and the sympathy betwixt the blood on the annointed Weapon, and the blood in the body causeth the cure' (p. 40). However, Foster denies that 'Scull-mosse or bones, Mummy and mans Fat have … any natural balsame or radicall humour (for so some call naturall balsame) residing in them, sympathizing with the hyposticall balsame remaining in living man' (p. 42). Here he uses the occult or arcane definition of *sympathize* as 'to respond sympathetically to some influence' (*OED*, 1). It is true, he says, that the sun beams move between heaven and Earth; but the sun is a giant celestial body, which is ordained by God and Nature 'to worke upon the terrestriall by light or beames, motion and influence' (p. 44). The unguent does not have the mass or potency of the sun: 'A little fire cannot burne or heat a great body, at a great distance … No more can a little Salve worke naturally on a Patient at a great distance, when many other bodies are interposed' (pp. 44–5). More importantly, the blood residing on the weapon is no longer alive: 'but that cold, dead, dry, corrupted blood, out of the body should sympathize with moyst, warme, living, perfect blood in the body, seemes to mee such a paradoxe, that I thinke I shall not beleeve in whilst I have blood in mine owne body' (p. 47).

In this way, Foster uses the terms *sympathy* and *sympathize* in their earlier, natural philosophical senses of correspondence and influence. But he nevertheless uses *sympathize* in a more metaphorical way to describe the way in which Fludd's salve persuades people to believe in its efficacy: 'And so Master Doctors argument of sympathy, and his sympathizing Salve, cannot be salved to be naturall and sympathize with reason, though he hath fetched an argument from Dyers and Lyers, from the Divell, the father of Lyers to maintain it' (p. 52). Even the word *salve* is reappropriated and is used in its verbal form to suggest 'To render tenable' (*OED*, 3). Foster's treatise is thus alive to the possibilities of metaphor, and displays a certain degree of creativity in its use of the very terms it criticizes by linking magical and intellectual sympathizing. Foster concludes his case by citing an example from Jean Roberti, a Belgian Jesuit who had written an attack on the salve in 1615.[15] He describes how one man, unable to obtain the supposedly necessary moss and mummy, created a version of the cure using herbs from his own garden:

> Where is then the sympathy? where's the Balsame residing in the Mosse, Mummy, and Mans fat? Where is the Magneticall operation? Where's the spirit of the blood? where the occult qualities? where's the invisible line carryed in the ayre? Surely all in the Divell. Hee is all in all in the businesse, and for my part to him I leave it all. (p. 55)

Foster's position is something of a paradox, then, in the sense that his scepticism falls short of a complete rejection of the weapon-salve and its properties. The cure works, he suggests, neither by natural means, nor divine operation, but through 'Magicke and an implicite compact with the Divell' (p. 56). His faith in the weapon-salve is thus competing with his religious faith, and the fact that he does not deny its efficacy allows space for a response from Dr Fludd himself.

Doctor Fludds answer unto M. Foster or, The squeesing of Parson Fosters sponge (1631) was Fludd's only work to be published in English. The main thrust of Fludd's argument is that his cure not only works but is also part of God's work; he thus counters Foster's accusation that the cure is unlawful or diabolical. Fludd emphasizes that they are the same religion, 'that I am his Brother in Christ, and his Country-man, yea, and not differing from him in Religion'.[16] In this way, Fludd begins by emphasizing the sympathy between the two men, so to speak, as well as

---

[15] See Debus, 'Robert Fludd and the Use of Gilbert's *De Magnete*', p. 392.
[16] Robert Fludd, *Doctor Fludds answer unto M. Foster or, The squeesing of Parson Fosters sponge* (London, 1631), p. 2.

establishing his own religious credentials. Fludd cites various passages from Scripture, including John's Gospel, to emphasize his belief that God is in all things: 'he is the Catholicke Actor of life, whereupon the Apostle teacheth us, that hee vivifieth all things, and therefore hee is said to bee in the spirit of the world, and also without it, no division of his divine Essence being made … tempering and uniting everie particle, as it were with the glew of perfect love and harmonie' (p. 8). God thus becomes the sympathetic force uniting everything in the universe. This religious approach is combined with the natural philosophical, as Fludd goes on to observe that there are various phenomena in the universe that work at a distance, including the loadstone, the sun and fire, and contagious diseases. The weapon-salve also works 'by a vertual contact, namely, by a Simpathetical property, which doth operate … betweene the beginning and end magnetically and occultly or mystically' (p. 29). This reference to a sympathetical property refers to the (now obsolete) occult understanding of *sympathetic* rather than the later affective or interpersonal meaning.[17] For Fludd, then, the weapon-salve can be explained by the concept of natural sympathy, which can be seen in various observable forms of action at a distance.

Fludd argues (contra-Foster) that because blood is part of the ointment it must therefore affect, or sympathize with, the blood of the individual it is being used to treat. Several passages from Job are employed to prove that the blood on the weapon 'is rejoyced in the nature of the other, forasmuch as both doe sympathise together, being that they are all of one consonance or degree, or unison in vitall love' (p. 93). Fludd employs the same musical analogy employed by Bacon to illustrate this concept: two lutes are placed on a table with a straw placed on one string of one lute; the corresponding string on the other lute is struck, and the observer will see the straw leap due to 'sympatheticall harmony' (p. 94). He compares this experiment to the workings of the weapon-salve:

> In which experiment you may note, that the string strucke, is aptly compared unto the blood of the wounded, being stil animated in his body, who doth by a secret emanation or emission, and that by a naturall inclination, and sympathy, cause in the selfe-same tone a secret communication between the still and occult spirit in the congealed blood, which is in the oyntment, which I compare to the string, which the straw hath on it … (p. 94)

---

[17] 'Relating to, involving, depending on, acting or effected by "sympathy", or a (real or supposed) affinity, correspondence, or occult influence; esp. in sympathetic powder' (*OED*, 'sympathetic', 1a).

In this way, there is harmony within difference: 'For as both are but one spirit, though they seeme to differ in distance, as doe the chord of both Lutes, so likewise are those two tones but one tone; though they seeme to differ: and therefore make but one unisone' (pp. 94–5). The same can be said of Fludd's analogy, which describes 'one mutuall consent of sim-patheticall harmony' (p. 98). Fludd presents this harmony as a kind of symphony of sympathies, and he quotes Acts 17:26 as evidence for his claim that humans are united in the same blood: 'for as much as the Text saith, *that all mankind is made of one blood onely*: and therefore this union of symphoniacall or sympatheticall harmony, is not easily to bee limited, by Master *Fosters* phantasticall sphaere of activity' (p. 128). The term *symphoniacal* is another obsolete word, which appeared in several texts in the mid-seventeenth century, meaning 'harmonious; consonant, accordant' (*OED*). Like Donne, then, Fludd makes an analogy between the concept of sympathy and the idea of a symphony between different elements. Indeed his metaphorical comparisons are a kind of rhetorical enactment of the mutual consent that he describes.

If anyone should be doubtful about the efficacy of the weapon-salve after these theological and natural philosophical arguments, Fludd treats his readers to several stories, usually second-hand, which illustrate his claims that bodies can affect each other at a distance. We learn that Lady Ralegh claimed that her late husband would stop the bleeding of any person, even at a remote distance, 'if he had a handkirchers, or some other piece of linnen dipped in some of the blood of the party sent unto him'. The status of this particular individual is further proof of the cure's genuineness; so wise a personage as Sir Walter could not have used such a cure if it were 'done by the divell' (p. 131). The most striking of these stories is the tale of a certain Lord or nobleman in Italy, who loses his nose in a fight, and has a replacement fashioned out of the flesh of a slave. The new nose works well for a time, and the slave is able to enjoy his freedom – though only briefly:

> The slave being healed and rewarded, was manumitted, or set at liberty, and away he went to Naples. It happened, that the slave fell sicke and dyed, at which instant, the Lords nose did gangrenate and rot; whereupon the part of the nose which hee had of the dead man, was by the Doctors advice cut away, and hee being animated by the foresaid experience, followed the advice of the same Phisician, which was to wound in like manner his owne arme, and to apply it to his wounded and mutilated nose, and to endure with patience, till all was compleate as before. He with animosity & patience, did undergoe the brunt, and so his nose continued with him untill his death. (pp. 132–3)

Regrettably Fludd does not offer any specific evidence – textual or pictorial – of this remarkable tale; but it is used nevertheless to counter Foster's scepticism about the distance between bodies being impairment to their sympathetical influence upon each other.[18] Strikingly, the text ends with a hymn to God, rather than further anecdotes or accounts of experimentation, and is thus a powerful riposte to Foster's treatise: 'Finis omnium & principium Deus. / God is the end and beginning of all things' (p. 64, second count). Fludd also includes a long quotation from Isaiah: 'Woe unto them that speake good of evill; and evill of good: which put darknesse for light, and light for darknesse: that put bitter for sweet; and sweet for sowre. Woe unto them that are wise in their owne eyes, and prudent in their owne sight' (p. 65). In this way, Fludd takes on the specific argument offered by Foster that the cure is the work of the devil, and presents various forms of evidence – natural philosophical, theological, and anecdotal – to support his claims. But what is striking in this controversy is the lack of agreement between these authors. Far from solving, or perhaps salving, the debate, Fludd's treatise simply added to the material at the disposal of English readers, and left the space open for further responses by James Hart and Daniel Sennert.[19] As we shall see in the next section, there were various creative responses to the debate in the wider culture, in which playwrights debated not only this curious medical practice but also the concept of sympathy more generally.

'How equally we two / Divide true sorrow, sympathize in griefe': Salves and Sympathy in Caroline Drama

When we turn to other cultural texts from the period we find that belief the weapon-salve was treated even more sceptically than in works by religious writers such as Foster and Sennert. But we can also detect a wider

---

[18] Lawrence Lipking writes that such stories should not be taken as 'mere flummery', because evidence in this period 'was demonstrative, based on testimony rather than on inductive logic supported by hard facts and statistics … The luminaries who vouched for the weapon-salve personified truth; the doubting Thomases in thrall to circumstantial evidence had lashed themselves to error' (*What Galileo Saw: Imagining the Scientific Revolution* (Ithaca: Cornell University Press, 2014), p. 133). And yet, as we shall see below, the idea of evidence based on mere testimony is parodied in Glapthorne's *The Hollander*.

[19] The weapon-salve was criticized from a medical perspective in James Hart's *Klinike, or The diet of the diseased. Divided into three bookes* (London, 1633) and by James Primerose in his *De Vulgi in Medicina Erroribus* (London, 1638). Daniel Sennert's *The weapon-salves maladie: or, A declaration of its insufficiencie to performe what is attributed to it* (London, 1637) concludes, like Foster, that 'this Cure is atchieved by the helpe or power of the *Divell* himselfe, drawne thereto by some close or open compact' (p. 29). Fludd returned to the subject in his posthumously printed *Philosophia Moysaica* (Gouda, 1638), which was translated into English some twenty years later as *Mosaicall philosophy: Grounded upon the essentiall truth or eternal sapience* (London, 1659).

scepticism about the workings of natural sympathy – particularly in relation to human desires and emotions. John Ford's *The Lover's Melancholy* (1626), which focuses on the melancholy state of Prince Palador following his father's death, contains a suggestive reference to the kinds of sympathetic relationships invoked by Bacon and Fludd. 3.2 depicts an encounter between Thamasta (Palador's cousin) and Eroclea, who is disguised as a boy named Parthenophill. Thamasta describes the unseen affinities between minerals and plants in the natural world as a way of explaining her desire for this apparently low-born youth:

> The constant loadstone and the steel are found
> In several mines, yet is there such a league
> Between these minerals, as if one vein
> Of earth had nourished both. The gentle myrtle
> Is not engraft upon an olive's stock,
> Yet nature hath between them locked a secret
> Of sympathy, that being planted near,
> They will both in their branches, and their roots
> Embrace each other. Twines of ivy round
> The well-grown oak; the vine doth court the elm;
> Yet these are different plants.[20]

Here Thamasta describes plants that seem to embrace or 'court' each other because of this 'secret / Of sympathy' in nature.[21] She goes on to relate such phenomena to her incongruous attraction to Parthenophill: 'these sleight creatures / Will fortify the reasons I should frame / For that ungrounded – as thou think'st – affection / Which is submitted to a stranger's pity' (3.2.88–91). The concept of natural sympathy is used by Thamasta to reflect upon the workings of human passions. And yet, as Tom MacFaul has emphasized, she is using all of her rhetorical skills to justify her affections, and as a result we should be suspicious of her reasoning.[22] Moreover, the fact that 'Parthenophill' is not what he seems, both in terms

---

[20] Quotations are from John Ford, *The Lover's Melancholy* in *'Tis Pity She's a Whore and Other Plays*, ed. Marion Lomax (Oxford University Press, 1995), 3.2.77–87.

[21] Elements of this passage appear to be derived from the third partition of Robert Burton's *The anatomy of melancholy* (Oxford, 1621), which describes the 'Sympathy or Antipathy which is to be seene in animate and inanimate creatures ... and is especially observed in vegetalls: as betwixt the Vine and Elme a great Sympathie ... the Olive and the Myrtle embrace one another, in roots & branches if they grow neere' (pp. 503–4).

[22] MacFaul, *Shakespeare and the Natural World*, p. 17. Ford's play also queries the idea that melancholy is the result of a humoral imbalance; as the physician Corax states, 'Melancholy / Is not as you conceive, indisposition / Of body, but the mind's disease' (3.1.100–2). He suggests that melancholy is first begot in the brain, 'The seat of reason' (108). See Lisa Hopkins, 'Staging Passion in Ford's *The Lover's Melancholy*', *Studies in English Literature, 1500–1900*, 45 (2005), 443–59 (p. 445).

of his status or gender, further complicates Thamasta's use of natural philosophy to explain her feelings for him.

Later plays from the period take a more specific interest in the weapon-salve and the idea of sympathetic cures. In Francis Quarles's *The Virgin Widow* (written 1640; printed 1649), for example, Jeffery Quibble describes the talents of his master, the apothecary Quack: 'He hath done rare cures by naturall Magick, Sympathies, and Antipathies; But this is Heathen Greek to you: Who would have conceiv'd that Sir *Walter Raleighs* blood should have cured *Goudomors* Fistula in *ano?*'[23] This appears to be a reference to Fludd's claim that Raleigh was able to stop the bleeding of others; but here the intent is clearly satirical, poking fun at cures based upon natural magic and the doctrine of sympathies and antipathies. As this example suggests, in order to paint a more comprehensive picture of cultural attitudes towards the weapon-salve, we need to investigate a range of printed texts beyond the Foster-Fludd controversy itself. Such texts also indicate the complex development that the word *sympathy* had already undergone prior to the 1630s. The fact that *The Virgin Widow* itself uses the word *sympathy* to describe a correspondence of suffering indicates that the affective meaning of the term coexisted alongside the natural philosophical concept. In 3.1 Queen Augusta reads a letter from King Evaldus which states that 'The ill Construction of our loves, enforces me to whisper my Affection in the Sympathie of thy sufferings'.[24]

We find a more extended exploration of sympathy – in both its magical and interpersonal senses – in Henry Glapthorne's *The Hollander* (written 1636; printed 1640).[25] The play certainly attests to the cultural awareness of the weapon-salve debate; but it also reminds us that it was a debate, and that dramatists satirised the pseudo-scientific beliefs espoused by writers such as Fludd.[26] The play might even be seen as instigating the mini-genre

---

[23] Francis Quarles, *The Virgin Widow. A Comedie* (London, 1649), 4.1 (p. 46).
[24] *The Virgin Widow*, p. 34. Quarles had used the affective meaning of *sympathize* in his narrative poem *Argalus and Parthenia: The argument of ye history* (London, 1629), which reworks the Argalus and Parthenia episode from Sidney's *Arcadia*. In book 2 Parthenia describes how the Queen responded sympathetically to an account of her misfortunes: 'At length, they did acquaint / The faire Queene Hellen with my strange complaint, / Whose noble heart did truly sympathize / With mine, partaking in my miserie' (p. 29).
[25] See Martin Wiggins and Catherine Richardson, *British Drama 1533–1642: A Catalogue, Volume IX: 1632–1636* (Oxford University Press, 2018), p. 449.
[26] In one of the few critical treatments of the play, William F. Bynum notes that Glapthorne's inspiration was the Foster-Fludd debate rather than Digby; see 'The Weapon Salve in Seventeenth Century English Drama', *Journal of the History of Medicine and Allied Sciences*, 21 (1966), 8–23. He comments that the play has 'slight artistic merit' but is nevertheless interesting for portraying 'the major outlines of a not unimportant chapter in Renaissance medicine' (p. 23).

of scientific satires that emerged in the Restoration period, which mocked natural philosophers and virtuosi.[27] It centres on Dr Artless and his wife, who run a successful hospital for women in London, which is in fact a house where female patrons can arrange and enjoy assignations with its male guests. Two of their patients are Lady Yellow and her sister, Mistress Know-worth, and the play opens with a discussion of the latter's ague; as Mistress Artless puts it, 'I should have found / Some lusty youth that would have given her physicke, / More powerfull to expell that lasie humour / Than all your Cordialls'.[28] Thus, while the Artlesses' business may be flourishing, with its own in-house Apothecary, the play acknowledges that Artless's cordials may be less effective than human interventions and relationships in curing the residents' ailments.

The action that follows resembles that of a city comedy, concerned with the Artlesses' attempts to find a husband for their daughter Dalinea, who eventually marries the young suitor Popinjay. But what is most distinctive about the play is its interest in the history of medicine and the weapon-salve. Sconce – the Hollander of the title – is a naturalised Dutchman who apparently desires the women of the house, but is actually far more keen to acquire Artless's magical cure, which he hopes will make his fortune. Sconce asks about Artless's credentials, and he is assured that he is a man experienced in the arts of medicine:

> And you perhaps labor of some disease,
> And come to seeke for remedy, I can
> As *Gallen* or *Hipocrates*, read a lecture,
> On maladies, their causes and effects,
> Tell by the countenance of a man, the ill oppresses him,
> You by that *Linea curva* ith' altitude of your horoscope,
> Should be subject to *Calentures*. (p. 84)

Artless thus underlines his ability to read both medical texts, including works by Galen and Hippocrates, and afflicted individuals. He suggests that, due to the curved line of his horoscope, Sconce is subject to calentures – a disease afflicting sailors in the tropics; it was also used figuratively to suggest 'Fever; burning passion, ardour, zeal, heat, glow' (*OED*, 2). However, this turns out to be a misreading: Sconce reveals that his only affliction is a 'gentile itch' that he acquired in the Low Countries (one

---

[27] See Al Coppola, *The Theater of Experiment: Staging Natural Philosophy in Eighteenth-Century Britain* (Oxford University Press, 2016), pp. 59–62.

[28] Quotations from *The Hollander* are taken from R. H. Shepherd (ed.), *The Plays and Poems of Henry Glapthorne*, 2 vols (London: John Pearson, 1874), vol. 1, pp. 75–157 (p. 76). Further references will be given by page number in the text.

does not need to be a medical expert to diagnose this condition). Indeed the play is just as interested in misreading and misdiagnosis as it is in the history of medical practice.

When Artless has departed, Sconce attempts to determine the whereabouts of the salve from Artless's man, Urinal. In 2.1 we discover the pair with a box of the weapon-salve, and Sconce enquires about its authenticity: 'But are you certaine *Urinall* this oyntment is Orthodoxall; may I without errour in my faith believe this same the weapon salve Authenticall?' Urinal assures him that it is 'infallibly the creame of weapon salves'. He continues:

> the simples which doe concurre to th' composition of it, speake it most sublime stuffe; tis the rich Antidote that scorns the steele, and bids the Iron be in peace with men, or rust: *Aurelius Bombastus Paracelsus*, was the first inventer of this admirable Unguent. (p. 93)

Paracelsus is named as the inventor of the salve, but his reputation as a physician and natural philosopher is less certain. Sconce suggests that he was seen as an 'Errant Conjurer', but Urinal defends him as 'an excellent Naturallist', and suggests that his master 'comes very neare him in the secrets concerning bodies Physicall, as Herbes, Roots, Plants vegetable and radicall, out of whose quintessence, mixt with some hidden causes, he does extract this famous weapon salve' (p. 93). Their discussion also contains some references to the Foster-Fludd exchange considered above: Sconce suggests that there is a Welsh doctor in the city who is reportedly skilful in compounding the salve; and this is almost certainly a satirical portrait of Robert Fludd, who was of Welsh descent.[29] Sconce reports that he does not like the Welsh doctor, who refused to hand over his weapon-salve, and stated that '*Hollanders* were *Jewes*' (p. 94). Urinal provides various anecdotes attesting to the efficacy of Artless's weapon-salve, including the tale of the Puritan who hanged himself on the bell ropes of his church, only to be miraculously revived by Artless by anointing the noose with his magical cure. In this way, the play replicates the rhetorical strategies of Fludd's treatise, but also exposes them as artless tales that offered as evidence by an unreliable narrator.

Later in the same scene, Sir Martin Yellow becomes jealous of Sconce, thinking that he is desirous of Lady Yellow, and wounds him in the arm. We discover Sconce at the start of act three, attending not to his wound but his weapon; yet the salve seems ineffective: 'this weapon salve,

---

[29] See Bynum, 'The Weapon Salve in Seventeenth Century English Drama', pp. 20–1.

so much extold by th' Twiball Knights, commended by *Mixum*, deified by *Urinall*, and adored by my believing selfe, procures no more miraculous effect, than if it were *unguentum album*' (p. 109). The unguent he mentions is a white ointment for inflammations and sores in common use in the period.[30] And yet, rather than questioning the efficacy of the salve or its enthusiastic proponents, Sconce attributes its ineffectiveness to his Dutch blood: 'Well, I am confident yet, there's no defect ith' *unguent*; my blood, my blood is sure anathemated; carries some curs'd impediment about it, that disannuls the vertue and incomparable force of the divine salve' (p. 109). Artless suggests that it was the dressing that was faulty rather than Sconce's blood; but more suggestive here is the intervention of Freewit, a suitor to Mistress Know-worth, who has seen the salve in action, but is dubious about its status and origins. He does not understand its workings, 'and therefore / Transcending naturall causes, I conclude / The use unlawfull' (p. 116). According to him, conscience and religion do not allow 'The assistance of a medicine made by charmes, / Or subtle spells of witchcraft' (p. 116).

Freewit's position thus resembles that of William Foster, who – as we have already seen – directs precisely these objections at Fludd's cure. The debate about whether the salve is natural or diabolical is recast into a dramatic dialogue between Freewit and Artless. Freewit's position is clearly stated:

> Out of your words sir Ile prove it Diabolicall, no cause
> Naturall; begets the most contemn'd effect,
> Without a passage through the meanes, the fire
> Cannot produce another fire untill
> It be apply'd to subject apt to take
> Its flaming forme, nor can a naturall cause,
> Worke at incompetent space: how then can this
> Neither consign'd to th' matter upon which
> Its operation is to cause effect;
> Nay at so farre a distance, worke so great
> And admirable a cure beyond the reach
> And law of nature; yet by you maintain'd,
> A naturall lawfull agent, what dull sence can credit it.   (p. 117)

Here Freewit articulates Foster's objections regarding the salve's ability to work at a distance. Like Foster, he does not dispute its operation but rather its naturalness. Sconce describes Freewit's argument as 'Very authenticke',

---

[30] See Juhani Norri, *Dictionary of Medical Vocabulary in English, 1375–1550: Body Parts, Sicknesses, Instruments, and Medicinal Preparations* (London: Routledge, 2016), pp. 1141–2.

and fears that his arm will be possessed with an 'evill spirit'. In this way Glapthorne's play not only stages the controversy between Fludd and Foster by converting their arguments into a dramatic dialogue but also includes figured responses from Sconce and Fortresse, who represent readers of, or responses to, that textual debate.

Artless offers a lengthy speech in defence of the cure, suggesting that Freewit speaks reason, but that 'every cause / Workes not the same way', and that some work by 'virtuall contact' (p. 117). This is a specific borrowing from Fludd's treatise, which also describes the workings of the salve as 'a vertual contact … a Simpathetical property'.[31] And, like Fludd, Artless uses the example of celestial bodies working on materials on earth: 'the bright Sun does in the solid earth, / By the infusive vertue of his raies, / Convert the sordid substance of the mold / To Mines of mettall, and the piercing ayre' (p. 118). He continues:

> The Load-stone so by operative force,
> Causes the Iron which has felt his touch,
> To attract another Iron; nay, the Needle
> Of the ship guiding compasse, to respect
> The cold Pole Articke; just so the salve workes,
> Certaine hidden causes convay its powerfull
> Vertue to the wound from the annointed
> Weapon, and reduce it to welcome soundnesse.   (p. 118)

Artless's eloquent defence compares the workings of the salve to the needle of a compass that is attracted to the North Pole, but we might also recall Bacon's concerns about using hidden virtues as an explanation for the behaviour of objects in the natural world. Sconce's response is comically fickle, inasmuch as he is easily swayed by the last position articulated: 'The salve is legitimate agen, Cosen *Fortresse*, O rare Doctor' (p. 118). Artless suggests that it is the blood in the salve that effects the cure, because 'there is a reall simpathy / Twixt it, and that which has the juyce of life, / Moystens the body wounded' (p. 119). Fortresse is happy with this explanation, describing the Doctor as a 'Rare *Paracelsian*' whose 'Annalls shall be cut in Brasse by Pen of steele' (p. 119).

These responses might seem to imply that ingenuous individuals are easily persuaded by rhetorically persuasive arguments; but it is worth noting that the final word in the scene goes to Freewit, and we do not hear

---

[31] Fludd, *Doctor Fludds answer unto M. Foster*, p. 29. Fludd goes on to write that 'the Sunne by his beames doth send out his spirit into a graine of corne in the Earth, and hath his lively influence or essentiall beames of Emission continuated with his like' (p. 36).

the reaction of Sconce or Fortresse.[32] Freewit also uses the term *simpathy* to suggest an occult relationship between things, but does so sceptically:

> You may as well
> Report a reall simpathy betweene
> The nimble soule in its swift flight to heaven,
> And the cold carkasse it has lately left,
> As a loath'd habitation; blood, when like
> The sap of Trees, which weepes upon the Axe
> Whose cruell edge does from the aged Trunke
> Dissever the green Branches from the Veines,
> Ravish'd, forgoes his Native heate, and has
> No more relation to the rest, than some
> Desertlesse servant, whom his Lord casts off,
> Has to his vertuous fellowes. (p. 119)

Freewit's speech thus recalls Foster's argument there is a decided lack of sympathy between the soul and body after the body has died. In the same way, he suggests, blood has no relation to the body after it has been removed. This point is made through a series of metaphors and comparisons with the natural world: when trees seemingly weep when struck by the axe, their sap soon grows cold once separated from the tree's body. A further metaphor involves a 'Desertlesse servant' cast off by his master – perhaps implying that he does not deserve to be dismissed – who has no relation to his previous comrades as a result. In this way, while Freewit's use of the term *simpathy* is still grounded in its natural philosophical definition, he has a more metaphorical understanding of the concept, and even uses a metaphor about interpersonal relations and social exclusion as a way of interrogating Artless's naive faith in the absolute likeness between medical and occult sympathies.

This interest in interpersonal relations is also apparent in the final two acts of the play, which involve acts of deception and cross-dressing that lead to marriages between Popinjay and Dalinea, and between Martha and Sconce. This part of the play has been dismissed by William Bynam as 'a series of rather contrived incidents'.[33] But what is significant about these final acts is their interest in affinity between individuals, which is marked by two appearances of the word *sympathize*. In 4.1, a disguised Popinjay encounters Dalinea, and recounts the tale of his 'younger brother', who

---

[32] Urinall describes Artless's rhetorical abilities in ambivalent terms in 4.1: 'Why looke you sir, my master has / Perswaded her as much as lay in him, and / He has a tounge able to cosen the divell' (p. 124).

[33] Bynam, 'The Weapon Salve in Seventeenth Century English Drama', p. 19.

professed his 'zealous love' for her (p. 132). Popinjay asks her to imagine a 'solitary Nightingale who sings / To her lost honour a harmonious ditty' (p. 133) and likens this bird's song to his brother's unvarying love for her. She is persuaded by Popinjay's speech, and compares this putative brother to him:

> Had your brother been
> Of the same disposition and soft sweetnesse
> That I perceive in you (though this be our
> First enterview) there could not have beene molded
> (Had I beene borne to entertaine loves heat)
> A man that would so fitly sympathize
> With my condition, nor whom I should fancy
> With more intire perfection. (p. 133)

Thus Dalinea expresses her admiration for Popinjay by comparing his qualities to those of this brother – who is of course a means of describing his own feelings for her. Dalinea implies that such a man is 'molded' while she is 'borne' to entertain love, implying that individuals have no choice in their affections and are acted upon by external forces – and yet, like Thamasta in *The Lover's Melancholy*, such arguments are often used by characters to justify feelings that they have willingly embraced.[34] The fact that Dalinea uses *sympathize* to describe their compatibility suggests a significant shift in emphasis: certainly in the first three acts the play is more concerned with the natural philosophical model of sympathy, but here the term is clearly being used to denote an affinity between people. Popinjay himself likens their relationship to the influence of heavenly bodies: 'Behold him Lady, / Whose every motion does as from the spheare, / Receive a lively influence from your lookes' (p. 133). However, this comparison is part of a highly metaphorical speech that uses a succession of astrological and natural metaphors to describe their love. This interest in the literary and philosophical possibilities of sympathy – together with the fact that Artless's weapon-salve is shown to be faulty – implies that Glapthorne's play is more concerned with interpersonal relationships than an arcane model of hidden causes and magical sympathies.

While Dalinea uses *sympathize* in its more general sense of agreeing and harmonizing with the other, we also find the term being used specifically in the sense of sympathizing with another's passions. In 5.1, Artless reports that his daughter has absconded with 'the younker Sconce' and is likely already married to him. Lady Yellow regrets Dalinea's decision,

---

[34] See also my discussion of Brandon's *The Vertuous Octavia* in Chapter 4, above.

implicitly suggesting that she has a considerable degree of agency: 'I pitty the poore girle / That she should be so suddaine in her choyce, / Enthrall her soule ith' manacles of fate, / (For such are nuptiall bonds) experience sister / Inforces me to lament her' (p. 145). This pity and grief is shared by Mistress Know-worth:

> How equally we two
> Divide true sorrow, sympathize in griefe,
> As in our blood and nature: sister you
> When your affectionate fancy fix'd your heart
> Upon your husbands love, had no suspition
> Of his unmanly jealousie, and I
> When I confin'd my love to *Freewits* breast,
> Judg'd him as void of falshood, as the spring
> When it has rested in green robes, the Earth is
> Of bare nakednesse, but we are both
> Deceiv'd by our credulity.   (p. 145)

The two sisters thus share in each other's woe as they contemplate Dalinea's situation. Her decision to enter into the bonds of matrimony reminds Know-worth of Lady Yellow's marriage to the jealous Sir Martin and her own commitment to the false Freewit. Dalinea's external situation thus increases the emotional bond between the two sisters. They 'Divide true sorrow', suggesting not only the strength and authenticity of their emotions, but also that they are shared between them equally. This is the context in which the term *sympathize* appears – that is, a sharing of feelings, and specifically grief. Indeed the term is used to describe an active and participatory exchange of feeling, which has its equivalent in Know-worth's description of agency and judgement in human relationships.

Thus the infidelities and irrational jealousies that the play dramatizes are cured – not by Artless's salve, but through acts of role-play and persuasion. When Sconce realises that he has married Martha, disguised as Lovering, he asks Artless to prescribe him an appropriate cure: 'Master Doctor you wish me well I know, I have married here I know not whom, you have excellent salves and unguents sir' (p. 154). However, when Artless tells Sconce that they are all at his disposal the latter appears to realise that they will not be effective: 'Thanke you good Mr. Doctor, have you never a one that will eat off the wen of manhood, make all whole before that will eunuchise a man, I would faine be a Hermaphrodite, or a woman to escape this match, I do not like it' (p. 154). A *wen* is a lump or protuberance on the body (*OED*, 1), or more figuratively a stain or blot (*OED*, 2). Clearly there are some things that Artless's magical salve cannot cure.

The Hollander is, then, a highly significant play both in relation to the history of medicine and its sceptical treatment of the weapon-salve, not least because it goes further than other commentators by denying that the miraculous cure works at all, and thus suggests that most early moderns encountering the salve would have recognized its somewhat preposterous edge. But it is also noteworthy in terms of the semantic and conceptual history of sympathy, demonstrating how the interest in natural sympathy could lead to a rearticulation of the imaginative and affective model. Indeed its narrative movement and shift in emphasis – from action at a distance to interpersonal sympathy – could be read as a metaphor for the rejection of the very ideas that lie behind Dr Artless's cure. Glapthorne's play thus provides us with further evidence that dramatic authors in the period were much more concerned with human relationships than with magical sympathies, even if the latter provided an imaginative springboard to define and describe the former.

'Their *passion*, our *compassion*': Charles Fitzgeffry's *Compassion towards Captives*

This fascination with sympathy for the other, combined with a sceptical awareness of natural sympathy, can also be found in the religious literature of the period. As we shall see below, the concept of sympathy at a distance was invoked as part of theological and ethical arguments as well as natural philosophical ones. But I want to begin this section with a sermon by the clergyman John Reading, printed in 1627, which makes a connection between the soul and music:

> melodies, and sweet harmonies (which are a musicall sound or consent of sundry duly proportioned notes, varied according to divers measures of time, with rising and falling of tunes) for the Analogie they have with the soule it selfe, and sympathie with the affections, which they doe both outwardly express, or resemble, and inwardly move.[35]

In addition to this musical analogy, which recalls Bacon's *Sylva sylvarum*, Reading uses *sympathy* later in the same text to refer to the feeling of another's misery: 'God commandeth sympathy, and sense of others miserie, (*Weepe with them that weepe*) and sorrow for our own: *Turne ye even unto mee with all your heart, and with fasting, and with mourning, and rent your*

---

[35] John Reading, *Davids soliloquie. Containing many comforts for afflicted mindes* (London, 1627), pp. 11–2.

hearts, &c.' (pp. 220–1). Quoting two key biblical verses, Romans 12:15 and Joel 2:12, Reading implies that sympathy is a godly commandment, even though the word itself does not appear in the Bible. The term was also used to describe Christ's compassion for others – for example by the writer and preacher Edward Reynolds in *An explication of the hundreth and tenth Psalme* (1632): 'Hee hath alreadie ascended up on high, and led captivity captive; yet in his members he still suffers, though not by way of *paine* or passion, yet by way of *Sympathy* or compassion, he is *touched with a feeling of our infirmities, Heb. 4.15*'.[36] Later in the same text, Reynolds again emphasizes Christ's compassion, describing '*his Sympathie*, for besides his *Essentiall mercy* as he is God, there was in him a *mercie which he learned* by being like unto us' (p. 393). As these examples suggest, religious writers in the 1620s and 1630s used the term *sympathy* to refer to an active form of compassion that involved having a sense or feeling of others' misery, and which could apply to individuals as well as Christ.

One of the most significant religious writers from this period to reflect upon this active form of sympathy was Charles Fitzgeffry, a Church of England clergyman and poet.[37] In 1603 Fitzgeffry became rector of St Dominick, near Saltash, where he remained until his death in 1637. Several of Fitzgeffry's sermons were printed, including his sermon given at the Cornish quarter sessions of 1630, which became *The curse of corne-horders* (1631). In this work, Fitzgeffry condemns the practice of hoarding corn and selling it for profit, which seems to him especially pernicious given the dearth of the previous two years.[38] He writes that 'Many Mens Barnes are full of Corne, but their brests are empty of compassion: their Garners are stuffed and stored; two yeeres graine under hand in many mens keeping, yet they still gape for a greater dearth, and doe their best, or rather worst to procure it'.[39] But rather than simply describing this situation Fitzgeffry invites his listeners to 'become officious Eves-droppers' outside the house of the poor neighbours, and 'listen to the pittious complaints that are among them'. He continues by imagining these sad complaints:

[36] Edward Reynolds, *An explication of the hundreth and tenth Psalme* (London, 1632), p. 116.
[37] Fitzgeffry wrote a poem commemorating Sir Francis Drake while still a student at Oxford, which was printed in 1596. The poem contains a rapturous account of Mount Helicon, describing it as 'Poets paradise, / Impressures of conceite, sap of delight, / Soules sweete Emplastrum, unguent of the eies, / Drops, making men with Gods to sympathize' (*Sir Francis Drake his honorable lifes commendation, and his tragicall deathes lamentation* (Oxford, 1596), sig. B4r). Thus Fitzgeffry was aware of the new English word *sympathize*, which had only appeared in print in 1594, using it here to describe the affinity between gods and men.
[38] See Anne Duffin, 'Fitzgeffry [Fitzgeffrey], Charles (c. 1575–1638)', *ODNB*.
[39] Charles Fitz-Geffrie, *The curse of corne-horders with the blessing of seasonable selling* (London, 1631), p. 34.

> Thus the feeble children doe call upon the wofull mother, shee complaines to the sad father, he answers her with pittious complaints against the pittilesse neighbours; Alas! What shall I doe? … I have beene over the Parish, I have beene out of the Parish, with money in my hand, and cannot get a pecke of Barley: they have it, but they say they cannot spare it. O miserable condition! (p. 36)

In this highly emotive passage, Fitzgeffry cultivates compassion amongst his listeners for the state of the poor – not simply by describing their predicament but rather by encouraging his audience to imagine themselves overhearing such piteous expressions of hunger and misery.

This kind of imaginative sympathy for the other is even more evident in *Compassion towards captives* (1637). This remarkable set of sermons was prompted by the increase in Turkish piracy on the south coasts of Devon and Cornwall in 1636. This is when the 'Turks' – pirates of various nationalities from the Barbary ports – resumed their attacks on small boats and on the coast itself, capturing and enslaving people.[40] This immediate context of Barbary-based piracy is certainly important, but it is also a chance for Fitzgeffry to extol his particular concern with imaginative compassion. The text contains three sermons on this theme, and begins with an address 'To the Compassionate, That Is, To the Truly Christian Reader' that aligns mercy and charity with Christianity itself, seeing the lack of these qualities as a particular hindrance: '*Want of charity*, want of the *bowels of mercy*, want of *Christian compassion*, want of feeling our brethrens wants, and consequently of true *Christianity*, these these are the wants that doe hinder us'.[41] We know that mercy was sometimes said by early moderns to be felt in the bowels, as Kristine Steenbergh has recently emphasized.[42] Fitzgeffry's emphasis upon the bowels of mercy may suggest a kind of physical sympathy or compassion with the other. But the greater emphasis in the three sermons is clearly upon remembering, imagining, and thinking about the other, through the example of Christ.

Fitzgeffry's text is Hebrews 13:3, which, as we have already seen, was a biblical verse deployed by preachers who wanted their audiences to imagine and reflect upon the sufferings of others.[43] And yet Fitzgeffry offers a far more detailed explication of and meditation on the constituent

---

[40] See Anne Duffin, *Faction and Faith: Politics and Religion in the Cornish Gentry before the Civil War* (University of Exeter Press, 1996), pp. 134–7.
[41] Charles Fitz-Geffry, *Compassion towards captives chiefly towards our brethren and country-men who are in miserable bondage in Barbarie* (Oxford, 1637), sig. **1v.
[42] See Steenbergh, 'Practising Compassion in Reformation England'.
[43] See Chapter 2, above.

parts of this significant verse. The first sermon takes the first part of the verse as its focus, '*Remember those that are in bonds as bound with them*' (p. 1). As Fitzgeffry writes, 'This is my text: whereof the scope and substance is *An exhortation* to pity and compassion towards them that are in bonds and captivity, especially for Christs sake' (p. 3). This leads him to reflect upon the misery of others and our duty to help them. As Fitzgeffry succinctly puts it, 'Their *passion,* our *compassion*'. The act of remembering involves reflecting upon their suffering from a position of freedom: 'Thinke upon their calamity and affliction. Let not your owne safety make you forgetfull of others misery: let not your enjoyed liberty drive out of your remembrance their calamitous captivity' (p. 3). In other words, Fitzgeffry invites his audience to remember the sufferings of others, not in spite but rather because of their 'enjoyed liberty'. The phrase '*As bound with them*' is glossed by Fitzgeffry as 'As if yourselves were in the same place and case'. He continues: 'Make their bondage your thraldome, their suffering, your owne smarting. Have a fellow-feeling with them, as being members of the same body, which is implied in the last part of the verse' (p. 3). Here Fitzgeffry employs the common metaphor of the members of the church being like the constituent parts of the same body. But rather than simply explicating these ideas or describing this fellow-feeling Fitzgeffry enjoins the members of his Church to action: 'But my text hath more need of *pressing* then of *paraphrasing.* The sence is obvious enough to our understanding, would God the substance thereof could as easily worke upon our affections ... first consider wee *others misery*, that so we may be the better incited to our owne duty' (p. 3). This is a central concern of all three sermons: that compassion should be a prompt for people to enact their Christian duty and actively attempt to relieve that suffering.

The second sermon, which is the most important for our purposes, focuses on the last part of the Bible verse, '– *as bound with them*', and as such extols the particular virtue of sympathy. This is the second duty we owe to our brethren, as well as remembering them: 'A *Sympathy* or *Compassion.* We must so remember them as if we our selves were in the same bondage with them, that so we may be the more feelingly affected towards them' (p. 21). Thus it is not simply a matter of reflecting upon such bondage, but rather through imagination and metaphor we should be, as it were, bound with then, in order to partake in and 'feelingly' experience their suffering: 'Their bondage must be ours, as if our feet were in their fetters, and their bonds upon our hands. Generally, there must be in all *Christians* a *Sympathy* in all their brethrens sufferings, a compassion in all their passions, a fellow-feeling in all their afflictions' (pp. 21–2). Fitzgeffry cites several biblical verses on this theme, including Romans 12:15 ('The Apostle exhorteth us as *to rejoice with them that rejoice*, so to *mourne with them that mourne*, and *to be of like affection one towards another*') and Galatians 6:2 ('*Beare ye one anothers burthens and so fulfill the law of Christ*' (p. 22)). As we have seen in previous chapters, the first of these two verses was often quoted by preachers in sermons that extolled the virtue of compassion. The second is more explicit about the importance of fulfilling Christ's commandments and following his example. And indeed, after citing various examples of compassion in the Bible, Fitzgeffry emphasizes the importance of remembering and emulating Christ's compassion: 'Our blessed Saviour presseth this duty upon us by his owne example as well as by his doctrine. He being free because bound with us; being rich, because poore with us, being God because man with us. This he did with us and for us, that though we cannot doe the same for our brethren, yet wee should doe the like with them' (p. 23). We share the sufferings of others, and thus imitate them, but we also have Christ to imitate: we imitate his actions of emotional imitation.

Fitzgeffry goes further by invoking the familiar analogy between the natural body and the mystical body of Christ. This presents us 'with a sound reason why there should be a *Sympathy* among Christians' (p. 24). We have seen this analogy made in other sermons from the early modern period, but Fitzgeffry adds an additional element whereby every member is like a surgeon, seeking to remedy the afflicted part:

> We are all members of one body, and we doe finde in our *natural body*, that *If one member doe suffer all the members doe suffer with it. A thorne pricketh the foote: what so farre off from the head as the foote? but though distant in situation they are neere in affection.* The heart being only in the foote, the whole body is busied, every member officiously offers to be a *Chirurgeon*, or to seeke and send for one as if it selfe were wounded. The head is whole, the backe is sound, the eyes, eares, hands are all safe, the foote only is grieved, yea the foote it selfe is well save in that very place where it is grieved. (p. 24)

Here Fitzgeffry invokes the idea of sympathy at a distance: even though the head and the foot are '*distant in situation*' they are near in affection. This is not the magical sympathy that we saw invoked by Bacon and Fludd, which connects objects at a great distance, but rather the natural sympathy that connects different parts of the body. And, while other preachers invoke this model as a way of suggesting affinity, Fitzgeffry suggests that these interconnected members actively seek to relieve the other's suffering:

'every member officiously offers to be a *Chirurgeon*'.[44] He uses a set of rhetorical questions to draw out the comparison between the physical body and mystical body of Christ: 'If thus in the naturall body, how much more in the *mysticall*? Why should not the smarting of any one be the suffering of every one, seing that the members are not more naturally compacted in the naturall body then the members of *Christ are in the mysticall*?' (p. 24). Such questions might imply that sympathy is a physical process, no different from the affinities and correspondences described by natural philosophers. Yet Fitzgeffry also makes it clear that this is an imaginative process, and he uses the specific term *sympathy* in this context:

> And surely without this *Sympathy* there cannot be in us any true touch of mercy and charity. To put our selves in our brethrens case is the only course to make us feelingly to pity them, charitably to relieve them. Then shall the bowels of our mercy be enlarged towards them, when we even feele our selves straitned in the same bonds with them ... they who have not this feeling can never truly conceive, much lesse daily remember, least of all charitably releeve others in their distresses. (p. 25)

He thus uses the same formulation that we have seen used by preachers such as Henry Holland, who we encountered in Chapter 2, whereby the congregation are encouraged to put themselves in another's case in order to imagine and thereby feel their distress. It seems that one has to imagine the state of the other, which allows one 'feelingly to pity them'; but this, in turn, allows us to 'truly conceive' of, and subsequently relieve, their distress. Thus feeling and conceiving – recalling Edgar's emphasis upon 'known and feeling sorrows' in *King Lear* – are intriguingly interdependent in Fitzgeffry's conception of sympathy.

It is even more striking, then, that Fitzgeffry reaches for a theatrical analogy in order to illuminate this idea further. He cites the example of the Greek actor Polus, who drew upon his own sufferings to more convincingly portray the suffering of a fictional character:

> *Polus* a famous Actor among the *Grecians* (as is recorded of him) being to represent on the stage *Electra* mourning for the death of her brother *Orestes* and bearing in her hands his *Urne*, insteed thereof he brought forth the *Urne* of his owne deceased Sonne, that by the apprehension of his owne, he might the more feelingly act anothers passion. Doubtlesse (deare *Christians*) we shall never act to the life the *Christian* part of sorrowing for our perplexed brethren, unlesse we looke on their thraldome as on our owne,

---

[44] Fitzgeffry uses the obsolete sense of *officiously* as 'Dutifully, duteously' (*OED*, 1) to emphasize the eagerness of the 'safe' parts to aid the member that suffers.

> as if their lashes did fall upon our loynes, as if our hands were galled with tugging their oares, and our selves stinted to their hungry diet of bread and water. (pp. 25–6)

This story was often quoted by orators and preachers in the seventeenth century.[45] The point for Fitzgeffry is that Polus draws upon his own loss and emotional experience in order to 'more feelingly act' the grief of Electra. The substitution of one urn for the other can thus be seen as a suggestive metaphor for the exchange of authentic and imagined sorrows: one can be used interchangeably with the other. Similarly, the audience is expected to use this anecdote as a way of understanding their own passions in relation to those of another. For Fitzgeffry, the '*Christian* part of sorrowing' is not a mere performance, but a genuine suffering for our afflicted brethren. The alliteration ('as if their lashes did fall upon our loynes') underscores the argument that there should be a felt affinity between the other's suffering and the listeners' bodies. Fitzgeffry's own performance of this anecdote may also have been deeply affecting, as he invites his audience to follow both Polus's example and his own in being moved by the plight of the 'perplexed'.

But while Fitzgeffry draws upon an example from Greek theatre he is not primarily concerned with art and feigned emotions (or so he claims). As we have seen, his central argument is that Christians must be tenderhearted and, furthermore, must practise active sympathy. It is not enough, he suggests, to be moved by fictional narratives – particularly at the expense of genuine suffering: 'Fabulous stories, faigned Tragedies will sooner moove them, then the true relation of their brethrens calamities. Such was that *Tyrant* who could not refraine weeping when he heard a player acting a passionate part in a Tragedy, but never relented at the many murthers committed by his command on his innocent subjects' (p. 26). We have seen in earlier chapters the importance of theatrical metaphors in early modern articulations of sympathy; but here Fitzgeffry points to the problems that arise when individuals are moved only by fictions and dramatic representations. He contrasts feigned compassion with genuine sympathy that involves combining words and actions:

> True affection (where meanes doe concurre with the minde) will not be without action ... It is a cold compassion that is not warmed with some

---

[45] Leofranc Holford-Strevens writes that by the mid-seventeenth century, Polus had 'become a stock example for those who wrote on the theory of rousing emotion on stage, the bar, or the pulpit'; see 'Polus and His Urn: A Case Study in the Theory of Acting, c. 300 B.C.–c. A.D. 2000', *International Journal of the Classical Tradition*, 11 (2005), 499–523 (p. 507).

contribution, a sorry *Sympathy* that restrains the bowels of charity. If the mouth only doe bemone them, and the hand endevour not to releive them, what is this but that painted compassion which S. *James* cals unprofitable? (p. 28).

There is arguably a tension here between the form and content of Fitzgeffry's sermon; as an orator he must rely upon words and stories to articulate this argument. He even implies that words on their own are deficient, or even lifeless: '*God helpe them, God comfort them*! *Good words indeed, but only words*; whereas men in misery need not words, but deeds of charity. To wish well only is but a livelesse carcasse' (p. 29). Thus his own sermon points to its own status as a mere text, inasmuch as it remains a verbal artefact until its audience converts its commands into deeds. As Fitzgeffry says, drawing upon another text (the Bible), 'So inseparably cleaveth this *Sympathy* with our brethren in their sufferings unto true *Christianity*, that we no sooner finde *Christians* to be named in Scripture but we finde in them this *active compassion*' (p. 30).

This emphasis upon active compassion is extended in the third sermon, which offers a critique of apathy and covetousness, and extols the virtues of humility, mercy, and charity. Fitzgeffry enjoins his listeners to 'Labour for a tender *heart*, apprehensive of the least frowne of our heavenly Father … then shall your compassion extend it selfe more viscerally towards your afflicted brethren' (p. 38). The heart is 'tender', suggesting that it is affected from outside; but this leads to an outward movement, whereby compassion extends itself towards the other. Fitzgeffry articulates a plausible counterargument, whereby a sceptical interlocutor points out that such people deserving of charity are strangers. This is powerfully answered: 'But they are of thine owne *religion*, thine own *nation*, thine owne *nature*: And is not the least of these sufficient acquaintance when they are in misery? Is it not both thine and their *Makers* charge?' (p. 40). Once again, Christ is the model for the listeners to emulate:

> Our *Redeemer* did not stand upon these nice points of kindred and acquaintance, when he freed us from our most miserable bondage. But though *We were Gentiles in the flesh, Aliens from the common wealth of Israel, strangers from the covenant of promise*; yet all this could not estrange his compassion from us, but he did and suffered more for us, then it is possible any man can doe for his brother, his father, or best benefactour. (p. 41)

This link between Christians and Christ is likened to the bodily sympathy between parts of the body: 'Doe we say that we are united to the *Head* and can wee bee unacquainted with any member of the body? Their hunger, their bonds, their burthens, their blowes are not these sufficient for commiseration, though we never saw their persons?' (p. 41). In this way, ethical sympathy for the other becomes, for Fitzgeffry, a form of genuine sympathy at a distance; people are unified not through magic but through Christ.

It is particularly suggestive, then, that Fitzgeffry refers at this point to other 'forcible incentives', including Fracastoro's ideas about contagion and the concept of natural sympathy: 'Nature it selfe incites us to this *Sympathy*. This naturall instinct we finde in our owne bodies. Whence is it that one in a company yawning or gaping, the rest doe so likewise unlesse they prevent it? That one eating bitter or tart meates others teeth doe water and are set on edge? Is there such a *Sympathy* in our bodies? Why not much more in our mindes?' (p. 41).[46] Fracastoro's ideas about sympathy and antipathy are thus invoked to bolster Fitzgeffry's theological argument.[47] In this way, Fitzgeffry makes a distinction between bodily and imaginative sympathy; he acknowledges the existence of the former, but suggests that the latter should be stronger:

> As in some things there is an *Antipathy*, so there is a *Sympathy* in others. Touch but one string in a lute, and another soundeth though not neare unto it. I omit the *Sympathy* betweene the *load-stone* and the *iron*, betweene *Amber* and *straw*, *jet* and an *hayre*, rare secrets in nature, common in triall. Out of the premises I argue thus: If our owne *naturall bodies*, if brute creatures, which are led only by sence, yea if senselesse creatures by an occult quality be thus affected one towards another, then what ought *Christians* to doe who are endued with *reason*, enlightened with *religion*, and led or rather drawne with naturall affection? (p. 42)

Fitzgeffry invokes the well-known example (also invoked by Bacon and Fludd) of musical sympathy and the strings of a lute that vibrate with each other. Earlier in the sermon he uses the word *senseless* to refer to men who are 'insensible of their own sufferings' and are thus unable to 'condole others' (pp. 37–8). Here *senseless* refers to inanimate objects and brutish beasts; if they can experience and be moved by natural or bodily sympathy then Christians can (and should) experience a higher form of sympathetic

---

[46] Cf. Joseph Hall's comments about yawning in his *Occasionall meditations* (London, 1631): 'It is a marvellous thing to see the reall effects and strong operation of consent, or Sympathye, even where there is no bodily touch; So one sad man puts the whole company into dumps; So one mans yawning affects, and stretches the jawes of many beholders' (pp. 286–7).

[47] See Vivian Nutton, 'The Reception of Fracastoro's Theory of Contagion: The Seed That Fell among Thorns?', *Osiris*, 6 (1990), 196–234. Fracastoro wrote two treatises – one on sympathies and antipathies, and one on contagion – and was clearly interested in the relationship between these two concepts. As Nutton points out, Fracastoro was sceptical about the idea of occult qualities but saw sympathies and antipathies as a kind of scientific principle that explained the workings of the universe (p. 199). See also Lobis, *The Virtue of Sympathy*, pp. 22–3.

affinity based upon reason and religion. What is most striking here is that Christ is not simply a model for our compassion but rather a mediator, and Fitzgeffry quotes Gregory I's *Moralia on Job* to make this point: 'Of this *body* the *Head* is *Christ*, who hath shewed this *sympathy* by his owne example … To which let this be added out of one of the ancients; *This forme of piety* (saith he) *Christ the mediatour betweene God and man hath shewed unto men*' (pp. 42–3). The word *mediator* certainly had theological connotations in the period, and was usually used to refer to Christ as a intermediary between God and man. But the term was also used in a medical context to suggest 'an intermediate agent' (*OED*, 3a); and here we might recall the workings of the weapon-salve – a rather different form of intermediate agent. Fitzgeffry does not offer a critique of the concept of natural sympathy in this passage but rather invokes it for a theological and rhetorical purpose: he proposes a more enlightened mode of imaginative sympathy that posits Christ as a mediator or agent between individual Christians.

The links that Fitzgeffry makes between disparate ideas and objects in the sermon enact this kind of thinking in relation to Christ: 'How can wee hope for salvation by him if we be not living members of his body? If wee be living members then are wee feeling members. As long as the member is in the body it is effected with the griefe of any part of the body. But if it be either dead or cut off from the body, let the body bee dismembred or cut into a thousand peeces, it feeleth not: so is every *Christian* who is not affected with the affliction of another *Christian*' (p. 43). We must be feeling members of the mystical body of Christ; and for Christians thinkers like Fitzgeffry this is more than a metaphor – it is a real feeling of another's pain, mediated through Christ. At the same time, however, the sermon makes considerable demands on the imagination of its listeners. In one astonishing passage, Fitzgeffry invites his listeners to go beyond simply imagining themselves in the situation of the other:

> Then from our sorrowfull brethren reflect wee our thoughts upon our selves, and in the scales of our owne estate weigh we the *equity of the precept*, which will not a little incite us to the performance of it. *Remember them that are in bonds as bound with them.* What more *equitable.* You might have beene bound with them, yea you might have beene bound and they free; if God had so disposed? You might have fallen into their bonds, and they enjoyed your freedome. And would not you then have desired of them what now is required of you towards them? (pp. 44–5)

What Fitzgeffry describes here is no less than an imaginative exchange of identities. His listeners are asked to imagine not only themselves in the subjugated position of the suffering other but also the other becoming the sympathetic self.[48] This act of imaginative transposition is part of the ethical argument of the sermon: imagining the oneself in the position of the other also involves imagining looking back at the self and seeing the other in one's place. Fitzgeffry thus anticipates Adam Smith's idea of sympathy involving 'changing places in fancy with the sufferer'.[49] But he even goes further than Smith by imagining an entirely different scenario in which the spectator is in bonds and in need of succour from the sorrowful brethren, who are free.

There are limits to Fitzgeffry's sophisticated model of sympathy, however, and it is possible to discern an anxiety that runs through the treatise about the racial other. In the first sermon we find that his demand for active sympathy for afflicted brethren is contrasted with – and indeed bound up with – Fitzgeffry's disdain for those who are responsible for incarcerating Protestants: 'especially remember them that are in bonds for *Christs* sake and his Gospels, either in the *Popish inquisition* or in *Turkish thraldome*' (p. 15). For Fitzgeffry at least, the Inquisition is far worse than Turkish bondage: 'All we can doe for them is to remember them, with our teares to condole them, with our prayers, that *Christ,* who cannot be excluded, will visit them with inward comfort, and confirme them to the end. The *Popish inquisition!* O it is a more barbarous bondage then any in *Barbary*' (p. 15). And, at the end of the close of the third sermon, Fitzgeffry articulates a familiar anxiety about turning Turk, whereby religious conversion is figured as a kind of contagion or disease that might infect the body politic. He refers to audacious pirates who mock English land dwellers from their ships: 'And who were these but some of our owne nation turned *Turkes,* threatning to bring us unto their owne condition because wee would not free them in season?' (p. 46). In this way, there is another form of sympathetic assimilation that Fitzgeffry acknowledges: the possibility that the self might be turned into the other without one's consent. But even here there is an active and ethical dimension to his anxiety: because we did not 'free them in season' there is a form of sympathetic revenge whereby the pirates forcefully turn English folk into Turks.

This dangerous form of sympathetic identification and assimilation is once again redirected towards a discussion of Christ's mercy for us.

---

[48] For a complex meditation on the relationship between the self and the other see Paul Ricoeur, *Oneself as Another*, trans. Kathleen Blamey (University of Chicago Press, 1992). Ricoeur argues that 'the selfhood of oneself implies otherness to such an intimate degree that one cannot be thought of without the other' (p. 3).
[49] Smith, *The Theory of Moral Sentiments*, p. 12.

Fitzgeffry even ventriloquises Christ as he compares our mercy to his own: 'I redeemed you, and you (in them) redeemed me: I you by taking on me your bonds, you me by freeing them from bondage' (p. 49). Fitzgeffry affirms the mercy that God and his son will bestow upon Christians – reminding us that any mercy that we bestow upon the other can only ever be a simulated imitation of Christ. And lest people doubt that this promise of mercy is a mere 'verball acknowledgment', Fitzgeffry assures his listeners that 'this verball acknowledgment shall be seconded with a reall recompence … by *God the Father*, and for none other, but for *you*, for you, who by your deedes of mercy have evidenced the sincerity of your faith' (p. 50). This promise of a Kingdom for those who perform deeds of mercy serves as a powerful end to a sermon that extols the importance of active compassion – one that must go beyond mere words, even if it is precisely those words that have the capacity to move audiences and readers to compassion in the first place.

Conclusion: 'here is no such magneticall and invisible Sympathie'

Fitzgeffry's *Compassion towards captives* thus lends further weight to some of the central arguments I have been making throughout this book. First, that the imaginative conception of sympathy, which some critics and historians have associated with the long eighteenth century, was not only present in earlier periods but also articulated and theorized in remarkably complex ways. And, second, that early moderns increasingly regarded emotions as an activity – something that individuals do – rather than environmental or humoral forces that act upon them. Fitzgeffry's passionate emphasis upon '*active compassion*' is a notable example of this view, whereby sympathy and fellow-feeling are presented as active processes, and which involve an outward movement from the self to the other – or even an imaginative exchange between the two. While there was undoubtedly a fascination with the idea of the weapon-salve, and its harnessing of the power of natural sympathy, it is surely mistaken to suggest that the views of writers such as Robert Fludd, and later Kenelm Digby, were representative of English culture as a whole. The evidence I have presented in this chapter suggests that ideas about sympathetic cures were complicated and satirized by other writers in the first half of the seventeenth century – particularly in more popular cultural forms such as drama. Thus, while the renewed interest in occult and scientific models in the Caroline period is an important chapter in the history of sympathy, it has arguably skewed critical understanding of sympathy in the preceding decades as well. The affective model of sympathy existed alongside the natural philosophical concept; and the relationship between these two models was highly complex, and could be complementary, mutually illuminating, or even oppositional. The situation is, of course, complicated by the overlap between scientific and religious discourses in the period, which we have seen in Fludd's insistence that his belief in natural sympathy is grounded in Scripture. But we have also seen how some dramatists and preachers – in particular Glapthorne and Fitzgeffry – drew upon scientific models in ways that distinguish them from interpersonal and religious conceptions of sympathy.

Some writers went further in making a clear distinction between natural sympathy, with its implications of passivity and involuntariness, and a higher form of sympathy between individuals and God. In a sermon printed in 1640, John Stoughton writes that fear of and love for God should be 'Not slavish, wire-drawn, and compelled affections: when our affections are extorted and drawn by force, without any naturall sympathie; but it should be a kindly, and a sonne-like affection towards God'.[50] The idea of natural sympathy provides Stoughton with a way of distinguishing between 'compelled' and 'kindly' affections; indeed individuals are enjoined to have a 'sonne-like' affection towards God the Father, thus placing them imaginatively in the position of Christ. In another sermon printed in the same year, but delivered some years previously when he was a preacher at Cambridge, Stoughton similarly elevates religious sympathy above the magnetical or magical:

> The first point of the Explication was, that *Christ is a sufficient Saviour*: out of it I deduced, 1. *That Saints are no Saviours*, nor therefore to be *invocated as Saviours:* here is no such magneticall and invisible Sympathie, that any man should wonder what necessity tyes these two together: neither is their any such forced deduction, that a man should need to pumpe or cherne to make it come: the dependance is easie as it is in the links of a chain, draw one, and the rest will follow …[51]

The ties Stoughton describes between Christ and the saints are not the result of 'magneticall and invisible Sympathie'. He employs another analogy – the links of a chain – to present this saintly sympathy as a form of interdependence and interconnectedness rather than action at a distance. In other words, this 'easie' dependence between Christ and the saints is distinguished from the mysterious forces of natural sympathy.

---

[50] John Stoughton, *The righteous mans plea to true happinesse. In ten sermons, on Psal. 4 ver. 6* (London, 1640), p. 41. Fifteen of Stoughton's works appeared in quick succession in 1640; he had died the previous year. See P. S. Seaver, 'Stoughton, John (bap. 1593, d. 1639)', *ODNB*.

[51] Stoughton, *XI. choice sermons preached upon selected occasions, in Cambridge* (London, 1640), p. 88.

This example provides further evidence that religious and dramatic writers were clearly aware of earlier concepts of sympathy, but these are sometimes employed as a way of defining and redefining the affective and religious senses of the term.

This increasing bifurcation of the natural philosophical and the emotional conceptions of sympathy would continue into the eighteenth century and beyond. But, as we have seen throughout this book, literary, dramatic, and religious writers from the sixteenth and seventeenth centuries played a vital role in this process, which involved a sceptical response to and creative engagement with earlier models and terminologies. Donne's comparison between sympathy and symphony – with which I began this chapter – highlights the suggestive overlap between various forms of affinity and correspondence in the period, which enabled (and complicated) the development of the affective model of sympathy. The emotional form emerges from this early modern fascination with harmony and agreement; yet it goes beyond mere correspondence, and involves an imaginative 'fellow-feeling of others miseries'. Donne's formulation, along with other articulations of sympathy that we have examined, clearly points towards our own understanding of the term. At the same time, however, Donne's comments remind us that, for early moderns, all forms of sympathy are loved by, and ultimately have their source in, the divine.

Coda

In the previous chapter we saw further evidence that Christ was one of the most important imitative models for understanding and practising sympathy in the early modern period, including Edward Reynolds's approving description of Christ's '*Sympathy* or compassion' in his *An explication of the hundreth and tenth Psalme* (1632). Reynolds also wrote a more extended exploration and defence of the passions, which appeared at the end of the chronological span of the present book: *A treatise of the passions and faculties of the soule of man* (1640). This treatise was an important text for seventeenth-century readers, and became a standard undergraduate text on Aristotelian ethics at Oxford; it has also proved to be important for later critics of the period.[1] After suggesting that it is better to have passions and moderate them than not have them at all Reynolds turns again to the example of Christ:

> And therefore our Saviour himselfe sometimes loved, sometimes rejoyced, sometimes wept, sometimes desired, sometimes mourned and grieved; but these were not *Passions* that violently and immoderately troubled him; but he, as he saw fit, did with them *trouble himselfe*. His *Reason excited, directed, moderated, repressed* them, according to the rule of perfect, cleare, and undisturbed *judgement*.[2]

The passage continues by suggesting that, while the passions of sinful men 'are many times like the tossings of the Sea, which bringeth up *mire and durt*', the passions of Christ 'were like the shaking of pure Water in a cleane Vessell, which though it be thereby *troubled,* yet is it not *fouled* at all' (p. 49). Reynolds suggests that there is nothing wrong with having a variety of passions – as indicated by the full range of emotions felt by Christ himself – but that they can and should be directed and moderated by reason and judgement.

---

[1] Ian Atherton, 'Reynolds, Edward (1599–1676)', *ODNB*. See Schoenfeldt, *Bodies and Selves*, pp. 9–10; Paster, *Humoring the Body*, pp. 1–19; and Tilmouth, *Passion's Triumph over Reason*, pp. 180–4.
[2] Edward Reynolds, *A treatise of the passions and faculties of the soule of man* (London, 1640), p. 48.

The latter part of this passage appears at the start of Gail Kern Paster's influential *Humoring the Body* (2004), and is used as evidence for Paster's central thesis: that early moderns passions 'are like liquid states and forces of the natural world'.[3] She argues that Reynolds's images – in particular the comparison of Christ's passions to water in a clean vessel – 'represent an entirely characteristic expression of seventeenth-century definitions of the embodied passions' (p. 6). Paster does concede that such images establish 'a theological and symbolic import for representations of the passions', but ultimately stresses their 'urgent practical character', which was 'just as important as their overarching theological significance' (pp. 6–7). It is worth emphasizing, however, that Reynolds's evocative simile has a biblical provenance, as indicated in a marginal note: 'But the wicked *are* like the raging sea, that cannot rest, whose waters cast up mire and dirt' (Isaiah 57:20). And while Reynolds compares the passions to the forces of the natural world this is part of an extended metaphor describing the 'middle temper' between tempestuous emotions and calm reason:

> As in the Wind or Seas, (to which two, Passions are commonly compar'd) a middle temper betweene a quiet Calme and violent Tempest, is most serviceable for the agitations of Passion, as long as they serve onely to drive forward, but not to drowne Vertue; as long as they keepe their dependence on Reason, and run onely in that Channell wherewith they are thereby bounded, as of excellent service, in all the travail of mans life, and such as without which, the growth, successe, and dispatch of Vertue would be much impaired.[4]

As Reynolds himself notes, the wind and seas are 'commonly compar'd' to the passions, but this does not necessarily imply that they are the same thing.[5] In this Coda I want to offer a brief reading of Reynolds's treatise as a way of exemplifying the methodology and approach advocated in the present book: in particular, tracing the usage of key emotion words; recognizing the importance of metaphorical language in descriptions of emotions; attending to intertexts and narrative exemplars; and acknowledging the coexistence of different emotional models in the same text (rather than reducing them to one). The fact that Reynolds draws upon variety of

---

[3] Paster, *Humoring the Body*, p. 4.
[4] Reynolds, *A treatise of the passions*, p. 60.
[5] Kirk Essary notes that similar metaphors involving water and other liquids 'were routinely drawn into theological contexts in sermons and commentaries from at least the early sixteenth century'. He suggests that this theological tradition 'forces us to question whether a materialist framework is adequate for understanding affective metaphors in this period' ('Clear as Mud: Metaphor, Emotion and Meaning in Early Modern England', *English Studies*, 98 (2017), 689–703 (p. 690)).

classical texts – including works by Homer, Virgil, Horace, and Seneca – as well as scientific and religious concepts, reminds us of the plurality and complexity of early modern emotional experience. The treatise also helps us to see how the concept of sympathy links to wider ethical and aesthetic debates about the passions.

Reynolds does refer to the earlier concept of natural sympathy in his discussion of love in Chapter 9. He writes that, in both nature and in the affections, there is a double attraction between objects:

> The first, is that naturall or impressed sympathie of things, whereby one doth inwardly incline an union with the other, by reason of some secret vertues and occult qualities disposing either subject to that mutuall friendship, as betweene Iron and the Loadstone: The other, is that common and more discernable attraction which every thing receives from those natures, or places, whereon they are ordained and directed by the Wisedome and Providence of the first Cause, to depend both in respect of the perfection and conservation of their being. (pp. 74–5)

The first attraction discussed here is the natural sympathy between things, or the 'secret virtues and occult qualities' that exist in nature, such as that which causes the attraction between the iron and the loadstone. The second is the 'more discernible attraction' that brings things back to their first cause, which is united through and derives from God. Reynolds goes on to present a theological vision of analogical harmony, comprising of 'the World, a God of Order, disposing every thing in Number, Weight, and Measure, so sweetly, as that all is harmonious' (p. 75). Clearly, then, Reynolds sees sympathy in this larger cosmological and religious context: the sympathy between people can be seen as part of the wider analogical order of the universe. His description of union also touches on this model, in which things are either unified from the outset, or find themselves combined with other objects or substances; this second form of union can be due to an '*accidentall aggregation*', or 'a *naturall* or *morall inclination* and sympathy which one thing beareth unto another. And of this sort is that *union* which ariseth out of *love,* tending first unto a mutuall *similitude* and conformity in the same desires' (pp. 99–100).

Such comments remind us of the complex interrelationship between theological and scientific discourses in period, which we also saw in the debates regarding the weapon-salve in the previous chapter. And yet we can also discern another form of sympathy at work in Reynolds's treatise, which is distinct from such natural philosophical and analogical models. Immediately after Reynolds's description of Christ's passions, which we considered above, he cites Aeneas as another example of moderation in the face of extreme emotion: 'He wept indeed, but in his stable mind / You could no shakings or distempers find' (p. 49). This passage is taken from book 4 of the *Aeneid*, when Aeneas fails to feel pity for Dido.[6] Pity and compassion, according to this example, are not simply automatic but can be repressed and moderated. And yet, as we saw in the case of Marlowe's dramatization in Chapter 4, this passage is emotionally complex and has the potential to increase the spectator's sympathy for the tragic Dido. Indeed Reynolds himself acknowledges there are times when sorrows need to be articulated; and we can see this in his discussion of grief and the '*communion* in *diverse objects*' (p. 54). He writes:

> For the first, we see in matter of Griefe, the *Mind* doth receive (as it were) some lightnesse and comfort, when it finds it selfe *generative* unto others, and produces *sympathie* in them: For hereby it is (as it were) disburthened, and cannot but find that easier, to the sustaining whereof, it hath the assistance of anothers shoulders. (pp. 54–5).

As well as referring to the idea of natural sympathy, then, Reynolds uses the term *sympathie* in a narrower sense to refer to the transmission of grief. He suggests that grief can be '*generative* unto others', in the sense of 'That generates, produces, or gives rise to something, or has the power or ability to do so; productive, creative; originating, causative' (*OED*, 2). In this way, Reynolds recognizes the value of transmitting grief from one person to the other, as well as the active and productive processes involved in sympathy.

However, he also notes that sympathy can be impeded when grief is especially great and therefore hard to articulate. This point is illustrated by two quotations from Seneca and Martial ('Curae leves loquuntur, ingentes stupent'; 'ille dolet vere qui sine teste dolet'), which are translated as two pairs of lines run together:

> Our tongues can lighter Cares repeat,
> When silence swallowes up the great:
> He grieves indeed, who on his friend
> Untestified teares doth spend.   (p. 55)

The first quotation, from Seneca's *Phaedre*, is precisely concerned with the difficulty of putting extreme emotions into words.[7] The import of the

---

[6] The passage in context reads as follows: 'But no griefs moved Aeneas. He heard but did not heed her words ... The hero Aeneas was buffeted by all this pleading on this side and on that, and felt the pain deep in his mighty heart but his mind remained unmoved and the tears rolled in vain' (*The Aeneid*, trans. West, p. 95).

[7] Hippolytus asks Phaedre 'Your spirit desires to utter something but cannot?', and she replies: 'Light cares can speak, huge cares are dumfounded' (Seneca, *Tragedies, Volume I: Hercules, Trojan Women, Phoenician Women, Medea, Phaedra*, ed. and trans. John G. Fitch (Cambridge, MA: Harvard University Press, 2018), lines 606–7, pp. 466–7).

second quotation, which derives from Martial's epigram 33, is somewhat different, inasmuch as it suggests that Gellia's private grief for her father's death is more intense, and perhaps also more authentic, than public demonstrations of woe.[8] Reynolds expands on these ideas: 'That *Griefe* commonly is the most *heavie*, which hath fewest *vents*, by which to *diffuse* it selfe: which, I take it, will be one occasion of the *heavinesse* of *infernall torment*; because there, Griefe shall not be any whit transient, to work commiseration in any spectator, but altogether immanent and reflexive upon itself' (p. 55). On the one hand, then, grief that is especially heavy or momentous can be 'reflexive' – that is, 'Of a mental action, process, etc.: turned or directed back upon the mind itself' (*OED*, 2a). On the other hand, however, giving vent to grief involves an outward movement from the self to the other that can lead to sympathy and commiseration; as the verb *diffuse* suggests, this process involves both dissemination (*OED*, 1a) and a reduction in intensity (*OED*, 1b). Thus, while Reynolds ostensibly advises the moderation and repression of grief, he recognizes the value of communicating it to others, which can bring about a diffusion or lessening of sorrow.

This ambivalence regarding the experience and articulation of grief is also apparent in Reynolds's extended discussion 'Of the Affection of Sorrow' in Chapter 22. In keeping with his overall categorization of the passions, Reynolds suggests that there are two types of grief: '*Sensitive* or *Intellectuall*' (p. 222). The latter is more 'quicke and piercing' because the spirit is more vital than the body: 'the anguish of the soule, findes alwayes, or workes the same sympathy in the body, but outward sorrowes reach not ever so farre, as the spirituall and higher part of the soule' (p. 222). Here Reynolds employs the term *sympathy* in its earlier sense of correspondence, although it is used to describe the transmission of grief between the soul and body – a familiar usage we have seen in other religious and scientific works from the period. But it is striking in his description that the anguish of the soul can affect the body but not vice versa; this complicates the idea that, for Reynolds, the passions are embodied in any simple sense.[9] It is also significant that, later in the same chapter, *sympathy* is used in the more imaginative and emotional sense, and once again this usage immediately follows on from several quotations from classical texts.

---

[8] The Loeb translation of the entire epigram is as follows: 'Gellia does not cry for her lost father when she's by herself, but if she has company, out spring the tears to order. Gellia, whoever seeks credit for mourning is no mourner. He truly grieves who grieves without witnesses' (Martial, *Epigrams, Volume I: Spectacles, Books 1–5*, ed. and trans. D. R. Shackleton Bailey (Cambridge, MA: Harvard University Press, 1993), pp. 62–3.
[9] Cf. Gowland's comment that the early modern subject 'is not simply "humoral", and the condition of the body does not simply determine that of the soul' ('Melancholy, Passions and Identity', p. 75).

Reynolds describes the detrimental effects of grief, including its capacity to '*indispose* and disable for *Dutie*' and to 'weakneth, distracteth and discourageth the Minde' (pp. 230–1). We have another passage from the *Aeneid*, which describes Aeneas's suppressing of his sorrows ('Although with heavy cares and doubts distrest, / His looks fain'd hopes and his heart griefes supprest' (p. 231)). Reynolds also quotes 'an excellent description in *Homer* of the fidelity of *Antilochus* when he was commanded to relate unto *Achilles*, the sad newes of *Patroclus* death'. The passage is taken from the *Iliad*, book 17:

> When *Menelaus* gave him this command,
> *Antilochus* astonished did stand.
> Smitten with dumbnesse through his griefe and feares,
> His voyce was stopt, and his eyes swamme in teares.
> Yet none of all this griefe did duty stay,
> He left his Armes whose weight might cause delay.
> And went, and wept and ran, with dolefull word,
> That great *Patroclus* fell by *Hectors* sword. (pp. 231–2)

This passage thus presents a similar predicament to the one explored in other classical quotations quoted in the text: extreme grief can lead to inarticulacy. But Antilochus's 'griefe and feares' do not prevent him from performing his duty: after all, his duty is emotional rather than martial, and he specifically puts down his arms in order to go to Achilles. In this way, the passage describes the difficulty yet necessity of articulating grief, and in this case putting it into narrative form. Furthermore, Antilochus's intense emotional response prefigures Achilles's huge sorrow at hearing the news, which is represented at the start of the next book.

This moment thus further underlines the combination of theological and classical elements that make up Reynolds's conception of the passions – and indeed is followed by further quotations from Seneca and the Bible. But it also points to a contradiction at the heart of the treatise, whereby Reynolds argues that passions should be controlled and regulated but simultaneously describes and invokes their power in order to persuade his readers. This tension is particularly apparent when he describes the physical 'inconveniences' caused by grief, and its effect upon the body: 'Grief in the heart, is like a Moath in a garment, which biteth asunder, as it were the strings and the strength thereof, stoppeth the voyce, looseth the joynets, withereth the flesh, shrivelleth the skinne, dimmeth the eyes, cloudeth the countenance, defloureth the beauty, troubleth the bowels, in one word, disordereth the whole frame' (p. 232). Thus, while Reynolds is at pains (so to speak) to catalogue these effects he nevertheless takes a rhetorical and creative pleasure in this description, employing the vivid metaphor of a moth gnawing its way out of a garment. This is not a straightforwardly literal description of emotional experience – signalled by Reynolds's 'as it were' – but rather a rhetorical attempt to convey these various disorders to the reader. Moreover, despite this emphasis upon the physicality of grief, the chapter concludes with a further list of subcategories, the first of which is sympathy: 'Now this Passion of griefe is distributed into many inferiour kinds, as *Griefe* of *Sympathy* for the evils and calamities of other men, as if they were our owne' (p. 232). In this way, Reynolds acknowledges the earlier, physiological model of sympathy as correspondence, and describes the physical effects of sorrow; but he also describes a specifically emotional and interpersonal model of sympathy, which involves articulating one's own grief and responding to the calamities of others.

Later in the treatise Reynolds returns to the occult understanding of sympathies and antipathies, in relation to God and the pursuit of knowledge. But it is clear this is quite different from the '*Griefe* of *Sympathy*' that he discusses in Chapter 22. The purpose of knowledge, Reynolds suggests, is to guide the soul to God. But there are some forms of knowledge that remain mysterious: he writes that 'there is scarce any Science properly so called, which hath not its *Arcana* to pose and amaze the Understanding, as well as its more easie Conclusions to satisfie it'. He goes on to provide a key example: 'Such as are in Philosophie, those *Occult Sympathies and Antipathies*, of which naturall Reason can render no Account at all: which overcomming the utmost Vigour of humane Disquisition, must needs enforce us to beleeve that there is an Admirable Wisedome that disposeth, and an infinite Knowledge that comprehendeth those secrets which we are not able to fathome' (pp. 448–9). These occult sympathies and antipathies are presented as an arcane form of knowledge that exceeds the grasp of normal individuals. The implication, however, is that they are comprehensible by God. This mysterious doctrine is invoked by Reynolds, as we have already noted, as a way of explaining human relationships – particularly in relation to love. But his discussion of grief, which draws upon classical and theological texts rather than scientific ones, uses the term *sympathy* in a more specific and narrower sense to describe the articulation and transmission of sorrow.

This final case study, then, points to a specifically emotional form of sympathy that exists alongside but is nevertheless distinct from cosmological or physiological models. As we have seen throughout this book, representations of interpersonal sympathy in the period involved – and cultivated – a sophisticated understanding of the emotional affinities between the self and the other. We have seen, for example, Philip Sidney's suggestion that individuals feel compassion for others because, 'under the image of them, they lament their own mishaps'. This kind of reflexive return to the self, which is also described by Reynolds, is somewhat different from Henry Holland's proposal that we should not simply feel pity for those in distress, but rather 'consider of them as if wee were in their case, for the time present' – an imaginative projecting of the self into the situation of the other. But we have also seen how the narrator of Shakespeare's *Lucrece* states that women often 'Griev[e] themselves to guess at others' smarts', which suggests a form of emotional and cognitive speculation about the thoughts and feelings of the other. Such examples add up to a kind of metacommentary on the different and complex processes involved in sympathetic experiences, including a recollection of one's own experiences; imagining the thoughts and feelings of the other; an imaginative exchange of places with the other; or even employing a theory of mind to determine the cause of another's grief. Taken together, they provide further evidence that sympathy in the Renaissance was not simply automatic or cosmological, but rather involved a multiplicity of responses to various complex interpersonal encounters. In other words, the range of perspectives and examples I have discussed in the present book suggests that the model of Renaissance sympathy as an external force or physiological phenomenon is inadequate.

Given this early modern fascination with the complexities of pity and compassion it seems particularly telling that the term *sympathy* was associated with human feelings from the outset. The fact that the first appearance of *sympathy* in an English printed text was in a collection of fictional stories – and describes the '*Sympathie* & attonement' of affections between friends – suggests that the term had an immediate and specific applicability to ideas of emotional correspondence. Perhaps, then, the idea that the concept of sympathy moved from the scientific and the physiological realms to the emotional and the ethical is not quite accurate. Rather, this new term was quickly taken up and absorbed by the culture as a valuable way of defining (and redefining) affective interactions and relationships. The advent of the verbal form *sympathize* in the 1590s continues this process, in which the emergence and subsequent development of an emotion word modifies the thing that it describes. It indicates that *sympathy*, which could imply a generalized form of agreement or harmony, became available as something that individuals could perform. These terms quickly replaced earlier emotion words such as *rue* and *ruth*, which implied a more passive form of pity and compassion. This phenomenon can thus be seen as a precursor to the semantic shift from *passions* to *emotions*; it suggests that a more active form of emotional experience and expression was already developing in the late sixteenth century, which was both reflected in and enabled by the emergence of *sympathy* and *sympathize*.

Alongside this semantic shift, the idea that an individual's emotions and desires were the result of occult or physiological sympathies became increasingly outdated; we have seen how plays such as Brandon's *The Vertuous Octavia* and Ford's *The Lover's Melancholy* depict individuals using the idea of natural sympathy as a way of explaining or justifying feelings that they have already embraced or acted upon. In both cases the earlier model of classical or occult sympathy is not simply invoked by writers from the period but rather employed to emphasize the complexities of human inclinations and affections. I have also suggested that Shakespeare's *King Lear* can be read as an essay on the separation of human beings from the natural world rather than their embeddedness in it. Such imaginative representations not only presented earlier concepts of sympathy in a sceptical way but also posited new understandings of identification and affinity between distinct individuals, as opposed to people being acted upon by external forces. Thus, while the concept of natural sympathies and the 'analogical worldview' remained compelling and even poetic as ideas, they were increasingly interrogated in the literary and dramatic texts of the period.[10]

But while imaginative texts – including plays, poems, and prose works – have been important case studies in the present book, it is worth emphasizing that religious writings have also been fundamental to this new history of sympathy. That is, both fictional and religious texts played a vital role in shaping the affective meaning of *sympathy*, which emerges as preachers, poets, and playwrights explore the word's metaphorical possibilities. The history of sympathy thus provides further evidence of the important cultural work performed by early modern sermons, which employed figurative language, rhetoric, storytelling, and performance to move and persuade their listeners. And it seems clear that there was a parallel development at work in both fictional writings and religious discourse, in which the term *sympathy* is increasingly associated with grief and compassion. Further research into this area might unearth more examples of cross-fertilization

---

[10] See Todd Andrew Borlick, *Literature and Nature in the English Renaissance: An Ecocritical Anthology* (Cambridge University Press, 2019), p. 110. Borlick comments that 'Writers as sophisticated as Marlowe, Shakespeare, and Donne never simply subscribe to received dogma; they also question or subvert it. Rather than a static and monolithic belief system, the "World Picture" would have experienced spikes and dips in popularity dependent on prevailing critical (and meteorological) conditions' (p. 110).

between 'literary' texts and sermons; but certainly individuals listening to, or reading, sixteenth- and seventeenth-century sermons were encouraged to associate the term *sympathy* with the process of imagining themselves in another's situation. At the same time, however, sermons from this period often point to an anxiety about the fact that the practice and experience of sympathy was not simply straightforward or automatic. The art of the sermon was thus an important part of the ways in which sympathy was explored and encouraged through cultural texts, representations, and performances.

This discussion returns us to the wider theoretical question of whether emotions are culturally produced or biologically hardwired. This is certainly one of the most intractable and complex debates in the field of emotion studies; but the case study of sympathy does provide some fertile material for reflecting upon this issue. On the one hand, mapping the history of sympathy does suggest that there have always been two distinct models of emotional engagement with others: a more automatic form of emotional mimicry, and a more complex and cognitive response to the sufferings of others. We have seen both of these models at work in the early modern period – for example in the maid's complex emotional response to Lucrece's grief – but they also characterise eighteenth-century debates about the nature of sympathy. In his *Treatise of Human Nature* (1739), David Hume describes how an impression of someone else's feelings 'acquires such a degree of force and vivacity, as to become the very passion itself, and producing equal emotion, as any original affection'.[11] Adam Smith also acknowledges that the effects of sympathy can be instantaneous or mimetic in *The Theory of Moral Sentiments*; but he emphasizes the imaginative work performed by the spectator, who must 'endeavour, as much as he can, to put himself in the situation of the other, and to bring home to himself every little circumstance of distress which can possibly occur to the sufferer'.[12] If we turn to present-day neuroscientific discussions of empathy we find that a similar dichotomy exists: that is, the interplay between our 'automatic tendency to mimic the expressions of others (bottom-up processing) and the capacity for the imaginative transposing of oneself into the feeling and thinking of another (top-down processing)'.[13]

---

[11] David Hume, *A Treatise of Human Nature*, ed. L. A. Selby-Bigge and P. H. Nidditch (Oxford: Clarendon Press, 1978), p. 317.
[12] Smith, *The Theory of Moral Sentiments*, p. 26.
[13] Claus Lamm, Daniel C. Batson, and Jean Decety, 'The Neural Substrate of Human Empathy: Effects of Perspective-Taking and Cognitive Appraisal', *Journal of Cognitive Neuroscience*, 19 (2007), 42–58 (p. 42). See also Jean Decety and Andrew N. Meltzoff, 'Empathy, Imitation, and the Social Brain', in Coplan and Goldie (eds.), *Empathy*, pp. 58–81.

Such examples might suggest that the interplay between these two forms of sympathy (variously defined) has always been part of what is loosely termed human nature. But we might argue that, while the first of these models (the instinctive or automatic) may be innate and perhaps universal, the second (the imaginative transposing of oneself into the situation of the other) can be nurtured and cultivated, and is thus more culturally specific. In this way, the advent of the word *sympathy* does not simply describe a pre-existing emotional experience but rather changes the nature of that experience. The enthusiasm with which the word was embraced by early modern writers working across different genres and discourses suggests that the culture required a new term for describing and conceptualizing the process of identifying with another person and sharing their emotions. As we have seen, this development was part of a wider fascination with, and theorization of, the workings of pity, compassion, and fellow-feeling. The relationship between such social and linguistic developments are hard to unpick: changes in culture and society may produce the demand for a new word; or a new word may itself produce changes in the culture; or – as I have argued in the case of sympathy – it may be a kind of sociolinguistic feedback loop in which one influences and amplifies the other. But certainly the development of this key emotion word reminds us of the relational and intersubjective aspects of human nature, whereby social emotions are necessarily shaped and modulated by our interactions with others, and how we describe those interactions.

At the same time, however, we have seen that exhortations to sympathy do not necessarily produce the cultural change they seek: hence the repeated lament – which extends beyond the early modern period – that sympathy and compassion are not as common as they once were. Such pessimism is evident in comments made by William Cavendish at the start of the Civil War in 1642, although this bleak context doubtless shaped his feelings about fellow-feeling: 'This Sympathy or fellow-feeling; this partner-ship or *companion-ship* with others in their misery is a rare grace, and, as faith, scarce found in the world'.[14] As with several other examples that I have examined, Cavendish takes a semantic as well as an ethical interest in sympathy, and provides various synonyms for it – *fellow-feeling*, *partnership*, *companion-ship* – suggesting that the concept was still being ruminated upon and redefined into the 1640s. And indeed other models of

---

[14] William Cavendish, Duke of Newcastle, *A declaration of the Right Honourable the Earle of Newcastle, His Excellency, &c in answer of six groundlesse aspersions cast upon him by the Lord Fairfax* (York, 1642), p. 31.

sympathy remained current at this time, while different perspectives coexisted within single texts, not least in Reynolds's *A treatise of the passions*. Such examples further suggest that the story of sympathy is not a straightforward or linear one, in which this interpersonal emotion becomes more sophisticated as we move into modernity; rather the affective and natural philosophical models coalesced and bifurcated in complex ways.

This history has been distorted by the effects of periodization and the critical desire to superimpose the development of sympathy onto larger narratives about the shift from the early modern period to the Enlightenment. This desire has also led to some generalizations and simplifications about the early modern period – particularly in terms of how early moderns understood and described sympathy, as well as an overreliance upon humoralism as a key to understanding the passions. As we have seen, conceptions of sympathy involved imaginative perspective-taking long before the supposed emergence of 'modern' notions of sympathy in the eighteenth century. This is not to say that early moderns are just like ourselves but to recognize that there are some models and representations of sympathy from the period that resemble present-day psychological and philosophical theories of empathy. In this way, the cultural history of sympathy may help us to reflect upon and interrogate the notion of modernity itself. Barbara Rosenwein has commented that 'Historians of modern emotions need to problematize their easy assumptions about the nature of modernity and the primitive nature of the premodern past. This will be hard to do. But because emotions do not depend on technology, the nation-state, or other factors associated with modernity, the study of emotions is a very good place to begin querying the very idea of modernity'.[15] As Rosenwein suggests, historians of emotion should remain sceptical about narratives of emotional 'development'; but perhaps there also needs to be greater acknowledgement of the ways in which different, sometimes conflicting, attitudes towards a particular emotion (and its intellectual contexts) coexist within a specific period.

While the story of the sympathy has not been a straightforward narrative of progress, then, it does seem clear that belief in magical sympathies and other occult qualities declined in subsequent centuries.[16] But we can

---

[15] Jan Plamper et al., 'The History of Emotions: An Interview with William Reddy, Barbara Rosenwein, and Peter Stearns', *History and Theory*, 49 (2010), 237–65 (p. 260).

[16] As Keith Hutchison has shown, however, the concept of occult qualities was not simply rejected but continued to be employed in some later scientific texts as a way of describing 'unintelligible' (rather than 'insensible') phenomena ('What Happened to Occult Qualities in the Scientific Revolution?', *Isis*, 73 (1982), 233–53). See also John Henry, 'The Fragmentation of Renaissance Occultism and the Decline of Magic', *History of Science*, 46 (2008), 1–48.

also see that a distinction between the physical and the emotional understanding of sympathy was already being made in the late sixteenth and early seventeenth centuries. A text like Reynolds's *A treatise of the passions* helps us to see something of this process at work; but it also highlights the remarkable variety of discourses and disciplines that early modern writers drew upon in order to explain the workings of sympathy and emotional experiences more generally. Reynolds, like many of the other writers we have encountered, reminds us that emotions were not simply the stuff of the body but understood in relation to theological, classical, philosophical, and literary frameworks as well as scientific or medical ones. His interest in classical texts, in particular epics such as the *Iliad* and the *Aeneid*, further emphasizes the importance of art, imitation, and narrative in cultivating emotions, as well as new emotion words. And this is where the early modern fascination with sympathy raises larger aesthetic questions, not least about the ways in which representations of emotion prompt us to reflect upon our own encounters with others, both fictional and real.

Looking forward into the later seventeenth century and into the eighteenth, we find that the capacity of art to move readers and audiences to sympathy and compassion would be highlighted by later commentators as one of the key characteristics of successful drama.[17] Shakespeare's particular ability to depict and stir the passions would become one of the great tropes of early criticism of the playwright, suggesting a certain affinity or synergy between his own interest with the workings of sympathy and his critical and cultural reception. But we might conclude by noting that the word *sympathy* is used in this context in a poem from 1647 to describe the work of John Fletcher, one of Shakespeare's key collaborators and his replacement as chief playwright for the King's Men. Here Thomas Stanley writes of Fletcher that

> *He to a sympathie those souls betrai'd*
> *Whom Love or Beauty never could perswade;*
> *And in each mov'd spectatour could beget*
> *A real passion by a Counterfeit.*
> *When first* Bellario *bled, what Lady there*
> *Did not for every drop let fall a tear?*
> *And when* Aspasia *wept, not any eye*
> *But seem'd to wear the same sad liverie.*[18]

---

[17] See Jean Marsden, 'Shakespeare and Sympathy', in Peter Sabor and Paul Yachnin (eds.), *Shakespeare and the Eighteenth Century* (Farnham: Ashgate, 2008), pp. 29–41; and Rhodes, 'The Science of the Heart'.

[18] Thomas Stanley, 'On the Edition', in *Comedies and tragedies written by Francis Beaumont and John Fletcher* (London, 1647), sig. B4v.

This poem proposes that a representation of grief, even if it is '*Counterfeit*', has the capacity to elicit a '*real passion*' in the spectator. It registers the power of dramatic art – specifically *Philaster* and *The Maid's Tragedy* – to move, and the importance of sympathy to aesthetic experience. And yet, at the same time, it is significant that these claims are made in a poem that appears in the prefatory materials of the Beaumont and Fletcher folio, which was printed after the theatres were closed. This prefacing of the plays with claims about their supposed emotional effect suggests that an imaginary performance might be regarded as just as moving as a real one; it also suggests that literary texts – or, here, a printed collection of plays – might produce sympathy in part by figuring sympathy.

Stanley goes on to claim that Fletcher's ability to depict the passions outdid nature herself: '*He Nature taught her passions to out-do, / How to refine the old, and create new*' (sig. B4v). In this striking couplet, Stanley suggests not only that Fletcher's plays surpassed nature in terms of their passionate expressions but also that they had the ability to refine old passions and even create new ones. He raises once again the intractable question of whether emotions are the product of biology and nature, or art and culture – and comes down more on the side of art. Stanley's poem thus implies that powerful works of art do not simply reflect our emotional lives but rather shape and cultivate them, and provide us with new words and vocabularies that may, in turn, beget new forms of passionate expression and experience. It also points to the particularly important role that early modern texts played in this historical process of understanding, redefining, and expanding our emotions – as well as higlighting their continuing capacity to move audiences and readers '*to a sympathie*'.

Bibliography

Primary Sources

Abbot, George, *An exposition upon the prophet Jonah* (London, 1600)
Anonymous, *Zepheria* (London, 1594)
Alexander, William, *The monarchick tragedies* (London, 1604)
Allott, Robert, *Englands Parnassus: or The choysest flowers of our moderne poets, with their poeticall comparisons* (London, 1600)
Andrewes, John, *Christ his crosse, or, The most comfortable doctrine of Christ crucified and joyfull tidings of his passion* (London, 1614)
Ariosto, Ludovico, *Orlando Furioso*, trans. John Harington (London, 1591)
Ariosto, Ludovico, *Orlando Furioso*, trans. Guido Waldman (Oxford University Press, 1983)
Averell, William, *A mervailous combat of contrarieties* (London, 1588)
Bacon, Francis, *The advancement of learning* (London, 1605)
Bacon, Francis, *A briefe discourse, touching the happie union of the kingdomes of England, and Scotland* (London, 1603)
Bacon, Francis, *Sylva sylvarum, or, A naturall history in ten centuries* (London, 1627)
Belleforest, François, *XVIII. Histoires tragiques: extraictes des oeuures italiennes de Bandel, & mises en langue françoise* (Paris, 1560)
Belleforest, François, *The French Bandello: a selection; the original text of four of Belleforest's Histoires tragiques*, ed. Frank S. Hook (Columbia: University of Missouri, 1948)
Bennett, John, *Madrigalls to foure voyces* (London, 1599)
Bilson, Thomas, *The survey of Christs sufferings for mans redemption and of his descent to Hades or Hel for our deliverance* (London, 1604)
Bodenham, John and Anthony Munday, *Bel-vedére, or, The Garden of the muses* (London, 1600)
Bodin, Jean, *Les six livres de la Republique* (Paris, 1576)
Bodin, Jean, *The six bookes of a common-weale*, trans. Richard Knolles (London, 1606)
Brandon, Samuel, *The Tragicomoedi of the Vertuous Octavia*, ed. Ronald B. McKerrow (Oxford University Press, 1909)
Bridges, John, *A defence of the government established in the Church of Englande for ecclesiasticall matters* (London, 1587)

Bright, Timothie, *A treatise of melancholie, containing the causes thereof, & reasons of the strange effects it worketh in our minds and bodies* (London, 1586)

Brooke, Christopher, *Two elegies: consecrated to the never-dying memorie of the most worthily admyred; most hartily loved; and generally bewayled prince; Henry Prince of Wales* (London, 1612)

Bullokar, John, *An English expositor teaching the interpretation of the hardest words used in our language* (London, 1616)

Burton, Robert, *The anatomy of melancholy* (Oxford, 1621)

Burton, William, *An exposition of the Lords Prayer made in divers lectures, and now drawne into questions and answers for the greater benefite of the simpler sort* (London, 1594)

Byfield, Nicholas, *The rules of a holy life* (London, 1619)

Cavendish, Richard, *The image of nature and grace conteynyng the whole course, and condition of mans estate* (London, 1571)

Cavendish, William, Duke of Newcastle, *A declaration of the Right Honourable the Earle of Newcastle, His Excellency, &c in answer of six groundlesse aspersions cast upon him by the Lord Fairfax* (York, 1642)

Cawdry, Robert, *A table alphabeticall conteyning and teaching the true writing, and understanding of hard usuall English wordes, borrowed from the Hebrew, Greeke, Latine, or French, &c.* (London, 1604)

Churchyard, Thomas, *Churchyards challenge* (London, 1593)

Chute, Anthony, *Beawtie dishonoured written under the title of Shores wife* (London, 1593)

Cicero, *De Oratore*, trans. E. W. Sutton and H. Rackham, 2 vols (Cambridge, MA: Harvard University Press, 1942)

Cicero, *On Invention. The Best Kind of Orator. Topics*, trans. H. M. Hubbell (Cambridge, MA: Harvard Universtiy Press, 1949)

Cockeram, Henry, *The English dictionarie, or, An interpreter of hard English words* (London, 1623)

Coeffeteau, Nicolas, *A table of humane passions. With their causes and effects*, trans. Edward Grimeston (London, 1621)

Colet, Claude, *The famous, pleasant, and variable historie, of Palladine of England … Translated out of French by A.M.* (London, 1588)

Cotgrave, Randle, *A Dictionarie of the French and English Tongues* (London, 1611)

Croll, Oswald, *Basilica chymica* (Frankfurt, 1609)

Croll, Oswald, *Bazilica chymica, & Praxis chymiatricae, or, Royal and practical chymistry* (London, 1670)

Daniel, Samuel, *Samuel Daniel: Poems and A Defence of Ryme*, ed. Arthur C. Sprague (London: Routledge and Kegan Paul, 1950)

Daniel, Samuel, *Delia and Rosamond augmented. Cleopatra* (London, 1594)

Daniel, Samuel, *The First Fowre Bookes of the Civile Wars Between the Two Houses of Lancaster and York* (London, 1595)

Daniel, Samuel, *The Poeticall Essayes of Sam. Danyel. Newly corrected and augmented* (London, 1599)

Day, Angel, *The English secretorie, or, Plaine and direct method, for the enditing of all manner of epistles or letters … now corrected, refined & amended* (London, 1592)

Dekker, Thomas, *The wonderfull yeare. Wherein is shewed the picture of London lying sicke of the Plague* (London, 1603)

Dickenson, John, *Arisbas, Euphues amidst his slumbers: or Cupids journey to hell* (London, 1594)

Digby, Sir Kenelm, *A Late Discourse … Touching the Cure of Wounds by Sympathy, With Instructions how to make the said Power; whereby many other Secrets of Nature are unfolded* (London, 1658)

Donne, John, *LXXX sermons preached by that learned and reverend divine, John Donne, Dr in Divinity, late Deane of the cathedrall church of S. Pauls London* (London, 1640)

Du Bartas, Guillaume de Salluste, *The Historie of Judith*, trans. Thomas Hudson (London, 1584)

Du Bartas, Guillaume de Salluste, *The Works of Guillaume De Salluste Sieur Du Bartas: A Critical Edition with Introduction, Commentary, and Variants*, eds. Urban Tigner Holmes, Jr., John Coriden Lyons, and Robert White Linker, 3 vols (Chapel Hill: University of North Carolina Press, 1935–40)

Dugdale, Gilbert, *The time triumphant declaring in briefe, the arival of our soveraigne liedge Lord, King James into England, his coronation at Westminster* (London, 1604)

Eliot, Thomas, *The Boke Named the Governour*, ed. Henry H. S. Croft, 2 vols (London: Kegan Paul, Trench, and Co., 1883)

Eliot, Thomas, *The dictionary of syr Thomas Eliot knyght* (London, 1538)

Erasmus, *Collected Works of Erasmus, Adages, vol. 31*, trans. Margaret Mann Phillips, annotated by R. A. B. Mynors (University of Toronto Press, 1982)

Erasmus, *Collected Works of Erasmus, Adages, vol. 33*, trans. R. A. B. Mynors (University of Toronto Press, 1991)

Fenton, Geoffrey, *Certaine tragicall discourses written out of Frenche and Latin* (London, 1567)

Field, Theophilus, *An Italians dead bodie, stucke with English flowers elegies, on the death of Sir Oratio Pallauicino* (London, 1600)

Fitzgeffry, Charles, *Compassion towards captives chiefly towards our brethren and country-men who are in miserable bondage in Barbarie* (Oxford, 1637)

Fitzgeffry, Charles, *The curse of corne-horders with the blessing of seasonable selling* (London, 1631)

Fitzgeffry, Charles, *Sir Francis Drake his honorable lifes commendation, and his tragicall deathes lamentation* (Oxford, 1596)

Flasket, John, *Englands Helicon* (London, 1600)

Fletcher the Elder, Giles, *Licia* (London, 1593)

Florio, John, *A Worlde of Wordes, or Most Copious, and Exact Dictionarie in Italian and English, Collected by John Florio* (London, 1598)

Fludd, Robert, *Anatomiae amphitheatrum effigie triplici* (Frankfurt, 1623)

Fludd, Robert, *Doctor Fludds answer unto M. Foster or, The squeesing of Parson Fosters sponge* (London, 1631)
Fludd, Robert, *Mosaicall philosophy: Grounded upon the essentiall truth or eternal sapience* (London, 1659)
Fludd, Robert, *Philosophia Moysaica* (Gouda, 1638)
Ford, John, *The Lover's Melancholy* in *'Tis Pity She's a Whore and Other Plays*, ed. Marion Lomax (Oxford University Press, 1995), pp. 1–80
Forset, Edward, *A comparative discourse of the bodies natural and politique* (London, 1606)
Foster, William, *Hiplocrisma-spongus, or, A Sponge to Wipe Away the Weapon-Salve* (London, 1631)
Four Revenge Tragedies, ed. Katharine Eisaman Maus (Oxford University Press, 1995)
Galen, *Certaine workes of Galens, called Methodus medendi*, trans. Thomas Gale (London, 1586)
The Geneva Bible: A Facsimile of the 1560 Edition, with an introduction by Lloyd E. Berry (Madison: University of Wisconsin Press, 1969)
Glapthorne, Henry, *The Plays and Poems of Henry Glapthorne*, ed. R. H. Shepherd, 2 vols (London: John Pearson, 1874)
Goclenius the Younger, Rudolph, *De vita proroganda* (Mainz, 1608)
Greene, Robert, *Ciceronis amor. Tullies love* (London, 1589)
Greene, Robert, *Greenes Groats-worth of Witte* (London, 1592)
Greene, Robert, *Menaphon. Camillas alarum to slumbering Euphues, in his melancholie cell at Silexedra* (London, 1589)
Hall, Joseph, *Occasionall meditations* (London, 1631)
Hannay, Patrick, *Two elegies, on the late death of our soveraigne Queene Anne With epitaphes* (London, 1619)
Hart, James, *Klinike, or The diet of the diseased. Divided into three bookes* (London, 1633)
Herring, Francis, *Pietas pontificia* (London, 1609)
Hind, John, *The most excellent historie of Lysimachus and Varrona* (London, 1604)
Holland, Henry, *The Christian Exercise of Fasting* (London, 1596)
Holland, Henry, *David's Faith and Repentance* (London, 1589)
Holland, Henry, *Spirituall preservatives against the pestilence: Or a treatise containing sundrie questions* (London, 1593)
Horace, *The Art of Poetry*, in D. A. Russell and M. Winterbottom (eds.), *Classical literary criticism* (Oxford University Press, 1989), pp. 98–110
Horace, *Horace, his Art of Poetry*, trans. Ben Jonson, in Gavin Alexander (ed.), *Sidney's 'The Defence of Poesy' and Selected Renaissance Literary Criticism* (London: Penguin, 2004), pp. 304–7
Hooke, Christopher, *The child-birth or womans lecture* (London, 1590)
Howell, Thomas, *H. His devises, for his owne exercise, and his friends pleasure* (London, 1581)
Huloet, Richard, *Huloets dictionarie newelye corrected, amended, set in order and enlarged* (London, 1572)

Hume, David, *A Treatise of Human Nature*, eds. L. A. Selby-Bigge and P. H. Nidditch (Oxford: Clarendon Press, 1978)
Ingelo, Nathaniel, *Bentivolio and Urania* (London, 1660)
James, I, *Basilikon Doron: Devided into three bookes* (Edinburgh, 1599)
James, I, *A counterblast to tobacco* (London, 1604)
James, I, *A remonstrance of the most gratious King James I* (Cambridge, 1616)
James, William, *A sermon preached at Paules Crosse the IX. of November, 1589* (London, 1590)
Jonson, Ben, *The Cambridge Edition of the Works of Ben Jonson*, gen. eds. David Bevington, Martin Butler, and Ian Donaldson (Cambridge University Press, 2012)
Knolles, Richard, *The generall historie of the Turks* (London, 1603)
Kyd, Thomas, *The Spanish Tragedy*, ed. Philip Edwards (Manchester University Press, 1959)
Kyd, Thomas, *The Spanish Tragedy*, ed. J. R. Mulryne (London: A & C Black, 1989)
Kyd, Thomas, *The tragedye of Solyman and Perseda* (London, 1592)
Lane, John, *Tom Tel-Troths message, and his pens complaint* (London, 1600)
La Primaudaye, Pierre de, *The French academie*, trans. Thomas Bowers (London, 1586)
Lawrence, John, *A golden trumpet, to rowse up a drowsie magistrate: or, A patterne for a governors practise drawne from Christs comming to, beholding of, and weeping over Hierusalem* (London, 1624)
Lemnius, Levinus, *The touchstone of complexions* (London, 1576)
Lightfoot, William, *The complaint of England* (London, 1587)
L'histoire de Palmerin d'Olive, filz du roy Florendos de Macedone, & de la belle Griane, fille de Remicius Empereur de Constantinople (Antwerp, 1572)
Lodge, Thomas, *The Complete Works of Thomas Lodge*, 4 vols (1883; rpt. New York: Russell and Russell, 1963)
Lodge, Thomas, *Euphues shadow, the battaile of the sences, Wherein youthfull folly is set downe in his right figure, and vaine fancies are prooved to produce many offences* (London, 1592)
Lodge, Thomas, *The famous, true and historicall life of Robert second Duke of Normandy, surnamed for his monstrous birth and behaviour, Robin the Divell* (London, 1591)
Lodge, Thomas, *Lodge's 'Rosalynde': Being the original of Shakespeare's 'As You Like It'*, ed. W. W. Greg (London: Chatto and Windus, 1907)
Lodge, Thomas, *Phillis: Honoured with Pastorall Sonnets, Elegies, and amorous delights. Where-unto is annexed, the tragicall complaynt of Elstred* (London, 1593)
Lyly, John, *Endymion*, ed. David Bevington (Manchester University Press, 1996)
Lyly, John, *Euphues: The Anatomy of Wit and Euphues and His England*, ed. Leah Scragg (Manchester University Press, 2003)
Markham, Gervase, *The most honorable tragedie of Sir Richard Grinvile, Knight* (London, 1595)

Marlowe, Christopher, *Dido, Queen of Carthage*, in E. D. Pendry and J. C. Maxwell (eds.), *Complete Plays and Poems* (London: J. M. Dent, 1976), pp. 191–234

Marlowe, Christopher, *Dido, Queen of Carthage and The Massacre at Paris*, ed. H. J. Oliver (London: Methuen, 1968)

Martial, *Epigrams, Volume I: Spectacles, Books 1–5*, ed. and trans. D. R. Shackleton Bailey (Cambridge, MA: Harvard University Press, 1993)

Medeley, Thomas, *Misericors, mikrokosmos, or, Medeleys offices containing an injunction to all duties of mercy belonging to the whole man* (London, 1619)

Meres, Francis, *Palladis Tamia. Wits Treasury* (London, 1598)

Middleton, Christopher, *The legend of Humphrey Duke of Glocester* (London, 1600)

Milton, John, *Paradise Lost*, ed. Alastair Fowler (London: Longman, 1968)

The Mirror for Magistrates, ed. Lily B. Campbell (Cambridge University Press, 1938)

Mitchell, Marea and Ann Lange (eds.), *Continuations to Sidney's Arcadia, 1607–1867*, gen. ed. Marea Mitchell, 4 vols (London: Pickering and Chatto, 2014), vol. 1

Montaigne, Michel de, *Essays written in French by Michael Lord of Montaigne*, trans. John Florio (1603; rpt. London, 1613)

Montaigne, Michel de, *Les essais de Michel de Montaigne*, ed. Verdun Louis Saulnier and Pierre Villey (Paris: Presses Universitaires de France, 1965)

Mosse, Miles, *The arraignment and conviction of usurie* (London, 1595)

Muggins, William, *Londons Mourning garment, or Funerall Teares* (London, 1603)

Mulcaster, Richard, *Positions wherin those primitive circumstances be examined, which are necessarie for the training up of children* (London, 1581)

Nicholson, Samuel, *Acolastus his after-witte*, ed. Alexander B. Grosart (Blackburn, Lancashire: Printed for the Subscribers by Charles E. Simms, Manchester, 1876)

Ovid, *Metamorphoses*, trans. A. D. Melville (Oxford University Press, 1986)

Painter, William, *The second Tome of the Palace of Pleasure* (London, 1567)

Paynell, Thomas, *The moste excellent and pleasaunt booke, entitled: The treasurie of Amadis of Fraunce ... Translated out of Frenche into English* (London, 1572)

Peele, George, *The Araygnment of Paris: A Pastorall. Presented before the Queenes Majestie, by the Children of her Chappell* (London, 1584)

Perkins, William, *The arte of prophecying, or, A treatise concerning the sacred and onely true manner and methode of preaching*, trans. Thomas Tuke (London, 1607)

Pliny, *Natural History, Volume VI: Books 20–23*, trans. W. H. S. Jones (Cambridge, MA: Harvard University Press, 1951)

Plutarch, *The Philosophie, Commonlie Called the Morals*, trans. Philemon Holland (London, 1603)

Porta, John Paptista, *Natural magick by John Baptista Porta, a Neopolitane: in twenty books ... Wherein are set forth all the riches and delights of the natural sciences* (London, 1658)

Prime, John, *An Exposition, and Observations upon Saint Paul to the Galathians* (London, 1587)
Primerose, James, *De Vulgi in Medicina Erroribus* (London, 1638)
Puttenham, George, *The Art of English Poesy*, in Gavin Alexander (ed.), *Sidney's 'The Defence of Poesy' and Selected Renaissance Literary Criticism* (London: Penguin, 2004), pp. 55–203
Quarles, Francis, *Argalus and Parthenia: The argument of ye history* (London, 1629)
Quarles, Francis, *The Virgin Widow. A Comedie* (London, 1649)
Quintilian, *The Orator's Education*, ed. and trans. Donald A. Russell, 5 vols (Cambridge, MA: Harvard University Press, 2001)
Rainholde, Richard, *A booke called the Foundacion of Rhetorike* (London, 1563)
Reading, John, *Davids soliloquie. Containing many comforts for afflicted mindes* (London, 1627)
Reynolds, Edward, *An explication of the hundreth and tenth Psalme* (London, 1632)
Reynolds, Edward, *A treatise of the passions and faculties of the soule of man* (London, 1640)
Rider, John, *Bibliotheca scholastica* (London, 1589)
Rogers, Thomas, *Gloucesters myte* (London, 1612)
Rollock, Robert, *Lectures, upon the history of the Passion, Resurrection, and Ascension of our Lord Jesus Christ* (Edinburgh, 1616)
Sandys, Edwin, *Sermons made by the most reverende Father in God, Edwin, Archbishop of Yorke* (London, 1585)
Seneca, *Tragedies, Volume I: Hercules, Trojan Women, Phoenician Women, Medea, Phaedra*, ed. and trans. John G. Fitch (Cambridge, MA: Harvard University Press, 2018)
Sennert, Daniel, *The weapon-salves maladie: or, A declaration of its insufficiencie to performe what is attributed to it* (London, 1637)
Shakespeare, William, *As You Like It*, ed. Juliet Dusinberre (London: Thomson Learning, 2006)
Shakespeare, William, *The Comedy of Errors*, ed. Kent Cartwright (London: Bloomsbury, 2016)
Shakespeare, William, *The Comedy of Errors*, ed. R. A. Foakes (London: Methuen, 1962)
Shakespeare, William, *The Complete Sonnets and Poems*, ed. Colin Burrow (Oxford University Press, 2002)
Shakespeare, William, *The History of King Lear*, ed. Stanley Wells (Oxford University Press, 2000)
Shakespeare, William, *King Lear*, ed. Kenneth Muir (London: Methuen, 1972)
Shakespeare, William, *King Richard II*, ed. Charles Forker (London: Methuen, 2002)
Shakespeare, William, *Love's Labour's Lost*, ed. H. R. Woudhuysen (London: Thomas Nelson, 1998)
Shakespeare, William, *The Poems*, ed. John Roe, updated ed. (Cambridge University Press, 2006)

Shakespeare, William, *Richard II*, ed. Andrew Gurr (Cambridge University Press, 1984)
Shakespeare, William, *The Riverside Shakespeare*, ed. G. Blakemore Evans, 2nd ed. (Boston: Houghton Mifflin, 1997)
Shakespeare, William, *Romeo and Juliet*, ed. Jill L. Levenson (Oxford University Press, 2000)
Shakespeare, William, *The Third Part of Henry VI*, ed. Michael Hattaway (Cambridge University Press, 1993)
Shakespeare, William, *Titus Andronicus*, ed. Jonathan Bate (London: Routledge, 1995)
Shakespeare, William, *Titus Andronicus*, ed. Alan Hughes, updated ed. (Cambridge University Press, 2006)
Shakespeare, William, *The Tragedy of King Lear*, ed. Jay L. Halio (Cambridge University Press, 1992)
Shakespeare, William, *The Two Gentlemen of Verona*, ed. William C. Carroll (London: Thomson Learning, 2004)
Shakespeare, William, *The Two Gentlemen of Verona*, ed. Roger Warren (Oxford University Press, 2008)
Sidney, Sir Philip, *The Countess of Pembroke's Arcadia (The Old Arcadia)*, ed. Jean Robertson (Oxford: Clarendon Press, 1973)
Sidney, Sir Philip, *The Countess of Pembroke's Arcadia (The New Arcadia)*, ed. Victor Skretkowicz (Oxford: Clarendon Press, 1987)
Sidney, Sir Philip, *The Oxford Authors: Sir Philip Sidney*, ed. Katherine Duncan-Jones (Oxford University Press, 1989)
Spenser, Edmund, *Edmund Spenser: The Shorter Poems*, ed. Richard A. McCabe (Harmondsworth: Penguin, 1999)
Smith, Adam, *The Theory of Moral Sentiments*, ed. Knud Haakonssen (Cambridge University Press, 2002)
Southwell, Robert, *The triumphs over death: or, A consolatorie epistle, for afflicted mindes, in the affects of dying friends* (London, 1595)
Stanley, Thomas, 'On the Edition', in *Comedies and tragedies written by Francis Beaumont and John Fletcher* (London, 1647)
Stoughton, John, *XI. Choice sermons preached upon selected occasions, in Cambridge* (London, 1640)
Stoughton, John, *The righteous mans plea to true happinesse. In ten sermons, on Psal. 4 ver. 6* (London, 1640)
Thomas, Lewis, *Demegoriai: Certaine lectures upon sundry portions of Scripture, in one volume* (London, 1600)
Thorne, William, *Esoptron basilikon. Or A kenning-glasse for a Christian king* (London, 1603)
Trussell, John, *Raptus I. Helenae. The First Rape of Faire Hellen. Done into poeme, by J. T.* (London, 1595)
Udall, John, *The True Remedie against Famine and Warres: five sermons ... preached in the time of the dearth* (London, 1588?)
Van Helmont, Jan Baptist, *De magnetica vulnerum curatione* (Paris, 1621)

Vicars, John, *Mischeefes mysterie: or, Treasons master-peece, the Powder-plot Invented by hellish malice, prevented by heavenly mercy: truely related* (London, 1617)
Virgil, *The Aeneid*, trans. David West (Harmondsworth: Penguin, 1990)
Virgil, *The 'Aeneid' of Thomas Phaer and Thomas Twyne*, ed. Steven Lally (New York and London: Garland, 1987)
Webster, William, *The most pleasant and delightful historie of Curan* (London, 1617)
Weever, John, 'Epigram 22, Ad Gulielmum Shakespeare', in C. M. Ingleby et al. (eds.), *The Shakespeare Allusion Book: A Collection of Allusions to Shakespeare from 1591 to 1700*, 2 vols (London: Oxford University Press, 1932)
Weever, John, *The whipping of the satyre* (London, 1601)
West, William, *The second part of Symboleography, newly corrected and amended, and very much enlarged in all the foure severall treatises* (London, 1601)
Wither, George, *Faire-virtue, the mistresse of Phil'arete* (London, 1622)
Wither, George, *Prince Henries obsequies or Mournefull elegies upon his death: with a supposed inter-locution betweene the ghost of Prince Henrie and Great Brittaine* (London, 1612)
Wilcox, Thomas, *An exposition uppon the Booke of the Canticles, otherwise called Schelomons Song* (London, 1585)
Wright, Thomas, *The Passions of the Minde in Generall. In Six Books. Corrected, enlarged, and with sundry new Discourses augmented* (1604; rpt. London, 1630)
Wyatt, Sir Thomas, *The Complete Poems*, ed. R. A. Rebholz (Harmondsworth: Penguin, 1978)

Secondary Sources

Alexander, Gavin, *Writing after Sidney: The Literary Response to Sir Philip Sidney, 1586–1640* (Oxford University Press, 2006)
Alberti, Fay Bound, 'Emotions in the Early Modern Medical Tradition', in Fay Bound Alberti (ed.), *Medicine, Emotion and Disease, 1700–1950* (Basingstoke: Palgrave, 2006), pp. 1–21
Arkin, Samuel, '"That map which deep impression bears": Lucrece and the Anatomy of Shakespeare's Sympathy', *Shakespeare Quarterly*, 64 (2013), 349–71
Armstrong, Kate, 'Sermons in Performance', in Hugh Adlington, Peter McCullough and Emma Rhatigan (eds.), *The Oxford Handbook of the Early Modern Sermon* (Oxford University Press, 2011), pp. 120–36
Auerbach, Eric, *Scenes from the Drama of European Literature: Six Essays* (New York: Meridian Books, 1959)
Austin, J. L., *How to Do Things with Words* (Oxford: Clarendon Press, 1962)
Bailey, Amanda, 'Speak What We Feel: Sympathy and Statecraft', in Amanda Bailey and Mario DiGangi (eds.), *Affect Theory and Early Modern Texts: Politics, Ecologies, and Form* (New York: Palgrave Macmillan, 2017), pp. 27–46
Baldwin, T. W., *William Shakspere's Smalle Latine and Lesse Greeke*, 2 vols (Urbana: University of Illinois Press, 1944)

Bakhtin, M. M., 'Bakhtin on Shakespeare: Excerpt from "Additions and Changes to *Rabelais*"', translation and introduction by Sergeiy Sandler, *PMLA*, 129 (2014), 522–37
Barish, Jonas, 'The Prose Style of John Lyly', *ELH*, 23 (1956), 14–35
Barthes, Roland, *S/Z*, trans. Richard Miller (New York: Farrar, Straus and Giroux, 1974)
Barton, Anne, *Essays, Mainly Shakespearean* (Cambridge University Press, 1994)
Bemrose, J. M., 'A Critical Examination of the Borrowings from *Venus and Adonis* and *Lucrece* in Samuel Nicholson's *Acolastus*', *Shakespeare Quarterly*, 15 (1964), 85–96
Borlick, Todd Andrew, *Literature and Nature in the English Renaissance: An Ecocritical Anthology* (Cambridge University Press, 2019)
Brammall, Sheldon, '"Sound This Angrie Message in Thine Eares": Sympathy and the Translations of the *Aeneid* in Marlowe's *Dido Queene of Carthage*', *Review of English Studies*, 65 (2013), 383–402
Brennan, Teresa, *The Transmission of Affect* (Ithaca: Cornell University Press, 2001)
Britton, Jeanne M., *Vicarious Narratives: A Literary History of Sympathy, 1750–1850* (Oxford University Press, 2019)
Brown, Georgia, *Redefining Elizabethan Literature* (Cambridge University Press, 2004)
Bruce, Yvonne, '"That Which Marreth All": Constancy and Gender in *The Virtuous Octavia*', *Medieval and Renaissance Drama in England*, 22 (2009), 42–59
Burrow, Colin, *Epic Romance: Homer to Milton* (Oxford: Clarendon Press, 1993)
Burrow, Colin, *Shakespeare and Classical Antiquity* (Oxford University Press, 2013)
Bynum, William F., 'The Weapon Salve in Seventeenth Century English Drama', *Journal of the History of Medicine and Allied Sciences*, 21 (1966), 8–23
Camenietzki, Carlos Ziller, 'Jesuits and Alchemy in the Early Seventeenth Century: Father Johannes Roberti and the Weapon-Salve Controversy', *Ambix*, 48 (2001), 83–101
Cavell, Stanley, *Disowning Knowledge in Seven Plays of Shakespeare*, updated ed. (Cambridge University Press, 2003)
Chandler, James, *An Archaeology of Sympathy: The Sentimental Mode in Literature and Cinema* (Chicago University Press, 2013)
Christian, Margaret, '*Zepheria* (1594; STC 26124): A Critical Edition', *Studies in Philology*, 100 (2003), 177–243
Clement, Jennifer, 'The Art of Feeling in Seventeenth-Century English Sermons', *English Studies*, 98 (2017), 675–88
Clough, Patricia and Jean Halley (eds.), *The Affective Turn: Theorizing the Social* (Durham and London: Duke University Press, 2007)
Cockcroft, Robert, *Rhetorical Affect in Early Modern Writing* (Basingstoke: Macmillan, 2003)
Copenhaver, Brian P., 'Magic', in Katharine Park and Lorraine Daston (eds.), *The Cambridge History of Science, Volume 3: Early Modern Science* (Cambridge University Press, 2006), pp. 518–40

Copenhaver, Brian P., *Magic in Western Culture: From Antiquity to the Enlightenment* (Cambridge University Press, 2015)
Coplan, Amy and Peter Goldie (eds.), *Empathy: Philosophical and Psychological Perspectives* (Oxford University Press, 2011)
Coppola, Al, *The Theater of Experiment: Staging Natural Philosophy in Eighteenth-Century Britain* (Oxford University Press, 2016)
Craig, John, 'Sermon Reception' in Hugh Adlington, Peter McCullough, and Emma Rhatigan (eds.), *The Oxford Handbook of the Early Modern Sermon* (Oxford University Press, 2011), pp. 179–93
Craik, Katharine A., 'Poetry and Compassion in Shakespeare's "A Lover's Complaint"', in Jonathan Post (ed.), *The Oxford Handbook of Shakespeare's Poetry* (Oxford University Press, 2013), pp. 522–39
Craik, Katharine A. and Tanya Pollard (eds.), *Shakespearean Sensations: Experiencing Literature in Early Modern England* (Cambridge University Press, 2013)
Crowley, Timothy D., 'Arms and the Boy: Marlowe's Aeneas and the Parody of Imitation in *Dido, Queen of Carthage*', *English Literary Renaissance*, 38 (2008), 408–38
Crystal, David, 'Verbing', *Around the Globe*, 7 (1998), 20–1
Cummings, Brian, 'Erasmus and the Invention of Literature', *Erasmus Yearbook*, 33 (2013), 22–54
Cummings, Brian and Freya Sierhuis (eds.), *Passions and Subjectivity in Early Modern Culture* (Farnham: Ashgate, 2013)
Cunningham, Andrew S., 'Was Eighteenth-Century Sentimentalism Unprecedented?', *British Journal for the History of Philosophy*, 6 (1998), 381–96
Csengei, Ildiko, *Sympathy, Sensibility and the Literature of Feeling in the Eighteenth Century* (Basingstoke: Palgrave Macmillan, 2012)
Danby, John, *Shakespeare's Doctrine of Nature: A Study of 'King Lear'* (London: Faber and Faber, 1948)
Davis, Nick, *Early Modern Writing and the Privatization of Experience* (London: Bloomsbury, 2013)
Debes, Remy, 'From *Einfühlung* to Empathy: Sympathy in Early Phenomenology and Psychology', in Eric Schliesser (ed.), *Sympathy: A History* (Oxford University Press, 2015), pp. 286–322
Debus, Allen G. *The Chemical Philosophy: Paracelsian Science and Medicine in The Sixteenth and Seventeenth Centuries*, 2 vols (New York: Science History Publications, 1977)
Debus, Allen G., 'Robert Fludd and the Use of Gilbert's *De Magnete* in the Weapon-Salve Controversy', *Journal of the History of Medicine and Allied Sciences*, 19 (1964), 389–417
Decety, Jean and Andrew N. Meltzoff, 'Empathy, Imitation, and the Social Brain', in Amy Coplan and Peter Goldie (eds.), *Empathy: Philosophical and Psychological Perspectives* (Oxford University Press, 2011), pp. 58–81
Degooyer, Stephanie, '"The Eyes of Other People": Adam Smith's Triangular Sympathy and the Sentimental Novel', *ELH*, 85 (2018), 669–90

Dent, R. W., *Shakespeare's Proverbial Language: An Index* (Berkeley: University of California Press, 1981)
Derrin, Daniel, 'Engaging the Passions in John Donne's *Sermons*', *English Studies*, 93 (2012), 452–68
Dixon, Thomas, '"Emotion": The History of a Keyword in Crisis', *Emotion Review*, 4 (2012), 338–44
Dixon, Thomas, *From Passions to Emotions: The Creation of a Secular Psychological Category* (Cambridge University Press, 2003)
Dixon, Thomas, *Weeping Britannia: Portrait of a Nation in Tears* (Oxford University Press, 2015)
Dubrow, Heather, '"Lending soft audience to my sweet design": Shifting Roles and Shifting Readings of Shakespeare's "A Lover's Complaint"', *Shakespeare Survey*, 58 (2005), 23–33
Dubrow, Heather, 'A Mirror for Complaints: Shakespeare's *Lucrece* and Generic Tradition', in Barbara Kiefer Lewalski (ed.), *Renaissance Genres: Essays on Theory, History, and Interpretation* (Cambridge, MA, and London: Harvard University Press, 1986), pp. 399–417
Duffin, Anne, *Faction and Faith: Politics and Religion in the Cornish Gentry before the Civil War* (Exeter: University of Exeter Press, 1996)
Eagleton, Terry, *Sweet Violence: The Idea of the Tragic* (Oxford: Blackwell, 2003)
Eagleton, Terry, *Tragedy* (New Haven and London: Yale University Press, 2020)
Enterline, Lynn, *The Rhetoric of the Body from Ovid to Shakespeare* (Cambridge University Press, 2000)
Enterline, Lynn, *Shakespeare's Schoolroom: Rhetoric, Discipline, Emotion* (Philadelphia: University of Pennsylvania Press, 2012)
Erne, Lukas, *Beyond 'The Spanish Tragedy': A Study of the Works of Thomas Kyd* (Manchester University Press, 2001)
Essary, Kirk, 'Clear as Mud: Metaphor, Emotion and Meaning in Early Modern England', *English Studies*, 98 (2017), 689–703
Essary, Kirk, 'Passions, Affections, or Emotions? On the Ambiguity of 16th-Century Terminology', *Emotion Review*, 9 (2017), 367–74
Epstein, Joel J., 'Francis Bacon and the Issue of Union, 1603–1608', *Huntington Library Quarterly*, 33 (1970), 121–32
Evans, Dylan, *Emotion: The Science of Sentiment* (Oxford University Press, 2001)
Evrigenis, Ioannis D., 'Sovereignty, Mercy, and Natural Law: King James VI/I and Jean Bodin', *History of European Ideas*, 45 (2019), 1073–88
Fairclough, Mary, *The Romantic Crowd: Sympathy, Controversy and Print Culture* (Cambridge University Press, 2013)
Ferrell, Lori Anne, 'Sermons', in Andy Kesson and Emma Smith (eds.), *The Elizabethan Top Ten: Defining Print Popularity in Early Modern England* (Aldershot: Ashgate, 2013), pp. 193–202
Floyd-Wilson, Mary, *Occult Knowledge, Science, and Gender on the Shakespearean Stage* (Cambridge University Press, 2013)
Floyd-Wilson, Mary and Garrett A. Sullivan, Jr (eds.), *Environment and Embodiment in Early Modern England* (Basingstoke: Palgrave, 2007)

Foakes, R. A., *Hamlet versus Lear: Cultural Politics and Shakespeare's Art* (Cambridge University Press, 1993)
Forget, Evelyn L., 'Evocations of Sympathy: Sympathetic Imagery in Eighteenth-Century Social Theory and Physiology', in Margaret Schabas and Neil De Marchi (eds.), *Oeconomies in the Age of Newton* (Durham and London: Duke University Press, 2003)
Foucault, Michel, *The Order of Things: An Archaeology of the Human Sciences* (1970; rpt. London: Routledge, 2002)
Fowler, Alastair, *Renaissance Realism: Narrative Images in Literature and Art* (Oxford University Press, 2003)
Fox, Cora, *Ovid and the Politics of Emotion in Elizabethan England* (Basingstoke: Palgrave Macmillan, 2009)
Fox, Cora, Bradley J. Irish and Cassie Miura (eds.), *Positive Emotions in Early Modern Literature and Culture* (Manchester University Press, 2021)
Frevert, Ute, *Emotions in History: Lost and Found* (Budapest and New York: Central European University Press, 2011)
Gaukroger, Stephen, *Francis Bacon and the Transformation of Early-Modern Philosophy* (Cambridge University Press, 2001)
Gibbons, Brian, *Shakespeare and Multiplicity* (Cambridge University Press, 1993)
Gillespie, Stuart, *Shakespeare's Books: A Dictionary of Shakespeare's Sources*, 2nd ed. (London: Bloomsbury, 2016)
Gilman, Ernest B., *Plague Writing in Early Modern England* (University of Chicago Press, 2009)
Gilman, Ernest B. and Rebecca Totaro, *Representing the Plague in Early Modern England* (London: Routledge, 2011)
Giovannelli, Alessandro, 'In Sympathy with Narrative Characters', *The Journal of Aesthetics and Art Criticism*, 67 (2009), 83–95
Goldberg, Jonathan, 'Fatherly Authority', in Margaret Ferguson, Maureen Quilligan, and Nancy Vickers (eds.), *Rewriting the Renaissance: The Discourses of Sexual Difference in Early Modern Europe* (University of Chicago Press, 1986), pp. 3–32
Goldie, Peter, *The Mess Inside: Narrative, Emotion, and the Mind* (Oxford University Press, 2012)
Gordon, Scott Paul, 'Reading Patriot Art: James Barry's *King Lear*', *Eighteenth-Century Studies*, 36 (2003), 491–509
Gowland, Angus, 'Melancholy, Passions and Identity in the Renaissance', in Brian Cummings and Freya Sierhuis (eds.), *Passions and Subjectivity in Early Modern Culture* (Farnham: Ashgate, 2013), pp. 75–84
Gray, Patrick, 'Shakespeare and the Other Virgil: Pity and *Imperium* in *Titus Andronicus*', *Shakespeare Survey*, 69 (2016), 30–45
Gray, Patrick and John D. Cox (eds.), *Shakespeare and Renaissance Ethics* (Cambridge University Press, 2014)
Greenstadt, Amy, *Rape and the Rise of the Author* (Farnham: Ashgate, 2009)
Gurton-Wachter, Lily, 'Sympathy between Disciplines', *Literature Compass*, 15/3 (March 2018), https://doi.org/10.1111/lic3.12443

Guy-Bray, Stephen, 'Rosamond's Complaint: Daniel, Ovid, and the Purpose of Poetry', *Renaissance Studies*, 22 (2008), 338–50

Guy-Bray, Stephen, 'Same Difference: Homo and Allo in Lyly's *Euphues*', in Contance C. Relihan and Goran V. Stanivukovic (eds.), *Prose Fiction and Early Modern Sexualities in England, 1570–1640* (New York and Basingstoke: Palgrave Macmillan, 2003)

HaCohen, Ruth, 'The Music of Sympathy in the Arts of the Baroque; or, the Use of Difference to Overcome Indifference', *Poetics Today*, 22 (2001), 607–50

Hadfield, Andrew, 'Edmund Spenser and Samuel Brandon', *Notes and Queries*, 56 (2009), 536–8

Halliwell, Stephen, *The Aesthetics of Mimesis: Ancient Texts and Modern Problems* (Princeton University Press, 2002)

Harris, Jonathan Gil, *Foreign Bodies and the Body Politic: Discourses of Social Pathology in Early Modern England* (Cambridge University Press, 1998)

Heald, Abigail, 'Tears for Dido: A Renaissance Poetics of Feeling', unpublished PhD thesis, Princeton University (2009)

Heavey, Katharine, *The Early Modern Medea: Medea in English Literature, 1558–1688* (London: Palgrave Macmillan, 2015)

Hendrick, Elizabeth, 'Romancing the Salve: Sir Kenelm Digby and the Powder of Sympathy', *The British Journal for the History of Science*, 41 (2008), 161–85

Henry, John, 'The Fragmentation of Renaissance Occultism and the Decline of Magic', *History of Science*, 46 (2008), 1–48

Hobgood, Allison P., *Passionate Playgoing in Early Modern England* (Cambridge University Press, 2014)

Holbrook, Peter, 'The Left and *King Lear*', *Textual Practice*, 14 (2000), 343–62

Holford-Strevens, Leofranc, 'Polus and His Urn: A Case Study in the Theory of Acting, *c*. 300 B.C.–*c*. A.D. 2000', *International Journal of the Classical Tradition*, 11 (2005), 499–523

Holmes, Jonathan H., '"To Move the Spirits of the Beholder to Admiration": Lively Passionate Performance on the Early Modern Stage', *Literature Compass*, 14/2 (2017), doi: 10.1111/lic3.12381

Honigmann, E. A. J., *John Weever: A Biography of a Literary Associate of Shakespeare and Jonson, Together with a Photographic Facsimile of Weever's Epigrammes (1559)* (Manchester University Press, 1987)

Hopkins, Lisa, 'Staging Passion in Ford's *The Lover's Melancholy*', *Studies in English Literature, 1500–1900*, 45 (2005), 443–59

Hunt, Arnold, *The Art of Hearing: English Preachers and Their Audiences, 1590–1640* (Cambridge University Press, 2010)

Hunter, G. K., *John Lyly, The Humanist as Courtier* (London: Routledge and Kegan Paul, 1962)

Hutchinson, Keith, 'What Happened to Occult Qualities in the Scientific Revolution?', *Isis*, 73 (1982), 233–53

Ibbett, Katherine, *Compassion's Edge: Fellow-Feeling and Its Limits in Early Modern France* (Philadelphia: University of Pennsylvania Press, 2018)

Irish, Bradley J., *Emotion in the Tudor Court: Literature, History, and Early Modern Feeling* (Evanston: Northwestern University Press, 2018)
James, Anne, *Poets, Players, and Preachers: Remembering the Gunpowder Plot in Seventeenth-Century England* (University of Toronto Press, 2016)
James, Heather, 'Dido's Ear: Tragedy and the Politics of Response', *Shakespeare Quarterly*, 52 (2001), 360–82
James, Susan, *Passion and Action: The Emotions in Seventeenth-Century Philosophy* (Oxford: Clarendon Press, 1997)
Karim-Cooper, Farah, *The Hand on the Shakespearean Stage* (London: Bloomsbury, 2016)
Kassell, Lauren, 'Magic, Alchemy and the Medical Economy in Early Modern England: The Case of Robert Fludd's Magnetical Medicine', in Mark S. R. Jenner and Patrick Wallis (eds.), *Medicine and the Market in England and its Colonies, c.1450–c.1850* (Basingstoke: Palgrave Macmillan, 2007), pp. 88–107
Kay, Dennis, *Melodious Tears: The English Funeral Elegy from Spenser to Milton* (Oxford: Clarendon Press, 1990)
Keen, Suzanne, *Empathy and the Novel* (Oxford University Press, 2007)
Keen, Suzanne, 'Empathic Inaccuracy in Narrative Fiction', *Topoi*, 39 (2020), 819–25
Keen, Suzanne, 'A Theory of Narrative Empathy', *Narrative*, 14 (2006), 207–36
Kerr, Jason A., 'The Tragedy of Kindness in *King Lear*', *Studies in English Literature, 1500–1900*, 61 (2021), 45–64
Kerrigan, John, *Motives of Woe: Shakespeare and 'Female Complaint'* (Oxford: Clarendon Press, 1991)
Kesson, Andy, *John Lyly and Early Modern Authorship* (Manchester University Press, 2014)
Kinney, Clare R., 'Continuations and Imitations of the *Arcadia*', in Margaret P. Hannay, Michael G. Brennan, and Mary Ellen Lamb (eds.), *The Ashgate Research Companion to the Sidneys, 1500–1700*, 2 vols (Farnham: Ashgate, 2015), vol. 2, pp. 113–23
Kinney, Clare R., 'Feigning Female Faining: Spenser, Lodge, Shakespeare, and Rosalind', *Modern Philology*, 95 (1998), 291–315
Kuzner, James, *Open Subjects: English Renaissance Republicans, Modern Selfhoods and the Virtue of Vulnerability* (Edinburgh University Press, 2011)
Lamb, Jonathan, *The Evolution of Sympathy in the Long Eighteenth Century* (London: Pickering and Chatto, 2009)
Lamm, Claus, Daniel C. Batson, and Jean Decety, 'The Neural Substrate of Human Empathy: Effects of Perspective-Taking and Cognitive Appraisal', *Journal of Cognitive Neuroscience*, 19 (2007), 42–58
Langley, Eric, *Narcissism and Suicide in Shakespeare and His Contemporaries* (Oxford University Press, 2009)
Langley, Eric, *Shakespeare's Contagious Sympathies: Ill Communications* (Oxford University Press, 2018)
Lawrence, Jason, 'Samuel Daniel's *The Complaint of Rosamond* and the arrival of Tasso's Armida in England', *Renaissance Studies*, 25 (2011), 648–65

Lee, John, 'Agency and Choice', in John Lee (ed.), *A Handbook of English Renaissance Literary Studies* (Chichester: John Wiley & Sons, 2017), pp. 56–69

Lee, John, 'Shakespeare, Human Nature, and English Literature', *Shakespeare*, 5 (2009), 177–90

Lipking, Lawrence, *What Galileo Saw: Imagining the Scientific Revolution* (Ithaca: Cornell University Press, 2014)

Lobis, Seth, 'Sympathy and Antipathy in *King Lear*', in Roman Alexander Barton, Alexander Klaudies, and Thomas Micklich (eds.), *Sympathy in Transformation: Dynamics between Rhetorics, Poetics and Ethics* (Berlin and Boston: De Gruyter, 2018), pp. 89–107

Lobis, Seth, *The Virtue of Sympathy: Magic, Philosophy, and Literature in Seventeenth-Century England* (New Haven and London: Yale University Press, 2015)

MacFaul, Tom, 'Friendship in Sidney's *Arcadia*s', *Studies in English Literature, 1500–1900*, 49 (2009), 17–33

MacFaul, Tom, *Male Friendship in Shakespeare and His Contemporaries* (Cambridge University Press, 2007)

MacFaul, Tom, *Shakespeare and the Natural World* (Cambridge University Press, 2015)

Mack, Peter, *Elizabethan Rhetoric: Theory and Practice* (Cambridge University Press, 2002)

Maclean, Ian, *The Renaissance Notion of Woman: A Study in the Fortune of Scholasticism and Medical Science in European Intellectual Life* (Cambridge University Press, 1980)

Magnusson, Lynne, 'Shakespearean Tragedy and the Language of Lament', in Michael Neill and David Schalkwyk (eds.), *The Oxford Handbook of Shakespearean Tragedy* (Oxford University Press, 2016), pp. 120–34

Mann, Jill, *Feminizing Chaucer* (Cambridge: D. S. Brewer, 2002)

Marcus, Leah S., '*King Lear* and the Death of the World', in Michael Neill and David Schalkwyk (eds.), *The Oxford Handbook of Shakespearean Tragedy* (Oxford University Press, 2016), pp. 421–36

Marcus, Leah S., *Puzzling Shakespeare: Local Reading and Its Discontents* (Berkeley: University of California Press, 1988)

Marsden, Jean, 'Shakespeare and Sympathy', in Peter Sabor and Paul Yachnin (eds.), *Shakespeare and the Eighteenth Century* (Farnham: Ashgate, 2008), pp. 29–41

Marshall, David, 'Adam Smith and the Theatricality of Moral Sentiments', *Critical Inquiry*, 10 (1984), 592–613

Marshall, David, *The Surprising Effects of Sympathy: Marivaux, Diderot, Rousseau, and Mary Shelley* (University of Chicago Press, 1988)

Martin, Kirsty, *Modernism and the Rhythms of Sympathy* (Oxford University Press, 2013)

Matt, Susan J., 'Current Emotion Research in History: Or, Doing History from the Inside Out', *Emotion Review*, 3 (2011), 117–24

Matt, Susan J. and Peter N. Stearns (eds.), *Doing Emotions History* (Urbana: University of Illinois Press, 2014)

Mazzio, Carla, *The Inarticulate Renaissance: Language Trouble in an Age of Eloquence* (Philadelphia: University of Pennsylvania Press, 2009)
McArthur, Tom, Jacqueline Lam-McArthur, and Lise Fontaine (eds.), *The Oxford Companion to the English Language*, 2nd ed. (Oxford University Press, 2018)
McGuire, Laurie and Emma Smith, 'What Is a Source? Or, How Shakespeare Read His Marlowe', *Shakespeare Survey*, 68 (2015), 15–31
Meek, Richard, '"Fabulously Counterfeit": Ekphrastic Encounters in *The Spanish Tragedy*', in David Kennedy and Richard Meek (eds.), *Ekphrastic Encounters: New Interdisciplinary Essays on Literature and the Visual Arts* (Manchester University Press, 2019), pp. 48–69
Meek, Richard, '"For by the Image of My Cause, I See / The Portraiture of His": *Hamlet* and the Imitation of Emotion', in Brid Phillips, Paul Megna, and R. S. White (eds.), *Hamlet and Emotions* (London and New York: Palgrave, 2019), pp. 81–108
Meek, Richard, *Narrating the Visual in Shakespeare* (Farnham: Ashgate, 2009)
Meek, Richard, '"Rue e'en for ruth": *Richard II* and the Imitation of Sympathy', in Richard Meek and Erin Sullivan (eds.), *The Renaissance of Emotion: Understanding Affect in Shakespeare and His Contemporaries* (Manchester University Press, 2015), pp. 130–52
Meek, Richard, 'Sympathy', in Katharine A. Craik (ed.), *Shakespeare and Emotion* (Cambridge University Press, 2020), pp. 224–37
Mercer, Christia, 'Seventeenth-Century Universal Sympathy', in Eric Schliesser (ed.), *Sympathy: A History* (Oxford University Press, 2015), pp. 107–38
Miller, Jacqueline T., 'The Passion Signified: Imitation and the Construction of Emotions in Sidney and Wroth', *Criticism*, 43 (2001), 407–21
Morrissey, Mary, *Politics and the Paul's Cross Sermons, 1558–1642* (Oxford University Press, 2011)
Mousley, Andy, 'Introduction: Shakespeare and the Meaning of Life', *Shakespeare*, 5 (2009), 135–44
Mousley, Andy, *Re-Humanising Shakespeare* (Edinburgh University Press, 2007)
Moyer, Ann, 'Sympathy in the Renaissance', in Eric Schliesser (ed.), *Sympathy: A History* (Oxford University Press, 2015), pp. 70–101
Mulhall, Stephen, *Stanley Cavell: Philosophy's Recounting of the Ordinary* (Oxford University Press, 1994)
Mullaney, Steven, *The Reformation of Emotions in the Age of Shakespeare* (University of Chicago Press, 2015)
Nevalainen, Terttu, 'Early Modern English Lexis and Semantics', in Roger Lass (ed.), *The Cambridge History of the English Language* (Cambridge University Press, 2000), pp. 332–458
Nevalainen, Terttu, 'Shakespeare's New Words', in Sylvia Adamson et al. (eds.), *Reading Shakespeare's Dramatic Language* (London: Thomson Learning, 2001), pp. 237–55
Norri, Juhani, *Dictionary of Medical Vocabulary in English, 1375–1550: Body Parts, Sicknesses, Instruments, and Medicinal Preparations* (London: Routledge, 2016)

Nutton, Vivian, 'The Reception of Fracastoro's Theory of Contagion: The Seed That Fell among Thorns?', *Osiris*, 6 (1990), 196–234

O'Connor, Marie Theresa, 'Why Redistribute? The Jacobean Union Issue and *King Lear*', *Early Modern Literary Studies*, 91/1 (2016).

Olmstead, Wendy, *The Imperfect Friend: Emotion and Rhetoric in Sidney, Milton, and Their Contexts* (University of Toronto Press, 2008)

Ortiz, Joseph M., '"Martyred Signs": *Titus Andronicus* and the Production of Musical Sympathy', *Shakespeare*, 1/1&2 (June/December 2005), 53–74

Paster, Gail Kern, *Humoring the Body: Emotions and the Shakespearean Stage* (Chicago University Press, 2004)

Paster, Gail Kern, 'Minded Like the Weather: The Tragic Body and Its Passions', in Michael Neill and David Schalkwyk (eds.), *The Oxford Handbook of Shakespearean Tragedy* (Oxford University Press, 2016), pp. 202–17

Paster, Gail Kern, Katherine Rowe, and Mary Floyd-Wilson (eds.), *Reading the Early Modern Passions: Essays in the Cultural History of Emotion* (Philadelphia: University of Pennsylvania Press, 2004)

Phillipy, Patricia, *Women, Death, and Literature in Post-Reformation England* (Cambridge University Press, 2002)

Plamper, Jan, *The History of Emotions: An Introduction* (Oxford University Press, 2015)

Plamper, Jan et al., 'The History of Emotions: An Interview with William Reddy, Barbara Rosenwein, and Peter Stearns', *History and Theory*, 49 (2010), 237–65

Potolsky, Matthew, *Mimesis* (London: Routledge, 2006)

Primeau, Ronald, 'Daniel and the Mirror Tradition: Dramatic Irony in *The Complaint of Rosamond*', *Studies in English Literature, 1500–1900*, 15 (1975), 21–36

Quinn, Kelly A., 'Ecphrasis and Reading Practices in Elizabethan Narrative Verse', *Studies in English Literature, 1500–1900*, 44 (2004), 19–35

Quinn, Kelly A., 'Mastering Complaint: Michael Drayton's *Piers Gaveston* and the Royal Mistress Complaints', *English Literary Renaissance*, 38 (2008), 439–60

Ratcliffe, Sophie, *On Sympathy* (Oxford University Press, 2008)

Reddy, William M., *The Navigation of Feeling: A Framework for the History of Emotions* (Cambridge and New York: Cambridge University Press, 2001)

Reiss, Timothy J., 'Cartesian Aesthetics', in Glyn P. Norton (ed.), *The Cambridge History of Literary Criticism, Volume 3: The Renaissance* (Cambridge University Press, 1999), pp. 511–21

Rhodes, Neil, 'Italianate Tales: William Painter and George Pettite', in Andrew Hadfield (ed.), *The Oxford Handbook of English Prose, 1500–1640* (Oxford University Press, 2013), pp. 91–105

Rhodes, Neil, 'The Science of the Heart: Shakespeare, Kames and the Eighteenth-Century Invention of the Human', in Stefan Herbrechter and Ivan Callus (eds.), *Posthumanist Shakespeares* (Basingstoke: Palgrave, 2012), pp. 23–40

Rickard, Jane, *Authorship and Authority: The Writings of James VI and I* (Manchester University Press, 2007)

Rickard, Jane, *Writing the Monarch in Jacobean England: Jonson, Donne, Shakespeare and the Works of King James* (Cambridge University Press, 2015)

Ricoeur, Paul, *Oneself as Another*, trans. Kathleen Blamey (University of Chicago Press, 1992)
Roach, Joseph R., *The Player's Passion: Studies in the Science of Acting* (Newark: University of Delaware Press, 1985)
Rorty, Amélie Oksenberg, 'From Passions to Emotions and Sentiments', *Philosophy*, 57 (1982), 159–72
Roughley, Neil and Thomas Schramme (eds.), *Forms of Fellow Feeling: Empathy, Sympathy, Concern and Moral Agency* (Cambridge University Press, 2018)
Rumbold, Kate, 'Shakespeare's Poems in Pieces: *Venus and Adonis* and *The Rape of Lucrece* Unanthlogized', *Shakespeare Survey*, 69 (2016), 92–105
Rusu, Doina-Cristina, 'Rethinking *Sylva sylvarum*: Francis Bacon's Use of Giambattista Della Porta's *Magia naturalis*', *Perspectives on Science*, 25 (2017), 1–35
Rusu, Doina-Cristina and Christoph Lüthy, 'Extracts from a Paper Laboratory: The Nature of Francis Bacon's *Sylva sylvarum*', *Intellectual History Review*, 27 (2017), 171–202
Ryrie, Alec, *Being Protestant in Reformation Britain* (Oxford University Press, 2013)
Sayre-McCord, Geoffrey, 'Hume and Smith on Sympathy, Approbation, and Moral Judgement', in Eric Schliesser (ed.), *Sympathy: A History* (Oxford University Press, 2015), pp. 208–46.
Scheer, Monique, 'Are Emotions a Kind of Practice (and Is That What Makes Them Have a History)? A Bourdieuian Approach to Understanding Emotion', *History and Theory*, 51 (2012), 193–220
Schoenfeldt, Michael C., *Bodies and Selves in Early Modern England: Physiology and Inwardness in Spenser, Shakespeare, Herbert, and Milton* (Cambridge University Press, 1999)
Schoenfeldt, Michael C., 'Shakespearean Pain', in Katharine A. Craik and Tanya Pollard (eds.), *Shakespearean Sensations: Experiencing Literature in Early Modern England* (Cambridge University Press, 2013), pp. 191–207
Schwyzer, Philip, 'The Jacobean Union Controversy and *King Lear*', in Glenn Burgess, Rowland Wymer, and Jason Lawrence (eds.), *The Accession of James I: Historical and Cultural Consequences* (London: Palgrave Macmillan, 2006), pp. 34–47
Scott, Charlotte, 'Still Life? Anthropocentrism and the Fly in *Titus Andronicus* and *Volpone*', *Shakespeare Survey*, 61 (2008), 256–68
Scott-Baumann, Elizabeth and Ben Burton, 'Shakespearean Stanzas? *Venus and Adonis*, *Lucrece*, and Complaint', *ELH*, 88 (2021), 1–26
Selleck, Nancy, *The Interpersonal Idiom in Shakespeare, Donne, and Early Modern Culture* (Basingstoke: Palgrave Macmillan, 2008)
Shaaber, M. A., '*The First Rape of Faire Hellen* by John Trussell', *Shakespeare Quarterly*, 8 (1957), 407–48
Shami, Jeanne, 'The Sermon', in Andrew Hiscock and Helen Wilcox (eds.), *The Oxford Handbook of Early Modern English Literature and Religion* (Oxford University Press, 2017), pp. 185–206

Shannon, Laurie, *Sovereign Amity: Figures of Friendship in Shakespearean Contexts* (University of Chicago Press, 2002)

Simonova, Natasha, *Early Modern Authorship and Prose Continuations: Adaptation and Ownership from Sidney to Richardson* (Houndmills: Palgrave Macmillan, 2015)

Skwire, Sarah, '"Take Physic, Pomp": King Lear Learns Sympathy', in Eric Schliesser (ed.), *Sympathy: A History* (Oxford University Press, 2015), pp. 139–45

Smith, Hallett, *Elizabethan Poetry: A Study in Conventions, Meaning, and Expression* (Cambridge, MA: Harvard University Press, 1952)

Sofer, Andrew, 'Absorbing Interests: Kyd's Bloody Handkerchief as Palimpsest', *Comparative Drama*, 34 (2000), 127–53

Somerville, J. P., *Royalists and Patriots: Politics and Ideology in England, 1603–1640*, 2nd ed. (London and New York: Routledge, 1999)

Staines, John, 'Compassion in the Public Sphere of Milton and King Charles', in Gail Kern Paster, Katherine Rowe, and Mary Floyd-Wilson (eds.), *Reading the Early Modern Passions: Essays in the Cultural History of Emotion* (Philadelphia: University of Pennsylvania Press, 2004), pp. 89–110

Stallybrass, Peter and Roger Chartier, 'Reading and Authorship: The Circulation of Shakespeare 1590–1619', in Andrew Murphy (ed.), *A Concise Companion to Shakespeare and the Text* (Oxford: Blackwell, 2010), pp. 35–56

Steenbergh, Kristine, 'Mollified Hearts and Enlarged Bowels: Practising Compassion in Reformation England', in Kristine Steenbergh and Katherine Ibbett (eds.), *Compassion in Early Modern Literature and Culture: Feeling and Practice* (Cambridge University Press, 2021), pp. 121–38

Steggle, Matthew, *Laughing and Weeping in Early Modern Theatres* (Aldershot: Ashgate, 2007)

Stephenson, Raymond, 'John Lyly's Prose Fiction: Irony, Humour and Anti-Humanism', *English Literary Renaissance*, 11 (1981), 3–21

St Hilaire, Danielle A., 'Pity and the Failures of Justice in Shakespeare's *King Lear*', *Modern Philology*, 113 (2016), 482–506

Stilma, Astrid, *A King Translated: The Writings of King James VI & I and their Interpretation in the Low Countries, 1593–1603* (Farnham: Ashgate, 2012)

Stockwell, Robert and Donka Minkova, *English Words: History and Structure* (Cambridge University Press, 2001)

Streete, Adrian, 'Elegy, Prophecy, and Politics: Literary Responses to the Death of Prince Henry Stuart, 1612–1614', *Renaissance Studies*, 31 (2017), 87–106

Strier, Richard, *The Unrepentant Renaissance: From Petrarch to Shakespeare to Milton* (University of Chicago Press, 2011)

Strier, Richard and Carla Mazzio, 'Two Responses to "Shakespeare and Embodiment: An E-Conversation"', *Literature Compass*, 3 (2006), 15–31

Strout, Nathaniel, '*As You like It*, *Rosalynde*, and Mutuality', *Studies in English Literature, 1500–1900*, 41 (2001), 277–95

Sullivan, Erin, 'The Passions of Thomas Wright: Renaissance Emotion Across Body and Soul', in Richard Meek and Erin Sullivan (eds.), *The Renaissance* of Emotion: Understanding Affect in Shakespeare and His Contemporaries (Manchester University Press, 2015), pp. 25–44

Sullivan, Jr, Garrett A., *Sleep, Romance and Human Embodiment: Vitality from Spenser to Milton* (Cambridge University Press, 2012)

Swärdh, Anna, '"Much augmented" and "somewhat beautified": Revisions in Three Female Complaints of the 1590s', *Modern Philology*, 113 (2016), 310–30

Thompson, Evan, 'Empathy and Consciousness', *Journal of Consciousness Studies*, 8/5–7 (2001), 1–32

Thorley, David, 'Towards a History of Emotion, 1562–1660', *The Seventeenth Century*, 28 (2013), 3–19

Tilley, Morris Palmer, *A Dictionary of the Proverbs in England in the Sixteenth and Seventeenth Centuries* (Ann Arbor: University of Michigan Press, 1950)

Tilmouth, Christopher, *Passion's Triumph over Reason: A History of the Moral Imagination from Spenser to Rochester* (Oxford University Press, 2007)

Tilmouth, Christopher, 'Passion and Intersubjectivity in Early Modern Literature', in Brian Cummings and Freya Sierhuis (eds.), *Passions and Subjectivity in Early Modern Culture* (Farnham: Ashgate, 2013), pp. 13–32

Totaro, Rebecca, *The Plague Epic in Early Modern England: Heroic Measures, 1603–1721* (Farnham: Ashgate, 2012)

Trilling, Lionel, *Sincerity and Authenticity* (London: Oxford University Press, 1972)

Tuckness, Alex and John M. Parrish, *The Decline of Mercy in Public Life* (Cambridge University Press, 2014)

van Dijkhuizen, Jan Frans, *Pain and Compassion in Early Modern Literature and Culture* (Cambridge: D. S. Brewer, 2012)

van Elk, Martine, '"This sympathizèd one day's error": Genre, Representation, and Subjectivity in *The Comedy of* Errors', *Shakespeare Quarterly*, 60 (2009), 47–72

van Engen, Abram C., *Sympathetic Puritans: Calvinist Fellow Feeling in Early New England* (Oxford University Press, 2015)

Vaught, Jennifer, *Masculinity and Emotion in Early Modern Literature* (Aldershot: Ashgate, 2008), pp. 1–16

Vaught, Jennifer, 'Men Who Weep and Wail: Masculinity and Emotion in Sidney's *New Arcadia*', *Literature Compass*, 2 (2005)

Waddell, Mark A., *Jesuit Science and the End of Nature's Secrets* (Farnham: Ashgate, 2015)

Wall, Wendy, *The Imprint of Gender: Authorship and Publication in the English Renaissance* (Ithaca and London: Cornell University Press, 1993)

Weaver, William P., '"O teach me how to make mine own excuse": Forensic Performance in *Lucrece*', *Shakespeare Quarterly*, 59 (2008), 421–49

Wells, Marion A., 'Philomela's Marks: Ekphrasis and Gender in Shakespeare's Poems and Plays', in Jonathan Post (ed.), *The Oxford Handbook of Shakespeare's Poetry* (Oxford University Press, 2013), pp. 204–24

Weststeijn, Thijs, 'Between Mind and Body: Painting the Inner Movements According to Samuel van Hoogstraten and Franciscus Junius', in Stephanie

S. Dickey and Herman Roodenburg (eds.), *The Passions in the Arts of the Early Modern Netherlands* (Zwolle: Waanders, 2009), pp. 261–81

White, R. S., '"False Friends": Affective Semantics in Shakespeare', *Shakespeare*, 8 (2012), 286–99

White, R. S., Mark Houlahan, and Katrina O'Loughlin (eds.), *Shakespeare and Emotions: Inheritances, Enactments, Legacies* (Houndmills: Palgrave Macmillan, 2015)

Whittington, Leah, 'Shakespeare's Vergil: Empathy and *The Tempest*', in Patrick Gray and John D. Cox (eds.), *Shakespeare and Renaissance Ethics*, pp. 98–120

Wiggins, Martin and Catherine Richardson, *British Drama 1533–1642: A Catalogue, Volume IX: 1632–1636* (Oxford University Press, 2018)

Williams, Raymond, *Keywords* (London: Fontana, 1976)

Wilson, F. P., *The Plague in Shakespeare's London* (Oxford University Press, 1963)

Wilson, Katherine, *Fictions of Authorship in Late Elizabethan Narratives: Euphues in Arcadia* (Oxford University Press, 2006)

Wilson, Katherine, '"Turne Your Library to a Wardrobe": John Lyly and Euphuism', in Andrew Hadfield (ed.), *The Oxford Handbook of English Prose, 1500–1640* (Oxford University Press, 2013), pp. 172–87

Wispé, Lauren, 'The Distinction between Sympathy and Empathy: To Call Forth a Concept, a Word Is Needed', *Journal of Personality and Social Psychology*, 50 (1986), 314–21

Woodcock, Matthew, *Sir Philip Sidney and the Sidney Circle* (Tavistock: Northcote House, 2010)

Wootton, David, 'Never Knowingly Naked', *London Review of Books*, 26/8 (15 August 2004), 26–27

Zunshine, Lisa, *Why We Read Fiction: Theory of Mind and the Novel* (Columbus: The Ohio State University Press, 2006)

Index

Abbot, George, 177, 213
Agrippa, Heinrich Cornelius, 6
  De occulta philosophia, 5
Alexander, Gavin, 67
Alexander, William
  Arcadia bridging passage, 69–70
  The Tragedy of Croesus, 186–9, 193, 210
Allott, Robert
  Englands Parnassus, 13, 133–5
Ariosto
  Orlando Furioso, 14
Aristotle, 35
Auerbach, Eric, 11
Austin, J. L., 21
Averell, William, 83, 180
  A mervailous combat of contrarieties, 76

Bacon, Francis, 180–1
  Sylva sylvarum, 218–22, 239
Bakhtin, Mikhail, 22
Bandello, Matteo, 36
Barish, Jonas, 39, 44
Barry, James, 211
  King Lear Weeping over the Dead Body of Cordelia, 200
Barthes, Roland, 58
Bate, Jonathan, 160, 161
Belleforest, François, 36
Bilson, Thomas
  The survey of Christs sufferings for mans redemption, 16
Bodenham, John and Anthony Munday
  Bel-vedére, or, The Garden of the muses, 133, 135–7
Bodin, Jean, 178
Brandon, Samuel
  The Vertuous Octavia, 168–71
Bright, Timothy
  Treatise of Melancholy, 7
Britton, Jeanne M., 3
Brooke, Christopher, 202–3
Brown, Georgia, 107

Burrow, Colin, 28, 116, 144
Burton, William
  An exposition of the Lords Prayer, 15
Byfield, Nicholas, 208
Bynam, William, 236

Cavendish, Richard
  The image of nature and grace, 15
Cavendish, William, 263
Cawdry, Robert, 182
Churchyard, Thomas, 106
Chute, Anthony, 114–5
Cicero, 35
  De Oratore, 26–7
Coeffeteau, Nicholas, 158
Colet, Claude. *See* Munday, Anthony
Craik, Katharine A. and Tanya Pollard, 140
Croll, Oswald, 216
Crowley, Timothy, 143
Crystal, David, 121
Csengei, Ildiko, 3
Cummings, Brian and Freya Sierhuis, 19
Cunningham, Andrew, 3

Daniel, Samuel
  The Complaint of Rosamond, 106–15, 124, 131, 135
  The Tragedie of Cleopatra, 120–1
Davis, Nick, 23–4
Day, Angel, 71
Debes, Remy, 12
Dekker, Thomas, 183
Della Porta, Giambattista
  Magia naturalis, 5–6, 218
Dickenson, John
  Arishas, 67–8
Digby, Kenelm, 25, 250
  A Late Discourse ... Touching the Cure of Wounds by Sympathy, 8–9
Donne, John, 215–17, 252
Du Bartas, Guillaume de Salluste Sieur. *See* Thomas Hudson

Dugdale, Gilbert, 176–7
Dutton, Richard, 174

Eagleton, Terry, 195
Edwards, Thomas, 165
Elizabeth I, Queen, 76, 78
Elyot, Thomas
  Dictionary, 6
Enterline, Lynn, 19
Evrigenis, Ioannis, 178, 181

Fenton, Geoffrey, 10, 38, 40
Field, Richard, 136
Fitzgeffry, Charles
  Compassion towards captives, 241–50
  Curse of the Corne-Horders, 240–1
Flasket, John
  Englands Helicon, 137–8
Fletcher, John, 265
Florio, John, 16–18, 173, 175. See also Michel de Montaigne
Floyd-Wilson, Mary, 19
Fludd, Robert, 222, 233, 235, 250
  Doctor Fludds answer unto M. Foster, 226–9
Foakes, R. A., 167
Ford, John
  The Lover's Melancholy, 229–31, 237
Forker, Charles, 29
Forset, Edward, 185
Foster, William, 234
  Hiplocrisma-spongus, 222–6
Foucault, Michel, 6, 20
Fowler, Alastair, 28, 157
Fox, Cora, 19, 162
Fracastoro, Girolamo, 247
Frevert, Ute, 4

Gale, Thomas, 6
Galen, 5, 6
Glapthorne, Henry
  The Hollander, 231–9
Goclenius the Younger, Rudolph, 216
Goldie, Peter, 28
Gordon, Scott Paul, 201
Greenblatt, Stephen, 22
Greene, Robert, 57, 129
  Menaphon: Camillas alarum to slumbering Euphues, 57, 61
Gurr, Andrew, 29
Gurton-Wachter, Lily, 10–11
Guy-Bray, Stephen, 41

Hannay, Patrick, 207–8
Harington, John, 16. See also Ariosto
Hart, James, 229

Herring, Francis, 209
Hobgood, Allison P., 140
Holland, Henry, 198, 260
  The Christian Exercise of Fasting, 88–90
  Spirituall preservatives against the pestilence, 90
Holland, Philemon. See Plutarch
Homer
  Iliad, 258, 265
Hooke, Christopher, 79–81
Horace, 25, 96, 163
Hudson, Thomas
  The Historie of Judith, 13, 134
Hughes, Alan, 160
Huloet, Richard, 38
Hume, David, 10
  Treatise of Human Nature, 262
Hunt, Arnold, 73, 99

James VI and I, King, 181
  A counterblast to tobacco, 181
  A remonstrance of the most gratious King James I, 210–11
  Basilikon Doron, 181, 186
James, William, 81–6
Jonson, Ben
  Cynthia's Revels, 171
  Horace (translation of), 25
  Volpone, 173–175

Kerr, Jason A., 195
Kinney, Clare, 69
Knolles, Richard
  The six bookes of a common-weale, 178–9
Kyd, Thomas
  Soliman and Perseda, 153
  The Spanish Tragedy, 148–53

Lane, John, 132–3
Langley, Eric, 23
Lawrence, John, 213–14
Lee, John, 24
Lemnius, Levinus
  The touchstone of complexions, 75
Levenson, Jill, 91
Lightfoot, William, 76
Lobis, Seth, 10, 217
Lodge, Thomas
  The Complaint of Elstred, 66, 113–14
  The famous, true and historicall life of Robert second Duke of Normandy, 66
  Phillis, 113
  Rosalynde, Euphues Golden Legacie, 56–66, 128, 130, 146

Index

Lyly, John
   Euphues: The Anatomy of Wit, 39–47, 49, 56, 149

MacFaul, Tom, 47, 230
Marcus, Leah, 189, 193
Markham, Gervase
   The English Arcadia, 68–9
Marlowe, Christopher
   Dido, Queen of Carthage, 141–8, 153, 163, 170
   Hero and Leander, 165
Martial, 257
Medley, Thomas, 208–9, 211
Mercer, Christia, 217
Meres, Francis
   Palladis Tamia, 112
Middleton, Christopher
   The legend of Humphrey Duke of Glocester, 30–1
The Mirror for Magistrates, 106
Montaigne, Michel de, 175
   Essays, 16–18, 173
Morrissey, Mary, 81
Mosse, Miles
   The arraignment and conviction of usurie, 86–7
Muggins, William, 182–5, 191
Mulcaster, Richard, 75
Mullaney, Steven, 20, 153
Munday, Anthony
   Palladine of England, 58
   Palmerin D'Oliva, 58

Nevalainen, Terttu, 36
Newton, Thomas
   The touchstone of complexions, 75
Nicholson, Samuel
   Acolastus his after-witte, 128–32

Olmstead, Wendy, 47
Ortiz, Joseph, 155
Ovid, 224

Painter, William
   The Palace of Pleasure, 35–8
Paracelsus, 216
Paster, Gail Kern, 18, 118, 189, 254
Paynell, Thomas, 37
   Amadis of Fraunce, 39
Peele, George, 137, 138
Perkins, William, 99
Petrarch, 64
Phaer, Thomas and Thomas Twyne, 142
Pliny the Elder, 5
   Natural History, 218
Plutarch, 5, 30
   Morals, 8

Prime, John, 72–3
Puttenham, George
   The Art of English Poesy, 215

Quarles, Francis, 231
Quintilian, 163
   Instititio oratoria, 25–7

Rainholde, Richard, 27
Ratcliffe, Sophie, 56
Rawley, William, 218
Reading, John, 239–40
Reddy, William, 20–2
Reynolds, Edward
   An explication of the hundreth and tenth Psalme, 240
   A treatise of the passions, 253–9, 264, 265
Roe, John, 120
Rogers, Thomas, 203–4, 214
Rollock, Robert, 184
Rosenwein, Barbara, 264

Sandys, Edwin, 77–8, 80, 84
Scheer, Monique, 81
Schoenfeldt, Michael, 18, 119
Selleck, Nancy, 22–3
Seneca, 256
Sennert, Daniel, 229
Shakespeare, William
   As You Like It, 59
   The Comedy of Errors, 166–8
   Coriolanus, 76
   Hamlet, 27, 98, 201
   Love's Labour's Lost, 166–8
   A Midsummer Night's Dream, 59–60
   The Rape of Lucrece, 27, 103–4, 109, 115–25, 129–32, 134, 135, 150, 151, 165, 166, 188, 260
   Richard II, 30, 165
   Romeo and Juliet, 90–1, 159, 165
   Sir Thomas More (contribution to), 92
   Sonnet 82, 123
   3 Henry VI, 129
   Timon of Athens, 80
   Titus Andronicus, 153–64, 166, 170, 199
   The Tragedy of King Lear, 61, 189–202, 206, 211–12, 244
   Troilus and Cressida, 171–2
   The Two Gentlemen of Verona, 139–40, 159, 164
   Venus and Adonis, 1–2, 134, 165
Sidney, Philip, 28–9
   Astrophil and Stella, 50, 52
   The Defence of Poesy, 54, 123, 163
   The Old Arcadia, 47–56, 65, 149, 260
Skwire, Sarah, 194

Smith, Adam, 10, 88, 140
    The Theory of Moral Sentiments, 54, 249, 262
Southwell, Robert, 94
Spenser, Edmund
    An Hymne in Honour of Beautie, 115, 134
St Hilaire, Danielle, 198
Stanley, Thomas, 265–7
Steenbergh, Kristine, 184, 241
Stoughton, John, 251–2
Streete, Adrian, 202
Strier, Richard, 19
Sullivan, Jr, Garret A., 48

Thevet, André, 37
Thomas, Lewis, 100–2
Thorne, William, 185, 213
Trilling, Lionel, 24
Trussell, John, 125–8

Udall, John, 78–9

van Elk, Martine, 167
Vicars, John, 209–10
Virgil
    Aeneid, 28, 141, 142, 163, 256, 258, 265

Weever, John, 165–7
West, William, 179–80
Wilcox, Thomas, 75
Wispé, Lauren, 12
Wither, George, 204–7
Woodcock, Matthew, 55
Wright, Thomas, 8, 94, 146
    The Passions of the Minde in Generall, 8, 94–100, 174, 218

Zepheria, 166

For EU product safety concerns, contact us at Calle de José Abascal, 56–1°,
28003 Madrid, Spain or eugpsr@cambridge.org.

www.ingramcontent.com/pod-product-compliance
Ingram Content Group UK Ltd.
Pitfield, Milton Keynes, MK11 3LW, UK
UKHW020347160925
462952UK00021B/831